Advance Praise for *Ben Sidran*

"Be warned: if you pick up this book and begin casually reading, you will be hooked—by Sidran's recollection of the 1960s, by his passion for music, and by his equally passionate pain at what has happened to it. But even if you never lived through the Sixties, or never listened to a note of music, you will be hooked by Sidran's passion for life; from his worldwide travels to his journey back to his Jewish roots. If Emerson was right when he said 'a man must share the actions and passions of his time, on peril of being judged not to have lived,' Ben Sidran has lived deeply—and set it down with perfect pitch."
— **Jeff Greenfield**, CNN's senior analyst for "Inside Politics" and host of "Greenfield at Large"

"Yes, Mr. Ben Sidran wears many hats; singer, writer, composer, journalist, lyricist, and the most important one, a jazz musician/pianist of the first rank! In all of these endeavors Ben's dedication to quality, generous spirit, street-wise intelligence, and loyalty to the memory of all those who preceded him remain a constant factor. I know something about hats and Ben wears all of his with élan and panache. His book gives the reader a glimpse of an energetic musician who can juggle them with passion and love. Write on! My man Ben!"
— **Phil Woods**, tenor saxophonist

"There are three kinds of people. Some people make it happen. Some people wait for it to happen. And some people ask 'what just happened'? Ben Sidran is clearly the first kind."
— **Benny Golson**, songwriter and tenor saxophonist

BEN SIDRAN

BEN SIDRAN

A LIFE
IN THE
MUSIC

TAYLOR TRADE PUBLISHING

Published by Taylor Trade Publishing,
An Imprint of Rowman & Littlefield Publishing Group.
200 Park Avenue South, Suite 1109
New York, NY 10003

Manufactured in the United States of America

LIBRARY OF CONGRESS CATALOGING-IN-PUBLICATION DATA
Sidran, Ben.
 Ben Sidran : a life in the music / Ben Sidran.
  v. cm.
 Includes discography (p. 315) and index.
 ISBN 0-87833-291-X (alk. paper)
1. Sidran, Ben. 2. Jazz musicians — United States — Biography. I. Title.

ML419.S43 A3 2003
786.2/165/092 B 21   2002013111

Manufactured in the United States of America.

⊛™ The paper used in this publication meets the minimum requirements of American National Standard for Information Sciences — Permanence of Paper for Printed Library Materials, ANSI/NISO Z39.48–1992.

For my mother and father,
SHIRLEY AND LOUIS SIDRAN,

and for my sister and brother,
MAXINE AND EZRA.

"I'll tell you the true whether I knew or not."

—**MEL BROOKS,** *The Two Thousand Year Old Man*

Contents

Acknowledgments

I would like to thank Judy and Leo, who encouraged me from the beginning and reassured me that the work was sufficient unto itself. I would also like to thank those who took a look at the work along the way, offered suggestions, and did not tell me to turn back, especially Howard Gelman, Jerilyn Goodman, Jeff Greenfield, Jim Hougan, Tommy LiPuma, Dave Maraniss, Jackie Mitchard, Lorrie Moore, Susan Pigorsch, Ken Robbins, Matt Salinger, Ralph Simon, Peter Straub and Terry Strauss. And finally, my thanks to Elaine Markson, who told me it was finally time to stop.

≈ Prologue

August 6th, 1991

RED ROCKS, COLORADO

I'm standing on stage in front of twelve thousand drunk, screaming teenagers. In the front row, a plastered sixteen-year-old girl is lifting up her T-shirt to flash me. I see her mouth open, she's screaming but I hear nothing. Up in the sky, up behind the churning sea of bodies, a helicopter lifts off, taking another poisoned kid to the neon room. But I hear nothing. In my ears, I have molded monitors that no sound can penetrate. I'm supposed to be plugged into the module on my belt, listening to the band, listening to myself. The greatest mix ever. On top of the world. But I'm unplugged. I look down at my hands. I'm still playing. But behind dark shades, in my cocoon of silence, on this bright hot August afternoon, I hear nothing, I see nothing, I feel nothing. Way in the distance, Steve Miller is singing "Big old jet airliner, don't carry me too far away...." But I'm already gone. Almost fifty years old. Man, I'm almost fifty years old. We're all almost fifty years old. Up on the hill in front of us, they're all fifteen and sixteen and they are absolutely pissing in their pants. I can only think about that cold November afternoon, some twenty years ago, driving Paul Pena home from the recording studio the day he first recorded "Jet Airliner." Him blind and me lost and he's directing me through the streets of Boston, and we get to his house and all his blind friends are there and we all get stoned and start playing music and then it gets dark outside and then there are no light bulbs in the lamps because, of course, they're blind, and suddenly, I am the one who is blind. And now it's twenty years later and "Jet Airliner" is one of Steve's big hits, and I'm on stage and I'm blind again, and deaf too, Oh Lord, up on this stage in front of a howling party mob....

Part One

EXPAND, EXPAND, KEEP EXPANDING

≈ Chapter One

1943–1955

In the beginning, you fall in love. It starts in your feet and pretty soon it's in your chest and then your throat and finally you can't think about anything else. For me it was boogie-woogie, specifically "Pine Top's Boogie" by pianist Pine Top Smith. My father had the record, and, by nine, I had it memorized. I played it over and over like some kind of personal litany, rocking back and forth, almost in a trance. I had been playing piano since...well, actually, I don't remember not playing the piano. My earliest memories include the piano, sitting at the keys, turning the pages of a comic book with my right hand and watching my left hand trace a boogie pattern. Slowly, unconsciously, I fixed the moves into my motor memory while my mind wandered. So even as a small child, jazz was, for me, the great escape: it spoke to me of something better, a world greater than the world I knew. To this day, I believe that alienation is at the heart of every jazzman's story.

I was born in Chicago in 1943. It was my father's city, but I didn't really know him. Sometimes it seems I awoke from a dream and he was gone. I do remember, as a small child, the sour smell of his sweat, the toasty odor of his cigarettes, and the roughness of his cheeks. These things are ingrained in me. But he himself is truly a ghost. And maybe he always was.

Before my second birthday, he enlisted in the army and left home. My mother moved us — my sister and me — to Racine, back to *her* mother and her childhood home. She was born Shirley Gordon in Racine in 1915. The Gordons first landed in Wisconsin around the turn of the century, when great grandpa Charlie Gordon got off the train too soon on his way from New York to somewhere else and decided he had arrived where he was going. He stayed, got a horse and wagon and went around selling vegetables. He had three sons; Max, the oldest, married Ida, who had arrived in Racine after her father abandoned their homestead in the Badlands of North Dakota. As a child, I remember my grandmother saying, *"Of course* they gave you the land for free if you stayed there; *nobody* could stay there." Max and Ida had two children; the youngest was my mother Shirley.

My earliest memories in Racine, then, are of being with the women, with my grandmother in the kitchen, fussing with pots on the stove, or with my mother, who told me a recurring bedtime story. It was about a magic place at the base of a big tree. Each night as she tucked me into bed, she would say, "You slip through a tiny doorway hidden at the base of the tree, and, down a spiral staircase, you go into a world where you can have anything you want." And each night, as she turned out the light, she would ask me, "Benny, what do you want?" And I always pictured this great lit chamber with people dressed in fantastic outfits, like cowboys and firemen, and there were fountains of ice cream everywhere...and there was music. Always music; music animated everything. At first it was "Tubby the Tuba," or "In The Hall of the Mountain King," but when my father returned from the war, it was Benny Goodman and Nat King Cole and Erroll Garner and Pine Top Smith. He was the one who brought these exotic voices into my head.

In our living room on Carmel Avenue there was an old upright piano, and it became the center of my universe. That's where I read my comic books, ate my snacks and watched time pass. I made up little songs and, eventually, I took piano lessons. Then I quit and refused to take any more. But I kept playing the piano. Next to the piano was a large Magnavox console with a radio and record player, and one day I heard Jimmy Forrest's "Night Train" roaring out of the speaker with a huge shouting saxophone and shiny trumpets, and I got so excited that I ran around the room in a kind of ecstatic frenzy until I broke something. It was my father's prized copy of Benny Goodman's "King Porter Stomp." When he found out, he was so angry he couldn't even look at me, but I didn't care: I had ridden the night train, and music was my driving wheel.

In general, I lived a pretty normal life for a Jewish kid growing up in a small Midwestern town — "The Central Stranded Time Zone," as Del Close once called it. On the High Holy Days and, occasionally, on Saturday mornings, I went to temple with my family and stood amongst a small gathering of Eastern European refugees and pretended to pray. I swayed with them as they davened and made soft chanting sounds, rocking back and forth, as if in a trance. I had no idea what we were saying but I loved the rise and fall of the voices and the feeling of being hypnotized. I've come to think of this as my first jam session. My father liked to comment on the action, and my sister and I were his best audience. Talking out of the corner of his mouth, like a bit player in an old gangster movie, he'd say something like, "See that fat narishkeit over there, Mrs. Baumblatt? Ted Savides is going to name a hog after her..."

Ted was my father's best friend. He lived on a farm outside of Baraboo, Wisconsin, a couple of hours north of Racine. Before Ted moved to the farm, he and his family had lived around the corner from us on Carmel Avenue. They had a big brick house with a large wooden barn out back. Ted was a Runyanesque character, an old baseball player, and one of my father's favorite pastimes was sitting with him around the radio on a Sunday afternoon, listening to the Cubs game. Pop would wear his Cubs hat, and the two of them would laugh and talk and swap stories or statistics that went back to Honus Wagner and came all the way forward to put Ernie Banks in his rightful place. In the background, Jack Brickhouse would be announcing, "From Bingo to Bango to Addison Street..." and Ted and my father would both laugh. I don't know if Ted ever actually had a hog named Mrs. Baumblatt, but I do know that he had a magic black baseball bat, beautifully balanced, easy to swing and rumored to hit a ball all by itself. He kept it in the hayloft out in the old barn.

I climbed up to that loft every chance I had. There I found the most amazing things: boxes full of ribbons and medals from the Civil War, from the D.A.R., and The Grand Army of the Republic. And there were old steel contraptions, small devices with spinning balls and webbed pulleys or wind-up keys that trapped animals or shot missiles or did other ingenious things. It was the long forgotten collection of Ted's father-in-law, Mr. Edmonds, who had built the house and the barn back in the eighteen-hundreds. Mr. Edmonds had been an inventor, and the loft was the final resting place for his work. Now, like the ribbons and the beautiful black bat, the contraptions were just gathering dust and waiting for history to claim them. That was me. I first discovered this sanctuary while climbing to the loft with Kathy Foote. We went up there to take off our clothes and hug each other. We must have been seven or eight years old and it is still among my most delicious memories. I can still smell the damp wood of the barn, see the sunlight poking through the walls, as we stood, silently caressing each other's naked bottom.

One day climbing down from the loft I came face to face with a snake. My sister Maxine and the Savides girls were already huddled around it, frightened and fascinated. I got closer to see what was going on and a small reptile tongue darted out at me. Without thinking, I picked up a brick and dropped it on the snake's head. Suddenly, the snake was no longer a magical thing. It was a lifeless piece of skin. I stood there, transfixed. Then my sister and I ran home to tell my father. He was sitting in his favorite chair with his Cubs cap on, reading the paper. After I told him my story, he just reached out and whacked me across the back of the head with the newspaper. "That's for ever killing a living thing," he said.

Maxine and I rarely wandered far from home. In the fall, we played on the grassy hill by McKinley Junior High school, a block from our house. We were told never to go down to the creek at the bottom of the hill because tramps came up from the railroad tracks. In the winter, McKinley hill was great for sledding. One winter, the snow piled up so high we could dig tunnels from our front door out to the street and never see the sky.

In the summer we tried to plant grass on the muddy patch we called our front "lawn." We put stakes in the ground and my sister and I hung string between them to keep people off. But we never managed to grow grass. Not even weeds would grow, only ruts from our bicycle tires. By July, the "lawn" was mud, caked hard as stone, and the roots of the big elm by the curb had spread under the sidewalk and jacked up the pavement. One day while riding my bike there, I hit a large crack and went sprawling to the concrete. By the next morning, my arm had swollen up like a vegetable, and several days later my mother became worried about me. I felt okay, but she kept asking me what was wrong. I was lying on the couch, feeling sleepy, drifting in and out of a dream where I was riding in an old convertible, the kind that the Keystone Kops used to drive down the streetcar tracks of L.A., and there were lots of kids in the car with me, and we were having a really good time, but something was wrong somewhere, and there was this loud buzzing sound in my head, and when I opened my eyes I saw the doctor. He was examining the inside of my arm and when he showed my mother a red line that ran from my elbow to the vein in my shoulder, she became frightened.

Quickly, I was wrapped in blankets and carried to the car. My mother acted kind of angry with me, except she was crying. I understood the red line was "blood poisoning," and if it crept to my heart, only inches away, I could die. The doctor drove very fast, ignoring us in the back seat. I fell back into a swoon as peaceful and happy as I have ever been. Everything was out of my hands.

Something in that moment stayed with me and made me more self-aware. After I had recovered and left the hospital, I still longed for that feeling of surrender, of letting go and falling upward, of trust and release. It was also around this time that I began having the distinct sensation that I was trapped inside a kid's body, looking out with older eyes. From that moment on, I was just putting in time.

Throughout the summer, our little neighborhood gang—my sister and me, Jimmy Anderson and his sister Heidi, Nancy Ruffalo, John Isbell—would play kick the can in the alley until dark, or ride bikes in the hot afternoon, or play war down on McKinley hill until they called us for dinner. Like the Mel Brooks line, hitting a tree with a stick was a good job back then. A stick could be a gun or a sword or a telekinetic Flash Gordon device, or you could take your stick exploring down by the creek, down where you weren't supposed to go, and you could use it to push aside the tangle of milkweed and thistle and wild strawberries to make a little clearing for yourself. That clearing would become your own little world for a while, and you could pretend that all of life was as safe and protected as that one small circle.

One day a group of us went to McKinley hill with cardboard boxes. We were going to go "sledding" on the grass, but pretty soon we had destroyed the boxes and were just rolling down the hill. Standing at the bottom, dizzy and covered with grass, I was about to walk back to the top when I heard a loud "crack" and found myself on the ground. John Isbell had been swinging around an old pair of World War Two binoculars on a leather strap, the strap had snapped and the binocs had hit me square in the head. All the kids ran over to see. I reached up and felt my head, and my hand came away red and wet. I screamed and we all ran to my house. Later that afternoon, after the doctor had put in the stitches and all the kids had gathered around to see them, John said he was sorry, really sorry. That was the day we became best friends. Years later, I also understood it was probably the day he became my protector.

I didn't see my father very much. Even before he got the job in Chicago and started riding the train every day he was mostly just a brooding presence. I can picture him standing in a doorway with his legs crossed, one hand on his hip, sticking out his lower lip to catch a peanut he had tossed. I can hear him whistling when he left the room. I don't know if these are true memories or merely imagined.

Sunday mornings, he would come downstairs and cook salami and eggs for my sister and me. It was his one culinary art but he made a ritual of it. Maxine was a year older than me, clearly his favorite, a smart, funny girl who had a lot in common with him. They talked and told jokes and kidded around the table, and I felt glad just to be along for the ride. Whatever she had, I wanted, too. That's how I started playing piano: she took lessons, so I took lessons.

On Sunday afternoons, the three of us, Maxine, Pop, and me, would take the '49 Buick and go to the bagel store. We were allowed into the back room where there was a huge oven. Deep inside its large open maw were rows of flames, which always made me think of Shadrack, Meshack and Abednego and the fiery furnace. On the floor were large buckets filled with murky water and pale, white circles of dough floating on the surface. We watched as Isabelle shoved a big wooden paddle into a bucket, lifted out a row of raw bagels and deftly slid them into the roaring furnace. The smell was heaven. We would buy a bag and eat as many as we wanted before we got home. Then Monday came and my father disappeared for the week.

Maxine and I loved Pop. He was a very complicated guy, and talking about him is hard, like blind men trying to describe the elephant; the truth depends on what part you were holding onto.

When I was small, he called me "Jonson." He called me Jonson, because he loved the writer Ben Jonson, but I was actually named for his father Ben, or Boruch, Sidransky. He called my sister "shorty," because she was shorter than he was, I suppose, and he called my mother "Chi Chi." I don't know why. I wish I did, because it would probably be a cute, loving, sexy story, and, if so, it would make the first and only one I ever heard about the two of them.

Around the house, Pop often seemed ill at ease, but in public, he relaxed and came alive. Out in the world, among his friends and admirers, he was fast and funny, a lady's man and a man's man. He radiated a hip nonchalance, and he was both playful and hardboiled. Many of my friends thought of him as the coolest guy they knew. He wasn't like other parents. He talked to you like an adult, about anything, movies, sports, music, whatever you liked. But when you stepped up to the plate, you had better be ready. His bottom line was that he broached no bullshit.

And he was movie-star handsome. Some folks say he resembled Jeff Chandler. In the old pictures, he has the same tight black curly hair and swarthy good looks. Even as a child, I remember people pulling me aside and telling me, in a conspiratorial kind of way, that my father "was really something special." They might be talking about his sense of humor, his remarkable memory, or his limitless store of anecdotes and information, but what they were really saying was that he made *them* feel special. He was a raconteur, and when he talked to you, when he focussed the power of his attention on you, you felt like you were at the center of some great ongoing drama.

But that was not the man I knew. At home, the man I knew was often withdrawn or out of control. It was like living in the eye of a storm and knowing it was gonna happen; it was just a matter of time. His relationship with my mom only made matters worse.

They fought bitterly and often, mostly about money I supposed, but sometimes, behind the closed bedroom door, about unnamed or unnamable things. The roar of their anger was like a distant thunder. Sometimes it burst out of their bedroom, and then Pop would come down loud through the living room where

I was sitting at the piano, and, for no apparent reason, he'd smack me across the back of the head. I thought maybe he suspected me of something and was just covering his bets. "Don't lie to me!" he'd say, and I remember more than once not having a clue what he was talking about. But of course, he wasn't talking about me. My mom, too, was often in her own world, like the day she stormed out of the house, and, turning to slam the door behind her, said to me, "Tell your father I've gone and it's all your fault!" I had no idea what prompted that either. I just kept my head down, and when my father came home, I said nothing.

They had met at the University of Wisconsin in the early1930s, when my father was a poor but promising young writer who loved jazz, and my mother was a well-to-do girl from Racine, with a car of her own and a dream of escape. She hoped, no doubt, that her future husband would become a famous writer and rescue her from the mundane life of a scrap-dealer's daughter, perhaps introduce her to cafe society and confirm her lifelong premonition that she was destined for something special. She had picked a promising candidate all right, but as the years went by, and he failed to deliver on his "promise," they both became bitter and vengeful, withdrawing into their own personal worlds of recrimination and denial.

To escape, in the cool of a summer evening, Pop and I would go into the alley and toss a baseball around. We had our gloves and our caps. Actually, he put on his Cubs cap the moment he walked into the house, and I was in bed long before he took it off. He wore it when he ate, when he listened to the radio, when he read the paper, and when we played catch, gradually stepping further and further apart from each other until it got too dark to see. When I would bear down with my fastball or try to break off a curve in the dwindling light and the ball sailed over his head, I would shout, "I'll get it!" and run past him to retrieve the ball. I didn't want him to chase it. He kind of lumbered when he ran, and it made me uncomfortable to watch. It was odd, because he had been an athlete in high school and as a young man had even considered trying to play semi-pro ball. But the weight of the world was clearly upon him, and pretty early on, even though he loved his Cubs and his jazz and his books and his pals, you could tell he was feeling the impending crush of his life.

He was born Louis Sidransky in the city of Drohiczyn, Poland, in 1916. He came to the United States when he was only four, after his father had fled The Pale by walking across Russia, then China, then taking a boat across the Pacific Ocean and a train across America to settle, finally, in Centerville, Iowa. There, Boruch (Ben) Sidransky opened a drygoods store and sent for his wife and children. Years later, my grandmother Tsipora (Cip) told me the story of her harrowing escape with two little children, my father and his sister. Bubby Cip said the only reason they made it past the soldiers on the train was because she had blond hair and blue eyes and didn't look like a Jew. I have a picture of my father standing with his first-grade class on the steps of his school in Centerville; he is wearing a miniature tuxedo and holding a violin, while all the other kids stood around in shorts and plain shirts, holding a book or a flag, like something out of a Grant Wood painting.

When my father was ten, the family moved to Humboldt Park on the near North side of Chicago, a close-knit neighborhood of Jewish émigrés. Years later, Saul Bellow, one of the kids who grew up on the block with my father, immortalized the underlying culture in *Humboldt's Gift*, a book that won the Nobel prize and captured something of Pop's own essential being. After my father's death, Bellow sent me a note that read in part, "I often feel, when I'm writing, that I'm a composite person, and your father is certainly part of the mixture. It comes over me now and then that I'm trying to do something he wanted done." What my father most wanted, of course, was to be a writer himself.

Like the generations that came before them, the kids in Humboldt Park reveled in the written word, but they also embraced the new era of the common man. Chicago in the 1920s and 1930s, Sandberg's city of broad shoulders, was a roaring place of gangsters and jazz clubs, where boogie-woogie piano players rolled 'em nightly, and Benny Goodman was the hero of many a Jewish kid. Goodman was a homeboy in short pants, a new kind of luftmensch, for whom the old status pyramid was inverted and the street action was exalted.

I somehow see this milieu—the jazz, the gangsters, the young Jewish intellectuals from Poland hitting the New World running—as having a very "Chicago" sensibility. To read, to write, to act, as Bellow wrote in *The Adventures of Augie March*, "first to knock, first admitted," was the culmination of a five-thousand-year-old drama. It was an ingathering of the Jew as street phenomenon, the American Dream fed through the mind of the Marx Brothers, the absurdity of modern life at a time when surrealism vied with socialism, and the soundtrack echoed daily with the latest refrain from a Jewish tin-pan alley. There were Jewish prizefighters, songwriters, musicians, gangsters (one of the Sidranskys was a member of Detroit's Purple Gang), doctors and merchants; the new American Jew could be anything he wanted to be. Unlike their parents, who fled the old country to avoid conscription, when the Great War eventually came, these new Americans were glad to volunteer to hunt down Hitler or Tojo or whatever evil was out there. It was an extension of their visceral love for their everyday freedoms, a new sense of sensuality, of entrance, of, finally, belonging. Think Jimmy Stewart in *It's a Wonderful Life*, a Jewish parable, or Irving Berlin (Israel Baline) writing *White Christmas*. Yankee Doodle meets Henry Roth: never before had being a Jew been as much a state of mind as a fact of life.

My father loved it all. He loved the Gillette Friday Night Fights—"look sharp.... feel sharp...be sharp"—the ball games, the infinite statistics of contemporary life, facts of all sizes that he gobbled up with a photographic memory, the arcane arguments of the Talmud rubbing up against the jokes of S.J. Perelman and the tough guys in Studs Lonnigan. It was all part of his Yiddishkeit, being uncompromisingly Jewish without being religious at all. Like so many Jews of his generation, he was an American first. For him, it was all about language, street culture, and the book. Not any book in particular—not a given philosophy or a particular interpretation of history, not communism or anarchism, or even the Torah. It was the book as an ideal, something that could contain the story of the past and sustain it into the future. Something you could write as well as read.

Intellectuals who could swing were my father's heroes, whether Benny Goodman or Hank Greenberg, and Pop took up both the clarinet and the base-ball bat seriously and with total élan. His offhand manner leant itself to playing, whether it was jazz or baseball—he could hit a fungo 300 feet and musically had perfect pitch. He seemed happiest when surrounded by other players. But none of this was his true passion. His real dream was to participate in the creation of a modern literature, to tell a story in the common tongue. This is what he and his friends must have talked about as young men, and surely promised each other they would dedicate their lives to achieving. Bellow did it, my father did not.

Instead, after the war, he moved to Racine, where his wife and children were living in his mother-in-law's house. There, he took a job as a copywriter at a small local advertising agency and spent his days crafting words to motivate people to buy stuff for their homes or their cars. At the same time, he remained very much aloof from the Racine Jews. He insisted on living on the west side of town, close to the train station and the Danish community, while the upwardly mobile Jews all lived on the north side, next to the lake, and not far from Meadowbrook, the one (restricted) country club. It was both a cultural and a geographical decision on his part. He probably felt, as his hero Groucho Marx had once so famously said, that he didn't want to be a member of any club that would have him. So while he was in Wisconsin, Wisconsin wasn't in him. A stranger in a strange land, a Jewish prince who, because of his quick mind and dazzling smile, qualified for special privileges, he hung out in Kringleville, cruised as best he could, and ducked life's daily bullets.

This never made sense to me and remained one of the biggest mysteries of his life: why, given his great sense of history and his breadth of knowledge, why did my father not fill his days with more meaningful work? Why did he hide out in the cultural tundra, slowly reading and drinking himself to death?

I remember a sign in the office of my dentist, Dr. Gorsky, which read some-thing like: "Courage is not rushing into great battles with drawn sword. Courage is facing the slings and arrows of everyday life." I would read that sign every week, as I sat there, counting the holes in the ceiling tiles and waiting for Gorsky to breathe his foul cigarette breath into my face and grind my front tooth into oblivion. I had smashed the tooth in the same alley where Pop and I played catch, falling off my bike one day face first into the concrete. Gorsky had the luxury of constructing my bridge in six or seven leisurely sessions, and I don't believe he ever used Novocain on me. "Wasn't necessary," he told my mother who brought me in. And besides, if he had asked me, I would have said, "No, I don't want anything for the pain. It's not that bad." Why would I say that? The pain of his drill haunted my dreams. It was excruciating. Why would I tell him, no, I'll just sit here with my mouth open, go ahead and rev that thing up? Because I was my father's son. Pop always bragged about how nothing hurt him. No pain bothered him. Life doesn't hurt. Rolls off a man's back, actually. Just passing through. That's the posture.

In his last writings, I found he had written, "I was lucky, I got through life and it didn't hurt at all." That's the same manuscript that starts, "Say what you will, cancer is not such a bad way to die...." I don't actually doubt that it didn't hurt him. I think maybe he had learned to lock up his feelings when it came to anything personal. Nothing was personal. It was all professional. A professional's opinion.

For me, however, it was highly personal. I wanted to know my father, and I wanted him to know me. He chose baseball (we never played music together), and he became the coach of my little league team, the Orioles. After school, I rode the bus downtown to the YMCA where tryouts and early practices were held. The Y was not far from his office at Western Advertising, and I would meet him there after tossing the ball around the noisy gym. Just across the street from his office, in the window of Porters Furniture Store, there was a round white rug designed to look like a large baseball, with red stitching and everything. It came to represent something huge to me. I stopped and stared at it every time I passed on the way to my father's office. It was connected to my desire to be a ballplayer, I guess, and to make my father proud of me. That summer, after I made the team, my mom bought me the rug.

As a coach, my father was tough, more so on me than the other kids. "Get your foot out of the bucket," he would holler when I stepped away from the ball. Or worse yet, when I hesitated before committing to the cut, "You've got a hitch in your swing!" That was the most flagrant violation a hitter could make, hesitating, not being in the moment when the ball met the bat; not flowing to the point of contact. Sometimes I wondered if this was why he was always slapping me across the back of the head, because he knew I had a hitch in my swing, and he was trying to wake me up.

Years later, reading Gurdjieff, I thought of the dreaded hitch — the moment of doubt. Wake up! "Jonson, you got a hitch in your swing. Get your foot out of the bucket, step into it!" I heard that voice in my head for years, not so much the words but the sound of it, the ring of frustration, the sense of disappointment. Long after he was gone, and I was making my first record, *that* voice seemed to come out of *my* mouth. Standing there in the vaulted expanse of Capitol Studios, the hallowed space where Sinatra had cut his classic records, to me, my voice sounded so much like my father's that I had to step away from the microphone. I didn't want to hear "that voice" anymore ("Get your foot out of the bucket!"). There are so many ways in which the sins of the father are visited upon the children.

My twelfth summer was the apogee of my baseball career. My father bought me a real glove and showed me how to form a pocket with prime neatsfoot compound, a ball and some string. After school, I worked lovingly on the glove, rubbing the oil into the palm with a rag, kneading it in, softening up the leather, making it so comfortable that the ball would naturally want to just plop into the pocket. It was almost as if, in time, the glove would catch the ball all by itself, and the hand simply had to deliver it to the right spot at the right moment. The smell of the oil as it ripened the leather was an aphrodisiac to me, and I worked on that glove religiously. Gradually, it lost its stiffness and became like an extension of my own arm. In the evenings when my father and I played in the alley, it didn't matter if I was pitching or catching, as long as the ball was changing hands.

The Orioles won a lot of games that year, and I was the starting second baseman and the leadoff hitter with a .400 batting average. Due to a great pitcher named Brian Bailee, who threw two no-hitters, we actually made it all the way to Thillens stadium in Chicago and the quarterfinals of the Little League World Series. It was a big deal. Earlier that summer, we had ridden on a float in the 4th of July parade in our Orioles uniforms, waving to friends sitting at the curb in lawn chairs, and now we took the two-hour trip to Chicago. I would like to say that Ted Savides gave me the magic black bat and with it, I won the big game in the last inning. But the truth is that Brian's arm gave out and we came up against a pitcher who threw 80 miles an hour and had his own no-hitter going against us.

And there was a nice, dramatic twist at the end. In the last inning, I became the first Oriole to get on base by virtue of a walk. Standing on the bag, I had a rising sense of destiny: I was going to steal second. I looked over at my father in the coach's box at third, but he didn't give me the sign to steal. I looked down at second. I took a step off the bag. The pitcher checked me over his shoulder, I crept another foot further, trying to worry him. I looked over at my father again; still no sign. When the pitcher looked back at the batter, I just went for it. In my mind, I saw myself executing a perfect hook-slide into second base, avoiding the glove and the ball, just like Ernie Banks on TV, but when I got there, the ball was already waiting. I was thrown out. And that was how it ended. The inning, the game, and my baseball career.

The car ride home was deathly. Pop was obviously sore at me for ignoring his coaching, but he said nothing. And I said nothing too. I wanted to say, "Sometimes, you got to go for it, right, Pop?" But I couldn't. Or he could have said, "Nice try any-way." But he didn't. As the miles passed, the gulf between us just seemed to grow and grow. When we finally pulled up in front of the house on Deane Boulevard, I jumped out of the car, ran in the basement, threw my glove in a corner, and went straight to the piano. I was actually glad that it was over.

But it wasn't really over. I have spent much of my life in pursuit of my father, or at least the man that I wanted him to be: someone who had it all, street smarts, book learning and a jazzman's cool. Ultimately, I set myself the task of succeed-ing where I thought he had failed, to imbue this life with some kind of purpose, and to create a loving family, where he had left behind only loneliness and iso-lation. I was going to be the healer, the prodigal, the revenge. Sometimes I feel like I was put on the path by a man who had no idea of the destination.

1955

The summer of '55, I began my first real job. Three times a week I took the bus across town to my Aunt Sarah's house, and she paid me ten cents an hour to pull weeds in her garden. I loved it, the freedom of leaving home, riding the bus, showing up as scheduled, sitting in the dirt, inhaling the sharp smell of marigolds. The little patch along the fence where lilies of the valley and black-eyed Susans grew became important to me; I felt proud to be contributing something. I think I learned everything I needed to know about record production by weeding my Aunt Sarah's garden: remove what doesn't belong, and make what is there beautiful.

In Racine that year, the Cadillacs had fins, the girls wore Angora sweaters, and there was a softness in the air. Life before sound pollution — with fewer cars, less construction and no constant TV chatter — was simply more peaceful: streets were quieter, houses were quieter, the whole world was quieter. Maybe because of this, the sound of a record just seemed to leap out of the phonograph at you, like a wild creature from a distant place, even though you knew it was only a steel needle vibrating in a wax groove. But that was it: I was called by the music. I wanted to be there in the worst way, in that place, that bar, that restaurant, that pad, that studio, that scene — it didn't really matter *where*, as long as it was where this sound was happening. Because, before MTV, before FM radio, before just about everything we know of today, there was that magical space where men like Louis Jordan and Erroll Garner and Dave Brubeck and Louis Armstrong and even Spike Jones were carrying on. They lived in many places at once, but they all came from that *sound*, and that sound came from the phonograph.

In the winters, there was a beautiful whiteness on the streets of Racine. At night, it was so quiet you could hear the snow falling, like the rustle of lace spreading gently over the neighborhood. The round globes cast shadows under the huge elms, and the trees bowed under the weight of the snow, while the occasional Buick hissed softly down the street on fat tires. For fun, I would stand on the corner by the stop sign, pretending to look the other way as a car pulled up. When the driver took off, I would swing down behind and grab on to the rear bumper. We called it "skitching," and we rode on the soles of our shoes, ten, fifteen, twenty miles an hour down the side streets of Racine, instant transportation over the ice and snow, like water skiers through the tundra. We all knew that one dry patch could kill you, but we were immortal, and I flew for blocks this way, going nowhere and anywhere. I came home later and later each evening having experienced the possibility of death and the feeling of a great motor pulling me forward.

I still rode the bus downtown in the afternoons, but now it was to go to Hebrew school to prepare for my Bar Mitzvah. My father had left his job in Racine and was commuting on the North Shore Railroad to Chicago, where he was a writer for the Leo Burnett Advertising Agency. He would leave home at seven in the morning and come home at seven at night. Now, instead of going to his office when I went downtown, I killed time in Trudy White's record store. With the money I made pulling weeds for Aunt Sarah, or baby sitting for the Kofsky kid, I started to buy records. Trudy White's wasn't really a record store. They sold everything from vacuum cleaners to sheet music, but they had a little record department in the back and I pawed through the two or three bins every time I was in there. One day, I found an album called *The Birdland Stars on Tour*. I don't know why it jumped out at me, probably because of the picture on the cover: four men in matching blazers under a distant spotlight. Maybe it was just the name "Birdland," which I had heard my father talk about.

I brought the disc home, went into my room, closed the door, and sat right next to my little record player, like an Eskimo huddling by a fire. I felt the heat coming from that music, from New York, Chicago, L.A. There was a saxophone player who was incredible, and I turned the jacket over to discover his name: Phil Woods. I couldn't get over the sound of his horn; it was so human, so physical. How did he do that? I held the album in my hands, staring at the photo and listening to Phil play. In between songs, the emcee, who was a midget, shouted, "Ladies and gentleman, the East meet West Septet! Let's hear it for 'em! The East meet West Septet!" Who were these guys?

The next week I went back to Trudy White's and discovered Horace Silver's album, *Finger Poppin*. That night I listened to Blue Mitchell's trumpet solo on "Juicy Lucy" so many times in a row that I started to feel like he was related to me; literally. I had the feeling that we were brothers. And I thought that he was calling my name.

One Friday night while I was babysitting for the Kofskys, I heard a car horn blowing out front. I looked out the window into the rain and sleet and saw a Buick Roadmaster idling at the curb with the windshield wipers going. Somebody inside was waving at me. I ran out of the house and leaned into the open window. It was John Isbell and he had stolen the Buick only minutes before. In those days, car lots simply left the keys in the ignition, and if you wanted to try a car, you just told the man in the office and took it for a ride. John had slipped into the Buick that afternoon, taken the key, had it copied, replaced it, and then returned later in the evening for the car itself. He just drove it off the lot. "Come on, Benny," he said, "let's go!" And just like that, I left the Kofsky boy alone in his bed, in the nice warm house with the television murmuring some old horror flick, and away we sped into the Racine night. We fishtailed through the cemetery and spun out at every stoplight, and eventually, afraid that we would be caught by the police, we ditched the car behind McKinley Junior High. I made my way back through the cemetery in the cold rain, and got into the Kofsky's living room before they returned. They never noticed a thing, paid me $1.50 and drove me home.

This started a round of petty auto theft that was made easier by the fact that my father left his red 1954 DeSoto at the train station every morning. By spring, John and I were regularly skipping school and easing down to the train station to drive off with the DeSoto. I was terrified that my father would notice his car was rarely parked where he had left it, but he never said anything. Much later, I understood that when he got off the bar car, braced for his return home, a parking spot was probably the last thing on his mind. When he walked in the front door of our house and saw me sitting at the piano, he gave me the ceremonial whack on the back of the head, and I felt we were even.

That spring, Bill Haley and the Comets launched "Rock Around the Clock" like a meteor across the teenage sky. Until then, pop songs on the radio were just tearjerkers like Teresa Brewer's "Music, Music, Music," or trivial, like Perry Como's "Find a Wheel." Sometimes, you got lucky and caught Tennessee Ernie Ford singing "16 Tons," or Peggy Lee singing "Fever" — or maybe even Sinatra singing "Learning the Blues" — inklings of a substream of sophistication. But generally, the radio played confections of the day, fitting the post-war mythology of a happy and safe world. Before Bill Haley, Middle American kids were not fighting to change the buttons on their dad's car radio. *Blackboard Jungle*, the movie that closed with the song "Rock Around the Clock," changed all that. It was a lightning rod for adolescent disaffection. Around the country, kids leaving the movie theater rioted in the streets, a phenomenon which expanded their access to the media, as the media took notice of their actions: rebellion quickly became a consumer item.

Simultaneously, black and white cultures were flowing together. It was no small coincidence that Milt Gabler, the producer of the song "Rock Around The Clock," was also the producer of Louis Jordan's earlier hits; his formula for combining the black shuffle groove with a white juvenile delinquent aesthetic became the industry standard for years to come. It was a turning point in American popular music, and it dramatically dialed up the heat. Soon it was Little Richard and Chuck Berry and, within months, duck tail haircuts, switchblade knives, tanker jackets and blue jeans made their appearance at McKinley Junior High School. Everybody wanted a piece of the blackboard jungle.

This new ache, like water, sought its own level. In my case, I was turning thirteen and I had my eye on a hot looking girl with extraordinary breasts named Marilyn. She was sweet and had a speech impediment—she said "w" instead of "l" so that she would pronounce her own name "Mariwyn"—and she never seemed to look at me or notice I existed. Then one night, the phone rang and I answered it and a girl's voice said, "Hewwo Ben? This is a fwiend of Mariwyn's. She wikes you." Suppressing my shock, I stammered that Marilyn should meet me after school and we would "do something."

The next day at lunch hour I told John my plan. He was torn between coming along "to stand watch" and dissuading me from my madness. My idea was that after school we would walk across the street to where an old lady always hung out her laundry, and there, in the soft white canyons of waving sheets, I would "do something" with Marilyn. I had no idea what. After school, Marilyn still pretending not to see me, followed John and myself into the alley, and without saying a word, as John hung back, she and I entered this snowy bower. Once inside the sheets, I simply turned to Marilyn and put my hand inside her fuzzy pink sweater. My heart stopped. Her breast was in my hand, warm and alive. It was an indescribable pleasure, like holding her beating heart itself. She just looked at me and smiled. Not a word was spoken.

Suddenly, an angry old lady appeared from nowhere. "What are you kids doing," she said. "You little criminals!" And then we ran. I didn't see where Marilyn went but John and I cut through the cemetery. We didn't stop running until we were out of range of the police or the FBI or whoever it was that old ladies sent after sex perverts like me. I was scared and out of breath, and, sitting on a tombstone, John earnestly informed me that I was probably going to go to hell for this. We sat there, and he talked to me about Christ and said that my only chance now to save my soul was to convert to Christianity and beg for Christ's forgiveness. He was dead serious. I actually gave it some thought, too, because I knew that all the hottest girls went to Luther League on Friday night. Maybe even Marilyn. The next day at school she didn't even look at me and we never spoke again.

1956

Life in Racine was generally slow, but it got more exciting when my schoolmates discovered anti-Semitism. I remember the first time I heard the word "Jewboy" whispered behind me like a cold draft in the locker room. Seemingly overnight, being a Jew became a complex thing, a subtext of so many situations, like the elephant in the living room that nobody notices. I don't have to go into the details, because anybody can imagine how creatively and thoroughly thirteen-year-old-boys can torture one another. But one example stands out.

Jim Rasmussen was a little weasel with perfect teeth and a brush haircut who palled around with the larger, more athletic kids. He had a fast mouth, and either started the "Jewboy" thing or ran with it when it took off. Soon he had everybody saying it, and he'd wait for me after school to say, "Hey Jewboy, what are you gonna do about it?" I tried to ignore him and he seemed to feel his part of the ritual had been fulfilled. One day, however, Jim goaded a quiet moon-faced kid named Jon Skow, who lived in the alley behind me, to start a fight. It was strange, because Jon was nice enough, and occasionally, we walked to school together. But apparently, this was his initiation into the cool gang. In any case, it was an offer he couldn't refuse.

He came up to me in home room that morning and said, "We're gonna fight after school."

I said, "What do you mean....why?" He said, "I can't tell you why, we just have to..." He looked really ashamed and said, "I'm sorry Ben, it's something I gotta do." After school, I went out to the playground and there he was standing at the edge of a ring of kids all waiting for something to happen. I walked up to him and said, "Jon, you don't have to do this, " and he said, "Yes I do," and pushed me down and sat on my chest and started swinging. I covered my face and he grabbed my arm and began twisting it as hard as he could. "Give up?" he said. I wouldn't. He kept twisting it harder, with both hands. My arm felt like it would come out of its socket any moment, and my eyes burned with salt water. "Give up?" By now he was pleading more than menacing. I wouldn't give him the satisfaction.

Finally, John Isbell stepped into the circle and pulled him off of me. Walking home with John, it wasn't the fight that burned my eyes and made my head swim: it was seeing a "friend" sell me out so quickly, just to be able to sit at a lunch table with kids who wore tanker jackets and put Brill Creme in their hair. That was it. The total substance behind Jon Skow's agreeing to hurt a friend was a better seat at the lunch table. The real pain was yet to come. The next morning, I met him on the street, and he wanted to walk to school with me as if nothing had happened. It was up to me to "understand" that it wasn't his fault, and that I shouldn't take it personally. I felt invisible. I saw that being a Jew was a deep river and it started with many small tributaries. But as they say, if you sit by the river long enough, you will see the corpses of all your enemies float by.

In the case of Jim Rasmussen, I didn't have to wait long. A couple of years later, when we had all moved up to Washington Park High School, and he was just another short fifteen-year-old in a Madras shirt, he and his pals went to Kenosha in a borrowed car to buy some beer. On the way back to Racine, they rolled the car, Jim was thrown out onto the highway and another car ran him over. The next day everybody at Park High was wringing their hands and swooning over the tragedy. I said nothing, but I had never been so sure that the great hand of justice did exist, and that it had risen up to smite mine enemy. And even though the text teaches that we are all reduced by a single death, that year, at the Passover Seder, when we put the drops of wine into the plate for the plagues — Dom, Kinim, Arov, Dever — I was no longer the foolish child who asked, "what did the Lord do for me?"

Taken one by one, these things were small, like drops of rain on the garden wall, but I remember clearly the moment when a friend said, "You can tell me, Ben, is it really true that Jews drink the blood of Christian babies?" That's when the whole edifice started to crumble, and I knew for sure that I was from some other place. And it was jazz, that was the place where I was from. Its voice whispered to me of a better life, where all men were brothers, and where having fun was not only a serious business but also the order of the day. The music itself was so warm and comforting, so free and on fire, and the players were so supportive of each other and the solos...well, the solos were like rhetorical flights where no words were necessary. It meant what it meant, and even as a young boy, I knew it would be a dream come true to be able to speak this language.

At this time there were two words that jumped off any printed page at me: one was "Jew" and the other was "jazz." And I noticed that these two words never appeared on the same page together.

I took solace in the sacred text of Charles Mingus' "Goodbye Pork Pie Hat" from the *Mingus Ah Um* album, with that great saxophone solo by John Handy. Here was the simple truth, stripped to its bones, just the way it is: the human condition. I was not alone. I wanted to understand what John Handy was saying. How could you play music like this? When I listened to Mingus, or Blue Mitchell and Horace Silver, I just fell in love with the possibility of meeting these men one day and of understanding this music from the inside. They may have been black and I was a Jew, but we were all marked, and we had done absolutely nothing to bring it upon ourselves. In this way, it was as if we had been chosen, that we were related, and that what I was living was not so different from what a black person would know.

When school ended that year, I rode the train from Racine to Chicago to see my father's new office. Standing on the rear platform of the old North Shore Railway, as I watched the past recede into a wild scramble of cattails and tiger lilies, I felt I was saying goodbye to something. Pop now worked in the Prudential Building, the tallest building in the Loop, and riding the elevator up to his floor, I sensed that our life had changed, that he was gone, that Racine was now pretty much over for him, and that I was on the way out, too. It was just a matter of time..."Goodbye Pork Pie Hat."

By July, I had a job at Gordon Auto Parts. As the owner's nephew, I was given the honor of working in a tin Quonset hut behind the store. There, in the blazing noonday sun, inside a windowless, airless shack, I hunched over a burlap sack, counting out used brake shoes or fuel pumps so that they could be sent back to the factory and be rebuilt. Time passed in a blur, like the filthy stinging sweat that ran into my eyes for hours on end.

One night, in the cool following a rainstorm, John Isbell and I took my father's car for a ride. It was the first time we had dared to take it at night. We had been sleeping in a tent in the backyard and around midnight, when everything was quiet and the moon was up, we just walked around to the front of the house and drove off. I spun the radio dial until we picked up Sid McCoy, the Chicago deejay who played jazz all night long. I rolled down the window and stuck my arm out, driving with one hand as I had seen my father do. We pulled into a gas station and bought soda and chips, then cruised by the lake. The wind was blowing through the car window, Sid McCoy was announcing a Cannonball Adderley song, and the world simply opened up. I felt as if I were flying, flying through a dream, I had left my body, and the car and the road and the music were one spatial thing, nothing but motion, as the headlights splashed through the darkness, showing a stop sign, which I ignored; we weren't going to stop, rolling along the lake, past the zoo, and then past another stop sign, which I also ignored, and then, in the rear view mirror, I saw the flashing red lights and for the longest time, I didn't connect them to anything, until at last, in a blast of awareness, I knew they were flashing for me.

Iced with fear, bathed in the surreal flashing red lights, I pulled the car over to the curb. Suddenly, I heard the radio really loud in the still night air, Sid McCoy giving his signature salute, "Hey hey old bean and you too baby, this is the time, this is the place, this is the real McCoy..." The cop came up to my open window and looked down at me. He took a long minute. I wasn't even five feet tall and could barely see over the steering wheel. He said, "May I see your driver's license, please," and I broke out laughing.

They took us home in separate squad cars. The cop who drove me was really nice. He told me not to worry, that a lot of kids get in trouble and it didn't mean that I couldn't be a police officer myself one day if I wanted to. We walked up the steps of my house and rang the bell. My mother opened the door. I was hiding behind the officer's legs. He said, "Ma'am, do you know where your son is?" and she said, "Yes, he's sleeping out back in a tent." He stepped aside to reveal me, and she became deathly silent. The cop explained that everything was all right and that they had found me driving the car. My mother called out, "Louis, come down! Benny is here and he's with a policeman." Instead of coming down, my father, who must have heard the whole thing, simply called out, "Tell him they can keep him."

The next morning John and I and our parents had a meeting at the police station, and it was decided that since there was no one pressing charges, we would be put under a kind of "house arrest," and our parents would guarantee our good behavior. Within days the word of what we had done spread around the neighborhood. Jimmy Anderson's parents would no longer let him hang out with us. They knew that but for the grace of God Jimmy would have taken that car ride too. As a preemptive strike, they enrolled Jimmy in St. John's military academy. It was a decision that ultimately led to his becoming a paratrooper, then going AWOL before he was sent to Vietnam, only to spend time in the brig and ultimately descend into a spiral of guilt that only stopped when he converted to Judaism and opened a little art gallery in Vermont. "I'm the only Yid in Burlington," he once said to me, "and I have your father to thank. I always thought he was so cool."

My mother and father discussed sending me to St. John's military academy too, and I thought it was ridiculous, but I was scared. Earlier that summer I had had a huge fight with my father. Pushed to the edge, crazed with rage, I had finally said to him, "Fuck you! You sold out!" I knew, I suppose, that this was the worst thing I could have said to him, his most tender, guarded, spot. He slapped me without thinking, full across the face, and then he broke into tears. So I was already on probation.

Eventually the idea of sending me to St. Johns died of its own weight. I bagged brake shoes at Gordon Auto Parts, kept my head down, and in the fall I had my Bar Mitzvah as planned. After the Bar Mitzvah, I left the Jewish temple and never returned. What had the temple ever given me? A few memorized lines to say on cue and a sense that the ghetto was still alive and well. Being a Jew was just one long, strange, lonely trek. How could it compare to the call of jazz? At age thirteen, I signed on at the temple of bebop.

That fall, my father found a good piano teacher for me in Milwaukee, and every Saturday morning we drove together the thirty miles from Racine so I could study with Milton Mieritz. Mr. Mieritz introduced me to theory, harmony and chord voicing, and helped me get my reading together. My father and I didn't talk much on the drive, but it was just about the only time during the week that we were together anymore. Squinting into the road ahead through the smoke from his Camel cigarette, he would sometimes sing fragments of curious little songs as we drove, snippets from his past like, "My name is Captain Spaulding, the African explorer," or "Well, I swan, I must be gettin' on, giddyup there Napoleon it looks like rain." But the most enigmatic of them all was something I heard him sing one rainy morning to the rhythm of the beating windshield wipers. "Looking through the knothole in grandpa's wooden leg," he sang, "who will wind the clock when I am gone?" It seemed so lonely and yet a kind of magical incantation. Splashing through the downpour, hearing his voice crooning softly, the wipers slapping back and forth, it became the biorhythm of my own escape. There was no question: I was gone. Years later, when I heard Professor George Mosse speak on the importance of alienation in the growth of personal conscience, I knew he was talking to me. "A little alienation," he said, "is not a bad thing." I am living proof.

The music carried me away, gently, steadily, one day at a time, like a dream within a dream: Thelonious Monk *Live at the Five Spot* with Johnny Griffin, that haunted record, that haunted space! Monk's piano intro on "Light Blue" was like an open wound; Johnny Griffin's saxophone solo was a litany describing everything in the room that night. You could actually hear the space. And Griffin's picture on the cover…just a shadow against the wall…who were these guys? Years later, the great Chicago bass player Richard Davis, who went to school with Griffin, told me, "In high school, when you saw Johnny Griffin coming down the hall, you ran the other way. I mean, people were afraid of him." In high school, I ran *toward* Johnny Griffin.

1957–1960

Seemingly overnight, everything changed. I was free. People who had tormented me earlier couldn't touch me anymore. I didn't care who was a jock or who was a hood. Or what anybody said. I had gone underground. I had learned how to hide my feelings and wear the mask. Then, at the end of my first year at Washington Park High School, I met a senior named Don Baldwin, a bass player, a great musician, and the leader of a little dance band. He had heard me fooling around at a piano one afternoon and introduced himself. He gave me some tips on how to play the song I was working on, and then hired me to play a dance that weekend. It was at the YWCA, and Don had professional-looking music stands with lights and a bandbook of standards. We played four-horn arrangements of songs like "Moonlight in Vermont," and "Laura" and "Smoke Gets in Your Eyes." I sat behind the piano and watched all the other kids trying to be cool and I knew something they would never know. I knew what it felt like to create a sound that made people want to hold each other and move together and dream of a time and place where they would be free. It was my introduction to the sacred hypnosis of jazz. I wore white socks and got paid $3.

Like everyone else, I drank beer behind the football stands and smoked Pall Malls in the parking lot, and the day we heard Ray Charles sing "What'd I Say" over at Todd Dahlen's house, with that exotic electric piano and those girls moaning in the background, Todd, John and I stole Todd's father's car and smashed it up. By the late fifties, music was starting to have this effect on a lot of people. And by then, I was dreaming the dream that Mose Allison sang about in "City Home," which was on my latest Trudy White purchase, *The Transfiguration of Hiram Brown*:

> "I'm thinking of a place
> I'm waiting for the day
> When I can make my getaway.
> Because as any fool can see
> There's nothing here for me
> But hurry up boy bring that water
> Don't do things you shouldn't oughta, but
> When I get away
> And find my easy street
> I'll have a smile for all I meet

And they will welcome me I know
Everywhere I go
I'll see the town in all its glitter
How could anyone be bitter?
And there's a chance
That I will find my real romance
When I get to my city home..."

That spring, we played the music from *South Pacific* at the high school talent show, and I organized the band. When the chorus line came out to sing "I'm Gonna Wash That Man Right Outta My Hair," I noticed a girl at the end of the chorus line. Her name was Terry and she lived right across the street from me, but I guess I had never seen her in cutoff jeans and a white rolled up shirt before. Or maybe it was finding her in this musical moment, away from the push and shove of the classroom, available to walk home with me after the show; either way, I was hooked.

The passing decades have witnessed America's inexorable descent into brutality — from the "peace and love" of the sixties to the "disco and sex" of the seventies to the "rap and violence" of the eighties and nineties — but the fifties were all about romance. Of course we believed in love too; love in the afternoon, in the basement on the pool table with her little brother peeking in the window and us not even caring; love in the park, in the bushes, behind the band shell, standing up in the garage, lying down in the front seat of a parked car. How can one girl's body be so infinite in possibility? But for all our clutching, promising and tears, nothing was so wrenching as finding the strength to hold her hand in public for the first time.

It happened one warm spring afternoon, while walking home from school with the birds singing and the bridal wreathes in bloom. I reached over for her hand and took it and she did not object and, for a moment, life was complete and at rest. It was such a small thing, really, almost invisible, but holding her hand in public finally released some deep emotional knot that I didn't even know I had been carrying. For a moment, I could breathe again. And then just as suddenly, a '51 Ford wheeled around the corner, driven by a kid named Gordy, a senior with a brush cut, and as he waved at Terry, she casually dropped my hand. The wind just went completely out of me. In that brief flash, I learned everything I needed to know about love, loss and desire. It is a well to which I've returned often over the years, and I am still amazed at how one small moment, taken at the right time and in the right place, can sustain you for your whole life. It's my Madeleine.

"My analyst told me
That I was right out of my head
The way he described it
He said I would be better dead than live
I didn't listen to his jive
I knew all along he was all wrong
And I knew that he thought
I was crazy but I'm not, oh no..."

Annie Ross, singing "Twisted," on Lambert, Hendricks and Ross's album *The Hottest New Group in Jazz*, was saying you can learn a lot by going crazy, and it became easy to believe she was right. Jon Hendricks, on the same record, taught:

"Take a look at me boy
Takes another look, take another look
Take another look,
Take another good long look at me
Love opened my eyes and now I see
Clouds of gray have silver linings when they're reversed
I found your love
And that's when the old gray cloud burst."

Words skipping like stones across the surface of time; love was a ball, and life was there for the taking. Advice from two "first degree searchers." I just had to get out of town and find them.

I wasn't driven to get to New York City or anywhere in particular. I just wanted out. I wanted to shake off this bizarre, macho, blue-collar city, where I was as out of place as I would have been at the only country club, which didn't allow Jews anyway. Most of the kids I graduated with went on to permanent positions at their summer jobs. In the summers, I, too, worked in the factories: Young Radiator Company, Acme Steel Company, and, the most brutal of them all, Eisendrath Tannery.

There, in a soot-covered building down by the river, we took shapeless animal skins and tossed them into a stinking vat of acid to strip them of their hair. But the worst job I had at Eisendrath's was on "the plating machine." My job was to haul tanned hides and throw them, one by one, into a huge press. The plating machine closed with ten tons of pressure and hundreds of degrees of heat in order to permanently stamp a grain into the leather. Before the machine kicked closed, a little gate swung down and swept past your fingers to make sure your hands were clear. The guy who worked across from me was missing two fingers. I would throw in a skin, trip the machine with my foot, and leap backwards. He would casually reach in and pull the skin out, muttering to himself. It was "piece work," we were being paid by the number of skins per hour, and I was obviously slowing him down, cutting into his take. I must have cost him a lot of money that summer, because during lunch hours, when everybody sat around listening to Paul Harvey on the radio ("Good Day!"), he would look me dead in the eye, shake his head and spit out the word "College!" That was his nickname for me.

All summer long, I counted the minutes until I could go home and put on the new Miles Davis record I had found, *Kind of Blue*. I listened to that record morning, noon and night. If the smell of leather had lost its charm for me, my love of the pocket was stronger than ever. The pocket is what musicians call the feeling when all the members of a group are working together like the fingers on a hand, and Miles' album was the epitome of manual dexterity. The liner notes, written by pianist Bill Evans, describing the delicate Japanese art of spontaneous painting—where something is captured that escapes all explanation, a knowing beyond understanding—captured my own sense that when you're ahead of your time, it's like never happening at all.

And then it did happen for me. Standing at my door was J.C. Holly, a junior at the University of Wisconsin and the leader of a little college band called "The Natural Five." He had heard me play at one of the local dances and had come to ask my parents if I could go to Madison on the weekends and play in his band. And my parents said yes. This was one of the greatest gifts they ever gave me. Sometimes history is made just because somebody said "yes."

That fall, my sister had gone off to Brandeis University—she was writing dramatic and illuminated letters back home—and my younger brother, Ezra, who had been born when I was eleven, was now a cute six-year-old occupying most of my parents' time. This made it easier for me to escape. I sort of got lost in the shuffle, and by the time they looked around, as if under the cover of darkness, I was gone.

On Friday afternoons, I rode up to Madison with the bass player, a wild character named Don Smith, who drove the back roads in his primered Ford with one hand on the wheel, sipping from a pint of blackberry brandy with the other. The whole way he would give me a play-by-play of his week's activity. "Last night, I fucked a girl right there, in that seat, right where you're sitting," he said to me one day. "Yeah, I fucked her so hard she actually took a shit, right there..." It was a wild ride down the blue line highways of Wisconsin.

In Madison, I slept on the living room sofa of the Kappa Sigma fraternity house, where J.C. was a brother. It was 1960, and the place was Animal House. By late Friday afternoons, the floor of the bar room in the basement was awash with beer. One memorable night, after I had returned from some sorority gig with J.C., I began playing a driving boogie on the old upright piano in the bar room, and the brothers became so happy that they got together, picked up the piano and threw it into the lake. Mike Murroch, a Kappa Sig linebacker who would soon go to the Rose Bowl, gave me some advice from his supine position that I have never forgotten. He said, "Do something, Ben, you got to *do* something." I took it for a kind of wisdom, yet when the Kappa Sigs asked me to pledge a few weeks later, saying I was the first Jew they had ever considered, I declined. Doing something is not the same as doing anything.

Chapter Two

Good judgment comes from experience
Experience comes from bad judgment.

— STEPHEN NACHMANOVITCH

1961

W e pulled into Madison on a muggy August afternoon, my father and I. It was a week before most of the other students arrived and the streets were empty and quiet except for the rise and fall of cicadas and the hum of an occasional plane in the sky: a sleepy Mid-West college town just before the storm.

The curb was littered with piles of chairs, desks and assorted household goods thrown out by departing students and waiting to be adopted by new arrivals. My father parked the Plymouth in front of the rooming house at 509 N. Henry Street where I was to live, and when we got out and stood on the curb, looking up at the old wood frame building, he said, "You know, I think I lived here once." It turned out he had, back in 1936, when the Rathskeller in the student union was for "men only," and the rooming house on Henry Street was at the edge of the known campus universe.

By 1961, however, it was smack dab in the middle of a flourishing rah rah culture, a block away from Langdon Street, where the fraternity and sorority houses vibrated with the hormonal pump of pre-rush activity. At the other end of Henry Street, on State Street, the scene ran from the state capitol to the University, past Martins Tailoring, where old Mr. Deutchkron sat mending pants, past Riley's Liquor Store, where old man Riley would sell anything to anybody as long as they came in the back door, past The Stop and Shop, where old Mr. Caputo cursed the kids as he took their money, past Victor Music, where they had a few jazz records hidden in the back, past The Pub with its window on the world, and past The Pad, Madison's only coffee house, where Murray made a bitter brew and the young Bob Dylan had stopped on his way from Minneapolis to New York City the year before.

I had rented a room along with another kid from Racine, but after only four weeks he had pledged ZBT and moved into the fraternity house, leaving me to my own devices. One of my favorite devices was playing the piano in Lowell Hall, an upscale girl's dorm on Langdon Street that had a nice baby grand in the lobby which nobody ever used. It didn't dissuade me that residents occasionally stopped to listen. That's how I met red-headed Candy Howe, with her sweet disposition, and exotic Jody Gottfried, with her sleek dancer's body, and ultimately, Lynzee Klingman, a fey, funny girl who looked like a knocked back Liza Minelli, with a wealth of New York Jewish style and humor. Through her, I met Peter Belsito from Whitestone, New York; Peter knew all about Cannonball Adderley and Charles Mingus, and the day we discovered our mutual love for alto player Jackie McLean, we went directly to The Pub and got drunk.

That autumn was the end of the era of campus innocence. I remember it as though through a golden haze of slowly falling maple leaves and spiraling punky smoke, mixed with the intoxicating smell of old wooden desks and the vision of young girls with pony tails. Student demonstrations still meant panty raids and homecoming floats. The first television generation was blithely playing out its "Spin and Marty" and "Leave It To Beaver" fantasies.

I had enrolled in the Integrated Liberal Studies Program, a kind of college within a college designed for about 300 students, and my first six weeks were an endless round of Greek history, anthropology and science. I would come back to my room on Henry Street and try to hit the books, but the place was its own distraction. Next to me lived a fast talking hustler from Brooklyn named Fields — he went by his last name only — who ran a string of beautiful girls through his room day and night. Typical was the afternoon when, trying to study, I was interrupted by a commotion in the hallway. I looked out and saw Fields ushering out a spectacularly beautiful Wisconsin blond. He turned to me and said, "They're all the same, they don't want you to think they're a who-ore, but they love it if you treat 'em like one." She just glared at him and flounced down the stairs.

We heard the screen door slam and we both knew what was coming next. From the front porch, we heard the deep baritone voice of Dave Hill, a.k.a. Dingus Zulu, as he started in with his best John Lee Hooker imitation: "Boom Boom Boom Boom...gonna shoot you right down..." Dingus was a large black man in his thirties, one of those guys who might have been a college student once but who now lived in the rooming house and bottom fished for chicks by spending his days on the front porch with an old guitar.

The ringmaster of this little circus was a guy in his sixties named Hans Jensen who owned the building and slept on a cot in the basement. One day, for reasons known only to himself, he took a garden hose and stuck it through the window of a first floor room, and when the student was flushed out like a gopher from his den, Hans blamed the whole thing on Fields. "He just ran upstairs," Hans told the confused kid, "You better go get him." The kid ran upstairs wet, flustered and pissed off and we could hear the sound of Hans laughing his head off down below. Just another bizarre Tuesday at 509 N. Henry.

On weekends, I played jazz gigs at fraternity houses. We would do three or four gigs a weekend, including a "beer supper" on both Friday and Saturday nights. These usually started out as polite affairs, with the fraternity brothers escorting their housemother, a middle-aged matron with the dubious task of looking after their moral development, into the dining room. They made a great show of holding her chair for her and serving her dinner. Then, after she had been escorted back to her room, the charade ended and the party began. By midnight, the brothers would be pouring beer into the piano, groping their dates, and just puking into the corners. As musicians, we got to witness the whole sorry affair and at the end of these long, "Mack the Knife" nights, packing up our music and smoking a last cigarette, we couldn't wait to get out of there.

After these gigs, I always went to The Pad to cool out and see what was up. The Pad was a dark, funky hole-in-the-wall with an old upright piano, a hip abstract mural and two rows of tables generally filled with dark-haired kids from New York City. The girls wore black tights and Fred Braun shoes, they pierced their ears to accommodate exotic dangling 8th Street jewelry and carried diaphragms in their purses. The boys grew beards, had shaggy hair and fingers yellowed from nicotine. Murray gave the regulars credit, a small detail that loomed large to all of us at the end of each month and ensured that the place was always packed.

I played piano there long into the night, either solo or at jam sessions with Elliot Eisenberg on drums and Bill Hannigsburg on bass. One night, for some karmic reason, several piano players were in the house, and we had our own little cutting contest. Until a completely unknown blind man was escorted into the room. He sat for a while, listening, then made his way to the piano and, intuitively avoiding all the bad keys, played an angular, soulful blues that brought the room to silence. When he was done, there was applause, the blind man stood, his companion offered an arm, and they went back out into the night. We never got his name. It was like an apparition of things to come.

1962

S ome of the regulars at The Pad ultimately achieved notoriety — Danny Kalb, for example, formed the Blues Project, and Marshall Brickman went on to write with Woody Allen — but most of its denizens simply dug their own deep local legends and live on only in the memories of those they touched. Regulars like "Boot" Jones, who delivered the food and a whole lot more, Joe Jackson, the sandal maker, and guitar player "Filthy" Phil Buss; these are names that still ring out loud and clear around the world to those who were there. But first among them were Gooch and Cindy.

Lowell "Gooch" Jenkins was a 300-pound black man, a football player and a terrific painter, and Cindy was his 95-pound girlfriend, white and from southern Wisconsin. They were a flamboyantly hip couple, a gathering of opposites, and they lived in a small walk-up a block from campus. One warm night in the spring of 1962, Peter Belsito took me there.

It was the first time I smoked pot. We all sat in a big circle, a few great looking Jewish chicks from New York dressed in black tights, black sweaters, and black eye shadow, Peter, me, a few others. We got so stoned. We listened to Miles Davis and Dave Van Ronk. I remember the dark wood of the old floors, the circle of people passing the pipe, holding my breath, feeling myself expand, expand, keep expanding, the freedom of hearing people talk about bebop and sex and history, living history, real intellectual history, the buzz about the freedom rides that summer, the latest Lenny Bruce routine on Philly Joe Jones, Dracula goes gourmet, the opening, opening, like a window letting in some fresh air, the feeling of finally being connected, wired, Cindy sitting cross legged on the floor called somebody "tow" for being against the current, the current being something you felt when you were plugged into the group antenna, hearing Jackie McLean in the background, and Lynzee whispering in my ear, "you taste like pineapple charms," opening, opening, there being no guides, nobody had ever been exactly down this road before, *On the Road* itself being just a few years old and Vietnam just a few years ahead, living in the middle, invisible because the rest of Madison was on its way to the Rose Bowl, they were so straight you could pass a joint in front of them on the corner of State Street at high noon and nobody would know the difference, because you were invisible and the only people who knew what was going on were all sitting around in a circle at Gooch and Cindy's, expanding, expanding.

For the first time, I knew what it was to be truly happy, a feeling of hope and possibility that opened to the horizon, the very real possibility that things could change, a thrilling sense of future. Change, hope and possibility all existed in the act of passing that hash pipe and listening to Jackie McLean.

The straight world might have called us beatniks, but to us the term was a pejorative — like "hippie" years later — nobody was self-identified as a beatnik (a self-identified beatnik is an oxymoron, or maybe just a plain moron). Maynard G. Krebbs was a beatnik. There was, however, a strong Bohemian strain, a mandate for self-expression and tolerance, the open, inquisitive spirit known locally as "the Wisconsin Idea" as it is written on the plaque in Bascom Hall: "We believe that the great state University of Wisconsin should forever encourage that fearless sifting and winnowing by which alone the truth can be found." That's what we were doing, sifting and winnowing. And rolling and smoking.

We revered the post-war Greenwich Village melange of jazz, literature, art and philosophy, and, as in New York, there was a decidedly left-wing Jewish cast to the affair. Much of the music played at the Folk Arts Society, for example, was learned in the Jewish summer camps on the East Coast. And although Jewish by definition, the spirit at these camps was secular, liberal and enlightened, reflecting the Jewish passion for social justice. Even the music of Mississippi Fred McDowell or Leadbelly was considered political inasmuch as the lyrics described a world of inequity and hardship. So when Bobby Zimmerman, the Jewish kid from Hibbing, Minnesota, arrived on the East Coast to sit at the death bed of Woody Guthrie, he was fulfilling his Yiddishkeit as well as his left-leaning politics, even as he was masquerading as a non-denominational Christian folkie from Oklahoma. Perhaps especially so. At that moment, they were one and the same, Jewishness and the left. And if this was the fire in which the persona of Bob Dylan was forged, then it was also the basis, within a few years, for the politicization of much of popular music. For a time, Jews and blacks rode the freedom train together.

In addition, there was a strong undercurrent of Jewish humor, which seemed to cross any ideological boundary. Not just the candid and profound observations of Mort Saul and Lenny Bruce, but also the ironic twist of phrase, the power of a seemingly offhand remark. A poem going around at the time said:

A brick not used in building
Can break a windowpane
For those who have ears to hear
Let it be said again
A brick not used in building
Can break a windowpane

It reminded me of the Stan Freeberg bit:

General: "Do you want this war to end on a note of triumph or a note of disaster?"

Stoned Soldier: "Either way, as long as it swings!"

Later, of course, one saw in these elements—Yiddishkeit, left-leaning politics, Jewish humor—the roots of a counter-culture, of people choosing *out* of the main game. And later still, one recognized in this impulse the concept of "Tikkun," the Jewish commandment to heal the world. But in the early sixties, in Madison, Wisconsin, it was just what was happening on a Saturday night, more like the Integrated Liberal Studies program of the streets than any planned or self conscious movement. Politics and bebop, pot and Ingmar Bergman, Gooch and Cindy, Lord Buckley and Franz Fannon, Gurdjieff and Jorge Louis Borges, Miles and Muddy Waters, sex and the blues, it was all up for grabs. It was a closed circle, but expanding, ever expanding.

It's difficult to describe the character and smallness of this scene at the time. Unlike the image of the drug culture today—the legacy of thousands of awful Cheech and Chong jokes and twisted crackheads—students who self-identified with this group were generally alert intellectually and driven by learning. Pot or peyote, whatever was at hand, was used as a way of intensifying the learning experience. (The line was you used drugs, they didn't use you.) Of course this was an ideal; we were not unaware that people often crossed over the line and, as Alan Ginsberg pointed out, many great minds were lost to the angry streets. But learning was the key. We were on fire. We kept stoned to keep cool.

I remember one afternoon, sitting on the flagstone terrace behind the student union, just watching the ducks paddle around Lake Mendota, when a young experimental psychologist named Ira Schneider became adamant that we all had to grasp the importance of the recent discovery of DNA. He began by haranguing us about this moment in time, the arrival of a human map, a key to everything from memory to meaning, and then, caught up in his sense of an historical fulcrum, he insisted that a group of us go to his house where he made his famous pot cookies in order that we might better understand the concepts he was describing. In the end, he wound up filming everybody doing bizarre acts in front of an American flag, but still, his initial impulse was correct; or at least, it did no harm.

At the time, we clearly didn't appreciate our extraordinary good fortune. To be alive when Miles Davis and John Coltrane, Art Blakey and Ray Charles, James Brown and the Stax and Motown stars were all making their classic albums—to us, it just felt like another day on planet earth. We couldn't know that thirty years later, this music would still seem like the best of the best. Still, within our little group, it was understood that the music was special, as true, as real, and somehow as life changing as anything else being presented to us at the University. Everything else — the pot, the politics, the interpersonal upheavals — seemed designed to bring this point forward.

Finally, the road led to the place where I lived. To this day, when people ask me how I can live in such a small town, I just smile and think, "The road leads from New York City to Madison, not the other way around."

It was a moment in time. A rare moment, it turns out. It seemed like it would last forever. It turns out, it did.

That summer, I returned to Racine to work at Young Radiator Company. There, I wore a white lab coat and used a slide rule to calculate the coefficiencies of cooling in a wind tunnel. In August, I quit and, following a time tested route of escape, I took a Greyhound to New York City. The bus arrived at Port Authority late on a Friday afternoon in August. I walked the few blocks to 52nd Street, found Birdland, and stood in front of the club until it opened. I watched as people came and went, drinking in the feeling at this historic spot ("the Birdland Stars on tour!"), and when the club finally opened and the musicians arrived with their horns and hats, I followed them down the long hallway and into the heart of jazz history.

That night, I saw Dizzy Gillespie's band and watched emcee Pee Wee Marquette, the same midget who shouted "The East Meets West Septet!" on my first jazz record, as he pretended to have a problem pronouncing Dizzy's last name (Gillepsie). Years later, I understood this happened often, especially if a musician didn't tip PeeWee a few bucks before each performance. These short-term memory lapses of his caused one irate jazzman to refer to him as "half a motherfucker."

I got a room at the Albert Hotel on 11th and University Place, and during the day I went to drink egg creams at the corner pharmacy and then rode the subway up to 238th Street to see my pneumatic girlfriend from Madison, Judy Rohmer. Judy had introduced me to the music of Dave Van Ronk and the Village culture and to guys who drank Robitussin, and the rocketing underground rides to see her in the Bronx were out of time and place, as if I was creating my own fiction; I remember it like scenes from a Shirley Clark film.

A few weeks later, I was back in Madison, at the rooming house on Henry Street, back for round two of ILS, without a thought in my head, just riding my Vespa

125 down Langdon Street to the student union one crisp autumn afternoon. I never made it there.

Instead, passing by the lakefront, I heard a four-piece band playing a rocking groove that reminded me of the kind of shuffle Louis Jordan would play, but with more raw energy, more like the boogie-woogie I loved as a kid. I rode my motor scooter right up to the edge of the stage and watched the band. They sang like angels. The two guitar players and the bass player had great vocal harmonies worked out. This was before the Beatles, and nobody had ever heard anything quite like it. The music they were playing was rough, urban, totally different from the Dave Van Ronk and Leadbelly being played by the New York crowd. This was Southern comfort, party music.

The band was really working the audience. The lead singer was just hammering the kids twisting in front of the stage; he was laughing, having a ball, insulting the guys, hitting on their girlfriends right in front of them, and everybody seemed to be loving it. They sang "Work with Me Annie," "Money," "Louie Louie," "Kansas City," "Fanny Mae," "Who Do You Love?" "Oo Poo Pah Doo," "Oh Charlena," "Got My Mojo Workin," "Long Tall Texan." It just kept coming, no intellectual pretensions, just good old animal magnetism. The more I heard them, the more I liked them. The clincher was they wore matching blazers and had no piano player.

I hung around and talked to them afterwards. Who were these cowboys? The lead singer was Steve Miller, from Dallas, Texas, and the bass player was his friend from home, Boz Scaggs, who had followed him to the University of Wisconsin. The drummer was a chunky guy named Ronnie Boyer, who turned out to be the manager of a hamburger joint out on the edge of town, and the third singer, who covered the Buddy Holly stuff, was Denny Berg, Steve's frat brother from the Chi Psi Lodge. They called themselves The Ardells, and they could make Joey Dee's "Peppermint Twist" sound like meaningful music.

At the time, I was making $35 a night leading my own little jazz trio, and when I joined The Ardells a few months later, I often got paid $50 a night just to have a ball. This lesson was not lost on me. From then on, I played at every fraternity and sorority house in town, and at most of the clubs within a hundred miles. Some nights, we roared through the Wisconsin back roads in Steve's VW microbus, listening to WLAC from Nashville, Tennessee, to Jimmy Reed and John R, "White Rose petroleum Jelly, poppa likes it 'cause it's easy on the pocketbook, momma likes it 'cause it don't stain the sheets..." I learned there and then, in Leadbelly's phrase, that "the blues is a feeling, and when it hits you, it's the *real* news." With The Ardells, I discovered the power of laying down a simple groove and watching people step out of themselves. It's what happens when you take your heartbeat and project it into a room full of people. When you get into that hypnotic space, a lot of magic can happen.

Of course, just as often, what happens is not magic at all. Like the night we drove down to Northwestern University in Evanston, Illinois. Joe Baldwin, a local singer who booked the gig for his own band, The Diablos, had double-booked himself that night, so Steve and I and some other guys drove the hundred miles to the Chicago suburb and pretended to be Joe Baldwin and The Diablos. We carried our instruments up a ladder into the loft of an old barn where the fraternity brothers had cleared out a space for a dance floor and set up beside a huge tub of white lightning (lab alcohol and Kool Aid.) Before the night was over, some of the sorority sisters had misplaced their clothes, some of the brothers had fallen out of the loft, and Joe Baldwin and The Diablos were forever banned from Northwestern University.

At the time, there were only a few bands around that played real blues or soul music. One was The Seven Sounds, from Milwaukee, and they used to come to Madison on weekends, very much like Otis Day and the Knights in *Animal House*. They traveled with their own scene, like gangsters, ten or twelve very sharp black dudes and some very flashy women, arriving in three big old Cadillacs, one pulling a trailer for the Hammond B3 organ. Usually, a rich fraternity like the Pi Lambs hired them and then everybody in town would try to crash. Those nights, the security was tighter than a pair of new shoes. These were fantastic parties, very segregated, with a smoky little Africa roped off in the back for the band, and the rest of the house crammed to the gunwales with bombed horny honkys.

One night, after a Seven Sounds gig, I was walking out of the frat house with Monte, the organ player. Earlier, we had played fourhanded at the organ and were in the midst of connecting on Bobby Timmons and Erroll Garner when somebody threw out the word "nigger," and suddenly, everything got real quiet. And then all hell broke loose. That night, the band put two Pi Lambs into the hospital just trying to get up the hill to their cars. As the Cadillacs pulled out, I leaned into the front window and said to Monte, "Man, I'm so sorry about what happened here," and he just looked at me gently said, "Don't worry man, my love is deeper than that."

I never saw Monte again, but I never forgot his words, nor that this music comes from a very deep love.

Shortly after I met Steve Miller, he too moved into the rooming house on Henry Street. The Chi Psi lodge where he had been living was just around the corner, but it wouldn't allow girls into the rooms, so Steve jumped ship. By this time, 509 N. Henry had become a full blown circus, with the great football player Larry Howard living there, and Hans Jensen going completely berserk at times. One day, Hans dragged my Vespa motor scooter into Larry's room and then accused me of driving it into the building. It was just lunacy. Everybody was trying to figure out some new outrage to pull on somebody else. And to make it even more exciting, 509 was adjacent to Dorothea House, a girls' dorm where young ladies from New York City lived and, occasionally, undressed with their window shades up. On weekends, the traffic on the fire escape that joined the two buildings could be pandemonium, with people climbing up and down the ladders at all hours.

From the beginning, Steve and I each seemed to have something the other wanted. I was completely taken with the strength and purity of his voice and his ability to connect to the people, those rocking shuffles that he just threw off with ease. He, on the other hand, was fascinated with my access to a bohemian underground. We spent a lot of hours talking and playing records for each other. He introduced me to Jesse Hill and Ernie K. Doe and Jimmy Reed, and I played him Horace Silver and Art Blakey and Charles Mingus. All of this music was actually connected through the blues, and it was not difficult for us to find common ground. It was only years later, after the record industry had taken over and sliced up the audience into a hundred little demographic strips that Steve and I, along with so many others, lost the ability, or the desire, to communicate.

At the time, Steve thought smoking pot was immoral, but he acted as though it was simply uncool. It's hard to imagine the guy who would later immortalize the line, "I'm a joker, I'm a smoker, I'm a midnight toker," being so against getting high, but he was. Pot was anathema to frat boys back then. It was somehow too dangerous, or decadent. One night, Steve and I were listening to music in my room, and when I went into my closet to get something, as a prank, or just to make me paranoid, he locked the closet door behind me. "Now how do you like smoking that shit?" he called out. I just opened the door to the little refrigerator I kept in the closet, and by the glow of a ten-watt bulb, I had my own little picnic. I said, "Oh please, Steve, don't throw me in that briar patch!"

Over the years, many fans of Steve Miller's subsequent recordings have asked me essentially the same two questions:

(1) Who was "Maurice"? As referred to in Steve's hit song "The Joker," Maurice was the smarmy guy in the middle of "The Duke of Earl" who probably wore a pencil-thin mustache and a cape and stepped out of the dark to deliver his soulful lyrics, speaking in big words that often made no sense but communicated the essence anyway, words like "pompetous," as in "the pompetous of love" (i.e. the profound dignity of a meaningful relationship) or "expoobedance" (make up your own meaning here). Steve loved this character, the pretentiousness of it, and had a lot of fun playing that role from time to time.

(2) What did it feel like back then, to be hanging out with Steve and Boz at age nineteen, playing this raw, prototype music? I always say, it felt just like this

feels, right here, right now. You breathe in, you breathe out. History only happens in the rear view mirror.

One night at The Pad in the fall of 1962, I met the great historian Harvey Goldberg. You would often see him there, or at The Pancake House, another place that stayed open late at night, drinking coffee. He was a night owl and a lover of jazz, and had lived in Paris at the Hotel La Louisianne when pianist Bud Powell and his wife Buttercup lived there. Before coming to teach European intellectual history at The University of Wisconsin, he taught at The New School for Social Research, where his friend Eric Hobsbawm was a major jazz scholar.

Harvey was an anomaly, a serious academic who preferred the company of ordinary folks to that of his colleagues, and he was one of the few teachers who anticipated the coming cultural firestorm and the role music would play. At that time, there were few serious studies being done on jazz, and virtually every respectable institution, including the University of Wisconsin, refused to even teach it in their music department. But in conversations at The Pad, Harvey made it clear that jazz was a key to understanding the American past, present and future. When he spoke, he was spellbinding; he made history come alive and everyday life seem important. To this day, when I go on stage, I take a piece of Harvey with me; I always try to let the audience know that *this* is what history feels like, right now, sitting here in this moment.

I was inspired to try my own hand at a kind of cultural criticism. I began writing a column for the student newspaper, *The Daily Cardinal*. My sister had found her way to the University and become friends with Jeff Greenfield, then the editor of the school paper. Maxine, who was the arts editor, and Jeff arranged for me to write a weekly jazz review. One week, I critiqued John Coltrane's album, *Ballads*. I said, in effect, that I thought it was boring, probably beneath the man and possibly an attempt to sell out. I can't imagine what made me say that. I was probably just trying to be clever, to fill up a few column inches, to get laid. I was young.

And then, a week later, I was at a friend's place. He had just purchased a big pair of Koss headphones, the kind that looked like the sound-absorbers worn by ground crews at the airport. After smoking a joint, I put on the headphones and he put on a record. Slowly, I came apart. It was the loveliest, most reassuring music I had ever heard, and I felt a panic in me subsiding, a panic I didn't even know I had been feeling. And of course, the record I was listening to was John Coltrane's *Ballads*.

How could I have been so stupid? How could I have missed something that beautiful? Are we all that blind to our own feelings? Or was it just that we are so often pulled by the need for acceptance from others that we will say anything to be clever, to be feared, or just not to be discovered? It was a dramatic lesson for me.

Taking the headphones off, I swore there and then that I would never again resort to the critics' cleverness at the expense of opening my heart. In the land of the blind, my radar may have been poorly defined, but at least I knew when I was in the dark. It would take years to fully appreciate just how dark it really was.

1963

Music was now at the center of my life, and with Harvey Goldberg helping me to contextualize it, I was in a rush to describe the social movements of the time in terms of jazz. There were an increasing number of like-minded people speculating on the political and cultural implications of this music, like Pallo Jordan, the son of a black professor who had been thrown out of South Africa and was now teaching at the University. Pallo and Elliot Eisenberg and I would talk long into the evenings about the role of jazz in America. It wasn't long before the nightlife overran the accumulation of college credits.

The denouement came in the spring of '63. It was triggered in part by a paper I wrote for a comparative literature class examining "The Introspection Toward Isolation." My premise was that the use of the first-person voice dictated content and subtext, and I went on to follow this up in the writings of Sartre, Pavese, Camus, Genet, and several others. It was a roaring, careening work that kept me up several nights in a row. And perhaps because these are not the sunniest of writers, I was plunged, at the end, into a profound despair. The paper itself concluded, "The disintegration of values so often discussed is nothing other than the reduction of Truth from a set social standard to one man's microcosm; there no longer exists a coherent, acceptable universal morality... it is too late."

I was struggling with the continuity of art and community, a major preoccupation of the times. I suggested that, "the widespread use of first-person writing is a significant indication of the growing anxiety and gap between

Man and his environment, and between one man and another. It is the ultimate stress on the penultimate existence...None of these authors show the least bit of faith in man's ability to create a worthy society; only resignation: 'History is blind. Man is not.'" Responsibility for moral development seemed to be taken out of the hands of institutions and thrown back on the individual. We were all alone.

Perhaps it was the long hours of struggling with this paper, or my spiraling into the events that were brewing on the streets, but after turning it in, I no longer felt like going back to class. The game of accumulating credits became transparent, and I started avoiding all my classes. Soon, I was having trouble getting out of bed in the morning. The following week, the paper was returned to me with an excellent grade and an invitation to come in and meet with the professor. But by that time, I had become anxious and depressed. For several nights, I had a recurring dream where I suddenly found myself naked in a classroom with no idea what the class was about.

Not long thereafter, my father and Saul Bellow came to Madison for a weekend. They were traveling the back roads of their own past, and had arrived on a damp March weekend to attend a social function being thrown by the English Department. They were clearly enjoying themselves, like a couple of kids, joking and telling each other stories that had so many arcane references I couldn't really follow the plot.

After lunch, I showed the paper to my father, to demonstrate, I suppose, that I was still working at the job he was underwriting. The next morning at breakfast, before the two of them pulled out of town, Bellow said he, too, had looked at it and thought it was good. And then he said, "You know, if you love to read, maybe you shouldn't be a literature major. It could put you off reading forever." He spoke a little about how his own work was often misunderstood, how academics often read things into his work that he had never intended. He seemed to be telling me that you must be careful about the size and shape of your devotions. You can either "know" something or "have" something. And perhaps we shouldn't know our loves too well. Like Heisenberg's uncertainty principle, our intense gaze alters the object of our attention, and nothing is without its consequences, not even love.

The next week, wandering down State Street to avoid going to school, I passed a store with papered windows and a sign reading, "Coming Soon! Discount Records." The door was unlocked and I went inside and found a middle-aged man unpacking boxes. I asked him if he needed help. He said, "What do you know about music?" A few minutes later I had a job. An hour later, I had dropped out of school.

Soon this record store had become the center of activity, not only for me but for the growing Madison counter-culture, a focal point much like the book stores must have been during the Paris uprisings. Working at Discount Records was a graduate education in music and the record business, which seemed to be arriving out of nowhere and mutating right in front of our eyes. This was the first full service record store in town. Up until then, records were sold in little bins at the back of appliance shops.

When Discount Records first opened its doors, most of the customers came in for classical music. I would stand in the back and wait for a potential jazz customer. It might be somebody asking about an old, corny show tune (*My Fair Lady* was one of the biggest selling albums of the day), or a pop album, but if I got to them first, they would walk out with something by Miles or Coltrane. I could sell a jazz record to practically anybody because my love of the music was so strong, and, at the time, jazz was fresh and new.

I would say, "Have you heard this album? Let me play it for you..." and then we would stand there listening to the music together. Pretty soon, someone else would come up and ask, "What's that music you're playing?" And then a little scene would develop. It was almost too easy. Jazz became a kind of litmus test: if people couldn't hear it, you didn't want to talk to them anyway. I met a lot of girls this way and helped many of them build nice record collections.

For the first year, the biggest selling albums were the classical titles, like Von Karajan's Beethoven set on DGG. But I remember clearly when a Peter, Paul and Mary album arrived with Dylan's song "Blowing in the Wind." It was a big seller and brought in a lot of new faces. Then Bob Dylan's albums started arriving, and the scene got bigger still. Suddenly, we were hosting a lot of after-hours parties at the record store. But then one day, the first Beatles album arrived and, as I sat in the basement with an exacto knife opening box after box, hundreds of Beatles records, I had a sense that something unprecedented was happening. This wasn't just about music. It was bigger than that. Soon, stickers appeared on every lamppost on State Street with the outline of four mop-tops, and nobody at the store could figure out why this British haircut band was moving so many LPs. Of course, several years later, with the release of *Rubber Soul* and *Sergeant Pepper*, it was obvious. Educated, white, middle-class kids had finally found peers making pop music.

In the store, we listened to all the new releases — jazz, folk, blues, classical. It was easy because there wasn't the glut that's on the market today. The manager of the store, a man named Don Ellis, was a consummate professional. He had come to Madison to civilize the natives, and he didn't just want you to listen to the music, he wanted you to know the product. We had to memorize the catalog numbers of every important record, so that when he shouted for you to bring "ML 6035," you were supposed to know he wanted Isaac Stern's *Prokofiev Violin Concertos* on Columbia.

Everyone who worked there was passionate about records and, generally, had left school for the opportunity to live in a world of music; none more so than Morgan Usadel, a former graduate student in anthropology. He was my hero. He knew jazz, classical, blues, opera, everything. When the store closed at night, Don, Morgan and I would often order a pizza and hang around for another couple of hours. Elliot Eisenberg or some of the other musicians would drop by as well. Nobody wanted to go home. We listened to *Clifford Brown with Strings*, or Bud Powell's *Time Waits*. It was a perfect life.

The basement of Discount Records became our own little clubhouse. Soon, Don Ellis, who was married with two small children, had pretty much gone native, and his marriage was in jeopardy. When I saw him one night out on the fire escape outside of Dorothea House, I knew he had crossed the line. Dope, sex and jazz. It was pretty hard not to love it.

Later in the evenings, we held jam sessions in somebody's pad, or in basements, schools, churches, the student union, anywhere there was a piano and they would let us play. We wanted to duplicate the *feel* of this music, the momentum, the swagger, the finely chiseled cool of the classic Blue Note recordings. Feeling this way was everything. I remember the first time I heard pianist Sonny Clark's *Cool Struttin*: it was like discovering a whole new way of walking.

I had no thoughts of becoming a professional musician. A recording contract was unheard of. Nobody knew, for example, that the original Ardells was probably as good a band as the original Beatles, because nobody had listened to the Beatles. And even if they had, it wouldn't have occurred to a bunch of college kids back then that their music had any larger significance. Except for Steve Miller. Not long after he heard the British invasion bands, he left school and began planning his assault on the record industry. And Tracy Nelson, too; she had some idea about recording, because as a "folk singer" it existed in the realm of possibility. However, one night in the summer of 1963, I took her home, got her stoned, and played her Joe Tex, Aretha Franklin and Otis Redding, and, I think, her "folk" career ended there and then. It was, however, the birth of *Mother Earth*.

For the rest of us, to play as good as Red Garland or Horace Silver or Sonny Clark was gonna take some time.

Then in the fall of 1963, George Brown came to town. He played drums in a trio at Joe Troia's Steak House, backing a singer billed as "Miss Fallout," not because her singing was so radioactive but because she had such enormous breasts that her low cut costume could barely contain them. She couldn't sing, but nobody cared, and the trio was burning. The group had been traveling throughout the

Midwest for some time, and when they got to this second-story club overlooking the chaos of State Street, they were happy to settle in for a while. George had recorded with the great jazz guitarist Wes Montgomery the year before and was only a little older than the rest of us. He was one of the best musicians to come through town, and was given such a warm welcome by the locals that when Miss Fallout left for her next booking, he decided to stay in Madison.

George was twenty-five years old, a handsome, articulate, impassioned black man, and when he landed in Madison, it was as if a messenger had been sent to alert the rest of us to a coming revolution. Whereas we had been digging the bebop scene pretty hard, buried up to our necks in the swing of drummers like Philly Joe Jones, Louis Hayes, Roy Haynes, Art Blakey, Max Roach, Billy Higgins or Pete LaRoca, everywhere that George went, he carried John Coltrane's latest album. For him, it was all about Elvin Jones, Coltrane's drummer. I had moved to a large apartment at 432 W. Mifflin Street, which I was sharing with Morgan and Marty Schwartz, a soulful-eyed ringer for Marcello Mastroianni, and at any hour of the day or night, George Brown would come knocking on the door, go directly to the stash, roll a joint and put John Coltrane on the box. For the next forty-five minutes, nobody would talk. We would just sit there and go to church on Elvin Jones, Jimmy Garrison, McCoy Tyner and John Coltrane. Then George and I would try to find a place to play and continue this new feeling, just the two of us. We were no longer searching for the chiseled cool; we were on the trail of a contemporary transcendence, starting to catch a very big wave.

One moment it was Coltrane *Live at the Vanguard*, with "India" and "Spiritual," "Impressions" and "Chasin' the Trane;" the next it was *Live at Birdland*, with "Afro Blue," "The Promise," and "Alabama." I had listened to these records before George's arrival, but I don't think I had actually heard or understood them until I heard them with George Brown. Listening to music is always like this. It changes depending not only on where you are but also whom you are with. I guess we are all emotional transmitters, and sometimes, when a 50,000-watt beacon walks into the room, we suddenly "get" what before we only sensed.

Coltrane's music, and the implications of playing jazz this way, of playing a music that was about a deep, emotional liberation — not just about swing — forced me to rethink a lot of things. People say this is what happened to them when they first heard Charlie Parker back in the 1940s. Wherever they were, they knew nothing would be the same again. Some even packed up and left home. This was serious business, and for us, when we got on the Coltrane, everything we knew to be true had to be re-evaluated.

Whereas bebop was linear, almost literary in form, Coltrane's music was rhapsodic, organic, rolling and subsiding on the sea of Elvin Jones' drums. It hovered in front of you like an apparition, kaleidoscopically changing form over and over again, only to return to the pedal point of the human heart, an emotional drama being played out on your own breath. Like Coltrane, pianist McCoy Tyner incorporated the advanced harmonies and swing of bebop in an entirely new way, so that his stacked chords were a stairway spiraling upward but never leaving solid ground. Furthermore, there was something clearly cantorial about this music. Even Jimmy Garrison's bass solos had a spiritual pacing and diction, moving in and out of time, keening over essential points, rhetorically asking questions that reminded me of something liturgical. This was no longer about fun. It was about life and death.

One day in October 1963, an eerie "coincidence" foreshadowed the end of our little idyll. That day, I was fooling around in the basement of Discount Records and, taking the calendar off the wall, I turned the page to the following month. With a red felt tip pen, I drew lots of daggers and dripping blood all over the month of November, just fooling around. Across the top, I wrote "the cruelest month" (in reference to T.S. Elliot's reflection on April) and then, for no reason at all, I circled one of the days and wrote "the worst day of the cruelest month." A month later, when I came into work on November 22, Don Ellis handed me the calendar. I had circled the date of John Kennedy's assassination. I grabbed the calendar from Don and ripped it up. We closed the store and like everyone else, wandered, stunned, through the gray afternoon.

Shortly thereafter, another bell rang to signal the end of the round: the death of Hal Hellmann. Hal was basically a nice kid, very good looking in a happy-go-lucky way, from Whitestone, New York, and he had followed his friend Peter Belsito to Madison earlier that year. He never enrolled in school, but seemed to be everywhere, in the middle of everything. He drove a jet black Jaguar XKE, sported a cowboy hat and assumed the cool sobriquet "Calvin." Many people thought that, because of his last name, he was the heir to the Hellmann's mayonnaise fortune, a supposition that while not true, he did not bother to correct. He was just a kid on a lark, blowing his college fund on an alternative lifestyle, and pretending, like many in Madison, that he was immortal, or, at least, that he could make time stand still. When the gun went off at the Edgewater Hotel and it was discovered that "Calvin" had killed himself playing Russian roulette with a drug dealer from Chicago, a palpable shudder went through the local counterculture. He was not the only one playing a life and death game, and his was not the only gun that was loaded. The other weapons, however, were often chemical or spiritual.

1964

By January, George Brown had moved to New York City. Within a few months, he was actually playing with Jackie McLean, then Sonny Rollins, and then hanging out with Coltrane himself. He sent back reports that "this music is getting ready to leap off." I re-enrolled in the University — in retrospect, it was like clutching to a log in the flood — and signed up for the usual classes, Contemporary Social Thought, The Modern American Novel, Advanced Old Dead White Guys. But it wasn't going to be easy to hide from the onrush of history. In the spring of 1964, Malcolm X came to town.

We all went to hear him speak in Great Hall at the student union. The room was crowded but not packed, and those of us who had read Malcolm's interview with Alex Haley in *Playboy* were prepared for a wild-eyed assault on the white devils. Instead, he made a lot of sense. He presented an impassioned call to arms, saying, "the struggle for civil rights is the struggle for human rights." He had made his pilgrimage to Mecca and he now felt that many white people displayed "a spirit of unity and brotherhood." This was exactly what John Coltrane's message was. These were becoming religious times.

Simultaneously, we had discovered some new sacraments. It started with peyote. We had sent off to a farm in New Mexico and received these gnarly little buds in the mail. We didn't know exactly what to do with them, so Ira, being the designated cook, ground them up and made an omelet. After we were through retching, the visions began, and the music took on new form and substance. Not long thereafter a fellow named Donny Simon learned how to synthesize DMT, DET and DPT in his apartment. These various esters could be smoked and gave an immediate LSD-like rush that only lasted for ten to twenty minutes. It was an extraordinary and wildly addictive high, because nobody wanted to surrender the pipe for fear of coming down. When one was high on DMT, everything was understood, but as soon as you came down, it was all forgotten.

Obviously, we were desperately searching for meaning. In retrospect, we were also trying to look fear in the eye, because those were fearful times. We were simultaneously being stalked by the military machine and were determined to be on the crest of whatever big new wave was about to break. In the meantime, we collected credits and fell in and out of love. Anna Taylor was a girl with huge brown eyes, long straight hair, the aura of a fawn, and the dark, quick mind of Sylvia Plath. A few weeks after we met, we were in a car together, on our way to San Francisco.

It was a bizarre trip to say the least. We drove with her mother, her mother's lover, and a young gay Puerto Rican fellow named Victor. Victor was going to San Francisco to spend some time with a large, black sketch artist named Earl Scarborough. Earl had been coming through Madison for years and we had met during his various stays at the fraternity houses. Five people were packed into a '62 Oldsmobile for two thousand miles. The first night we stayed in North Dakota and the five of us slept in the same room. It got funkier from there. Arriving at Earl's on Haight Street a week later was like finally entering Oz.

At the time, Haight Street was a quiet Italian neighborhood, very pleasant and low key. Earl liked to cook soul food and sashayed around in a silk robe while his boyfriends applauded the act. He claimed to be a personal friend of Johnny Mathis, and when he wasn't singing along in his deep baritone, he was making sure everybody had plenty to eat, smoke, drink, or whatever they needed to wallow in their own sensuality. Earl also loved the singer Nancy Wilson. He listened to her records for hours on end, and when she sang "Happy Talk," Earl, a big cool cat, would do this little tippy-toe dance that was so hip, so gay, so outrageous, that hanging at his house became wonderful theater.

I stayed there for several days, in the afternoons walking up the street to the Blue Unicorn Cafe to read books and daydream, and, at night, haunting North Beach, where I heard jazz at the Workshop and saw Lenny Bruce at Basin Street. One night, I saw Lenny take the microphone out onto Broadway. That night, he told the crowd, "You can only know the good about yourself if you know the bad about yourself..." I was listening.

After a few days, Anna and I moved to Berkeley, where I got a job for the summer at a new Discount Records store on Telegraph Avenue. It felt very much like being in Madison. The Free Speech Movement was on, and there were gatherings in front of Sather Gate, where Mario Savio reminded the students they were not "raw material"—they were people, and if the university machine could not recognize their humanity, it was time to "throw themselves upon the gears of the apparatus." Except for the foliage and the juice bars, it could have been State Street. For the next month, Anna and I lived in a pad on Parker Street, as if this was the most natural place to be.

It was a tremendous struggle to return to school in the fall, not because the course work was so daunting, but because the distractions of life were so seductive and the curriculum seemed archaic, irrelevant. Unlike today, when the majority of students at universities seem focused on making a pile of money, and the universities are providing them the wherewithal to achieve this, during the sixties, the universities were still operating as if it were the 1930s: classically educating students to become teachers to educate more students. Ours was a search for self, rather than for employment, and there was little practical context or direction for what we were going through.

In my case, I never felt completely at ease either in or out of the university, as if my natural place was somewhere in between, on the way to becoming, rather than being the thing itself. Later, one would call this "perpetual learning," or recognize in it the earnest rootlessness of our generation. But in August of 1964, with a hint of ozone and a taste of gunpowder in the Berkeley air, I returned to Madison and the safety of collecting college credits.

That autumn, George Brown returned to Madison, too, and he brought Rahsaan Roland Kirk with him. Rahsaan was a legendary saxophone player who gained fame by playing three horns at once, and although blind, he was not without vision. His *We Three Kings* album had been on and off our turntable for years. George called to say they had booked a gig in town and that Rahsaan was interested in smoking some DMT with us.

That night, various folks came and went through 432 W. Mifflin, thrilled to meet the legendary Mr. Kirk. For hours, we passed the pipe to him, and for hours, he reached for it unerringly. And even though, one by one, we all fell to the floor in ecstatic stupor, Rahsaan kept saying, "Pass me that pipe again, damn it! I want the real shit. You cats are holding back. Pass me the pipe!" Our world kept swirling in more and more bizarre patterns but, amazingly, the chemicals had no effect on Rahsaan's brain. Perhaps he had altered his own chemistry through years of ocular compensation and circular breathing, but in any case, he never felt the DMT, and he ended up storming out of the pad, leaving the rest of us paralyzed on the floor.

That was the year the drug thing got out of hand. It wasn't just the DMT and the peyote and the pot and the mescaline. It was also the heroin. Some of our crowd had discovered the truth of Charlie Parker's dictum: "You don't play better high but you do hear better." Since listening to music was a major occupation, smack became a kind of adjunct. One could hear into the music, separate the bass from the drums, isolate the piano and suspend it in time, consider all aspects of the shape of the tenor sax. Nothing could interfere with the act of listening, but of course this was retrograde, passive rather than active, back to the chiseled cool instead of forward toward self-revelation. And, inevitably, once you went far enough down that particular road, you couldn't get back so easily. The bridge to real life was washed out. My roommate Marty found himself on the wrong side of the bridge.

1965

In January, I got a phone call from Anna saying she had found this great apartment on Baker Street and why didn't I come back to San Francisco and live there with her. Marty was the first one to say, "I'll go check it out for you." He needed a purpose, and, also, to get out of town for a while, so he flew to the coast.

A few weeks later, George Brown, Jim Hougan and I got into Don Ellis's Mercury convertible for the long drive west. Don was taking the job as manager of Discount Records in Berkeley and needed somebody to drive his car there. Hougan was going to Los Angeles for no apparent reason, and George was tired of Madison and didn't much care where he went next. Hougan had no driver's license, and the one time we let George drive, we woke up on the wrong side of the road watching a truck coming directly at us, so I became the designated driver. We lost a muffler in Oklahoma, and, except for the fact that all the public bathrooms in Texas mysteriously seemed to be broken when people saw George, we got to Los Angeles in only 52 hours non-stop. We had used a lot of bennies and coffee to stay awake and were wired like a Christmas tree when we barely slowed down to drop Hougan off at the side of a freeway in downtown L.A. Then George and I roared up the coast to San Francisco. After almost three days of nonstop driving, I found the address on Baker Street, backed into a parking space in front of the house, and smashed Don's car into a truck.

Twenty minutes later, like some gorgeous giraffe ambling through the veld, Lolita glasses perched fetchingly on the tip of her nose, her perfectly straight hair swinging in stop time, along came Anna Taylor. Marty was trailing behind, and from the first glance, I knew something was wrong. George put his hand on my arm to steady me, knowing how wired we both were, and Anna started telling me a story about some Israeli guy named Yosi and how she really wanted to explain this exciting news to me, but why didn't we go inside first because she had something very special for me. George and Marty disappeared down Baker Street and I found myself lying on a mattress in an otherwise perfectly empty room on the second floor of an old Victorian house.

Anna had a way of making the outrageous seem perfectly reasonable. She handed me a glass of water and a small pill and suggested we each take one so that we would be in the same place. It would help me understand what she was about to tell me, she said, and I looked at her innocent face, with her little chipmunk overbite and those large doe eyes, and I swallowed the pill. She had just handed me my first dose of LSD.

She began gently unwinding a long complicated story about how wonderful it was all going to be, and I was trying to nail down just what she was getting at when there was a knock on the door. A big round bald black head, with a broad flat nose and a bright oriental smile, peered around the corner. Anna said, "Ben, this is John. He's our landlord. John, this is Ben." The acid was coming on and I was hearing an increasingly loud buzzing in my ears, like the approach of a thousand cicadas from some distant planet, but I recognized the face of John Handy immediately. He was the saxophone player who had delivered the haunted solo on Charles Mingus' "Goodbye Pork Pie Hat," the recording that had helped me though so many hard days in Racine. And now Anna was telling me that John Handy was my landlord.

John smiled and said hello. He had an enormous ring of keys in his hand, and with great patience, he was slowly trying one key after another in the lock of our door. "Just looking for your key, man," he said. I was lying about ten feet away on the mattress, in the clean white room on the polished wooden floor, with Anna propped up next to me, still taken with the shock of seeing John, when the acid came on in a rush. John just smiled his sweet oriental smile, going from key to key, looking for the one that unlocked my door. It was too much. Anna was chattering away about something or other but I could no longer hear her. I looked down at the beautifully polished blond oak floor and the squares of sunlight flooding in, and I started to cry.

Anna had no idea who John was. She had simply walked into a grocery store one day, seen an ad for a place to rent, and rented it. It was just a fluke, a fortuitous calamity in the making, that the place she rented belonged to a great jazz musician who was married to a very tough broad. Because while Anna and I were very bad together, John's wife, Nancy, either had eyes for Anna or simply enjoyed making matters worse. She went out of her way to keep us off balance. And of course, the mysterious Yosi was never far from the picture.

Maintaining a dangerous, potentially destructive relationship like the one I had with Anna was like peering over a 1000-foot cliff—half of you is fascinated, hypnotized; the other half is saying, "Man, are you crazy? Get back." It's like the old hipster's story: two stoned jazzmen are in a room on the fifth floor of a hotel when one of them decides he can fly. He jumps out the window and falls to his death. Later, a friend asks the surviving musician, "Man, why didn't you try to stop him?" "Stop him," says the musician, "Man, I was betting he could make it!" I guess I was betting I could make it.

I was too busy to know any better. I had studied "Language and Meaning" the previous year at the University of Wisconsin, and since the guru of semantics, S.I. Hayakawa, was at San Francisco State, I enrolled in a class there. One night the instructor threw me an orange and said, "Tell me something about this." I said, "It's orange." He said, "What does that mean?" I said, "Well, okay, it's round and has weight." He said, "What does that mean?" Well, obviously, if you reduce everything to its simple constituent parts, all "facts" dissolve in your hand, and you wind up trying to describe the physical properties of quarks and photons. Hence, "language and meaning," nothing inherently means anything. It was like having a conversation with Anna all over again.

Once a week I took a piano lesson from Fred Satman, a Bay area legend who had instructed Dave Brubeck. I rented a piano, and since John's piano was being rebuilt, there were nights with great jam sessions in our apartment. One night Freddie Redd came by; he was a pianist who had made several dark, disturbing records on Blue Note with Jackie McLean in the early sixties, including *The Connection*. I sat directly against the piano as he stomped it off. Another night, Norman Simmons played my piano. One day, I answered the front door and it was Dizzy Gillespie. I was too stunned to speak.

I kept trying to unravel the intimacies of playing jazz, practicing but not knowing if I was getting anywhere. I noticed that John never practiced. I asked him about this and he said, "I'm at the point where I just play, I don't have to practice." Then I asked him to show me the chord changes to "Goodbye Pork Pie Hat," and he said, "Charles never gave us the changes. He just sang our parts to us and we had to figure out what to play." I knew there and then that I had been given a key to an inner mystery of this music, but it would take years to fathom what it really meant to rely so thoroughly on your own sense of self. Style: where does it come from? Voice: how do you find your own? Suddenly, these questions opened up and became real. To learn how to play, one had to learn how to listen, and the very first voice each of us hears is the voice inside our own head.

I again took a job at Discount Records, this time in San Francisco, and spent a lot of time standing on the corner of Fillmore and McAllister, waiting in the fog for a bus to take me from one labor to another. San Francisco is not an easy place to be broke. Anna took a job as a waitress in a new jazz club that had opened on Divisidero Street called The Both And. It was the first jazz club with a light box on the wall — a couple of hundred colored bulbs that somehow beat in time to the music. One night, I went there to hear Rahsaan Roland Kirk, and George Brown came with me. We had a little reunion in the dressing room.

I still cannot believe what I saw Rahsaan do that night. Holding one note on a couple of horns (through circular breathing), he walked off the stage, across the room to the bar (still playing the notes), where he grabbed a patron under the arms, lifted him up with his free arm (still playing the notes), and walked the length of the bar carrying this dumbfounded customer (still playing the notes). Eventually, he returned the guy to the very stool from whence he had plucked him (still playing the notes), and walked back to the stage, continuing his solo as if nothing strange had happened. The solo itself was nonstop burning. And, yes, he was blind. No wonder our little chemicals had had no effect on him.

One day late in the spring, as I was opening boxes in the shipping room of Discount Records, George and Anna showed up. Anna and I had not been communicating well for weeks, and I was losing my ability to dance around a subject with her until no one remembered what it was. (Like Piet Hine's little "grook" says, "We dance around in a ring and suppose, while the secret sits in the center and knows.") We had been having long conversations, but I could never understand where they were going. The essence was always shadowed in desire, allusion and some vague, unspoken hunger. Somehow, I always wound up in a rage or in tears.

This time, Anna started talking and for some reason, out of nowhere, I just belted her in the face and she fell over backwards. George grabbed me. I felt like I was losing consciousness. I had never hit a woman in my life. I had practically never hit anybody. It's not something that I would do. In a flash, I realized what I had only been sensing for months, that while Anna made me feel like I was going crazy, she was really the one who was not balanced, who was manipulating my sanity. I knew I had to get away. Something bad was happening to me. The voice inside my head said, "This is not you — save yourself."

Within the week, I had moved out of the house on Baker Street, out of San Francisco entirely. I went home to see my father. I didn't know who else to talk to. He and my mother and my brother Ezra had moved from Racine to Winnetka, a suburb of Chicago. I found my father sitting on the screened porch at the back of the house, reading a newspaper. I had heard from my mother that he had had a "small operation" for some internal problem, but he looked fine and relaxed, sitting with his feet up on a coffee table and his bulldog fast asleep on the floor.

We made small talk for a while. I told him I was going to return to Madison, that I had made up my mind to finish my degree and get on with it. He seemed to be half listening. Then I told him about my drug use. I said I was scared about my life. I didn't know if I was in trouble or not. He put the paper aside and asked me, "Are you using heroin?" When I said I was not, he shrugged and said, "Illegitimata non Carborundum" (a favorite expression of his, meaning "don't let the bastards wear you down") and picked up the paper again. It might have been the coolest thing he had ever done: by not showing me panic (whether or not he felt it I'll never know), he let me know that, somehow, I would be all right.

I returned to Madison and enrolled in summer school. That summer, I spent eight weeks studying Wittgenstein's *Philosophical Investigations* with Professor Ray Lucas, a wunderkind in the department of philosophy who had developed an abiding interest in the music of John Coltrane. The book was a revelation. It illuminated the problems only hinted at in my study of semantics, and then took the discussion to an entirely new level: there was only one human language, incomplete, an open set. The various forms of music and speech were all part of this continuum.

According to Wittgenstein, there was simply a deep knowing that we are all born with, and from this knowing, we communicate with one another. Further, he saw all language as just a game, and laughter was at the very heart of it. It occurred to me then that this was also true of jazz. Maybe not laughter as such, but a sense of humor, seeing the absurd as well as the profound in life. "Maybe you should just flip out," as Del Close's hipster said, "then you won't have that to worry about anymore." This ironic edge was the wave upon which a lot of great jazz improvisation was born; if you were not having fun, you were doing it wrong.

In Wittgenstein's formulation, "essence is expressed by grammar," so, I asked myself, what is the grammar of jazz? And how is music like speech? "Understanding a sentence," he wrote, "is much more akin to understanding a theme in music than one might think." What, then, is this music *saying*? These thoughts occupied my thoughts all summer long, and ultimately came to form the basis of my book *Black Talk* years later.

Finally, there was Wittgenstein's famous duck-rabbit, a drawing that when looked at one way appeared to be a duck and looked at another way, appeared to be a rabbit. So which was it? The drawing itself does not change, only our perception of it does. "What is different," he asked. "My impression? My point of view? But how is it possible to see an object according to an interpretation?" In a very direct and simple way, he had demonstrated that we are all bringing the world into being, moment by moment, and our emotions are the constant filter through which this transformation occurs.

Wittgenstein's book just pushed me over the edge. I saw that one could never understand how one understands. It's like pulling the wings off a butterfly to see how it flies; the act destroys the possibility. Ultimately, then, the only criticism of a poem or piece of music is another poem or piece of music. (Finally, a resolution to the quandary posed by my Coltrane review.) I was on fire with the possibility that I had found a new way to understand my love for jazz.

All summer long, these ideas raced through my mind. At the same time, the music itself was getting more fractured, more deconstructed. Albert Ayler, Ornette Coleman, The ESP catalog, so-called "free music" were affecting musicians everywhere. Even Jackie McLean, that prototypical bebopper, was on the way to *Destination Out*. Ray Lucas and I spent many hours together that summer talking about these things, taking acid together, playing music. Of course trying to grasp an *a priori* understanding of the world by taking LSD was like fighting fire with gasoline. But if we were spinning our wheels, the result was still incandescent.

My other course that summer was the study of Milton's *Paradise Lost*. Nothing could have been more apropos. One evening in late July, I laid out my favorite records, I prepared something to drink and a few pieces of fruit to eat and I took some mescaline. I waited an hour, and then I took some LSD. It was an insane thing to do and, I believe now, I was motivated by fear, not the quest for knowledge. It was the fear that my world was making less and less sense, fear that I was slowly going crazy. I wanted to know there and then whether it was going to happen. As the Buddhist Monk Pema Chodron has written, "Only to the extent that we expose ourselves over and over to annihilation can that which is indestructible be found in us." I guess I wanted to know if there was anything at the core of my being that was indestructible, that could be counted on, even staring into the yawning face of infinity. What was me? It was now or never.

That night, I entered a souk where Hamza El Din jammed with Pops Staples, Sufis danced to bebop and muezzin chanted the blues. I looked out of my window and saw that the bushes in the front yard had become a thicket of horses' heads, their great manes blowing in the wind, their huge lips pulled back, exposing spittle and teeth. The faces of people on the street were grotesque cartoons, wildly familiar and yet horrifying. I heard the roar of the wind and it was Elvin Jones playing "The Drum Thing," but there were human voices in the drums, and I saw the generations of humanity, my father's father, his father, the original father. The sky opened and there was a city of gold. To this day, I am not sure that this city existed, but I cannot say for certain that it did not. I died. I did not die.

By morning, there was a great calm. I put John Coltrane's *A Love Supreme* on the KLH and had the sensation that Coltrane was "talking" to me. It was like being hit with a bolt of lightning, because it was my mother's voice that I heard coming out of his horn. She was calling me from inside the music. How could this be?

For several weeks thereafter, I had the disquieting sensation that virtually all aspects of the physical world were actually symbols of a greater knowing, a hidden truth. I felt if we could only learn to read the trees, we could understand the meaning of life. Walking to class, I would occasionally be stunned by the hidden significance of an ordinary elm. Thankfully, this compulsion gradually subsided, and I settled back into the bliss of my ignorance.

Years later, when I asked a former astronaut, Rusty Schwiekert, if there was ever a fear of falling from such great heights when he was circling the earth or doing a space walk, he said, "The sky begins at our feet. Aren't we brave just to walk around?" Yes, we are very brave indeed.

That autumn, for the first time, I enrolled in one of Harvey Goldberg's classes. Up until then, I had only known him as a friend, talked to him long into the evenings or over a leisurely lunch. I felt I was finally prepared to take on his academic performance, for that is what everyone said his lectures were.

They were held in the largest auditorium on campus, and students would arrive a quarter of an hour early just to get a seat. By the time Harvey arrived, people were hanging from the rafters. He would stride into the room and wait off to the side of the stage, all eyes on him, but nobody approaching. When the bell rang, he walked to the podium, hesitated for a moment as if to gather his thoughts, and then, removing his glasses — he appeared myopic without them — he looked into the middle distance and declared "The point is, you know...." And he was off, painting a picture of life during the Paris Commune in such detail and context that it became as real as the life we were living. He brought home to us the literal truth of *la condition humaine*, decades before "Les Mis" brought the cartoon version to the masses.

When he was on stage, he was transformed by the information. This was his relationship to jazz, this transformation. His timing was exquisite. Remarkably, his last sentence would end as the final bell rang. It would stop you cold. Week after week, I walked out of his lectures in a daze, and it would take awhile to become aware of whether it was warm outside or cold, wet or dry. He had hypnotized all three hundred of us. He was, he said, "rousing the historical consciousness" of his students, to destroy our passivity and to crack the belief that, "the present is so frequently considered to be eternal and unchanging." The revolution was a long revolution; it began at the beginning of time and continued to the end, and along the way, we are all part of this great chain of human events. This is what history feels like, he implied, and you're living in it. Do not shut your eyes to your own life!

I never took a course in music at the university, but the variations and spells that Harvey Goldberg wove each week prepared me for my future in jazz. And there were times when jazz seemed to be all that stood between chaos and me. Because jazz is chaos controlled, a way to give meaning to the madness of life, to turn the howling at the edge of the universe into a beautiful ballad. Jazz was not just a musical grammar, it was a blueprint for living, a way of moving through the world, and the principles one had to master in order to play this music would also help you to survive the daily assaults. At least that is what I began to believe during this time.

By the fall of 1965, what had once been a relatively small counter-culture was becoming a major movement. The anti-war activities, the Beatles, the affluence of the baby-boomers and their concomitant reluctance to "grow up," everything was conspiring to push it forward. My reaction was to go underground. I stayed home a lot, in the apartment on Mifflin Street, and fell headlong into the world of books and music. In particular, Mose Allison's album *The Word from Mose*, became my watchword, the most important record in my collection. Before going to class, I would listen to him sing "the Fool Killer's coming, he's getting closer everyday," or, "if you want to make your own breakthrough, you're going to have to lose a few," and his lyrics just pinned me. It was both a healing and a challenge. Like Bob Dylan's "Subterranean Homesick Blues" ("Look out kid, it's something you did, God knows when but you're doing it again..."), Mose's words were hip, to the point, poetic and life altering.

That fall, I also spent several weekends in Chicago with Steve Miller, who had moved there and was playing in a funky club called Big Johns. His band included other refugees from college life — Roy Ruby, Barry Goldberg, young middle-class Jewish musicians who were choosing to live the blues. Shooting pool in the back room at Big Johns, I met guitar players Elvin Bishop and Mike Bloomfield, and I discovered that the scene was definitely changing. Up until then, playing blues or jazz wasn't a serious option for a college kid; it was more of an avocation. But it was clear that Mike and Elvin and Steve and Barry were all bright, educated, and totally committed to this way of life.

I could relate to them; I, too, refused to reduce music to the pedagogy of teaching students to become teachers to teach more students. I continued to learn what I learned on the streets, from great players, some of whom remain forever nameless, others who became recognized in time, but all of whom shared their knowledge with me, whether black or white, young or old, clean or hooked; their generosity still shines like a beacon in my life. But unlike Steve and the others, I continued to study literature, history and philosophy, to read "secondary sources," to plumb Shakespeare. It never occurred to me to quit. I was searching for something else, a higher understanding, I thought, a more definitive way to live my life.

I continued to carry the idea of "first degree searchers" with me. It was an idea that had been with me since high school. My thought was that they walked among us, looked like you and me, and never identified themselves, yet they recognized one another when they met and were obligated to offer a word or a gesture to help each other along the path. I sensed I was often being extended a hand. But who really knew? One had to have faith, and I tried to have it, but the act of trying is a double-edged sword. Sometimes it felt like I was just wandering, blindfolded, and then, bang, after a long period had passed and I saw that an obstacle had been avoided, I wondered if a hidden hand had been operating.

I was simultaneously trying to become myself and to save myself. It may sound melodramatic, but in the sixties, there was every chance that one could lose one's life, to drugs, to the killing fields of Vietnam, to the mistakes of one's parents' past, to the mistakes of one's friends' future. Today, young people look back at the 60s as an era of "flower power." I never understood Alan Ginsberg's term: there was no power in flowers and I never thought he swung on that stupid harmonium. He was just as lost as the rest of us. We were all alone and searching.

In *The Self in Transformation*, popular at the time, Herbert Fingarette wrote, "Cease striving; then there will be self transformation," and I understood the concept. But I also saw how hard everybody was trying not to try hard. Similarly, Carlos Castanada's *Teachings* made a great read, but unless you could learn to jaunt yourself into another dimension when the draft board called, you had better have a back-up plan. It was like taking LSD: the philosophical fashions of the day, while they expanded your consciousness and nourished your sense of the divine, ultimately left you lonely and unprepared for the real tests, which we all knew were coming.

It was around this time that I first started hearing the voice inside my head, particularly when I thought I was at rest, repeating, "I need something...I *need* something." Over and over, a nameless wanting, a gnawing hunger. I had no idea what I wanted.

It was there the afternoon I went to talk to Professor Ragsdale about why my assignment for his class in Journalism would be late. Helmut Ragsdale was a former World War II correspondent, and although he was tough as nails, his exams tended to be wonderfully open-ended, like "Art is a lie that tells the truth, or the truth that tells a lie; discuss." I told him that we were demonstrating in the streets against the war, that I was confused, that I didn't seem to be able to focus. He looked at me with compassion and said three words that not only helped me get through his class, but also put me on the path I still walk: "Work. Don't think." These three simple words are as true and powerful today as they were thirty-five years ago.

One day, the most beautiful girl I had ever seen walked into Discount Records with Marty Schwartz. She had short black hair cut in a dramatic Sassoon flip, huge eyes, a brilliant open smile, and an incredible body. Marty was so handsome, he was like a pilot fish for the rest of us. He would attract these gorgeous women and, not being particularly interested in what happened next, he would abandon them in the pool where the rest of us casually circled. I approached her and asked, "Are you Marty's girlfriend?" She said, "I don't know." A few weeks later, she came to my apartment with another friend, and we got to know each other. The next week when I saw her in the Rathskeller —it was right before Christmas vacation—we decided to go to Lorenzo's steak house and wound up spending the afternoon there. After about four hours of eating, drinking and talking, I walked her back to her dorm and she said, "Can't I come home with you?" I said, "Give me a half hour." I went to my house and asked the woman who was essentially living there to leave. Judy and I have been together ever since.

1966

In March, Steve Miller came up from Chicago and brought with him some of the good pot he was now smoking. After we shared a joint, I asked him if he had ever tried LSD. He had not. I described what it was like, told him that you could learn a lot about yourself, and that could be both good and bad. I told him that I had mixed emotions about it, but if he wanted some, I could arrange it. It was each one teach one, and I assured him that if he wanted to try it, I would stay with him all the way. When he said yes, I handed him a glass of orange juice and a small white pill. I went to the record collection and started sequencing the trip. To start off, I put on The Staple Singers' "Motherless Children." Then Mingus' "Self Portrait in Three Colors." For twelve hours, I took him through the stages of the ego dying, of fear, grief, remorse and acceptance. At six o'clock the next morning, we walked down State Street and there, in the pale dawn, we heard the first robin of spring, perched high on a blinking red light, singing his heart out.

That spring, a group of us started playing softball in a field by the student dorms, and semiregular teams quickly formed. Usually, it was the lefties vs. the drug-gies. As musicians, Elliot Eisenberg and I could float (a metaphor for our place in the culture I suppose); one week we played for one team, the next week for the other. There were some interesting moments, like the time Steve Shapiro, an historian and a regular on the "lefties" team, hit a long fly ball to center field, and the kid out there, who had clearly not come down from the previous evening's activities, didn't know which one of the several balls he perceived fly-ing through the air to catch. You could see his confusion as he watched this incoming MIRV. In the end, he fell to the ground and covered his head. But these games had a serious edge to them too. The difficulty of the period, like the problem of our friend in center field, was that too many ideas, too much information and too many alternatives were incoming at the same time.

As large as Vietnam loomed, it would be a mistake to think of the war as the single issue of the sixties. The one overriding issue, perhaps, was freedom, and the various subgroups—war protesters, blacks, gays, Jews, communists, feminists, weathermen—all gathered together under this banner. In truth, they were all pretty much in the same closet. Not even Harvey Goldberg could reveal to the world that he was a homosexual. It was a genuine crisis of consciousness.

Back then, the world often appeared to be black or white, us or them; you were either on the bus or off the bus. It was this central duality of our existence, the greater battle being fought on all fronts, that caused many artists, from Archie Shepp and the Last Poets to Bob Dylan and The Rolling Stones, to see their work as confrontational. That is why the music of the sixties, even the love songs of Al Green or the charged sexuality of Aretha Franklin, seem today like songs from some long forgotten war. For some, they are all that's left of the moments of trial, passion and pushing the boundaries of the possible. Once so powerful, they are now merely melancholy.

Music was the common denominator for all these social struggles, those spoken and those unmentionable. As historian Raymond Williams wrote at the time, "There is great danger in the assumption that art serves only on the frontiers of knowledge...*It is often through the art that the society expresses its sense of being a society* (my Italics)." In 1966, when I first read those lines, rumors were flying that Lyndon Johnson was considering rounding up anti-war protesters and putting them into camps in the Southwestern desert. At the time, even kids who were not part of the political action would have chosen to go to the camps rather than remain outside the fences. Why? The music would have forced the decision.

For the working jazz musician, however, there was a downside to this newfound adulation of their craft. As the rhetoric of the times vaulted the notion of "freedom" above all others, real musicians soon discovered that "freedom" often came to mean that anybody who had taken enough LSD and could still pick up an instrument was considered qualified as a "free jazz" musician, i.e. able by birthright to express themselves by producing bleating sounds they could not control. Or, alternatively, ragged kids who believed the literal truth of the Beatles' lyrics "all you need is love" demanded that since music" belonged to the people," no musician should get paid for playing; hence, "free music." These were small prices to pay, however, for what we believed was the central role musicians would play in the new society.

A crystallizing event came that spring during the occupation of the University's administration building. As the war in Vietnam ratcheted up, government agencies put pressure on the University to cooperate with the Selective

Service System by providing information that could be used to determine which students should be drafted. This put the University in bed with the local draft boards. As we were paying the University, and in many ways we *were* the University, this collusion was unacceptable. The demonstration started as a small thing, a rally with Evan Stark, Bob Cohen and a few other campus radicals using a bull horn and urging kids at the student union to join them in a protest at the Administration Building. It would be a sit-in, a tactic straight out of the civil rights struggle, the first time the freedom movement had crossed directly into the path of the white middle class, and it caught fire. By six o'clock that night, the halls of the building were jammed with kids, milling around, sitting against the walls. Nobody knew what to do.

I wandered in and heard a few people make speeches and after an hour of this aimlessness, I ran the few blocks to Harvey Goldberg's apartment to tell him what was happening. When Harvey heard the news, he understood immediately that a bridge had been crossed. When we returned, the crowd seemed to part for him like the red sea for Moses, and Harvey spent the next twelve hours meeting with groups of students and giving those assembled the historical context they needed to understand what they were doing. Suddenly, the party had a purpose, and a musician had in some small way helped to deliver the news.

Smoking pot and resisting the draft: these two issues, by redefining average middle-class kids as deviants, forced many who were simply looking to have a good time to see themselves in a new way, to become marginalized in the world of their parents. They sensed intuitively that pot was not dangerous and that the war in Vietnam was not like previous wars, and the call to distrust those over thirty had an instant logic. As writer Malcolm Gladwell has suggested, major movements like this often do not require a lot of people at first, only a few people in key places. During this period, at college campuses all across the country, there were only a few at first, but within months, whole sections of the demographic had scuttled to the fringes.

When the sixties started, musicians were the outsiders, the geeks, sometimes having to fight their way up a hill to get home. By the middle of the decade, they were leading the parade, and everybody wanted to be in the band. By the end of the decade, of course, it was every man for himself.

In May, I got a phone call from Steve Miller. He was moving to San Francisco and he wanted me to join him. "Man," he said, "most of the bands out there, they don't even know how to play, and they're making a lot of money. " Within days, a tape arrived in the mail with a letter. "Here are some of the tunes I've been working on," he wrote. "I know joining my group would be in some senses a step down for you, but I also believe it would give you an opportunity to grow into a much more serious musician.... God knows where you would end up." He was right, of course. I *was* playing at being a musician and he *was* making the commitment, and God only knew where it would lead me if I joined him. But by then, my life had become consumed by a more far-reaching fire, and music was only one element; meaning was the ultimate goal. I wanted to learn to read the trees, to understand the music from the inside, to synthesize the study of language with the socio-politics of jazz. Listening to the music on Steve's tape, I realized how little rock and roll had to do with my ultimate goal.

This would not be the last time I was offered a port in the storm but decided instead to stay the course in the leaky little boat of my own invention. I had no idea where I was headed, but I believed I would recognize it when I arrived. We are all, I think, basically Magellans on a singular voyage.

That summer, Judy and I went to New York and were down at Slugs, a funky club on the Lower East Side, when George Brown introduced me to McCoy Tyner. He said, "McCoy, this is my friend Ben. He's a piano player." McCoy extended his huge warm paw and said hello. I said, "Mr. Tyner, it's an honor." He looked at me for a long slow second and said, "Don't do that to me..."

What had I done? Well, for a start, I had put him on a pedestal, and perhaps he was telling me that we are all just people, an exalted enough position and a difficult enough problem. And maybe he was also letting me know that by raising him up to be a hero, I was simultaneously attempting to let myself off the hook. We all pull on our pants one leg at a time; after that, it's all about the journey we take. He was telling me it was time to move on.

1967

A fter almost six years of wandering the physical and emotional map, I finally graduated from the University of Wisconsin. It seemed like several lifetimes since I had first walked into the rooming house on Henry Street. Now where would I go? One thing was sure: without a plan, the answer was

Vietnam. Back in Madison, Marty had come into a small inheritance and had opened a nightclub called the Uptown Cafe. He had also become a serious junkie. Morgan had left town to run a record store in Champaign, Illinois. Steve was in California. Me, I made one last ditch effort to avoid the inevitable. I enrolled in graduate school as an English major. I was a dismal failure. When the instructor droned on about gerunds and fricatives, I actually fell asleep.

George Brown came through Madison once more, this time with saxophonist Pharaoh Sanders, who had just recorded *Kulu Se Mama* with Coltrane. The record was an astounding meeting of the primitive and the avant garde, incorporating Africanisms, chants, burning straight-ahead music and prayerful lyricism. "The man has a halo around him when he plays," George said. "You can see it. Sometimes, when we play, we're two feet off the ground."

I took George and Pharaoh to the Uptown Cafe. Pharaoh's favorite expression at the time was "Everything is everything," and he said it enigmatically as an answer to several of my questions. When he removed his little skullcap for a moment I noticed that he had a mirror on the inside (to reflect the energy back into his brain?). From time to time, his eyes seemed to roll back up into his head of their own accord. I learned that he did not indulge in pot or any other mind-altering substance, but George was as wild as ever. That night at the concert, he was a one-man thunderstorm, soloing for almost twenty minutes as the band played just one composition for over an hour. There was no name to it. There was nothing you could sing on the way out. You could barely speak. Your mind had been blasted.

What did all of this mean for someone who still loved classic jazz, like the pianists Sonny Clark and Bud Powell and Erroll Garner and Horace Silver? That night, I went home and listened to them all, as if seeking advice from old friends. I couldn't reconcile the elegance and lyricism of the past and the chaos and unrestrained passion of the present. It seemed there was no middle ground. The next morning, I went directly to Bascom Hall and again withdrew from school. From there, I went to the Rathskeller in the student union to contemplate my future. The Vietnam War was breathing down my neck, and the world was becoming very real. It seemed I was doomed to be either tense or past tense.

I was listening to Otis Redding on the jukebox when Harvey Goldberg sat down at my table. I told him what I had just done and he asked what I planned to do next. I said I had no plans. In the ensuing silence, as we both pictured the alternatives: Canada, prison, Vietnam, Otis was singing his sad, sad song, "Fa, fa-fa fa-fa fa-fa fa-fa." Then Harvey said, "Don't forget, Ben, the first obligation of a revolutionary is to remain free." Then he told me about the University of Sussex, a new redbrick University in England with an interdisciplinary graduate program in American Studies. "You could design your own agenda," he said, "And I'll write you a letter."

And once again the road forked. Within weeks I had sent off my application, along with Harvey's recommendation and one other, and then spent the rest of the spring waiting to learn my fate.

One day in April, in the midst of this emotional stasis, I took a drive to Chicago with my friend Lenny, who was delivering another friend of ours, Helen Rothbaum, to O'Hare airport. She was going to catch a flight for San Francisco. The song "A Whiter Shade of Pale" was just becoming popular, and when it came on the radio for the second time, with it's reference to "the Miller's tale," I thought about Steve and the others out in San Francisco. By the time we got to O'Hare, I had decided to get on the flight with Helen. No luggage, no ticket, nothing. I flew "student standby" for $25, and that night, I went to the Fillmore Auditorium to hear the new Steve Miller Band.

The Fillmore in the spring of 1967 was like a huge high school gym with a raised stage at one end and a screen with goofy, amorphous blobs of light projected behind it. The floor was littered with zonked kids. The sound was terrible, booming and echoing throughout the place. It was possibly the most unmusical environment I had ever stepped into. I know it has been romanticized over the years, but without the patina of history, it really was just a big drafty hall. The opening act was up, so I went to find the boys in the band.

Steve had recruited a collection of Madison's best rock musicians — drummer Tim Davis and guitarist Curley Cooke from The Chordaires, keyboard player Jim Peterman from The Playboys — and the band was backstage learning to eat fire. After big greetings, Curley showed me how you soaked a rag in alcohol, tied it to an unbent coat hanger, lit the end and then breathed out as you inserted it into your mouth. Theoretically, alcohol burned with a cool flame and you felt no pain if you exhaled properly. Steve was wearing a flowing shirt and "love beads," and his hair was long, down to his shoulders.

Harvey Kornspan, Steve's new manager and another old friend from Madison, came up and asked what I was doing there. I said I had no idea. The whole thing seemed to me like a circus without a ringmaster. Many years later, when I told him my memory of this experience, Harvey said, "Of course you felt that way. You were already in a professional consciousness; the rest of us were in game time." At the time, however, I only remember feeling like the odd man out.

The next morning, I awoke in the band's huge Victorian house on Pierce Street. I met Jim Peterman wandering through the kitchen, and together we took a walk through the old neighborhood. What had once been a quiet and charming street when I had stayed at Earl's place just a few years before, was now a seething medieval fair of hustlers and runaways, bikers and dealers, well-intentioned Diggers and freaked out locals.

A few blocks away, on Page Street, we came upon a group of young guys sitting on the steps of a Victorian house, tearing into a loaf of white bread. Jim introduced me: they were musicians who also played at the Fillmore and the Matrix and some of the other places around town. One guy was sprinkling salt on the bread. Then he pinched it between his thumb and forefinger, making a little paste out of it before he swallowed it. I asked him what he was doing and he said, "When you pinch the bread and add the salt, it tastes like peanut butter." Apparently, they had so little money that day, they couldn't afford both. This was how I met Jerry Garcia and some of the guys from The Grateful Dead.

As we sat on the stoop talking, I told Jerry I was facing an impending draft physical, and he asked me if I knew "Dr. Keith." I said no. He said Keith Bogost was a psychiatrist who had helped a lot of musicians he knew. The doctor lived in Milwaukee. I said I just happened to live seventy miles away, in Madison. Jerry said, "There you go."

Returning to Madison, I found the letter from Sussex in the mailbox. Judy sat with me as I tore it open. The first words were "We are pleased..." and we read no further. The rest of the spring and early summer was like one long, nostalgic picnic. Judy would not be coming to England with me so we tried to make the days we had special. We stayed close to home, laughing and talking and listening to records. The soundtrack of those months included Dr. John's *The Night Tripper*, James Brown's "Cold Sweat" (who was that funky drummer?), and the Beatles' *Sergeant Pepper's Lonely Hearts Club Band*; it was the magic of the past, the funk of the present and the mystery of the future. Lying on the porch, reading Marshall McLuhan's *Understanding Media*, I began to sense the scope of the global village I was about to enter.

Before leaving Madison, I had one final lunch with Harvey Goldberg. On the way to meet him at the Union terrace, crossing the library mall where kids were splashing in the fountain or sunbathing on the grass, I heard an advertisement blasting from a student's portable radio. It was for "The Big Love In at Lord Jim's clothing store!" I was appalled that the counter-culture had so quickly and so easily been co-opted by an advertising agency. When I sat down at Harvey's table, I was still seething about this. He said, "Ben, never underestimate the ability of the American system to absorb dissent."

He went on to say that in other countries and at other times, dissent was confronted, and this confrontation was healthy, an essential and useful tool for social change. But here in America, dissent was simply more fuel for the fires of consumerism. Here, dissent is marketed as a hip new product; even the concept of hip was being sold back to the community that had encoded it. It was reminiscent of Daniel Boorstin's dictum: "counterfeit happenings tend to drive spontaneous happenings out of circulation." Clearly, it was just a matter of time before everything we knew to be true was up for sale.

Also that summer, John Coltrane had come to Madison. He played at the student union, and the place was packed with all the regulars. It felt like a graduation ceremony for the old crowd. Not long thereafter, we were all in New York—Judy, Marty, George, me—attending a round of send-off parties. At one of them, Marty came over. He didn't look good. He said he was really strung out and he had to get off the scene for a while. I said I understood.

And so, a couple of days later, following the final party on board the student ship the SS *Aurelia*, after the huge horn had sounded and the gang plank had been pulled up, Marty and I waved good-bye to Judy and the others on the dock. At the last minute, Marty had decided to sail for Europe too. On our third day at sea, he spent the afternoon throwing up overboard. Everybody thought it was because he was seasick.

By the end of that summer, John Coltrane had died.

~ Chapter Three

*"The value of an education in a liberal arts college is not
the learning of many facts but the training of the mind to
think something that cannot be learned from text books."*

—ALBERT EINSTEIN

1967

By the time the SS *Aurelia* had docked at Southampton, Marty was "engaged" to an attractive, first-year French major on her way to Nancy. I had performed a brief wedding ceremony mid-crossing, so that just in case the ship went down their union would be blessed. Marty, however, was still motivated to see England, so he disembarked with me and together we found our way to Brighton. We arrived on a bank holiday when there was not a hotel room to be had, so we slept that night on the floor of the Palace Hotel, a grand old whitewashed dame on the sea front. In the morning, we awoke to the sound of the surf crashing on the hard rock beach and the voice of an elderly cleaning lady asking, "Some tea, luv?"

We set out to find more permanent lodgings, and after a day of trudging up and down the warren of lanes, we came upon a hovel in Kemptown that, for some reason, seemed to be just right. It was large — two bedrooms — and quite bright, with sparse furnishings and balls of dust under the beds. I signed the papers, delivered some pound notes to the landlady, who had seen too many students come and go to care about one more, and was handed the keys. We sat blissfully amidst the tattered furniture and ratty carpeting and watched the sky turn to dusk. Gradually, the place went dark. And stayed that way. Because there would be no electricity until we put some shillings in the meter. The landlady had failed to explain to us the subtleties of the system — without constantly feeding coins to the thing, the place was without power.

Within a few days, Marty had left for France to pursue his girlfriend, and I had enrolled at University of Sussex. It was clear I would have to move; the place in Kemptown was too far from the train station and also from the twentieth century. I reinstituted the search and came up with a nice modern bed-sitter on Clifton Street. It, too, had a shilling meter, but at least the water worked, and there was an electric heater in the bathroom down the hall. From here I launched my assault on a graduate education.

Each morning, I rode the train to campus, a ten-minute jaunt into the rolling Sussex countryside. My breakfast ritual was to stop at the Railroad Cafe, a small diner adjacent to the sprawling train yards, and order the mixed grill — charred tomato, petrified sausage, a bacon rind and one sad little egg, fried to a cinder. It was terrible food but wonderful sustenance, and spending a few moments each day in this cozy room crowded with ordinary working men, behind windows so steamed you often couldn't see the world beyond, gave me the sense of knowing, for the first time, the humility of truly being an alien. Not just an internal, psychological émigré, but a literal one. Gradually, America's grandeur was revealed to me, and her outrageous indifference to history and her people was even more stark.

I was in a program with only ten other students, and we spent several hours of the day together. There was a seminar on "The American Identity," which I found amusing — I didn't even know Americans had an identity. But when other students would make judgments about America that were too abstract or based on hearsay or some narrow secondary source, as the only American in the room, I felt compelled to say, "that may sound good, but that's not true." I became very conscious of being this thing called "an American," and I learned that to Europeans, we all looked the same: we were frightening and fascinating, powerful yet awkward, naive and dangerous, existing somewhere both in the future and in the past. I was out of the bowl and saw what exotic fish we were. I was floating free.

Professor Marcus Cunliffe, a distinguished British historian, was the chair of the American Studies program, and he held weekly sherry parties for us at his luxurious flat overlooking the Channel. One afternoon, as I was standing around making small talk, he sidled up next to me and said with conspiratorial bonhomie, "That letter Saul Bellow wrote on your behalf was really glowing. How did you come to know him?" Sipping my sherry, looking out onto the cold green sea, I said as little as possible, hoping my diffidence would pass for a greater knowledge than I actually had. In short, I had become a graduate student.

In England, the pieces of the past started to fall into place for me, reverberating like huge steel doors being slammed shut down a long concrete hallway. A key seminar was the one on "Deviant Behavior," taught by a wonderfully open sociologist named Rupert Wilkinson, who made it clear that "to the other guy, you are the other guy," and that any notion of deviancy depends upon the small patch of psychological territory on which you stand. A lot of people prefer not to be seen as "normal," and that's normal too.

Another remarkable seminar was taught by Leslie Fiedler, a brilliant and outrageous critic of American literature, who was in England following a bad pot bust at the State University of New York. He had been set up, he told us, by conservative forces on campus and had originally been on his way to teach in Scandinavia when, like me, he had washed up on the shores of Brighton in the fall of 1967.

Fiedler was spellbinding. One day he delivered his well-known exegesis on Mark Twain's *The Adventures of Huckleberry Finn* to a small group of us gathered around him like children attending story hour. When the period ended, we begrudgingly left the raft on the Mississippi River and ran for the train back to Brighton. For Fiedler, I wrote a paper on Richard Farina's book *Been Down So Long It Looks Like Up to Me*, examining the underlying proposition, based on a fictional University's collusion with the Selective Service System, that it no longer mattered "how" one plays the game but only "if" one plays the game. Farina focussed on the chiseled cool of bebop: "Polarity is selected at will," he wrote, "for I am not ionized and I possess not valence." It was a disengagement so aggressive that it redefined passivity.

Perhaps coincidentally, and for the first time in my life, I stopped playing piano. I hadn't wanted to join Steve Miller in San Francisco, and I was listening non-stop to the music of John Coltrane, whose piano player, McCoy Tyner, was just so brilliant that he shut me down. That was it. There was no way I was gonna get there, and if that was the wave of the future, then I was out of it. The piano had been part of my life since I was aware that I even had a life, and giving up playing was like losing a limb. But even as I felt this loss, I felt an opening, a sharp wind blowing in new possibilities. It was as if I had stopped smoking and the air had suddenly turned cold and fresh. A significant emptiness entered my life. There can be no true surrender until and unless there has been a true desire to possess — as one must clutch and grasp before one can release and set free. I had tried everything in my power to play this music and now I let go of it with everything I had.

In this release came a surprising discovery. After several months of ignoring every piano I passed, one day I entered a room in Falmer House, the student union, and there was a grand piano sitting quietly, at rest, next to a window that overlooked the campus green. For some reason, I sat down and started to play, with nothing in mind. I played for hours, to pass the time, as I had done when I was very small. And the next day, I came back and did the same. And the next.

I was playing to find me. Or to feel me. To feel whatever it was I felt, to get in touch with that part of me that had grown old. I had accidentally stumbled on the real meaning of music in my life. Playing piano was an extension of my own self, and for the first time, I no longer wanted to sound like McCoy Tyner or Horace Silver or Sonny Clark. I just wanted to discover what I was feeling. As inconsequential as it may seem, I was listening.

I went back to playing. But this time, I accepted my limitations. I played because it was simply better than not playing. I did it with a sense of discovery. Each problem that came up was my own, something interesting to solve rather than an indictment of my lack. Owning my bad habits and being entertained by my lines, I was able to hear myself, perhaps for the first time, and to say what I wanted to say with authority.

I didn't sound like anybody else. I sounded like me, for better or worse. The birth of a personal style, it seems, comes from this acceptance of who you are rather than who you dream of being. Not from your triumphs, necessarily, but often, from how you recover from what you perceive as your failures. Jazz, as they say, is the art of recovery. Without the "accident" (the mistake) there is no jazz. Or, better put, in jazz, there are no mistakes, only opportunities.

And then in December, the Steve Miller Band came to England. They had scored a big record deal and were coming over to work with Glyn Johns, the engineer for The Who and The Rolling Stones. I found myself commuting from seminars at Sussex to recording sessions in London, riding the fabulous Brighton Belle, a train with overstuffed chairs and a dining car that served kippers, perhaps the most luxurious one-hour excursion on the island. In London, the band had rented an elegant home at 3 S. Eaton Place, deep in Belgravia. There, in the midst of rolled 'brollies and stiff upper lips, these Left Coast freaks had encamped like a band of gypsies.

My first recording session was a revelation. I spent equal time out in the studio and in the control room watching Glyn work. At one point, he taped a piece of cardboard over the v.u. meters on the mixing board so as not to be distracted by such technical details as recording level. His recording style was built on intuition. My chance to actually record came late at night, after the full band had gone back to the house and I was left at the studio with Glyn and Boz Scaggs.

Boz had spent a long couple of years during the mid sixties living in Sweden and wandering through Europe. From time to time, he had lived rough, sleeping under the bridges of Paris and, finally, making his way to India, where, exhausted, he was taken in by monks and nourished back to health. During this period, he had written a haunting little song, which he played for us that night. I don't think Steve had intended to record it—it was out of keeping with the band's harder image back in San Francisco—but that night, as Boz sat in a chair with his twelve-string guitar and sang, "Baby's calling me home, and she keeps on calling me home..." Glyn and I were mesmerized.

Something of Boz's loneliness while wandering the globe came over us like a spell. Glyn asked me if I could play a harpsichord, which I had never even seen before, but I said yes, and he rolled this ancient keyboard over to where I was sitting. Boz began teaching me the chords, and Glyn silently and efficiently set up the microphones and disappeared into the control room.

As we were casually talking, and Boz was singing the verses softly into the microphone, I was aware of Glyn twisting dials in the control room. He told us to put on the headphones and, suddenly, time stood still. For the three minutes and thirty seconds it took to record the song, I entered a magic realm that to this day still takes my breath away. Up until that moment, music had always been live, in the air, going away from me as it normally does. But that night, well after midnight, with only myself and Boz and Glyn in the room, I heard the vintage harpsichord I was playing spread out against Boz's voice and guitar like some kind of aural painting. The music had a three dimensionality and a permanency that it did not normally have. Every note I played hung for a moment in my consciousness. I could consider it and reconsider it before playing the next phrase. I knew I was playing, and at the same time, I was observing the music as if from a distance.

Very few musicians are able to completely ignore the "red light" when they are in the recording studio. There is something unnatural about an event in time being captured as an event in space; there is always a hint of virtual reality in the frozen moment of the recording process. But in this first moment, it seemed a kind of miracle. I put on the earphones, heard the first notes leap off the strings, and I was hooked on the recording process forever.

Boz and I went into the control room to hear the song, and instead of the little tune we had just recorded, a huge guitar and an enormous harpsichord came stomping out of the speakers that hung on the wall. Somehow, Glyn had made the little song into a great moment. Glyn smiled and said "Small always plays big on tape."

Boz went back into the studio to double his vocal, singing a phrase here and there along with his original track to make the chorus more full, and I asked Glyn if he thought the song would fit on the album. He said there was a big difference between playing live and recording. A lot of things that worked great on stage didn't come off in the recording studio, while even more things that sounded just plain silly on stage were the stuff great records were made of. Six months later, when *Children of the Future* was released, Boz's song opened side two and segued directly into the album's strongest rocker. Glyn had made his point.

In time, Olympic Studios, where we did that recording session, became the subject of legend. Like Abbey Road, much of the great British music of the era was recorded there. And although during the period that I was on the scene there was a sense of history, an awareness that this music had a life of its own, it was all very off-hand and nonchalant. On a typical afternoon, one might find Pete Townsend or Eric Burdon, recording or just having tea and scones. In fact, at 4 P.M., the "tea boy," who was 70 years old, would come around to each studio with a tray and people would simply enjoy a civilized moment. Not exactly the image of bad-boy British rock. Upstairs in the loft, Glyn's younger brother Andy spent hours practicing guitar with Peter Frampton and listening to Booker T and the MGs. There was a great hunger to absorb American R&B and blues. It would be several more years before the star-making machinery would divide all these musicians into separate little ships that passed in the economic night. At the time, it was "mates" and "lads," and rolling tape was cheap.

That December, the Steve Miller Band had an unfortunate run-in with Scotland Yard. It seems a friend from San Francisco had sent a satin pillow through the mail to Harvey Kornspan, the band's manager, and, perhaps because the comings and goings at the house were somewhat notorious, the postal service interdicted the package and placed it in front of a dog trained to sniff out marijuana. He reacted positively to the package, and on the word of a dog, the band was busted. Judy had recently arrived from the States and that morning we had taken the train from Brighton to London for the weekend to hang out with the band. As we walked up the steps to the house, we were greeted by a very correct gentleman who said "Come in, the others are in the dining room." Sure enough, seated around the huge oval table were all the band members and their various friends. They were being guarded by a few Bobbies and the very same canine that had dropped the dime. "It's a bust," drummer Tim Davis announced, and for the next several hours, anybody who came into the house was added to the group sitting around the table. By evening, everybody was hauled off to jail, but because Judy and I had an address in Brighton, we were released with a warning to avoid such unpleasantness in the future.

1968

Months after Steve and the others had returned to San Francisco, I was still going up to Olympic Studios to record with various musicians from bands like Spooky Tooth and Blodwyn Pig, or just to spend some time with Glyn. Judy had enrolled in the London School of Weaving and was commuting on the Brighton Belle several days a week. We would meet in London for dinner, or walk down Kensington Church Street to Harrods, or just spend time on Kings Road or Carnaby Street, goofing on the "swinging London" scene. We went to the Marquee Club and The Speakeasy; we saw Jimi Hendrix sprawled like a pasha with two large blondes; we saw Paul McCartney while we were standing on line at the American embassy. The smell of coal smoke was always in the air and England was on top of the world.

As an American, a child of the cultural revolution, I was slow to understand that to Glyn and the rest of the British musicians, the term "commercial" was not a pejorative, as it was back home. Since the 1940s, jazz musicians in America had consciously stopped being "entertainers." Their attitude toward the audience was "you come for the music or you don't have to come at all." In some ways, it was unhip to be accepted. Bob Dylan, too, seemed to cut commercial music precious little slack, and most of my heroes, like Mose Allison, were well out of the money hunt. But at Olympic Studios, the music was clearly a commodity. Glyn always listened to the music in pieces — first just the bass, then just the drums, one at a time, then all together, then the guitars, then the vocals — then everything together — all very very loud. When music is played this way, it becomes something other than translated emotion; it becomes a physical thing. Something to be manipulated; packaged; marketed. Glyn was the first person I ever met who said the words "commercial music" in a positive way. If something was commercial, it meant you had succeeded.

By spring, I had completed the course work for my Master's Degree in American Studies and had written a brief thesis on the social history of Black music in America. My adviser, Rupert Wilkinson, encouraged me to continue on for a Doctor of Philosophy, using this paper as a guide for my dissertation. I had never even considered a Ph.D. — I had gone to Sussex to maintain my student deferment — but I understood that I was being presented with a significant opportunity. If I stuck it out for another two or three years, I would have a degree that would allow me to teach at the university. Suddenly, this seemed like the most wonderful prospect, to be a colleague of men like Harvey Goldberg and Helmut Ragsdale, to be privy to this world. Perhaps it would lead to the higher understanding I had been seeking for so many years. The gnawing hunger in my mind was still there, whispering, "I need something...I *need* something" at seemingly random times. Driven by this void, and the sense that my mission was somehow to fill it, I signed on as a doctoral candidate.

Later that May, Harvey Goldberg came to Paris. He had called to say it would be an interesting time to visit, and we arranged to meet him at the Hotel La Louisianne in the 6th arrondissement, the heart of bohemian Paris. Judy and I took the train to Dover, then the boat across the English Channel, and finally another train from Calais to Paris. We arrived mid afternoon at the Gare du Nord, where we transferred to the Metro and came up out of the underground at Boulevard St. Michel. Emerging into the glare of a sunny afternoon, we found we had arrived smack at the center of the revolution.

On the left, a mob of jeering students was throwing stones and chanting; to the right, a phalanx of police officers began charging them, swinging great batons and shouting "Allez! Allez!" For a frozen moment, we were poised at the fulcrum of the Paris uprising. And then we were running as fast as we could down the Boulevard St. Germain, along narrow lanes with a ragged group of kids, pursued by the police. I grabbed for Judy's hand so we wouldn't be separated just as we were both struck on the back of our legs by a great baton. Shouts in French rained down on us from windows above, and the sound of the police, heavy with their chains and battle gear, was just behind us. Suddenly, the Rue du Seine opened on the right. We turned up the narrow street, hearing the hooting and hissing of old French women taunting the cops, and, as we passed a large outdoor fish market, the Hotel La Louisianne appeared on the left. We ducked into the lobby and there was Harvey. Out of breath, I said, "So this is what history feels like," and he didn't crack a smile.

Several months later, in August, I returned to Winnetka, Illinois, where my father was very offhand about the terms of his illness. He denied there was anything to worry about. He said he had bursitis in his shoulder, that was all. He had just returned from a long car trip with my younger brother, Ezra, visiting all the major Civil War battlefields, a passion they both shared, and on the way home, the two of them had stopped to visit Saul Bellow in New England. He told me a little about the trip, but the subject of his health never came up. In fact, he mentioned to me that he was thinking of taking a new job and I managed to say, "That's great. Change is a sign of life," and immediately, I felt like a fool for uttering such a stupid remark. He was very thin and gaunt and was spending a lot of time in bed reading. Something was terribly wrong.

Over the next several weeks, I went back and forth from Madison to Winnetka, trying to be casual, trying to get some hard information from anybody about my father's condition. Nobody was talking, not my mother, not my father, not his friend Dr. Schuster who came periodically to meet with him behind the closed bedroom door. In those days, nobody would say the word "cancer," as if saying it would make it come true.

Then one weekend, I came to the little white house on Spruce Street and walked up the winding stairway to the second floor just as my father was coming out of the bathroom. He had a look in his eyes that was indescribable, a baffled, fifty-yard stare. The bathroom was paneled in mirrors, and there was no way he hadn't seen what he looked like. He looked like a dead man.

That day, I spent the whole afternoon sitting in his bedroom with him as he read. He said nothing to me. I said nothing to him. Dying was not mentioned. Life itself was in a state of denial. The pages turned. He was reading as if to blot out memory, to set aside the pain. I sat there and he simply ignored me. It grew dark. To this day, it remains the most inexplicable, desolate day of my life. I was waiting for him to say goodbye. Perhaps to tell me I had not failed him. Or perhaps to pass along some words of wisdom, encouragement, direction. Anything.

He must have been terrified. I suppose he was holding on for dear life and, at the same time, trying desperately to surrender to death. But his face showed nothing. He was impassive. Tough to the end. This was his final message to me: "don't let the bastards wear you down." It's not much to hang on to when you're looking for a talisman. But perhaps it was all he had.

After midnight, my mother woke me up, panicked. My father was raving, incoherent. We called for an ambulance. Two paramedics came with a gurney and they lashed him to it. The stairs from the second floor were so steep that they almost dropped him going down. It was awful, a nightmare. I told my mother to stay home and I got in the car and drove to the hospital.

When I got there, he was already in a large white room, hooked up to tubes and bottles. There was no medical attendant. Just the two of us in a large neon room. I said, "Pop, can you hear me?" He didn't react. He had stopped shaving days before, and it was the first time I had seen him with a beard, as the bohemian he might have been. I touched his hand and said, "Your beard is looking good...." He said nothing. I left the room and returned home to get my mother. By the time we got back to the hospital, he had died. Alone and cold in an empty room hooked up to a morphine drip.

The next day, my sister and I started making the phone calls. I drew the job of explaining to our thirteen-year-old brother Ezra that his father wouldn't be coming home, an act for which he has never completely forgiven me. I took him out to the front curb and sat him down. I said, "You know pop was very sick..." He didn't want to hear what was coming next. He said, "Call Mr. Bellow." Their car trip together to the killing fields of the Civil War, ending at Bellow's house, had been their last galvanizing experience, and he had seen the love between Bellow and my father. Now Ezra was grasping at anything just not to see the inevitable. I said, "Mr. Bellow can't help him now."

That day, the house was bedlam. My father's sister and mother arrived; his sister Judy was just plain hysterical, and his mother Cip chanted over and over, "You'll never know what we lost," like some kind of mantra that would help bring him back. Maxine was all business with the funeral home. My mother was strangely distant, acting as if, somehow, my father had done this to her, just the latest in a long line of betrayals and abandonments. I felt my shoulders begin to bend under the weight of the chaos. Two days later, I sat at his funeral and sobbed uncontrollably. At the gravesite, when we were supposed to toss dirt on the casket, I couldn't do it. I couldn't bury him.

In the ensuing days, I began to go through my father's personal effects. There was almost nothing. It was incredible. He had left a wallet and a stopped watch. That was it. Sitting in his bedroom, staring into this small box of artifacts, I remembered the song he used to sing on our car rides, "Who will wind the clock when I am gone?" It would have been ironic if it wasn't so sad. The answer was now clear. Maxine thinks it's the reason I've spent my whole life being on time and producing artifacts as if there's no tomorrow. She says I'm covering for my father. With a man of ideas, one longs for some tangible evidence, something to hold on to as a hedge against the ravages of time. And though, months later, I did find a few boxes of his papers, it was small consolation.

Louis Sidran (born Sidransky) died September 22, 1968. He was fifty-two.

One month later, almost to the day, I received the notice from my draft board informing me that my student deferment had been canceled and that I was to report for my pre-induction physical. I had been going back and forth between Madison and Chicago, helping my mother organize her life, and as my father had left no will, it was taking a huge toll. I was becoming a zombie, and the draft notice sank me into a darkness I had never known before. It was upon me the rainy night I entered a small, wood-panelled bar in downtown Chicago to have drinks with my father's friend.

Saul Bellow was waiting for me in a padded leather booth. He looked as distraught as I felt. There were tears in his eyes. He shook my hand and said, "Poor Louie, poor Louie," his big sad eyes brimmed with sorrow. When I sat down, his first words were, "Never forget, your father was a great man."

My whole life, I had been hearing this from people. I knew all about his brilliance, his fast, funny humanity. But at home, he had been such a different man.

When he put on that Cubs hat and settled into his chair, he was silent, withdrawn, imprisoned. He had obviously lived more than one life.

"You know," Bellow said, "your father did not love his life but he embraced his fate." I said I didn't really know him. What I meant is that I didn't understand.

Bellow sighed. "He kept his distance from you, because he didn't want his problems to become your problems. But he talked about you, always."

That seemed so strange to me, a father expressing his love for his son by avoiding him. I wanted to say something, but I also wanted to believe it too. Love is a conundrum. We know the world is a hard mean lie, and we want to protect those we love from it. But to do so is to perpetrate a bigger lie. What to do? And how to survive this gift of omission?

The drinks came. Bellow asked after my family. I told him my sister was holding up, my brother was in denial and my mother seemed disconnected. He told me my brother was a good kid and not to worry about my mother, "she's tough as nails." Then he asked after my own situation. I told him I had just been called for my draft physical. He asked what I was going to do.

I had heard that Bellow had wanted to enlist in the army during World War Two but had a medical condition that prevented it. All the young Jewish men at the time wanted to do their part in bringing Hitler down, and up until the very end, even my father had remained strangely gung-ho and patriotic about Vietnam. In fact, we had had terrible raging fights about this and about Lyndon Johnson. I had said to him, "Instead of bombs, why don't we just drop Buicks and TVs on the Vietnamese? Then they would have to come to us for spare parts, and, voila, we win!" He was so mad at this he refused to talk to me about it any more. His generation, they were the best and the brightest, and now it had turned to shit. In his final papers I found a scrap that said, "These kids, they're going to inherit tomorrow, but why must they also own today?"

In that soggy booth, with the wooden taste of scotch in my mouth and the smell of wet wool in the air, I told Bellow I didn't know what I was going to do. He said, "Whatever you do, Ben, remember: don't do anything that you'll be ashamed of later." I knew it was not going to be that easy.

The last thing I mentioned to him was that my father was growing a beard when he died. This seemed to bring him to a precipice. He got very quiet. Tears emerged in his eyes again. "Poor Louie," he said, "Poor Louie." Finally, we shook hands and I walked out into the cold October rain. There is an old Chicago blues lyric, "the sky is crying..." That night, the whole world wept.

The next week, I went to see the doctor that Jerry Garcia had recommended. A no-nonsense psychiatrist, he had worked for the military before becoming disenchanted with the war in Vietnam. After talking with him for an hour, he said, "There's no way going in the army is going to be good for you. I will see you a few more times, and when you receive the date and time for your physical, let me know." The week the notice came, I went to see him and he handed me a letter. He said, "No matter what happens, do not say anything. Insist on seeing their psychiatrist and hand him this letter. Remember, do not say anything." I thought of what Bellow had advised; I felt a chill go up my spine.

I had to go to Racine to board the bus for Milwaukee and the induction center. In Racine, I went to the house of my friend John Isbell, who had agreed to stay up with me through the long night. It was a tradition to avoid sleep before the morning of your army physical. Back in Madison, the Draft Resistance Union often enlisted beautiful girls to pull young men aside before they boarded the bus, asking them, "Do you know what your options are?" But in Racine, you were on your own, and John was the closest thing I had to a support system. He laid in a case of beer, and we spent the night drinking and talking about old times, the stolen cars, the fights, the girlfriends. At 6 A.M., he drove me to the bus depot where dozens of young men were gathered in little groups. Some of them were acting joyous, roughhousing with one another as if they were going off on a great adventure. Others were quiet, holding small Bibles. I saw no one I knew. I got on board and with a great lurch we set off for Milwaukee.

A half hour later, we stumbled off into the growing dawn and were ordered into a large hall, lined up, stripped down, and put on the conveyor belt of conscription. They moved us through as fast as possible, with little or no opportunity for comment or objection. At one point, standing naked in a line of young men, some already posing as marines, a few others wild eyed on LSD or strung out on speed, I asked the corporal in charge to see the psychiatrist. He looked at me, went away and came back with a sergeant. The sergeant made me repeat the request and then took the letter I was holding. He said, "Stand over there."

I stood shivering by a wall as the other recruits filed by. A young soldier walked past me and said out of the corner of his mouth, "Don't give up." When I looked at him, he looked away. Eventually I was ushered into the office of the psychiatrist who asked me a few questions, which I answered as briefly as possible. He wrote a few things down and handed me a form. Then he said, "I want you to know that we're going to get you. And you can tell Dr. Bogost that we're going to get him, too. That's all." I was shown to the final station and my card was stamped "1Y." I had been temporarily deferred from the nightmare in Vietnam.

Back on the bus to Madison, I felt a terrible remorse. I was distraught, and I felt humiliated. I would never wear a soldier's uniform like my father had. By the time I got back home, strung out from days of no sleep, my head was swimming in confusion. On the street, I saw Elliot Eisenberg and I told him what I had just gone through. I said I knew it was crazy but I couldn't shake this sense of guilt. He said, "Man, don't ever forget that our music was invented by a lot of cats who did *not* go into the army," and immediately I felt better. You just have to stand for something or you'll fall for anything.

1969

I spent that spring in Madison working on my dissertation. It had turned into a full-blown social history of jazz, an investigation of the African-American oral continuum in the context of literate America, the coming together of McLuhan's thesis and Coltrane's sound. When I wasn't at my typewriter or in the University library, I was spending a lot of time with our dog Harold, a small brown poodle with a striking resemblance to Errol Flynn. He was so smart that on more than one occasion, he conned grown men into giving up their meal. I came to realize there was never any reason to raise my voice to Harold, because his hearing was better than mine. I worked on it and eventually, I was able to talk to him in a conversational tone under any circumstances and he would always respond appropriately — as long as I shared my food with him. It was a variation on the oral tradition.

In April, Judy and I went to San Francisco for her spring break. Steve Miller had broken up the band and was living in Stinson Beach, while the other guys were living in the city. For several nights, we stayed in town with Jim Peterman, the organ player, who was now living across the street from Jann and Janie Wenner. Jann had recently started *Rolling Stone* magazine and was very open about his plans to expand and become a major player in the publishing industry. One day, we were sitting at his desk, looking at a potential ad layout, and he asked me what I thought about it. I looked at the copy and saw Pete Townsend's name. I said, "Well, for one thing why not refer to him as *Mr.* Townsend. Why not bring some respect to the scene?" He said, "Why don't you come to work for me?"

Over the next few days, we talked about it. We hit a crucial difference of opinion when he asked what I would do if I were an editor of the review section. I told him I would do away with all purely negative record reviews. I said that if a writer simply didn't like something, or if he couldn't find some social or historical context in which to frame his remarks, he should say nothing at all. Ignore a record rather than trash it. Obviously, I was still smarting from my own review of Coltrane's *Ballads*. Jann was taken aback. He said, "We are in the business of informing the public." I said, "Yeah, well I think the negative stuff is often just the easy way out, somebody complaining about what *isn't* happening rather than explaining what *is*."

We agreed to disagree, and then a week later, when I was back home, a letter arrived in Madison. It was from Jann, offering me a job as a reporter-writer-record-review-editor. "We're ripe for a change," he wrote, "and I really hope you can make it." I thought about it; I loved writing and I could picture myself in that thriving San Francisco warehouse where Jann held court. But, again, I wasn't looking for a job. I was looking for a purpose. I called Jann and passed. And then I grabbed a flight to L.A.

Steve Miller was going back into the studio, this time with just his bass player and drummer, and he had called to say I should come out, play keyboards and work on the songs with him. Our relationship by this time had become more poised, more professional. I was perhaps the only guy from the old days who had refused to join his band, which somehow made me even more valuable to him in the studio.

In L.A., I was met at the airport by Steve's drummer, Tim Davis, who handed me a joint as soon as we left the baggage claim. When we arrived at the studio, Glyn and Steve and the bass player, Lonnie Turner, were already listening to a playback in the control room. When they finished, Steve said, "Let's try it again with a keyboard." I went out into the studio and sat behind a clavinette, and Steve kicked off the groove which had just a few basic chords and a bass line that sounded suspiciously like the first couple of bars of the Beatles' "Lady Madonna." I doubled the bass line in spots and covered the chords in the bridge. It took an ungodly long time to get the track recorded. At one point, Glyn, trying to cheer us up, started renumbering the takes, going back to "one" again rather than saying, "Okay, boys, lucky take number forty two." There was an open section in the middle of the song and, to keep myself entertained, I began playing the melody of Dizzy Gillespie's "Birk's Works" every time it came around. Of course nobody in the room recognized it.

Finally, the track was cut, and Glyn said, "I've got an idea. Why don't we make this record a science fiction concept? You know, like sometime in the future, when robots might rule the world?" He was just throwing it out, but that afternoon, Steve and I went back to the hotel to smoke a joint and kick it around. I said, "Well, since you stole the bass line from "Lady Madonna," why don't we cop the Beatles' "Looking Through a Glass Onion," you know, where they say 'We told you about Strawberry Fields, the place where nothing is real....' Well, we can say, "I told you about Living in the USA and you know that I'm the Gangster of Love..." I went on spinning a little yarn, with Steve listening:

"I told you 'bout livin' in the USA and you know that I'm the gangster of love

Well let me tell you people I found a new way and I'm tired of all this talk about love

'Cause it's the same old story with a new set of words about the good and the bad and the poor. But the times keep on changing and I'm keeping on top of every bad guy who walks through my door..."

I looked up at Steve to see what he thought, and he said, "Cause I'm a Space Cowboy..." I started to laugh. Where did that come from? He said, "Bet you weren't ready for that." I said, "That's good. Let's keep that line too." That night, Steve went in and sang "Space Cowboy," even harmonizing the little Dizzy Gillespie melody I had played in the middle section. Eventually, the royalties from "Space Cowboy" paid for my graduate education.

A couple of weeks later, Glyn was unexpectedly called back to London. The Beatles wanted him to mix their new record (*Let It Be*), and it was an offer he couldn't refuse. The Beatles had also agreed to cover any of out-of-pocket expenses for the Steve Miller Band during Glyn's absence, including studio time and charges on the bungalow we were renting at the Chateau Marmont Hotel. This was a license for us to go nuts. Rock and roll will do this to you. Ideas you would never consider in the real world can take on a kind of reasonable, adventurous patina in the parallel universe of rock and roll.

Once Glyn was gone, after endless hot fudge sundaes from room service, we decided to go into the studio on our own, take some LSD and roll tape. It seemed like a good idea at the time. That night, playing on acid, feeling the instrument playing me, I came away with a sense of what it must be like to be a genius. Only on acid, you don't play that good, you just get to feel that way: the next day, we discovered that the tapes were unusable, a sorry chaotic mess of confusion and erratic tempos.

Even more troubling was the trip Tim Davis and I made late one night to the Whiskey A Go Go. We had been sitting in the bungalow at the Chateau, and around 1 A.M., we decided to take a little drive and see who was playing at the club. Tim calmly got behind the wheel of the rent-a-car, politely wheeled into the flow of traffic on Sunset Boulevard and stepped on the gas. And he never took his foot off the accelerator for the fifteen blocks to the club. By the time we arrived at the Whiskey, he had run every red light on Sunset, achieved a top speed of 86 miles an hour (according to police records) and had gathered a small flotilla of California Highway patrol in his wake. We pulled into the parking lot, and two cops jumped out of their squad car with guns drawn and said, "Don't move!" We were thrown into the back of the cruiser, all the while Tim was threatening the cops with bodily harm. "You motherfuckers," he kept saying, "you motherfuckers."

He had just kind of snapped. But by some miracle, the cops ignored him and instead of beating him senseless, they booked us for grand theft auto and threw us in a cell. Sitting there with Tim, I realized this was yet another consequence of rock and roll madness—you came to feel that the laws of everyday life simply didn't apply to you anymore. Within a few hours, after it was established that the car wasn't stolen and Steve had bailed us out, Tim was his gentle old self again. As we left the police station, he thanked the officers for not killing him, and they looked at him as if this might be their last chance.

That summer, Judy and I got married. She had graduated from the University of Wisconsin in June, and we were planning to return to England in the fall so that I could finish my degree at Sussex. But when we went to Los Angeles and told her father, he said to me, "How long does my daughter have to follow you around the world?" I said, "Well, we could get married on the boat going over." Judy looked at me and smiled. We had never really discussed getting married but she was clearly for it. Her father said "fine" and called the Holland American Line. They told him the captain no longer performed weddings at sea. That weekend, Judy and I went to San Francisco and, passing a jewelry store, we went in and bought a wedding ring. The next day we went to city hall and filled out the paperwork. We planned to keep it a secret, wait the mandatory two days, get married by a justice of the peace, and then go back to L.A. and tell the family.

When we got back to Stinson Beach and told Steve what we were planning, he said, "Wait! I want to get married, too!" The next day he took a plane to Denver and returned twenty-four hours later with a stunning sixteen-year-old girl named Kim whom he had met on tour. Apparently, he had gone to her house in Colorado and within hours had convinced her father to essentially grant him custody of his beautiful young daughter. Three days later, the four of us went to city hall—Kim in a flowing white gown, Judy in a deadly black fringed outfit—and stood in front of the judge. Afterwards, we had a little reception at the Fairmont Hotel, attended by Jann and Janie, Glyn and a few other friends, and the next week, there was an announcement in the Random Notes column of *Rolling Stone* saying "eat your hearts out girls..." Judy thought the whole thing was ridiculous, but it got us back to England. And as a wedding present, her father gave us the equivalent of what he would have spent on the wedding. We took it and bought a brand new Porsche.

Returning to Brighton was like returning to a familiar cave. We rented the large ground floor flat at our old address, 5 Clifton Street, and again I holed up with my typewriter. I rarely went out except to take the train to the university to meet with my adviser. Once a week, Judy and I gathered with friends around the television to watch *Monty Python's Flying Circus*. The first couple of weeks I simply didn't get it, but by the third week, there it was, in all its twisted, perverse glory: British humor, as Spike Milligan once described it, based on "one man shouting gibberish in the face of authority, and proving by fabricated insanity that nothing could be as mad as what passes for ordinary living." It fit well with the rest of our lives and henceforth we planned our social calendar around it.

That autumn, when I wasn't actually sitting in the corner writing the dissertation, I was lost in thought, endlessly turning over the concepts of the thesis or waking up in the middle of the night to scribble them down. I was on to something, this notion of an oral continuum being fostered, invisibly, by black music in America, in the face of Western literary tradition. It was like discovering a whole new way to look at the stratification of American society, not along traditional economic or social lines but along perceptual matrices. Reminded of Wittgenstein's "duck / rabbit," I thought that the essences of black and white America were perhaps simply invisible to one another, requiring a perceptual shift in order to become "real." After several months of work, and some serious discussions with my adviser, I threw out the first three chapters and started over. I was finding that the traditional language available to the discussion of jazz in America simply would not hold up — often, the ideas would seem to fold back into themselves, much as Marshal McLuhan had once described a chicken as just "an egg's idea to get another egg." I was searching for a new way to tell the story of this music.

1970

If I were meeting Judy in London, I would often drive up early and spend the afternoon with Glyn at Olympic Studios. The more I watched him work, the more convinced I became that record production was something I could do. One needed the ability to communicate with musicians, an intuition about where the music was going and a sense of how to get there. Other than that, there were no rules. From time to time, Glyn called me to play on sessions, and I discovered that on tape, simplicity loomed very large.

This was brought home to me one day when Glyn called and asked if I was free to come up to London that evening. "The Stones are recording, and they need a piano player," he said. "And by the way, would you mind stopping in Lewes to gather up Charlie? He doesn't drive, you know." A couple of hours later, I pulled the Porsche up to a small castle in the Sussex countryside and knocked on a giant oak door.

It opened, and the familiar tough-guy's face of drummer Charlie Watts smiled and invited me in, with a voice that was all tea and sympathy. Miles Davis' *Kind of Blue* was playing on a hidden sound system, and Charlie's wife Shirley was playing with two of their dogs. The home itself was furnished in various antiques, with collections of dolls, silver spoons, books, and all sorts of British kitsch. A great roaring fire was going in the walk-in fireplace; the atmosphere was that of a hip elderly country squire.

As we got into the car to drive to London, I confessed to Charlie that I really didn't listen to the Rolling Stones' records very much. He said, "That's all right mate, neither do we." Instead, we talked jazz. He loved bebop most of all—"I was listening to the radio last night," he said, "and everything sounded like Charlie Parker,"—but he could get quite sentimental about the older stuff too, particularly the jazz of the 1920s and 1930s: Yank Lawson, Billy Butterfield, Eddie Condon, Gus Johnson. "Man, nobody can swing like Gus Johnson," he said. He was surprisingly humble: he told me that he had once met Oscar Peterson's drummer, Ed Thigpen, at Chicago's London House. "And do you know what he said to me? He said, 'Do you love the drums?' And I told him, 'Well, you know, I just hit 'em.'"

When we arrived at Olympic Studio an hour later, Charlie, always the gentleman, held the door open for me. Inside, we found Mick Jagger sitting alone at a grand piano in the huge space of Studio One. He was playing something pretty, and after Charlie introduced us, I asked Mick if that was the song we were going to record. Like Charlie's home scene, it seemed so different from the public image of The Rolling Stones. He said "Oh, no, mate, this is just something I'm fooling around with."

Within the hour, we were set up in a row, me at the far end on a Wurlitzer electric piano, Bill Wyman on bass, Charlie on drums, Keith Richards and Brian Jones on guitars, and Mick leaping up and down in front of us for all he was worth. We started hammering away at three simple chords—there were no lyrics at the time, not even a melody, just a kind of nasty pattern that kept churning over and over—and we played those three chords all night long. It went beyond simplicity; it was one of the most mind-numbing experiences I've ever had, and if that rhythm track ever appeared on a Rolling Stone's album, I'm sure I couldn't recognize it today. But forty-six takes and some Chinese chicken later, it was over, and I came away with a lot of respect for the kind of physical strength and concentration it took to cut a hit record.

Driving home, as the sun was coming up over the Sussex downs, I asked Charlie how long he thought he could keep this up. The demands of a rock drummer were so different from the person he seemed to be. I said, "What do you think you'll be doing when you're fifty years old?"

He said, "When I'm fifty, I'll be up there...crying." Then he paused and reconsidered. "When I'm fifty? No, I doubt it. It takes a lot of strength. You know...I think I'll pack up by the time I'm thirty, it's too much...it's just too much."

All winter long and into the spring, I had been composing songs with the idea that perhaps Steve Miller would want to record them, and while he did record one called "Midnight Tango," I found myself with a collection of musical orphans. One day Glyn said to me, "Why don't we do a demo for you?" It hadn't occurred to me that I could pull off a solo recording. But Glyn went ahead and arranged a demo session at Olympic Studios, calling on Peter Frampton and Mick Abrahams to play guitar and Charlie Watts to play drums. And so, while waiting for the verdict on my dissertation, which I had submitted that May, I recorded a half dozen of my own songs.

When the session was over and we had listened to the final playbacks, Glyn turned to me and said, "Ben, I don't know how to tell you this, but I can't produce you. Your music isn't really pop and it's not simply jazz. I think you'll do just as well by yourself as you would with me." And then he handed me the master reel and smiled. It was the first, but clearly not the last time that I was given the good news and the bad news simultaneously: I don't sound like anybody else.

The next week, I was called in to defend my dissertation. I knew every single sentence by heart, had written and rewritten each word several times. Still, entering the room and facing four affectless academics made me nervous. For almost three hours, they probed and parsed and asked me to relate my assertions to their more traditional areas of expertise. When they were done, I was asked to leave the room, and after a brief moment, Dr. Postgate, came out and said, "Congratulations, Dr. Sidran."

I don't know what I had expected to feel. I know that my whole life, I had held formal learning in such high regard that the idea of becoming a Ph.D., a doctor, a colleague of my academic heroes, seemed out of reach. Perhaps I had never really anticipated arriving at this point. But, in fact, as I walked to the train to tell Judy the good news, what I felt was nothing. Nothing at all. The world had not changed, and I had not become any wiser by devoting myself to the academic process.

Actually, what I felt was cheated. I must have been harboring the notion, absorbed in early childhood, perhaps from watching my father and his friends, that formal learning was a magical thing, and that through it, one could arrive at the essential nature of things. In retrospect, it was a very Jewish notion. Now, with the exception of the "Dr. Sidran" part, I was walking out of the University pretty much the way I had walked in. No profound insight, no real understanding and no resolution to the ongoing, gnawing "need" inside my head. On the train ride home, I chanted the little mantra, "Them that knows don't talk, and them that talks don't know."

Judy and I began making plans to return to the United States, and we decided we would let fate choose where we landed. I began by sending out dozens of letters to universities across the country, seeking a basic teaching position. But as the weeks went by, it became painfully obvious that we were landing nowhere. Of the fifty or so letters I mailed, I got only two guarded responses: one a possible offer to teach freshman English at Cal State and another too ludicrous to even mention. It appeared that many young men had stayed in graduate school to avoid going to Vietnam, and were all now graduating and seeking employment at the same time. This glut of newly minted Ph.Ds, and the fact that I was in American Studies, a field not generally offered, made my prospects pretty bleak.

Then one day, while wandering through the warren of old shops in Brighton known as The Lanes, I passed a small record store. Standing there looking at the shiny album covers in the window, it dawned on me: I was missing the obvious; it was time for me to stop studying the secondary sources, to stop trying to "understand" the information. It was time for me to *become* the information. I went home and told Judy we were moving to Los Angeles and I was going into the record business. Twenty-four hours a day, I was going to feel what a musician felt, taste the food they tasted and get paid the way they got paid. To this day, I am terribly moved by the transformative power of adversity and by the potential triumph that lurks within every failure.

Ben and Maxine on Carmel Avenue (1946)

The last ball game (1954)

Conducting the band at Park High School (1960)

On the Terrace of the University of Wisconsin (1963)

With Judy,
summer 1967

With Harvey and Judy in Paris (1968)

With Jann Wenner (1969)

First day of recording, Capitol Studio A (1971)
Jim Keltner and Gary Mallaber on drums, Ed Davis standing with guitar

Ibiza (1973)

With Bob Krasnow in Chicago (1973)

Mingus gets the key to the city from Mayor Soglin (1974)

With Jane Fonda on "The Weekend Starts Now" (1974)

Part Two

BECOMING THE INFORMATION

≋ Chapter Four

"Time is a river
Our bodies are canoes
When you go in wading
Please remove your shoes."

—Written on the rear window of a VW
microbus on the island of Ibiza

1970

That September, we sailed back to the United States on the new *QEII*. Whereas several years before it had taken nearly two weeks to sail to England on the SS *Aurelia*, this monster of a liner took barely five days to make the return trip. Once docked, we went into the hold of the ship, got in the Porsche and drove up the gang plank, through customs and out into the steaming streets of New York City. Before leaving town, I dropped off photocopies of my dissertation at several publishing houses, hoping, who knows, perhaps I'd get lucky. Now that I was self-employed, casting bread upon the water was the name of my game.

It took nearly a month to drive to Los Angeles. On our way West, we stopped to visit friends along the way, in Boston, in Chicago, in Madison; we even spent a couple of nights in a teepee outside of Missoula, Montana. Finally, in early October, we drove south from San Francisco, down Highway 1 and into the flaming heart of the beast. It had been a hot, dry summer, and the fires were raging as we approached Los Angeles. The skies were choked with angry black smoke, and here and there, fingers of flame crawled down the hillside toward the highway.

Outside of Malibu, we actually saw a man calmly pumping one last tankful of gas into his Mercedes even as the flames licked at the walls of the filling station. It was like arriving in the ninth circle of Hell, only this inferno had palm trees.

Once in L.A. the fires were just a dim haze on the horizon, and we set to work finding a place to live. We discovered a cozy little house in the flats of West L.A., but just as we were about to sign the lease, Glyn arrived from England and said he was thinking of renting a place in L.A. too and would we consider sharing something with him? He would only be spending a week or two each month and, as we didn't have much money, it made sense. So we recast the search — Glyn was not a West L.A. flats type — and ultimately, we discovered a large ranch house high in the hills of North Hollywood. We signed the lease and moved in with only a hundred dollars left in the bank and fifteen copies of my demo tape from London. I felt like the kid who had just traded in the family cow for a handful of beans.

I got to work knocking on doors. I woke up every morning and made phone calls, starting with the "A's" — A&M Records, Atlantic Records — and worked my way through the alphabet...Capitol Records, Columbia Records...down through Little David and Mercury and ultimately arriving at United Artists Records. On a good day, I didn't get very far down the list because somebody had taken my call and agreed to see me. I would show up with my demo tape and do my dance. Sometimes, the meeting was put off by a very nice secretary who herself took the tape and promised to get back to me. I gathered a long list of names, mostly of secretaries, and eventually built up some very nice relationships with the women who guarded the dens of power.

To pay the rent, I got work in recording studios, doing a lot of faceless sessions where they wanted me to imitate Jerry Lee Lewis. I would leave these studios with fingers bleeding. I did one session for Gene Clark of The Byrds and another for James Taylor, but mostly, I did demo work for music publishers. And, for a while, to pick up some cash, I joined Jesse "Ed" Davis' band.

Ed was a Washitaw Indian from Oklahoma whom I met in London when he arrived with a contract from Atlantic Records, a reputation as one of the fastest guitars in the West, and a briefcase full of cash. His sessions were actually a lot of fun. For one of them, he had us all sitting around in a circle on the floor of Olympic Studio — me, guitarist Eric Clapton, bass player Billy Rich, even Judy joined in — and then he gave us this "Indian" chant to repeat, something that sounded like "Li-ah Ho-ni Ba Na Na." We were all chanting away very seriously while Ed conducted us with "authentic Native American" movements. Finally, I asked him what the chant meant. "It means," he said, "you have a banana in your ear." He fell out laughing; the whole thing had been a put-on. At the end of the session, he reached into the briefcase and passed out the cash.

Ed's band was an extension of Leon Russell's "Mad Dogs and Englishmen." Leon was also from Oklahoma and had arrived in L.A. early on, playing piano on many hits during the sixties. At the time I met him, he was Joe Cocker's "music director." Ringmaster was more like it. I remember going to his house in the Hollywood Hills one afternoon where half-naked women and babies wandered languorously around a swimming pool and Leon held court behind mirrored shades and a flowing white beard.

On another afternoon, I went with Leon and Glyn to A&M studios to record a new song Leon had written. He had the words and music spread out on several pieces of paper, and I was enlisted to sit in the studio with him and turn the pages at the appropriate moments. I sat there silently as Leon played this gorgeous two-handed piano and sang, in his strangled Oklahoma drawl, "Are we really happy here in this lonely masquerade..." It was the first recording of the song that would eventually become a huge hit for George Benson. Where Leon had an artistic depth and a kind of guru's way about him, Ed Davis was all raw slide-guitar and rock and roll insanity.

The band rehearsed in his garage, a block from the ocean, where a couple of drummers from out of town, Gary Malabar and Sandy Konikoff, were crashing in his garage. They became the heart of the rhythm section. On bass we had a brilliant lunatic named Wolfgang Meltz, a Hungarian refugee with unbelievable technique, and there was also a wonderfully soulful, if erratic, saxophone player in the band named Jim Gordon. We worked in places like the El Monte Legionnaires Club and the Topanga Corral and occasionally went on the road. Every gig was an adventure, and at the end of the night, my ears were ringing and my hands were raw. My last memory of this particular tribe of outlaws was watching them stagger through the Seattle airport early one morning following a long night of the blues, combined with the sound of a girl's voice as she pounded on the door of the motel room next to mine at 5 A.M., pleading "Let me in, come on, man, let me in. Or just throw out my clothes..."

Over those early months in California, I learned well the meaning of the "Hollywood Slow No." The Hollywood Slow No is.... "yes." "Yes, he'll call you back." Or, "He's in a meeting now but, yes, he's considering the project." Or, "Yes we should have lunch." It's the Japanese heart of the Hollywood mind — nobody will actually say the word "no" to you. But whereas the Japanese won't tell you "no" in order that you not lose face, in Hollywood they won't say it just in case your face turns out to be a viable commodity in the future. Everybody is hedging his bets and the deal is always left open, but rarely closed. Living with the "slow no" is like swimming in oatmeal; a lot of your energy is spent just trying to keep breathing.

It was something Glyn and I discussed often down at Mike's Pool Hall. Particularly on boiling hot afternoons in the San Fernando Valley, we would slip away to Mike's and cool out underneath a slowly rotating fan. Sipping a cold bottle of beer, chalking his inlaid mother-of-pearl cue, then looking down the long green table before executing another languid stroke, Glyn would say, "Relax, Ben, these things take time."

Then one day in the middle of this endless L.A. autumn, I received a letter from Oxford University Press. They had read my manuscript and were interested in publishing it. They offered a five hundred-dollar advance (four months rent!), and they clearly understood the premise of the work and seemed excited about it. Along with the letter, they sent a contract. It was all very low key, and not knowing how these things worked, I let the contract sit on my desk for a week so as not to appear too eager. I was about to sign it and send it back when another letter arrived, this one from Holt, Rinehart & Winston.

Unlike the quickly typed note from Oxford, this letter was written on embossed stationary and came from a man with two middle initials—Steven M.L. Aronson. It said, "We have read your very impressive manuscript and would be interested in discussing it with you if ever you are in New York." This time, I picked up the phone and called Mr. Aronson directly. I said by a strange coincidence, I planned to be in New York the very next week. We arranged to meet and I hung up, ecstatic. Then I picked up the phone and dialed my father at his office to give him the good news. And as the phone rang and rang down some long forgotten corridor at the Leo Burnett advertising agency in Chicago, I realized what I had just done. I dropped the receiver back on its cradle like a hot rock. The breath went out of me. I still hadn't buried him.

The next week, Steven Aronson, a dapper little fellow in a bow tie, took me to The Palm restaurant in New York. Over a huge hunk of charred meat, he told me, "We like your manuscript. We think it could be an important work. If you want to rework it that's fine, but we'll publish it as is..." Then he offered me an advance of five thousand dollars. Suddenly, I was rich. The following week I wrote a brief introduction, thanked Harvey Goldberg, Pallo Jordan, Elliot Eisenberg, Ray Lucas and George Brown for their help in formulating the ideas, and dedicated the book to my father. I titled it *Black Talk, or How the Music of Black America Created a Radical Alternative to the Values of Western Literary Tradition*. Finally a magic bean had sprouted.

Back in Los Angeles, I kept knocking on doors and calling executives. When their secretaries told me they were out, I was polite and said I would call back. I suspected that few of these guys ever bothered to listen to my demo tape; I had no manager, no big money connections, and the music, as Glyn had pointed out, was unlike anything else that was around. I was a gourmet item, a taste that would have to be developed. In the record business, as in many other businesses, people are working full time at not looking bad. That's what it meant to "go with the go and flow with the flow," one of the more popular expressions at the time. And signing an oddball like me was clearly going against the flow.

One hot smoggy day, after a round at Mike's pool hall, Glyn and I cruised into Hollywood to visit some friends recording at Capitol Records. On the way to the studios, Glyn wanted to run up on the seventh floor to drop off something with Artie Mogul, then president of the company. A darkly handsome man, Artie was notorious in the industry for his raffish approach to the business. Some people would say, "Artie, when you leave the company, please leave a little something behind for the rest of us." Since he was one of the men I had been pestering regularly (actually, his secretary, Felice was the one I usually spoke with), Artie and I had a cordial relationship. That is, he wouldn't say no to me — perhaps because of Glyn — but he certainly wasn't about to say yes.

On this day, he was in an expansive mood. He was going to meet a friend of his for lunch at the Brown Derby, and he invited us to come along. The three of us walked the few blocks down to Sunset, and there we met his friend, Albert Grossman. Albert, a huge man with a long gray ponytail, managed Bob Dylan and Janis Joplin among others, and was one of the prime movers of the new music. If Mogul was notorious, Albert was infamous, both for his methods of negotiating (his friends called him the "gray cloud" because he was so hard to pin down) and his opulent hippie style (others suggested that his last name should have been hyphenated).

After we were seated and the waiter had taken the orders, Artie turned to Albert and said with a twinkle in his eye, "You know, Albert, there's only one girl left in this world that I want to fuck."

"Who's that," asked Albert.

"The Queen of England."

Glyn's ears pricked up.

"The Queen of England," said Albert, "But she's a dog. Why would anybody want to fuck the Queen of England?"

"Because," said Artie, "I want to hear the Queen of England say, 'Give it to me Artie, give it to me.'"

Albert found this enormously funny. The two of them laughed uproariously. Glyn looked away and asked the waiter to bring him a telephone. And, sitting there in this flamboyant showbiz retreat, I realized I had finally found my way backstage in the record business.

A few days later, when I called his office, Artie took the call. He said, "Come on in, let's talk." When I came in, he was on the phone, and he motioned me to sit down. On his desk, I noticed a picture of an attractive young girl and a middle-aged woman, which I took to be his daughter and wife. I thought about the Queen of England. Artie went from one call to another. After about half an hour, he hung up, looked up to find me sitting there, and said, "So you want to make a record?"

I said, "Yes."

"Tell me about it." He obviously had never listened to the demo tape.

I said, "I write these songs, and I want to use jazz musicians and rock musicians, famous musicians who have never played together...and I'm going to have my friends Steve Miller and Boz Scaggs sing..." He stopped me right there.

He said, "Kid, we're only interested in singer/songwriters. Do you sing?"

"Well...."

"If we're gonna work with you, you gotta sing."

I immediately changed tack. "Of course, I *can* sing," I said.

A few minutes later, I was going down the hall to discuss my "deal" with his assistant, Michael Sunday. Within one month I had my first recording contract. Within two months, Artie had left the company. He had thrown me a bone before he closed the door behind him.

Looking back, I don't think he had any reason for signing me. I think that before I had had lunch with him, I simply didn't exist, no matter what Glyn told him or who played on the demo, or how many times I called. But once I had borne witness to his fantasy (his obsession?), his personhood, I had somehow materialized in his universe. I existed. As Groucho used to say, "In the halls of justice, all the justice is in the halls."

1971

The first time I sang "in public" was several months later, in the famous Studio A at Capitol Records, the room where Frank Sinatra often had his picture taken, tie open, head tilted back in front of a big Neuman U47 microphone. I have a memory of me in the same spot, same microphone, wearing earphones, listening for the first time as this voice, which almost thirty years later has become a kind of trademark, first emerged. It was not a beautiful thing. Particularly in earphones. First of all, it reminded me of my father's voice, which was more than problematic. Further, it sounded naked, untrained and vulnerable. But after three decades, these are the qualities that have come to be my strengths rather than my weaknesses, and in any case, this voice has become my closest friend, my biggest asset.

At the time, I figured I would probably only get to make this one record. I had no illusions or ambitions about becoming a pop star. I felt I had snuck in the back door, and if this was going to be my one shot, I was going to make *my* record. The first phone call I made was to find Blue Mitchell. After a dozen tries, I located him in Hawaii, playing with the Ray Charles orchestra. I said, "Blue, you don't know me, but I'm recording here in L.A. and you're the first person I'm calling." And he said, "Baby boy, I don't know why more people don't call me. I'd love to play on your record." Until his death, that's what Blue called me: "Baby boy."

I cut the initial tracks with various rhythm sections: the blues tracks with Ed Davis on guitar and two drummers, Gary Malabar and Jim Keltner; the jazz tracks with bass player Willie Ruff and John Pisano on guitar; and the R&B tracks with Boz Scaggs and his band (George Rains on drums). Both Ed and Boz were very helpful, as was Bruce Botnick, the engineer Glyn had recommended I use and who became my co-producer. Bruce had previously recorded The Doors, a band with a jazz influenced piano player and a narrative sense, and together, we crafted a dramatic premise for the record. It opened with a solo piano / vocal song called "Leo's My Name," a fictional piece set up to represent a guy working at a piano bar, singing his nightly appeal for sympathy. The song began:

"Leo's my name, music's my business, it's all I know to do
Although I've had few
Hits you'll recall, or not at all
So like a peddler displaying his wares, let me appeal to you
I'm on the road it's true
But then so are you...."

The rest of the album mixed jazz, pop and blues in a way that I had not heard before, and which, a few years later, might have been called "fusion" music. At the time, however, I was just bringing together all the idioms I had been listening to for the past ten years. For example, the song "Poor Girl" was based on a Bobby Blue Bland rhythm figure; "About Love" was a funky Howard Roberts jazz thing; "My Wife" was clearly influenced by Mose Allison; and the title track, "Feel Your Groove" was filmic: the house lights go out, the spotlight hits the stage, the curtain goes up and there's a piano player singing this little love song. I couldn't wait to come into work each morning; Capitol Studio A had become a kind of playground.

One day, Glyn showed up at the studio with a slight, pretty young girl with dark brown eyes and a haunted aura. He introduced her as Mimi Fariña. Of course I recognized the name. The first thing I told her was how much I had loved her husband Richard's book, *Been Down So Long....* By the end of the day, she was singing on the track "Feel Your Groove." My idea was to have her provide a sexy answer voice on the fade of the song, but when she got in front of the microphone, she was anything but carnal. Her voice was airy and ethereal, almost ghostly. I got on the talkback and said, "Come on Mimi, more sex," but she just giggled like a schoolgirl and kept floating this sweet sound onto the track. A lamb among wolves

A few weeks later, Blue Mitchell arrived in Studio A. He was much smaller in person than I had imagined, and very friendly. I played him the track we were working on—the same one Mimi had sung on—and, after he listened to it a few times in the control room, he went into the studio. At first, he played a few tentative notes. Then he messed around with his horn and asked to hear the track again. Then he readjusted the music on the stand. Then his earphones seemed to be uncomfortable. This continued for about twenty minutes, with nothing put down on tape. I became worried; I thought maybe there was a problem with the music I had prepared. I went into the studio to talk to him. I checked the charts. They seemed okay. I asked him if there were any problems. He said everything was fine.

More time passed, and we were still getting nowhere. All the while, Blue busied himself by blowing the spit out of his horn, adjusting his glasses, making little gestures that indicated he was getting prepared, listening to the track. And then suddenly, all at once, he played brilliantly, a completely lyrical solo, typical of Blue Mitchell and nobody else. Bingo! It was as if he had arrived all at once from some far away place. Then suddenly I understood: Blue Mitchell couldn't read music. He had been stalling, just waiting for the song to settle into his memory, to fall naturally under his fingers, and once he had it, he was able to play any number of variations that were wholly his own.

Later that afternoon, after we had smoked a joint together and listened back to the music ("Baby boy!"), I asked him, "How were you able to record all those intricate compositions with Horace Silver at those breakneck tempos?" He said, "Horace was very patient with me, and we always played the songs for several months before we recorded them."

I miss Blue Mitchell. I made five records with him over the years. He was the most melodic musician I ever knew, a self-invented jazz player whose name was engraved on every note he played. And he was my first musical brother.

I had been given a budget of $20,000 to make the album, and, in the end, had spent just $17,000 to complete it. After the cover photo was taken (Judy and me in a dramatic black and white portrait by Ethan Russell), and the liner notes were written, I went into Capitol to discuss the marketing plans. I settled into Michael Sunday's office on the seventh floor with a list of ideas.

"I have $3,000 left from my budget," I said, "and I'd like to talk to you about spending it on an advertising campaign in *Rolling Stone*."

"Wouldn't you like to go to London and record another track?" he countered.

I wasn't sure if he had understood me. "The record is done. You have it here on your desk. It's finished. I have this money left in my budget and I've checked with *Rolling Stone*...."

He cut me off again. "Isn't there something you would like to record in London?"

"You don't understand," I said.

"No, you don't understand," he said. "This is the seventh floor, A&R. We make records. Marketing is on the ninth floor. They sell records. You were given a recording budget of $20,000. If you don't spend it on the record, you can't just take the balance and spend it on ads. It will go back into the A&R fund and somebody else will piss it away, on tape, on guitar strings, on catering, on whatever they want. Now, don't you want to go to London and record another track?"

I took a long breath and looked out the window of the Capitol Tower. In the foreground, traffic was flowing nicely on the Ventura Freeway. In the background, the smog obscured the San Bernadino Mountains. In the hallway, I heard Felice, formerly Artie Mogul's secretary, now administrative assistant to his successor, Herb Belkin, talking to somebody on the phone. "He's in a meeting," she was saying, "can he call you back?" Only weeks before, that had been me on the other end of the phone. I told Michael to keep the money, I wasn't going to London, the record was finished. I was going home.

The completion of my first recording and the impending release of my book *Black Talk* had me in a kind of fugue state. I had taken to driving aimlessly through the streets of L.A, without a thought in my mind, listening to jazz on radio station KBCA, deejay Tully Strode saying, "another hazy day in L.A." while Gene Ammons and Jackie McLean played his theme song, "The Happy Blues." I did this for about a week until one day, I got a phone call from Herb Belkin, the new president of Capitol Records.

Herb was an articulate, gentle man who liked the sound of my record. Further, he thought I had some talent as a producer, and he had called the meeting because he had a proposition for me. He got right to the point. "Ben," he said, "how would you like to work here as a staff producer?" As he said the words, he passed a long list of names across the desk to me: it was the Capitol Records artist roster.

"Who on this list would you like to produce," he said. It was a great bit of theater. I looked down and my eye fell on the name "Nancy Wilson."

That's what I said. "What about Nancy Wilson?"

Herb said, "I'll see what I can do." Out his window, the L.A. sky had never seemed so blue.

In truth, however, there were storm clouds on the horizon. One had been the Silmar earthquake that had roared through town a few months earlier. Like millions of other folks, Judy and I were awakened around 6 A.M. on February 9th by what sounded like a freight train roaring through the living room. "What was that?" she asked, but I just held on to her tight for what seemed like forever; the bed pitched and yawed as if we were back on the North Atlantic. And then suddenly everything went terribly dark and very quiet. We thought we could hear the ocean, ten miles away.

Carefully, we picked our way through the house to look out the big living room window into the valley below. Outside it was totally black, not a street light nor a house light anywhere, where normally a whole galaxy would be twinkling like stars. Instead, the only break in the darkness, running like a river of light, a liquid snake, was the Hollywood Freeway. The sound of the traffic several miles away was the "ocean" we thought we had heard. Then a dog barked and Judy shivered in my arms.

Another storm cloud on the horizon had been the Charles Manson affair. Today, the level of horror in our society has elevated to the point where we are inured to a few butchered people more or less, but in the early seventies, and coming on the heels of the political assassinations of the late sixties, the two-night spree of the Manson Gang cast an aura of impending chaos that outshone even the cinematic excesses of Hollywood. There was a palpable sense of evil floating over the city.

When I came home after my meeting with Herb Belkin and told Judy about his offer, she was happy for me. But in general, she was miserable. For one thing, she was not part of the whole music-business compact. She thought many of the people she met were one-dimensional and shallow. "Who are these guitar players who think they're so special?" she would say. "They don't read books. They don't even go to movies." She was right, of course. I was also not in love with all these guitar players in tight pants who thought they were the next big thing. It was a cultural desert, and although I was meeting some interesting people, I didn't care about them like *they* cared about them.

And while I was spending time cruising Hollywood and hanging out in the studios, Judy was often home alone, weaving on her handmade London School of Weaving loom and staring out the window into the smog of another "hazy day in L.A." In the Hollywood hills where we lived, you couldn't walk to a store, much less anywhere for pleasure, nobody knew their neighbors, and nobody seemed to care about social issues. One day, for example, we wanted to make a fire in the fireplace but Judy was concerned about the open field of dry grass across the street. In light of the recent fires, she called the local fire department to ask if it was okay. They told her, "Lady, you got a fireplace. Make a fire." She was getting spooked.

But what finally pushed her over the edge was a party at our house for a few of our friends and several of Glyn's show business associates. It was a relatively innocuous affair from my point of view, but at the end of the evening, I found

Judy in the kitchen, seething. Apparently, a singer named Rita Coolidge, who had come as Glyn's guest, had been introduced to her, and when Rita discovered that Judy was not in "the business," she treated her like the hired help. L.A. was like that, a company town with little patience for anyone that wasn't fully engaged in the game of self-promotion. Over the next few hours, Judy talked to me about leaving Los Angeles. She was feeling like a stranger in the city, in the neighborhood, and in her own home.

"Where would we go?" I asked.

"Let's go to Madison," she said. "I'll go to summer school. And then we'll see what happens."

Over the years, people have asked me how we could have left L.A. just as my so-called "career" was taking off, and I'm reminded of Mose Allison's answer, when asked by a fan why he wasn't a bigger star: "Just lucky, I guess."

The long answer is that I was completely in love with Judy, I wanted to be with her, and I wanted her to be happy. She could just as easily have said, "I want to go to San Francisco," and we would probably still be there today. The longer answer is that clearly I was not invested in the Hollywood hustle or the dream of becoming a star. And the final answer is that I have always been intrigued by the unknown. And after a single year in L.A., it was becoming all too familiar.

The record business is brutal on marriages. You are always the meat in somebody else's sandwich, and either you are the latest and greatest or you're garbage. There isn't really a middle way. But as all spiritual teaching insists, the middle way *is* the way. Judy became my middle way. She was never a big fan of the music; she liked it well enough, Van Morrison and Miles Davis and The Ronettes and Carole King and a lot of others, but to her, people were just people. If at any point I had decided to surrender my life in music and done something entirely different, that would have been just fine with her. Aside from her physical beauty, this has always been part of her great attraction for me. She has always had great faith in the proposition that our life together is unfolding the way it was meant to. A positive attitude like that often proves prophetic; Judy has the greatest karma of anybody I've ever met.

Before we left L.A., we had dinner with friends to say good-bye. One by one, we told them what we were doing, and one by one they all said we were crazy. But by the end of the night, however, they often confided that they too were planning to leave L.A., "just as soon as we finish this next project." Many of them are still there. Almost none of them are still together as couples. I remember telling one friend at dinner, "Don't blow your youth on your early years. You'll have nothing left for later."

We left town on June 21st, 1971, the longest day of the year. It was Africa hot in Southern California, and Judy was wearing short shorts and what looked like a handkerchief across her chest as we flew over the San Bernadino Mountains and down into the desert. With the windows rolled down and a hot wind blasting in our faces, we held hands and sang along with Van Morrison, "Love, love, love, love, crazy love…" Suddenly, cresting a hill, the car seemed to choke. I looked down at the tachometer and saw it go flip-flip-flip and then fall to zero. The temperature outside was over 100 degrees and the air-cooled engine of the Porsche had simply started to seize.

I pushed in the clutch to keep rolling and looked down the road for a place to pull over. And there, like a mirage, way in the distance, I spotted a gas station. We barely managed to coast onto the blacktop where a dozen cars sat steaming with their hoods open and their drivers looking dazed. Nearby, a couple of goons covered in grease quietly surveyed the scene. Judy stepped out of the car and both of these guys just turned and locked on to her...and then on the Porsche. I thought, "Oh, God, we're in a Hitchcock movie now."

Slowly, one of the boys walked over to us and put his head inside my window. His face was expressionless.

I said, "You ever work on a car like this?"

He said, "Nope. But they're all the same. Just fuel and fire."

I popped the rear lid and he seemed surprised that instead of a trunk, there was an engine back there. The power plant of the Porsche was full of solid-state electronics, and when he took a huge screwdriver off his belt and started chipping away at something, I said, "OK, thank you very much," and closed the lid. I noticed a little shady area behind the gas station and I thought if I could just push the car into this spot, maybe it would cool off. I said to the mechanic, "When does it cool off around here?"

He said, "September."

Judy and I pushed the car behind the building and waited a few hours. It was absolutely quiet, the desert just baking in the sun and all these broken down cars cooking in the quiet glare. Nothing was moving, except for the two goons who kind of floated around, wiping their hands on their trousers from time to time, casually checking us out. We knew we definitely did not want to be standing there when the sun went down. Just before dark, I got the car started and we drove across the desert as carefully as you might drive through a Wisconsin blizzard, tucked up behind a big truck for protection. Around midnight, we finally pulled into Las Vegas, and the big thermometer on the bank said it was still 100 degrees.

From Los Angeles to Las Vegas; we had gone from the fire into the frying pan.

A few days later, we arrived safely back in Madison. On the first morning, I awoke in a rented bed in a rented house truly aware of what I had just done. It was as John Coltrane once described playing with Thelonious Monk, like stepping into an empty elevator shaft, and the challenge now was to go up rather than down. That day, I had lunch with my old friend Jim Hougan, who was now writing for the local newspaper. We sat on the Terrace of the student union, watching the sailboats lean into the wind on Lake Mendota, and Hougan filled me in on what had been happening since we were last in town.

The main thing was the bombing of Sterling Hall. A group of ex-students had called the police early one morning and said, "Warn the hospital!" and then an explosion rocked the entire city, almost leveling the math research building. A homemade concoction of fertilizer and diesel fuel had been driven in an old van into the service ramp of the large brick structure at an hour calculated to avoid harming anyone, and the "bomb" was detonated.

"The kids figured nobody would get hurt," Hougan said, " and it would make their point—the University was in collusion with the war machine, and they were going to bring the war home. Only there was somebody in the building at that hour, a graduate student named Robert Fassnacht, who was killed in the explosion. It became a watershed moment in the whole anti-war movement, and the tide at once began to turn against the radical student elements, the SDS and the Weathermen."

As Hougan was bringing me up to speed, Judy arrived from her weaving class, radiant and gorgeous. I realized I hadn't seen her look this happy in more than a year. The three of us spent the rest of the afternoon talking, looking out at the boats, and letting our good fortune warm us like the sun sparkling on the lake.

That summer, my first record, *Feel Your Groove*, was released, and, not surprisingly, our move to Madison did not inspire Capitol Records in their promotional efforts. They were more accustomed to an artist hitting the road or hanging out on Sunset Strip, where they could be discovered by agents, managers and the rock press. The fact that Holt, Rinehart & Winston had just published *Black Talk* only confused them further. They simply had no idea what a book had to do with a record, and in truth, neither did I.

But I had banked the book and record advances, and life in Madison was cheap. It was a shortsighted way to look at a career, perhaps, but love *is* blind. By fall, I began picking up the phone to hustle work, slowly at first, and then with some urgency. And I began to hear the question that would follow me for many years to come: "Area code 608...where's that?"

Madison may have been a backwater by show business standards, but the music scene was not stagnant. The Jazz Workshop had opened and wild sessions were taking place there every night. The club had a Hammond B3 organ and drummer George Brown was back in town. While Judy and I were in England and Los Angeles, George had been experiencing rough times in New York City.

He had gone to New York to play the music ("I'm gonna play," he had told me, "and I don't care what happens"), but he called one day from a pad on the lower East side "just waiting for the revolution to come downtown." And instead of talking about the music, he was now talking about the money. "I'm gonna get me some money," he said "Cause this shit ain't living, not this part of it. You can play soulful as you want with some money. I'd rather own this building than play anyway, cause it's all down to the money in this world."

George was reporting a fundamental shift in the communal vision. Whereas in the past, it had always been a question of who was playing the music of the future, in the future, it would be a question of who was getting paid the most for playing the music of the past. But what finally drove George out of New York, and caused his descent into anger, bitterness and disorientation, was getting mugged in broad daylight. He had gone to a concert to hear George Benson ("George used to hang around when I was working with Wes Montgomery," he told me, "back when he wasn't anything,") and when he came out three Black men approached him, took his money and beat him up.

He told me on the phone, "My clothes were covered in blood and about five hundred people were standing around. The police were more afraid of them than I was." They took him to the hospital, and after his release his first call was to us. We sent him some money to come back. When I picked him up at the bus station, George said "If you're too light to fight, you're too thin to win."

One might ask what this little vignette of a black drummer living rough in New York had to do with the music business, and the answer is — practically nothing. And that's exactly the point. By the early 1970s, the music business was already moving away from the music and toward the business, and musicians like George, powerful innovators who once roamed free were now being pushed off their native territory. The next week, George and I started playing at the Jazz Workshop. He could still create powerful waves of rhythm that carried a single song for over an hour, and by the end of the evening, the crowd was hoarse from screaming and wrung out from dancing. But George was clearly not in the same spiritual place he had been only a few years before.

Fate, however, always seems to provide great drummers for me just when I need them most. Only a month after George's return, James Brown's band came through Madison, and when they left, their drummer, Clyde Stubblefield, stayed behind. He had been on the road with Brown for almost five years, and was tired of the exhausting schedule and the personal abuse. That week, he too found his way to the Jazz Workshop, fell in love with the scene, and suddenly, my musical horizons were expanded in several directions at once. I started writing new songs and looking forward to playing again.

By late autumn, *Feel Your Groove*, had made some interesting friends. For example, it was getting a lot of play on radio station WPLJ in New York, where Ann Sternberg and Michael Cuscuna were championing my cause. When Judy and I went to New York that fall, we discovered my music was well known by a small but very hip group of people. It was reassuring to think that while we were living this very quiet, very normal life in Madison, the music was out in the world, working.

Gradually, the phone began to ring again. First, it was Jann Wenner calling from San Francisco with a proposition. This time, he wanted me to produce a record for him. He had discovered a six-foot-tall black transvestite singer named Sylvester who worked, along with his group, the Cockettes, at a drag club in North Beach called Bimbos. Jann said he had a feeling Sylvester could become a national sensation, and I had the feeling that if Jann put *Rolling Stone* behind it, my dog Harold could be a star. The world of rock and roll was becoming so strange that a black drag queen singing falsetto love songs didn't seem that far out of line.

Judy and I went to San Francisco and met Sylvester, who was very nice, relatively masculine and quite striking looking. He claimed to be a long lost relative of Billie Holiday (he wore a gardenia in his hair some days) and said his dream was to live in a mansion in Beverly Hills and walk Rodeo Drive with two Afghans on a leash. I trusted he was referring to two dogs. We went to work trying to make his dream come true.

Sylvester actually had a beautiful baritone voice, but he refused to use it, insisting instead on this piercing falsetto which, at times, was interesting but often veered off into the horrific. The male falsetto has been with us for centuries, ever since it marked the beginning of secular singing as a departure from the monotony of the Gregorian chants, but particularly in its early 1970s, post Marvin Gaye incarnation, the falsetto has often suggested a slightly sinister glorification of the adolescent male. (One need only recall The Four Seasons' "Sherry Baby.") In Sylvester's case, hearing it emerge out of a muscular six foot cross-dresser was downright bizarre.

I called friends in the bay area to play on the sessions, guitar players Mike Bloomfield and Curley Cooke and drummer Bill Meeker, and we went to work at Wally Heider's studio. From day one, it was odd and quickly became more so. Sylvester arrived the first morning dressed as a woman, full drag, long flowing dress, hair piled high and neckline plunging. Accompanying her was a stunning six-foot, absolutely drop-dead beautiful Asian woman. The first song we recorded was Leon Russell's "Super Star" ("Long ago and oh so far away, I fell in love with you up there on the silver screen...."). Sylvester sang her heart out and her friend sat in the control room next to me, swooning. By the end of the day, we had recorded several heart-wrenching versions of the song, and one of the musicians (whom I cannot name) had become completely smitten with Sylvester's girlfriend. He couldn't take his eyes off her. Soon, he was bringing her drinks and sitting solicitously near by. Finally, I had to pull him aside and say, "You know that is not a woman, don't you?" He looked at me with sad, helpless eyes, and I could see that he didn't care.

Meanwhile, Judy and Sylvester had become fast friends, spending time in between takes discussing make-up and fashion. I walked past them at one point and heard Judy say, "If more women were like you, it would be fine with me." We were clearly not in Madison anymore.

Later that month, after returning home, the phone rang again, this time at 3 A.M. It was Michael Cuscuna from New York. Through the fog of post REM sleep, I heard a song from my record playing way in the background and Michael was saying, "Listen man, you got to talk to this cat. He made me call you..." and then he passed the phone to someone and I heard a voice which was all hipness and hustle say, "This is Bob Krasnow, I own Blue Thumb Records and I've been all around the world looking for somebody like you. What do I have to do to sign you?" I said, "Call me in the morning."

The next morning, Michael called back and apologized. He said, "Krasnow and Charlie Green were at the pad and we got totally ripped. Man, first they wanted to play cards. So I said, 'What should we play?' And Charlie said, 'Let's make up a game.' And in ten minutes, he and Bob had invented a card game that actually worked. That's how good these crooks are. Anyway, we were listening to your record and he couldn't stop talking about it. You should call Bob." By the end of the year, I had signed to Blue Thumb Records.

1972

Blue Thumb Records was the epitome of inmates running the asylum, artistic types in search of other artistic types to turn loose. Krasnow had originally been a promotion man for James Brown, and had formed Blue Thumb Records back in 1968. The company lasted a scant six years, until 1974, and its existence marked the end of the beginning of the record industry. After Blue Thumb came the deluge of lawyers and accountants, and the business became about "units" instead of albums, "acts" instead of artists.

From its inception, Blue Thumb had an outlaw mentality. Bob had this wonderful way of saying to people who had a nucleus of an idea, "Do it!" Never how to do it, when to do it, or how much will it cost. Just do it. All aspects of Blue Thumb seemed to be based on this principle of "go for the light." As Krasnow's partner, producer Tommy LiPuma once told me, "We didn't have the funds, but we sure had the fun."

The first day I arrived at Blue Thumb in Beverly Hills, I knew this was not going to be your standard record business experience. The offices were on the second floor of a small, New Orleans-style building, and to get to them, one had to cross an outdoor courtyard, ride up to the second floor in a minuscule, wrought-iron elevator, and then walk down a long, narrow corridor, exposed to the elements. Bob welcomed me with both hands and escorted me into his inner sanctum, where the walls of his office were painted a dark gray, almost black, and on one wall was a floor to ceiling painting of Jimi Hendrix. He sat in a large antique chair behind his desk, wearing a fringed leather cowboy vest, and offered me the barber's chair across from him. I took the barber's chair, and got my psychic hair cut.

Bob said, "Ben, you can have whatever you want here. You just have to know how to ask for it." I said, "How do I ask for it?" He said, "I can't tell you that. That's what you got to find out."

Blue Thumb was a clearinghouse for musicians of every persuasion, and that week I ran into several of them. One afternoon, for example, stepping out of the elevator, I literally bumped into Sly Stone. When we shook hands, his great warm paw seemed to be covered in baby oil. I had with me a tape of something I had just cut with Clyde Stubblefield, and knowing Sly loved James Brown, I said to him, "Man, you got to hear this, it's gonna kill you." He looked at me with the cold glaze of a man who had already seen too much and said, "Man, I don't want to die..." and he was gone.

Before returning to Madison, I went to the studio to hang out with Tommy LiPuma. Tommy was working on a record for the legendary Chicago guitarist Phil Upchurch, and a couple of hours after walking in, I was sitting behind a B3 organ, recording the song "Love and Peace." That's how Blue Thumb worked. It was an extended family that ultimately grew into a substantial artist's roster, including The Crusaders, Captain Beefheart, Dan Hicks, The Pointer Sisters, Dave Mason, Hugh Masakela and a dozen other self-invented musicians who invariably crossed whatever arbitrary musical boundaries were being drawn at the time.

I recorded my first Blue Thumb album in Madison later that year. It required flying both Bruce Botnick and a sixteen-track tape recorder in from Los Angeles;

Phil Upchurch came up from Chicago and everybody stayed at our house on the city's funky East Side. Every morning, Judy made breakfast and sent us off to the studio. It was a time of great camaraderie. We approached jazz and R&B as one and the same thing, and the rhythm section of Clyde, Phil, Curley and myself was so "locked in" that at the end of each song, we often couldn't stop playing. Many of the songs wound up as extended jams which we later faded out electronically. The four of us loved these moments so much that we talked about making an album of just fades — starting each song at the point where it would normally end and going from there. (The musical equivalent of selling the holes rather than the donuts.) We should have done it; it would have been called disco a few years later.

Ultimately, we did plan a few arrangements with this technique in mind. One song even faded up on the drum groove, and then after a few minutes, faded out on an entirely different groove. It was a little trick that seemed to imply to the listener that the song had no beginning or end, but was just a constantly evolving presence somewhere out in psychic space.

Several months after the release of the album *I Lead a Life*, this particular song caught the attention of the great drummer, Tony Williams. Tony had burst on the jazz scene in the middle-sixties as a sixteen-year-old kid out of Boston, and before his eighteenth birthday, he was working with Miles Davis' band, helping Davis to reinvent jazz on several occasions. He was there when Miles told the press, "I could have the world's greatest rock band if I wanted," and Tony's Lifetime group was a model for several of Miles' subsequent groups. By his early twenties, Tony had already joined the ranks of drum innovators like Kenny Clarke, Max Roach, Philly Joe and Elvin Jones. My simple little trick of fading up the drums had triggered something in him, and he called to ask if I would produce his next record. I couldn't believe it, but he said, "I think you hear the drums the same way I hear the drums."

By November, Tony and I and the rest of his band were living in a rented house in Rowley, Massachusetts. There was virtually no furniture in the place, just some beds for sleeping, a kitchen, and in the living room, a piano and a drum kit. Tony loved getting up in the morning and bashing. He was fond of playing big, open backbeat grooves, almost like Led Zeppelin rock and roll. One morning I asked him, "Tony if you can play bebop like God, why do you want to play rock and roll?" He said, "Man, this feels just as good to me as playing straight ahead..." and he went on to tell me how as a kid he had loved the Beatles and all the British invasion bands. It was obvious that because his musical gift was so large, he had become pressed into the service of bebop early on, but he was still a kid at heart.

Some mornings we played duets. Tony never told me what to play, but once he told me what *not* to play. "Throw away your left hand," he said, and when I tried it, I found I felt much freer, more able to respond to him musically. It was the kind of advice Miles Davis would give his musicians. Miles would never tell musicians what to play, but would often react to something that didn't seem to fit. Years later, Miles would tell me, "What it is is balance. If you make a drawing on a page, you have to balance it, you know. And that's the way most everything is. Art, music, composition, solos, clothes...."

For several weeks, we recorded Tony's album at Intermedia Studios on Newbury Street in Boston. One morning before going into the studio, we were talking about Miles Davis and Tony said, as so many other musicians have, "Miles really changed my life." I asked him how—was it something Miles said or something he did? Tony paused for a long minute and then said, "No, it wasn't anything he said or did. It was just him. Just being around Miles...you knew you could be anybody you wanted to be. As long as it was you."

When the record, called *The Old Bum's Rush*, was released, Tony took a lot of heat in the jazz press for making an album that was not simply an extension of his work with Miles. The irony of Tony being freed by Miles to be anybody he wanted to be, and then having the jazz press cut him down for it, and, in particular, for not following in Miles' footsteps, was not lost on either one of us.

1973

B ack in Madison, my old college friend Paul Soglin had been elected mayor, and it seemed like the city was becoming a playground for refugees from the sixties. There was a wonderfully open feeling. In the Marquette neighborhood, where Judy and I had purchased our first house, there was an eclectic mix of working people, students, professionals, politicos, artists, writers and folks just passing through town. Paul himself lived a couple of blocks away, and on Sundays, there was always a volleyball game that gathered up these elements and jangled them together. Millionaires and carpenters, doctors and cab drivers, bartenders and politicians were all doing the bump, set and spike.

One weekend that spring, an old friend from England, Chris Hodenfield, who often wrote for *Rolling Stone,* came through town on a cross-country trip, traveling with Daphne Davis, a writer for *New York* magazine. After spending the afternoon at the volleyball game and the evening at our house, Daphne said, half exasperated, "You are too normal. You are never gonna make it in this business. There is absolutely nothing here to write about. You should be raising rats in the basement or something."

This pretty much confirmed what we knew. While my recordings were getting good reviews it was obvious that not being in New York or Los Angeles gave the rock press and the fashion press a good reason to ignore the story behind the music. And the story, as Daphne had immediately sussed, was that life here was good. My reaction was to sleep in, love my wife, have dinner with my friends and play gigs at night. None of which improved record sales.

In fact, throughout this period we were staying just a month or two ahead of the mortgage, and while we were never in dire financial trouble, there were many nights when I would wake up with a start, realizing I was almost thirty years old and still unemployed. Looking to take off some of the pressure, and also to live out my former fantasy, I approached the University of Wisconsin about a teaching position. In short order, I was made a visiting lecturer at the handsome salary of $3000 and told to prepare a syllabus for a three-credit upper level course in the Department of Communication Arts. That spring, the catalog of classes listed "Communication Arts 611 — The Social Aesthetics of Record Production," a course that purported to explain the process by which America decides what music lives and what music dies. I was swamped with requests from students to get in. Ultimately, I chose thirty seniors and graduate students, and twice a week, we gathered together in Vilas Hall, the large cinder-block building that covered the spot where Lorenzo's once stood. Talk about irony; it was at Lorenzo's bar that I had first communicated so well with Judy.

Com Arts 611 was a way for me to reformulate my relationship to the music business, while it also provided an opportunity for some of the people I was working with — engineers, lawyers and executives — to visit Madison and speak to the class. I made it a point to let the students know that this was the real world, and while there would be a final exam, their true grade might well be several years in the making. Right away, I discovered the difficulty of talking about the business of music at a regular time in a normal classroom, replete with neon lights, a chalkboard and students taking notes to prepare for the grading cycle. This setting had nothing to do with, for example, the free-form environment of Blue Thumb Records, or the intensity of the recording studio, and I despaired at ever presenting anything concrete and useful. I began dragging the class down to a local recording studio just to have a windowless, clock-less space in which to talk.

Blue Thumb had recently released my album, *Puttin in Time on Planet Earth*, a collection of eight songs recorded the previous October. The album featured my three favorite drummers, Tony Williams, George Brown and Clyde Stubblefield. There was even one track on the album that sought to combine both Tony and Clyde, bringing together the men who had helped invent the emotional axis of the sixties, the music of Miles Davis and James Brown. Years later, I learned that back in 1969, Miles had asked Tony to recreate Clyde's groove on "Cold Sweat," and then I understood why Tony seemed so shy when meeting Clyde. He was going to school on "the Funky Drummer."

To celebrate the release of this record, Bob Krasnow came to Chicago, where I was opening at a club called The Quiet Knight. Naturally, I invited Bob to come to Madison to talk to my class, and he seemed pleased to accept. That week, I prepared the students for his arrival, outlining the history of the record business and placing Blue Thumb in context. "This label is truly on the fringes of the industry," I told them, "an artist's enclave, and Krasnow is a pioneer of the first order. He dresses in fringed leather, outhangs even the wildest artist, and is known as a man of the streets, a guy who really has his ear to the ground." The students couldn't wait to meet this gunslinger from the Wild West. That afternoon, when I went to the airport to pick Krasnow up, I was shocked to see him get off the plane sporting a conservative haircut and a bespoke three-piece suit.

I said "Bob, what happened?"

He said, "What do you mean?"

I said, "The hair, the suit, the whole thing."

He said, "Oh that, well you know, nothing is forever."

We arrived at the Com Arts building, took the elevator up to the third floor, and entered a hushed classroom. I had promoted the arrival of Jesse James and, instead, was walking in with a guy who looked like the sheriff. The students were confused but polite. Krasnow sat at the desk, faced the class, and made a few perfunctory remarks. "The record business is an artist-oriented business," he said, "and everybody, from the accountants to the kid in the stock room, eventually starts to think like an artist." Then he asked, "Does everybody here agree with the philosophy of the record business?"

Now, the students and I had been talking for weeks about various philosophies: the philosophy that popular music was one of America's significant cultural treasures and was no longer simply "captured" in the wild but was being manufactured in the studios and shipped to the people; the implications of this on the social organization of young people in particular, but also on the society in general; the tension created by this disparity or conflict of interests, which culminates in the 'art' of record production. We were examining the Western conception of 'art' to see whether recordings were an exception to the rule that art has to be separated from ordinary life, and were deep into discussions about the rarefied atmosphere of the recording studio. I had shared my own thinking freely. "Record production is always a statement of social commitment," I had told them prior to Krasnow's arrival. "The product speaks of the process. Production becomes a metaphor for social aesthetics. The record and its promotion become a tool to make manifest a particular world view." So when Krasnow asked the class if they agreed with "the philosophy" of the record business, it took a few moments for one graduate student to timorously raise his hand and ask, "Excuse me, Mr. Krasnow, but what exactly is the philosophy of the record business?"

"Why, to make money, of course," said Krasnow. "That's the philosophy of every business."

The room erupted in protest. Several people spoke at once. "That's not a philosophy! That's just greed plain and simple...." Krasnow sat there with a cat-that-ate-the-canary grin on his face. He had delivered the news.

And news it was. By 1973, it was becoming clear that there was a major change in the zeitgeist of America. As a country, we were experiencing the oil crisis, the gold crisis and the spectacle of Watergate, and even though many of us would cheer the afternoon Alexander Butterfield revealed that there were tapes of all of Nixon's oval office conversations (thank God for technology!), there was a feeling abroad that we were sliding backwards down the slippery slope of history, and that the innocent righteousness of the sixties was rapidly becoming an anachronism. It was perhaps not insignificant that both George Brown and Bob Krasnow were now saying the same thing: it's all down to the money.

For most of us, however, it would take several years for the news to sink in. We continued the idyll of post-sixties America, the volleyball games and the media schemes. I started working on the production of a television program called, "The Weekend Starts Now," a late-night talk show that aired Thursday nights at midnight and ran classic movies, like Ernie Kovacs' *Our Man in Havana* or Bogart's *Casablanca*, without interruption. The impetus for the program had been a project initiated by several of my Com Arts students who did a survey on why television went dark in Madison after *The Tonight Show*. They discovered that a lot of people were still up at midnight and would watch, so we took the information to the local NBC affiliate. Within weeks, we were on the air.

It was my first experience hosting an interview program, and I was generally terrible at it. After spending the week trying to sell ads and scheming with Bob Halper, my friend and so-called producer about what the week's show would be, I usually found myself on camera, unprepared, unscripted and unabashed. I would stare into the camera and just start talking. But, as we were the only talk show being produced in the market, we quickly attracted anybody who was passing through with a gig to promote or an ax to grind. Jane Fonda, Dan Hicks, McCoy Tyner, Father Phil Berrigan, The Firesign Theater, Kinky Friedman, Mayor Soglin, Harold the Poodle wearing camping gear, every kind of everything went on the air Thursdays at 11 P.M.

Occasionally, we pushed the boundaries of taste. For example, we often included a late night benediction by our designated spiritual leader, "The Reverend L.J. Sloman of the Last Exit Before Freeway Church of God." Reverend Sloman, a.k.a. Ratso, was a friend of mine who dressed in a Hawaiian shirt and clerical collar and stood in front of a chroma-keyed American flag delivering the good news of the kingdom. "Friends," he said, "I have seen the future... and it is condominiums! Yes, join us here at God's Own Landgrab where the future is selling out now at yesterday's prices." Patriotic music blared in the background and Sloman, wearing little hippie shades and a demonic grin on his face, delivered his pitch, and then the station signed off for the evening. It must have been a rude shock for the few farmers out in the countryside who happened to be watching television at that hour, because one day, following one of Sloman's "benedictions," I was called in by the station manager and read the terms of the NAB's "Seal of Good Practice."

Technically, according to the Arbitron ratings, we had no viewers at all. But these rating services didn't canvas students and plenty of folks who worked second shift and stayed up late. And, as Sloman's rants proved, not everybody was covered by the rating services. I was constantly being approached on the streets by folks with comments or suggestions. I knew the program was having an impact. Our sponsors told us, too. One of them, a pizza place that delivered late at night, did land-office business every Thursday evening when their ad ran: the ad was simply 60 seconds of me, Judy and Sloman sitting around a table eating a pizza while their phone number flashed in the lower portion of the screen. In Madison, late at night, that was a hard sell. In fact, it was when people starting coming up to me in restaurants, acting as if we had been together in their bedrooms the previous night, that I knew it was time to get off the air. I hadn't moved back to Madison to become notorious — I had moved there to be invisible.

In the summer of '73, a restaurant called Good Karma, a hippy co-op that served soy burgers and fruit smoothies, decided to feature music. An enterprising co-op member named Josh Levenson moved in an old upright piano and start booking bands. One of the first artists he brought in was Mose Allison. I had never met Mose before, and to have him performing in my hometown for a week was a gift, an education and a golden opportunity. I had the chance to talk to him about life and song writing, and by the end of the week, I had heard fifteen sets and we had become friends.

The next band Josh brought in was Charles Mingus. There was little money for lodging, so Josh housed the band at various homes around the city. He asked me if I would look after Mingus' drummer, Danny Richmond, and of course Judy and I were delighted to host this dapper, urbane gentleman. In the mornings, Danny would come padding downstairs in his silk robe and slippers, and around the breakfast table, he charmed us with long, drawn-out recountings of his years with Mingus. "Sometimes, I feel like I'm married to Mingus," he said. "Charles often introduces me as the only friend he has in the world. I mean we're tight!" They were so tight, in fact, that they could do the seemingly impossible together, like accelerate and decelerate tempos simply by giving each other a look. "It finally got to the point," Danny said, "where we could do it without looking at each other. Then people really got spooked."

One morning, I asked Danny why he thought Mingus had not been more successful financially. After all, Mingus had even started his own record label, so he was clearly a musician who thought about the business side. Yet he was always scuffling. Danny said Mingus never got the recognition he deserved, while others, like Miles Davis, for example, had become huge celebrities, because, "Charles is not beautiful to look at. It sounds stupid, but that made a difference." He also suggested that it could be because Mingus was overtly political: "Charles speaks his mind."

I said, "You can call it that. But I once saw Mingus throw Jackie Byard off the piano bench to 'show' Jackie the part. And he has been known to assault musicians who are not playing parts the way he wanted."

Danny smiled and became very political himself. He said, "Well, it's all part of the Jazz Workshop concept. You know, Charles started that so people could bring in new music and have cats play it, at rehearsal, even on the job. So the idea was if something wasn't going the way the composer wanted, he could stop the performance and explain it to the musicians. That's what Charles is doing a lot of the time."

In general, Madison was becoming more and more like Del Close's vision of Times Square: all you had do was stand there and eventually the whole world would pass by.

In July, I returned to Boston to produce an artist named Paul Pena. Paul was a blind, black guitarist who wrote songs of incredible passion and range. His playing and singing were reminiscent of Jimi Hendrix, and while still only in his twenties, he had already become something of a legend in Boston, a hero to local singers, like Bonnie Raitt. Paul's manager, Gunther Weil, was an oddity in the record business, a Harvard educated Ph.D. in psychology, and an intellectual with both a deep appreciation for jazz and a spirited love of show business. He had been a teaching assistant for Tim Leary during the sixties, and had been part of the social experiment at Millbrook that ultimately got Leary removed from the faculty. He had also produced Paul's first album for Capitol, and was looking for fresh ears to produce the second one.

Judy had decided to spend that summer studying weaving at the Haystack Mountain School of Crafts on Deer Isle, Maine, so we packed up Harold the Poodle and drove east in the Porsche. It was a terrific trip, with Harold standing in the back watching the road roll by for hours, and then letting us know when it was time for all of us to stop for water and exercise. Nights, we checked into a motel, and the three of us watched television on a vibrating bed. It was an uneventful, lackadaisical trip until the afternoon we arrived in Maine. That day, Harold jumped out of the car at the home of some friends and was immediately attacked by two large Alaskan Malamutes, who took him for prey. We quickly gathered him up and rushed him to a hospital where he survived the surgery, but for the rest of the summer, I had to administer various medications to him at regular intervals. So Harold too became very much a part of Paul Pena's recording sessions.

He and I lived with Gunther and his family in Cambridge. Gunther was a student of Chi Gung, the Chinese martial art of channeling energy flow through breath control, so every day, we followed breakfast with fire breathing, progressed to the studio and, after long hours of recording, concluded the day with more martial arts forms and conversation about music, literature and spirituality. Working with Paul was a constant wake-up call as well. He was funny, profound and totally focused on his music, but he wore his heart on his sleeve and could be wildly quixotic. And because of his glaucoma, he smoked pot non-stop. It was a volatile mix and days in the studio were always unpredictable.

I had gathered together a wonderfully sympathetic rhythm section, including drummer Gary Malabar, who had played with me in Ed Davis' band and also on Van Morrison's *Moondance* album, and bassist Harvey Brooks, part of Bob Dylan's "Like a Rolling Stone" sessions and a member of the Woodstock music community. But it was Paul himself who kept opening my eyes.

Paul lived in a communal house with four other young blind people. One day, after we had cut two great songs — one called "New Train," about Paul's growing up in a Boston suburb, and another called "Jet Airliner," a heartfelt lyric about Paul's desire to return to San Francisco — I drove him home. I had no idea where he lived, but Paul was totally comfortable directing me through the streets of Boston. It was remarkable that a sightless man could negotiate the city with such comfort. He would say, "See that gas station two blocks ahead on the right? Make a turn there, then go through two sets of lights and make your first left...." Driving along, listening to music and chatting, it was hard to believe he was blind.

We arrived at his apartment, and I went in with him to hang out for a bit. Shortly, his roommates began arriving, and pretty soon, a party was going on. A lot of pot was smoked, beers were passed out, and a jam session began in the living room. They had a piano, a drum kit and some guitars and everybody grabbed something and started to play. Looking around, I realized I was the only sighted person in the room. And yet the music was grooving, people were passing around cold drinks, calling out songs, and generally, there was no sense of disability anywhere.

Until it grew dark outside. I reached behind the piano to turn on the light, but of course, there was no bulb in the fixture as nobody in the house had thought to replace it. Light bulbs meant nothing to this crew. The party really started to wail then, the music cranked up to the next level and everybody was having a ball. Except for me. I was becoming gradually terrified, as, slowly, I couldn't see a thing. The room got quite dark in a matter of minutes, black in fact, and I was now very stoned. While the others were still passing drinks and joints and calling out songs, unaware that one among them had become disabled, I was pretty much backed up against a wall, unable to see anything, let alone a joint or a cold drink.

With a slam of recognition, I entered the everyday world of my companions. The fragile surface of my reality gave way and I felt the hollow irony of all the years spent studying Wittgenstein and the others. If ever I needed proof that my world was a projection of my own perceptions and assumptions, this one moment provided more than all the years at school. That night, when I finally made my way back to take care of Harold at Gunther's place, it was hard to know which one of us was nursing the other.

The following September, Paul and I went to San Francisco to record a couple of things with Jerry Garcia, and then down to Los Angeles to record a string session. In L.A., we checked Paul into the Tropicana Hotel on Santa Monica Boulevard. Judy and I lead Paul by the arm up and down the seemingly endless exterior walkways of the Tropicana to his room high up on the third floor, where, once inside, he turned on the television and said good night. We left him there to make his way back down to Duke's Restaurant for dinner, a trip requiring hundreds of steps and many turns, but Paul said not to worry, he had everything under control. After my experience in Boston, I had no doubt that he did, but when he failed to show up at the string session the next day, I became worried. I found him later that night back in his room, with a long explanation about why he had missed the recording session, but no apparent problems with getting around the Tropicana, or the city of Los Angeles for that matter.

Late that December, after the record was mixed, Gunther and I went to Woodstock to deliver the finished product to Albert Grossman, who was scheduled to release the album on his Bearsville Label. Albert loved Paul's music, and he wanted Paul to move to Woodstock and become part of his "stable" of artists, which included Paul Butterfield, Bob Dylan and The Band. Paul did not want to do this; he wanted to move to San Francisco where the weather was better. He had spent a lot of time on the road — difficult for any musician, often a night-mare for one who is blind — and indeed, one of the most famous lines of his most famous song "Jet Airliner" is about this: "My heart keeps pushing me backwards as I jump aboard that 747...riding high but with a tear in my eye, you got to go through hell before you get a little heaven." It became something of a standoff between Paul and Albert, and we had gone to see if we could resolve it.

The night before the meeting, Gunther and I holed up in a little motel off the main drag in Woodstock, and tried to focus our energy on the coming con-flict. Gunther spent a good part of the evening standing on his head, reminding me of Frodo the Hobbit preparing to do battle with the dark forces of Mordor. Together, we worked through the potential scenarios, but when the meeting came the next day, it only lasted moments. If Paul was not willing to move to Woodstock, Albert was not going to release the album. Period. We were stunned. Weeks went by and gradually we all realized that Paul's record would not be released. It was effectively the end of his recording career and a tremendous injustice. We all felt a sense of loss and betrayal.

A few months later, I was back in L.A., working with Steve Miller on his album *Journey from Eden*, and when Steve heard the tape of Paul's music, he immediately recognized the commercial potential of the writing. Steve soon recorded the song "Jet Airliner" and, whereas Paul's version was a raw, dark paean to freedom, his became a hooky anthem that all teenagers could get with. To date, Steve's version has sold millions of copies, and, at times, the royalties have been all that stood between Paul and destitution.

1974

By early 1974, the winds of change were blowing hard through the eco-nomic landscape. In the record business, one could say the high front that had propelled creativity only a year or two earlier had passed and now a troubling low was stationary and dominant. The smaller labels, like Blue Thumb, sought shelter from the coming storm in the arms of larger corporate entities (in the case of Blue Thumb it was Gulf & Western), and the only line these corporate parents were interested in was the bottom line. A kind of lifeboat mentality developed among the men who ran the record business. When push came to shove, they ultimately saved each other and tossed the artists overboard. In fact, in the eyes of the executives, like Krasnow, Mogul and the others, *they* were the stars of the industry, the franchise for their backers, and the musicians just came and went with the prevailing winds.

There was still a lot of talk about "artist development," but the real momentum was shifting from the recording studios to the boardrooms. One day, I walked into the Blue Thumb office and heard Bob Krasnow delighting in the fact that Clive Davis, the lawyer who had been running Columbia Records, had been fired in a scandal over the mismanagement of funds. Krasnow called out to his secretary to get Clive on the phone. "I want to offer that motherfucker a job," he said. "I want that crook to work for me." It was like Artie Mogul wanting the Queen of England to say "Give it to me, Artie..." Pure power ultimately respected only pure power. Within the year, Krasnow, too, would be gone and not under dissimilar circumstances.

Back in Madison, however, life retained its timeless quality, an island of possibility in a sea of reality. Indeed, that spring, Good Karma brought the Charles Mingus band back to town, and this time, Josh asked us if Mingus himself could stay at our home. I was thrilled at the opportunity to host Mingus and, having just read his autobiography, *Beneath the Underdog*, was more than a little intimidated. In that book, his own words paint a picture of a flamboyant, hedonistic, race-driven man. But Charles in person was quiet and gentle, and, at the time, suffering from a bad cold. Grossly overweight and trying to regain his health, he came down each day around noon for "breakfast" and sat at the dining room table. Judy would say, 'Charles, would you like a nice salad this morning?" and he would say, "Thanks, Baby," and light up a cigar.

As Judy prepared his meal, I would go to my record collection and select things to play for him, usually beginning with Art Tatum and then working my way up through Duke Ellington and Thelonious Monk and Bud Powell. Charles would rarely say anything during these music sessions, but every time I left the house, Judy told me, he got very loose and not only played the piano, but also played with Harold the Poodle for long periods. She said he called home regularly, and she heard him say to his wife Sue, "Yeah, everything is fine and they're taking good care of me here." But when I would return home, he would again grow silent and withdrawn.

At night, we drove to the club where Mingus and his band — George Adams on saxophone, Jack Walrath on trumpet, Don Pullen on piano and Danny Richmond on drums — conjured up great spirits and a moaning, rolling emotional release. The seventy-five or so patrons of the little health food restaurant would leave stunned and happy. And the next day, the cycle would be repeated.

Finally, on Friday afternoon, after a long week of salads and concerts, I asked Charles if he would like to see a movie. There was a very funny comedy that had just opened in town that I thought he might enjoy. He said, "Okay, let's do it." We were practically the only two people in the theater that afternoon, and as the house lights went down and Cleavon Little rode his horse across the screen, I suddenly realized what I had done. I had taken Charles Mingus to see *Blazing Saddles*, a film about a black sheriff in a racist Western town, where the Indians spoke Yiddish and the bad guys were campy stage actors. About a half-hour into it, Mingus turned to me and said, "Is this supposed to be funny?" I said, "Wait, Charles, it will get better." Just then the Basie Band showed up in the desert and Mingus started clapping. And then, a little later on, when Mongo knocked out the horse, Mingus hollered "That's what I'm talking about." Otherwise, he was nonplused by the entire Mel Brooks experience.

That night, in between sets at the club, Mayor Soglin gave Charles the Key to the City. Later, back at the house, looking at the key, Mingus asked me, "You know where the lock is?"

On Sunday afternoon, after a final performance the night before that featured a long soliloquy by Mingus on "Fables of Faubus," a stinging response to racism in America, Charles prepared to go. He gave Judy a big hug and said good-by to Harold. He gathered up his leather briefcase with all the music stuffed in it and I saw, on the top of the pile, a chord chart for "Goodbye Pork Pie Hat," the very song that John Handy told me was not written down the day it was recorded.

I said, "Charles, would it be okay if I took a look at 'Good Bye Pork Pie Hat?'" After a long moment, he said, "Okay," and handed me the music.

I held the single, handwritten page for less than one minute, but in that time, I memorized the complete chord sequence as Mingus had intended it to be played. Over the years, I have heard many variations on this theme, and most of them have been extravagantly speculative. But Mingus' chart was simple and direct, almost a blues in E minor, with the beautiful melody hovering over the basic changes. I handed it back to him and said, "Thank you, Charles." and we shook hands. As he disappeared into the night, I took out a blank piece of manuscript paper and wrote down exactly what I had seen. A major piece of the puzzle was in place.

I began rehearsing a band to go on the road in support of my next album, *Don't Let Go*, but preparations were interrupted by a call from Bob Krasnow who told me he had a record he wanted me to produce first: he had signed Sylvester.

By the end of the month, in which I had moved into the "Sunset Riot House" in L.A. (The Hyatt House on Sunset Boulevard) for three weeks, subsisted on room service club sandwiches and hot fudge sundaes and spent long days at the studio with Sylvester and his band of androgynous whackos, I was seriously contemplating jumping off the roof as the quickest way to end my misery. In the couple of years since I had last seen him, Sylvester had become a different person, or, perhaps, simply more of the person he had always been. He was bitchy, star-struck, arbitrary, self-impressed and, from time to time, simply evil. In the end, the album was released, but I refused to put my name on it (it is listed as produced by my production company, "Bulldog Productions.") And when, a few years later, he became one of the premier disco "divas," I was happy for him and even happier for myself that I was well clear of it.

The following summer, I began to tour in earnest. I had no way of knowing it would be the start of a quarter-century run that to date has kept me away from home for twelve of the past twenty-five years. Playing the music for three or four hours a night has always been a joy; but surviving the other twenty gracefully, that has been a challenge.

It began as a kind of lark with a band of Madison musicians in a couple of rented vans. *Don't Let Go* was released in the spring of 1974, and started getting a lot of airplay, and we played at all the so-called "showcase" clubs across the country. These were the unofficially sanctioned clubs, clubs that the record labels considered the "right ones" to play. One went from the Quiet Knight in Chicago to Bogarts in Cleveland to the Main Point in Philadelphia to Paul's Mall in Boston to the Bottom Line in New York, following an endless line of bands during the period. Later, this concept of record company supported night clubs came to haunt us all, as it ultimately reduced both the money we were able to make and the number of clubs that were able to stay in business. At the time, however, it made touring relatively simple. You had a record, it got airplay, you plugged into the circuit and off you went.

The tour actually started in Minneapolis, where we opened for guitarist Ry Cooder at the Marigold Ballroom. Just before we went on stage, the room seemed to go electric. The buzz reached the dressing room: Bob Dylan was in the house. We did our normal set and the crowd loved it. In the interval, I decided to screw my courage to the sticking post and go meet Bob. I found him sitting in a back booth with a friend, sending off vibes like a caged animal. He was hunched in the far corner of the booth, wearing black shades and a black leather jacket, totally on guard. I said, "Bob, I just want to say how much your music has meant to me." He said, "Oh yeah?" He seemed so uncomfortable that I became increasingly embarrassed. His companion gave me a sympathetic look, and finally I said, "Well thanks again, Bob," and left him there, radiating paranoia like a microwave tower. (Years later, describing this encounter to Barry

Feinstein, who had once made a cross-country car trip with Dylan, he said, "Yeah, well you can get the best of Bob Dylan for $5.98 in any record store.")

By the time we got to Philadelphia several weeks later, I had discovered that I had foolishly brought a bunch of kids into an adult situation. The band had checked into an old Main Line hotel where, coincidentally, the DAR (the Daughters of the Army of the Republic) were having their annual ball, and as I walked into the lobby one night, the elevator doors opened and my guitar player rolled out onto the carpet holding a drink in one hand and a flaming fish in the other. It occurred to me then that I needed to start working with musicians who weren't necessarily from Madison.

Originally, the plan had been for us to go from Philadelphia to Boston, then on to New York and Washington, D.C. However, when we got to Boston, I received an emergency phone call from Tommy LiPuma at Blue Thumb Records. He said, "Ben, I don't know how to tell you this, but you better turn the van around. The label is out of business. As soon as you get back, you'll fly out to L.A. and I'll explain everything." We had been so near — the tour was selling records and the records were getting airplay and, despite the lunatics from Madison, we were getting great reviews. But clearly this run was over.

The next week, sitting at the bar of Sportsman's Lodge in the San Fernando Valley, an old record business haunt where it was always midnight, even at noon, Tommy told me a story that began, "Krasnow must have been out of his mind..." and ended with the news that Gulf and Western had come in, changed the locks and thrown everybody out of the office. Thus, a great adventure had come to a screeching halt. By the time I arrived in town the parent company had practically pulled the logos off the records, and the catalog, including my three albums, had been absorbed into the larger pool at ABC Records, also owned by G&W.

Tommy sat at the bar, angry and dazed, and cursing the fact that he had not even been given the chance to put together a group of investors to buy the company back. "We were profitable," he said, "and this was going to be our best year. Krasnow...well, in his own mind, Bob has always been above the law." This had been the case with a lot of first generation record men, and was perhaps brought to its logical conclusion at Blue Thumb. As Don Graham, an early partner in the label told me years later, "We didn't really have any competition except ourselves. We were our own competition." And in the end, the competition won.

A few months later, I happened to be sitting backstage at a concert with singer / pianist Randy Newman, a good friend of both Tommy and Krasnow. Randy knew the story of Blue Thumb, and he seemed as shell shocked as the rest of us. "What kind of business are we in," Randy kept saying, "where guys can do things like this?" And I thought to myself, that's a really good question. What kind of business is this? The next day, I called Jann Wenner at *Rolling Stone* and proposed an investigative piece on the current state of the business. Jann agreed immediately and we set up a fee, an expense account and a deadline.

Working on the story gave me a vehicle to focus my anger and a channel for my frustration. With Blue Thumb gone, my recordings were quickly becoming "cut out" and were disappearing from the shelves of record stores around the country. There was a thriving business in "cut outs" and if you found your records in this category, it was a message from the business that your services were no longer required. My music became a collector's item virtually over night. For the next few years, as more and more fans came up to me at concerts and said that they couldn't find my albums, I joked that I was now "the king of the cutouts." But from a business standpoint, it was no joke at all. If you were cut out, you didn't exist.

In fact, from a business standpoint, many "progressive" artists, the category into which I had fallen, were having a similar experience. The shift in the economy that had precipitated the demise of Blue Thumb Records had also sent a lot of "marginal acts" (that was me) searching for a home. As the momentum of the sixties ground into the inertia of the seventies, Bob Krasnow, like many of his peers, got other lucrative job offers — Bob washed up at Warner Brothers Records — but in the artistic community it was every man for himself. Singer / songwriters were scattered to the breeze. Some reappeared, reinvented at "alternative clubs" like CBGB's or Max's Kansas City. For others, it was just another tightening of the hand-tooled belt. In my case, it was an opportunity to continue thinking about the music in a more global way, as I had begun to do at the University.

As I progressed with the interviews for the *Rolling Stone* piece, it was clear that the record business was in the process of changing into a "real" business, based not on the unpredictability of the artists but on the repeatability of the content: not coincidentally, disco music was sweeping the nation. In Madison, we had been playing long-form dance music for several years, extended jams that went on for hours at clubs like the Nitty Gritty, and it was fun to watch what happened to a dancer when you changed the groove; it felt like you were actually generating metaphysical power in the room. The only way I can describe the exhilaration of these moments is to compare it to the feeling of long distance running, after the endorphins have kicked in and one shifts into that space where there is no pain or fatigue. You felt as if you held the force that binds the nucleus of all matter, the mysterious Hobbes Bowson, in the palm of your hand. When we found these emotional spaces, it was the realization of the sixties made manifest and we hung where the free music of Pharaoh Sanders met the groove of James Brown.

But "disco" soon became a kind of machine music, a formula played in clubs by disc jockeys, based on pre-determined tempos. Each season, there was a new "beat per minute" that was supposed to be the latest thing. In 1974, it was 120 beats per minute; that was the tempo that was required for the dance floor. Whereas the rhythm grooves that we had been putting down at the Nitty Gritty were focussed by the emotion in the room, this new metronomic music was emotionless focus, a kind of mindlessness that, along with the cocaine plague, set the tone of the times.

At the same time, by the early seventies, America was deep in the throes of the great Volume Boogie. Inexperienced musicians were using volume as a cheap substitute for excitement, bringing the music down to the lowest common denominator (or up to the lowest common denominator, as the case may be). This focus on volume had a parallel in the world of sports, where pro football was taking over from baseball as the media's game of choice. Baseball, a game of subtlety favored by the rational side of the brain, was supplanted by football, an exhibition of speed and brute strength. In baseball, a pinch hitter who was 5'6" and a Ring Lardner aficionado had the chance to come across your radio as the hero of the day. In pro football, huge men in battle gear roared up and down the television screen, identified mostly by their numbers, generating a hundred times the visceral excitement. Volume, size, emotionless focus; America was coming into its own.

Volume and technology had a profound effect on jazz. For one thing, a musician can only play so loud. A drummer can only hit the drums as hard as he can hit them. But his ability to play soft and express nuance is infinite. And it's well known that nuance is what sucks people into the music, into the emotional heart of the moment. This is why jazz was incubated in small clubs, where the acoustics of the room determined the shape of the experience. Hence clubs like the Village Vanguard in New York City became legendary, almost sacred spaces. On the surface, they may have looked like nothing special, but when you closed your eyes, they turned into temples of focused emotion. Not coincidentally, by the mid-seventies, every small club we played, even the jazz rooms, had a "sound man" who immediately turned up the volume when you tried to play soft, defeating the nuance and taking away the control that musicians had spent years trying to perfect.

This "sound man" mentality, wherein a microphone was placed on the kick drum and it immediately became the loudest thing in the room, was the harbinger of even worse things to come. In the fifties, it was said that Philly Joe Jones played "too loud" with Miles, and then in the sixties, Elvin Jones came along and played even louder with Coltrane. By the seventies, sound men, often twenty-year-old kids with partial hearing loss were making the esthetic decisions and by the eighties, it no longer mattered: jazz musicians who once walked into the room five minutes late and still arrived light years ahead of the audience were now spending pointless hours during long afternoons laboring through mind numbing "sound checks."

Perhaps the first shot across the bow was fired the day in 1973 that Shelly's Manne-Hole, an intimate jazz room in Hollywood, shut its doors. What closed the club was not poor attendance — the club was drawing well — but the fact that upstairs, above the club, was a recording studio. And apparently, the live music from the club on the first floor was leaking into the echo chambers of the recording studio on the second floor. Echo chambers are used to create artificial space around recorded instruments. The choice was clear: the living space (the jazz club) was sacrificed for the artificial one (the echo chambers) because of the economics of scale. Only seventy-five people could fit into the club at any one time, but many thousands could purchase the recording.

Coincidentally, even as I was experiencing the new reality of the record business, the record business was being very good to Steve Miller. In 1974, he finally sold a million records with a song called "The Joker" (which starts out with the lyric, "Some people call me the Space Cowboy..."). On a trip to California to research the article, I stopped in the Bay Area to see him. That night, he opened the case of Chateau Lafitte Rothschild that Capitol Records had sent him, and the two of us sat and watched a video of his performance on the Wolfman Jack TV show. Without his trademark pair of dark shades and acting dead sober, he said to Wolfman, after being congratulated on selling a million units, "I may have sold a million, but I don't have a million...yet."

That would change by the end of the year. But that night, in a stupor of superior red wine, Steve said to me, "What the record company wants is for my record to go up the charts as fast as possible and then disappear as fast as possible. They want it to go away so they can sell whatever is next." Entering the higher strata of that rarefied air, the top ten, he had discovered he was still disposable, and he glimpsed the plan of his own obsolescence. In his moment of triumph, he could feel the cold breath of the marketing machine on his neck, even as his hit record was about to be certified platinum.

1975

In January 1975, I got yet another phone call from George Brown. This time, he had been thrown out of Amsterdam, actually picked up off the streets, and, he said, taken to the airport and put on a plane to JFK. For the tenth time, I sent him money to get home. He was raving about being the victim of some great social injustice, although he was hard-pressed to define exactly what the injustice had been, and knowing George's habit of burning his bridges *before* he crossed them, one suspected that in Amsterdam he had finally surrendered to his various weaknesses, and his erratic nature had turned into a full blown anti-social episode.

Seeing George, once a proud, articulate innovator, get chewed up like this, I began to have a real sense of just how dangerous the jazz life can be. It was like riding the back of the tiger: you don't know where it will take you, and your only options are to dismount and be devoured or to ride on. All because, in the beginning, you fell in love. Over the years, we've lost so many great men and women to this journey. People often speculate on why jazz musicians turn to drugs. I think maybe jazz itself is the drug and the heroin, cocaine and pot are simply substitutes for this mainline addiction.

They say there are two things you can't talk about to a man: his woman and his religion. To a true believer, jazz is both. How many have fallen in love with this music only to get trapped in their dream, to have surrendered to the intoxication only to wake up one day, old beyond their years? The music is like a labyrinth, or like absinthe: it's easy to lose yourself within it. Perhaps this is why, among musicians, it is often called "the curse." George Brown's inability to function in the new economic landscape was a symptom of a larger plague, and unlike the heroin plague that had swept the jazz world during the fifties, the plague of the seventies claimed its victims silently, invisibly.

My story for *Rolling Stone* appeared in the May 22, 1975 edition. In the piece, Art Mogul was quoted as saying, "I fear that guys like me are kind of over. Within five years, the president of every record company in America will either be legally or financially oriented. The record business has become too big and too complicated for the creative guy to run it anymore." Jerry Moss, the "M" in A&M records, reported, "I wouldn't have said this two years ago, but because of the high cost of everything nowadays, for somebody to do as we did, you know, to work in small numbers and establish some kind of growth potential, is almost impossible." The legend of the "one motivated man," which had long dominated the history of the business, was giving way to the motivated conglomerate.

This long-term trend toward consolidation brought with it some interesting Catch 22s: for example, a record company won't sign an artist without "good management," but most artists can't attract good management without a record company's commitment. The Yosarian complex was further complicated by radio. As conglomerates are less motivated by "feel," charts became more important: but a record won't sell without airplay and it won't get airplay until it starts selling. As a creeping homogeneity of music spread from coast to coast, record companies, that would normally have taken chances and developed new talent, cut back instead. By 1975, automated radio was sweeping the country (no actual live personalities, just tapes giving prerecorded intros to songs and time checks), and there was a rating service using computers to predict what a record's chances were of making a given chart position weeks in advance. Kind of like running an exit poll minus the inconvenience of people exiting.

Outside of radio play, the only way for a musician to gain exposure was through live performances, but that too was a shrinking market. The competition had become so fierce at the important showcase clubs that it took a strong booking agency just to arrange for a musician to play for next to nothing. Showcase clubs like the Bottom Line in New York, the Troubadour in L.A., and the Boarding House in San Francisco, became reliant on record companies, who kept large running tabs for their guests, bought ads when one of their bands performed, and gave the bands recoupable money to play the gig. By refusing to subsidize the band if it didn't play at the favored club, this system hurt all the other local venues and limited the field of play dramatically.

So the record companies wound up subsidizing the bands, subsidizing the booking agencies, subsidizing the important clubs, the promoters and even the radio stations. They were in partnership with too many people and were bankrolling every aspect of the business with high interest money. In the great American tradition, their response was to expand further. They began to manipulate the distribution pipeline.

For years, record companies had sold their product to anywhere from one to three middlemen, each providing a service and taking a small slice. As profit margins narrowed, the conglomerates set up their own branch distribution networks. Large companies got better at seeing what was selling and put the push on stuff they wanted to promote. But branch distribution also increased the operating overhead and large record companies became volume junkies just to keep the cash flowing. They needed the billing to keep the doors open, even if they had to lose money in the end on the product. Like most junkies, they spent more time trying to score than getting off; they were doing tremendously more volume without increasing their net profits. Likewise, branch distribution downplayed "art" or "esoteric" records, which had a smaller sales potential.

It was an eye-opener: I and many other smaller acts were being thrown into a kind of economic abattoir. Reflecting on the situation, John Hammond, an elder statesman of the industry, told me, "In the early twenties, the record business proliferated then flagged, electric recording revived it in 1925, radio killed it in 1928, the Depression buried it in 1932, jukeboxes revived it in 1935, Petrillo killed it again with the strike in 1942, and the long-playing record in 1948 revived it permanently. I think," he said, "it will always be with us as a real mass market for new and experimental music and for the staples in music too. We're the only industry that's discovering and promoting musical talent these days. Radio does nothing. Television does nothing, nothing live. The theater is too square. *So if there's going to be evolution in music, it's going to be through recording*" (my emphasis).

Hammond had, inadvertently, hit upon what was perhaps the most troubling aspect of the situation: musical innovation had become, by and large, a function of the record business. Whereas only a decade before most new music was discovered on the street and brought into the studio, by the mid-seventies, it was more often created in the studio and shipped back to the streets. What had once been "captured" was now being manufactured. This put an enormous burden on the creative talents of top industry executives, and as more of these guys were now money men, not music men, their ears were often not up to the task.

By the second half of the seventies, the question had become not whether various forms of "popular music" could survive this concentration of power, but whether it had actually existed in the first place, or was simply a projection of the technology and the marketing hype.

The response to the article in *Rolling Stone* was immediate and widespread. Ironically, even as the article clearly spelled out the demise of "marginal acts" like myself in a business that was increasingly disposed toward mega-stars, it also, inadvertently, created my own next opportunity. I got many calls, and one was from Clive Davis, the owner of Arista Records, who had read the piece and liked it. He called, he said, to congratulate me, but, ultimately, it led to a recording contract.

But first, Steve Backer, Clive's director of jazz A&R, called to offer me a simple gig. Jon Hendricks, the lyrical mastermind behind the fifties vocal group Lambert, Hendricks and Ross, had been signed by Arista and, apparently, Clive had succumbed to Jon's charm and had delivered the full $20,000 production budget into his hands. To date, Arista had not seen or heard anything in the way of recorded music, and, fearful that the money was not going into the recording, Steve called to ask if I would go to San Francisco where Jon lived and take over the production of the record.

I went to San Francisco the next month and began work on the album that would later be released as *Tell Me the Truth*. The day that I arrived at Wally Heider's studio, the band was in place, the engineer was in place, but Jon was nowhere to be found. Two hours later, Jon came running up the stairs, said "Hey man, nice to meet you. Say, lend me some bread, I've got a cab waiting," and after I laid the money on him, he disappeared down the stairs and didn't return that afternoon.

But Jon was, and still is, one of the hippest, funniest, most literate, most swinging musicians on the face of the planet, a master story teller and an old-school singer, who reaches into his heart every time he approaches a song. Blessed with a huge musical gift, he is always aware that it came from somewhere higher up, and there was always, even in the darkest moments of the hustle, a sense of a spiritual purpose about him.

My favorite moment in the recording sessions, and there were many, came the afternoon he taught me the song "Old Folks." We were sitting alone together in the studio and he asked me if I knew it. I said no and he said, "Here, I'll show it to you." We went over to the piano where he sketched out some chords to me and then started singing. I followed him as best I could. Jon, being the great jazz musician that he is, completely gave it up on the vocal, throwing back his head and letting the anguish and the nostalgia of the song soar into the room. When it was over, the engineer in the control room said, "Would you guys like to hear that?" We hadn't known it was being recorded.

Hearing the playback, Jon loved his vocal. He said, "That's it! That's going on the record."

I said, "Wait a minute, Jon, I'm clearly making some mistakes there. The piano is leaking into the vocal so there's no chance we can replace it."

He said, "No, that's as good as I can ever sing that song. It's great. We've got to use it."

I tried to play the producer. I said, "Jon, I think it's a great song, but that take really isn't good enough. Let's recut it."

He looked at me and said, "Ben, sometimes, the mistakes are the only part that's jazz."

And of course that take wound up on the record.

During these sessions, Jon also explained to me his technique for creating "vocalese," the art of putting words to well-known jazz solos. The skill, later popularized by The Manhattan Transfer, was pioneered by Jon, along with singers Eddie Jefferson and King Pleasure. We were talking about the musical flow and intense literacy of his writing, and he said, "Well, you see, I'm not trying to fit lyrics into the line, like a jeweler fits stones into a setting. What I do is I listen to the music, over and over, until it's part of me, and pretty soon that line starts to speak. I hear the story as it's being told and the words just come on up. The music is talking and I'm listening." He became the vessel.

Following the on-time, on-budget production of Jon's record, I was offered my own recording contract at Arista.

I got the idea for the record in the spring of 1975 while lying in a hammock in my backyard, watching the breeze blow apple blossoms off the trees. I was thinking about the impending American bicentennial and the blizzard of red, white and blue that was coming in a matter of months; by the next summer, it would be a full blown marketing storm and they would be selling patriotic toilet paper before this party was over. The idea of a "Bicentennial Bebop Band" popped into my addled reverie. I could imagine recording a jazz take on the American experience, an alternative to the standard fare that was being planned. I got out of the hammock and went into the house and by evening, I had written the title song.

Free in America

"The nicest thing about the United States
Everybody is free to make their own mistakes
You don't have to look far but then there you are
Everyone's free in America
Yes, you're free to vote, free to hope against hope
Free to split if you don't like the stroke
It might not sound like much but it will do in the clutch
Step right up sucker, it's your turn to touch
Cause you're free
Free to make a new life
Free to change your name, free to change your game
Free to change your wife
You never give it a second thought
But what your money's bought
Coast to coast they call it the most
Shore to shore we got lots and lots more
Sea to shining sea!
Freedom, freedom...
Roll down the highway in your big shiny car
You got the radio telling you just where you are
It might be cold advice but then you can't beat the price
Step right up sucker and roll the dice
'Cause you're free..."

A few months earlier, while on a trip to Los Angeles, I had been handed another good piece of Americana. I was in the office of a song publisher, and he passed a pile of sheet music across the desk. "Here," he said, "maybe there's something you'll want to record." Most of it was junk but one thing jumped out at me, a song called "New York State of Mind."

He said, "Oh, that's a song Billy Joel wrote. We tried to get it to Sinatra but he never responded."

I said, "Has it been recorded yet?"

He said, "Nope, it's all yours."

That's how I became the first person to record one of Billy's most well known songs. In fact, a lot of people assumed that I had written it because mine was the only recorded version for some time. Unlike subsequent recordings, mine was very dark, almost a junkie rendition, featuring the great trumpet player Woody Shaw and Richard Tee on organ. Not exactly your standard bicentennial celebration theme, but, hey, I was on a roll.

1976

By the middle of May, the record was finished, the band was thoroughly rehearsed and Judy was three months pregnant. I had read somewhere that the first of our senses to be switched on is hearing, which begins approximately four months after conception. For the remainder of the term, sound remains the baby's primary sense: the mother's voice, the in and out of her breathing, the beating of her heart. To this I added Miles, Coltrane, Horace, Monk, Mingus, James Brown, Percy Mayfield and a dozen others. It was a joyful spring, as Judy and I took leisurely walks to the lake to watch the mother duck and her new baby ducks swimming all in a line. We had long lazy dinners at restaurants, had the baby's room painted and started collecting small furniture. When it was finally time for me to go to New York to launch the next tour, I was almost unable to do it.

One afternoon, I found myself sitting by the side of the highway in my car, crying, sobbing actually. I had no idea I felt this way. It felt like something deep, an almost primordial longing for another time and place that I didn't know I had been carrying with me, had finally broken free.

The tour started in early June. This time, I had a great band, a major booking agency (American Talent International) and a major record label behind me. Well, partially behind me. Arista had agreed to help finance the first half of the tour, and if they got the kind of record sales they were looking for, they said they would help finance the second half as well. This did not inspire a lot of confidence — what would happen to us if they pulled out? — and I called Clive Davis to discuss the situation.

Clive asked a few questions. Where were my strong markets (Minneapolis, San Francisco, New York), what had my previous LP sold (20,000 copies), what did this one cost to make ($35,000), how much had Arista committed to support the tour ($7,500). After some quick calculations, he said, "If we get some sales action from the first half, don't worry about the back half." When I hung up, I felt like Charlie Brown about to kick the football that Lucy was holding.

The tour started on Long Island, at a club called My Father's Place. It was a double bill with a glitter sado-Masochist who called himself Wayne County. Following this, we went to Washington D.C. where we played at the Cellar Door on another double bill. The first night was pretty empty, but business got better as the week went on.

From *The Washington Star*:

"There are club dates and then there are showcases. Showcases are those rare occasions when record companies choose to put their newer acts into a club to simply get them in front of a paying audience...This weekend the Cellar Door is hosting a showcase — two acts that, by themselves, would draw only meager audiences...Last night one of the few paying customers to show up was Elton John, and the crowd was probably a good deal bigger than it might have been because of his presence. Elton, who is in town to rehearse the start of his 1976 tour, is friend and mentor of Leslie Duncan, the opening act on the bill...Though Elton was there to cheer on Duncan, the musical honors for the evening went to jazz pianist and vocalist Ben Sidran. Sidran is a unique figure in pop music. Sidran is, in fact, a fine player. Working a vein similar to Mose Allison, he creates a most interesting sort of bluesy jazz. Sidran's vocals are perhaps most related to those of Tom Waits — breathy, without striving to be more full than they can possibly be...."

In Washington, the folks from N.O.R.M.L. (The National Organization to Reform Marijuana Laws) came down to the show; they had heard I was talking about them. I would often say, somewhere in my set, "I'm here for my favorite cause, the National Organization to Reform Marijuana Laws..." And, indeed, it was; I had long thought that the prohibition against pot smoking was among the most stupid, wasteful and, ultimately, damaging of public policies and I would say it — in a nice way — from the stage.

Keith Stroup, N.O.R.M.L's director, came back after the D.C. show and said the problem was money, of course; many of the fat cats who were his natural supporters assumed the fight had already been won, and they lived above the marijuana laws. Also, he said, the flourishing of coke had clouded the whole issue of getting high.

"The fight for individual liberties is disappearing up a lot of big time noses," he said. I told him I had read in Judith Exner's book that JFK had once offered her coke.

The gig in Baltimore the next night was bizarre; we played in a bowling alley as the opening act for a rock band called Heart, two chicks screaming their hit song, "Crazy On You." We barely got out with our lives.

From there we went to the Jazz Workshop in Boston for a few nights, a double bill with George Benson, and then down to the Other End in New York City. It was the July 4th weekend, the big Bicentenial celebration, and the streets in the Village were full of hookers having a field day with the sailors from the Tall Ships. One enterprising girl stood on the corner of Bleeker Street wearing a "happy birthday America" ribbon, hot pants and a see-through American flag for a top, working the traffic. The first night at the club, Billy Joel came down to hear me sing "New York State of Mind." He had been hearing it on WRVR, and he sat at a front table with his wife, getting drunker by the minute. They were loud, arguing and fussing, and I put off singing the song until the end of the second set, by which time, they were in a roaring fight.

From *Variety*:

"Ben Sidran, one of the most talented of today's pianists with specialties in jazz, blues and rock, has an excellent turn in his first gig in this Greenwich Village cabaret room.... A disk switch to Arista from Blue Thumb should speed his career. Calling his act a 'good bar band' Sidran has a good comic rap and, more important, good performance of his own material and others' tunes...a good act."

After New York, we went up the coast to Hartford and a great double bill with an R&B band called NRBQ. There, I felt the first air escaping from Arista's balloon of hype. The Arista promo man came in drunk, had never even heard my music, and basically spent the night talking about selling his house in Cherry Hill. When he left, the club owner presented me with his bar bill.

From *The Walrus*:

"Audience Reaction: Rave; Reviewer's reaction: NRBQ is like God around here — crowds automatically get off. But nobody expected Ben Sidran to be that good, despite his excellent string of lps. But he was, and the crowd screamed and stomped for him too, causing the management to try to get him back as a headliner..."

By the time we got to the Midwest, to the Agora in Cleveland and Bogarts in Cincinnati, the band was like a hot car, all tuned up and ready to run, and the songs were just roads to rip up for the fun of the trip. We couldn't wait to play each night, but financially, we were scuffling. The record company was becoming scarce. One night in Cincinnati, Michael Franks, a singer who had just released a record not dissimilar to my own, came to the taping of a radio show. In passing, he told me he had already sold 50,000 albums, 20,000 singles, and that Warner Brothers had booked his whole tour for him and given him $40,000 to defray the costs. I felt like I was still playing sandlot and talking to somebody who had made it to The Show.

It made the phone call I got the next morning from Arista's lawyer even harder to swallow. He said they would agree to give me some of the money I needed to continue the tour in return for half of my publishing rights. I said forget it. I called Steve Backer to complain, but he told me, "Man, you should feel grateful."

I said, "They can kiss my ass," and hung up.

From there on out, the rest of the tour was guerrilla warfare. We continued playing each gig like we were storming a military objective, taking no prisoners and pushing further into the jungle to achieve some vague philosophical objective. Working our way through the Midwest, we were running on fumes, but we found crowds packing the rooms. In Des Moines, people were hanging from the rafters, strange faces peering out from everywhere. It was like playing to a wildly animated Breughel painting.

From *The Des Moines Register*:

> "One does not listen to Ben Sidran, one surrenders. Musically and personally, Sidran seems an infinite pool of inspiration. A chat with the talented pianist before his show Tuesday at So's Your Mother shed some light on why. And his set before some 500 persons who crammed every nook of the bar bolstered initial impressions. In conversation and in concert, Sidran is a philosopher. He is not of the 'heavy rap' school; rather, his music and conversation is engaging, erudite discourse...Despite his doctoral degree, Sidran in no way qualifies as a snob. In fact, he is slightly anti-intellectual...Sidran, considered a jazz performer by most music buffs, religiously rejects that label. 'I play bebop influenced dance music,' he insisted. But he also insisted that labels aren't important or relevant anyway. 'There is no good or bad music,' he added, 'Music touches the listener or it doesn't.'"

Leaving Des Moines for Denver was a bad movie. After a few hours of sleep, a trip to the local Country Kitchen for some bad hash browns, a dash to return the rent-a-car, we all poured onto the plane, pretty well out of it. Curley Cooke, the guitar player was hung over and wearing shades, and kept growling, "Where's my junk!" loud enough for strangers to hear him. Zappa, the bass player, was saying to nobody in particular, "Let's get this turkey in the air. Tell the captain to put on another log, pour on the coal..." It was eight o'clock in the morning and I felt like I was about to fall off the planet. And only a few weeks ago, everything seemed so sure.

That morning, I had received the check from Arista for the second half of the tour support. On the bottom was written, "advance against any and all monies, including mechanical royalties for controlled compositions...for tour deficit financing." Of course, I had not agreed to this. In order to cash the check, I would have to betray myself.

The gigs in Denver the following days were another series of gaffs and fire drills. The club owner claimed he thought I was a solo act because of the way ATI had filled out the contract. In truth, ATI probably told the club, "The band will play the gig under any circumstances, don't worry, it's important to the record company." It was what is known as "jam booking." That's where the agency shoehorns an act into a venue and plays dumb when the musician screams; by then, it's too late and the agency has already collected its commission. So once again, we became the opening act for a loud rock band, this one called Mountain, a bunch of over-the-hill heavy metal thugs. For several days, I was held hostage in Denver to the machinations of "jam booking."

That week, there were monsoon rains in Denver, and the streets were flooding to unheard of depths. From time to time, it seemed like the sky simply lowered and great sheets of water buried everything. Cars were swept away at intersections and children were lost in ditches. I holed up, smoked pot and watched a lot of television. One news report, the big international story of the week, was about an earthquake in China. A journalist doing a standup in front of a cage of lions was saying, "before the temblor hit, the animals in the Peking Zoo were acting nervous, and scientists suspect that they sensed the big one coming." I wondered if maybe human behavior, too, some of it at least, might not be a kind of nervous premonition of coming events as well. Maybe mass movements, like rock and roll or the hula-hoop, were actually cultural manifestations that if properly understood could predict coming disasters. What if the study of art and mass communication — the art as the news, the news as art — could uncover this prescience in our pack behavior? If so, I wondered, what could I learn about my own future in the situation I was now in, jam booked and opening for some rock dinosaurs in a flooded city? Absolutely nothing came to mind. I switched to cartoons.

By early August we had arrived in L.A. Sweet L.A. The palm trees were blowing in a warm wind outside the baggage claim at LAX, and driving the rent-a-car down Sunset Blvd. to the Ryatt House, we passed a beautiful, Cartier-bedecked blond in her Mercedes 450 SLC convertible, top down, windows rolled up, air conditioning blasting. Free in America!

On the radio, Boz's "Lowdown" was playing. Like Steve, Boz too was scoring big that summer. I had heard that "Lowdown" was the third single released from his record. The first two had stiffed. Likewise, Steve had told me if it wasn't for a particular A&R woman at Capitol named Jean Riggens, who believed in him, "The Joker" never would have happened either. Or as Tommy LiPuma always told me, "In this business, you got to have a rabbi." I guess Steve Backer needed to go back to the musical seminary: Arista never even released one single for me.

In fact, when I got to my dressing room at The Troubadour that night, I found that the Arista promo person had sent over a basket of wine and cheese, but the card in the basket spelled my name wrong (Cidran). As a rule, if you get to the dressing room and there are flowers from the local promotion person, you know you are in trouble. On this tour, there had been flowers everywhere. No records in the stores, no ads in the papers, no radio spots. But flowers enough for Clive's son's Bar Mitzvah .

Playing in L.A. always held the potential to be a real circus. My opening night, Tom Waits came crawling through the club (we talked about the movie "Stormy Weather"), and John Mayall came backstage to say hello. He had been playing with Blue Mitchell, who I hadn't seen in some time. And finally, after the first set, Tommy LiPuma dropped by for a few minutes with Michael Franks, but they couldn't stay long either. They were leaving early the next day to fly to Brazil to record Michael's next record.

From *The Los Angeles Times*:

> "Ben Sidran, musical scholar and author, opened this week at The Troubadour with a show that was anything but academic. Sidran himself, anchored firmly at the piano, does look more professor than showman, but the full-bodied music offered by his quartet is strong, sharp and impassioned. The group covers a range of jazz styles whose borders exclude free-form exercises and stale rehashes. The swirling disco-jazz of "Let's Make a Deal" comes closest to the former, but the bulk of the set emphasizes freedom within a varied, disciplined framework. Sidran offers both instrumental jazz and jazz-directed pop with a heavy blues influence. Ballads like 'New York State of Mind' recall Paul Simon in attitude and structure, while some doses of Mose Allison and 'Gangster of Love' (Johnny Guitar Watson via Steve Miller) illuminate Sidran's ultimate sources."

The next afternoon, I went to Tower Records on Sunset to buy a Louis Jordan record. I had been thinking a lot about Jordan and the way he combined bebop chord changes and dance rhythms. It was something I thought I could update.

The chick behind the counter told me "If it ain't in big bands we don't have it." It wasn't there. I told her Jordan was an older blues-style singer. She said, "If it ain't in the blues section, we don't have it." I tried there and failed. I said he was from the forties. "If it ain't in big band nostalgia we don't have it." I asked if I gave her the number of the record would she locate it for me in back stock. She said there was no back stock. And besides, "The number won't do no good. It's all arranged in piles." What was happening to our collective history?

Two weeks after the Israelis did the rescue at Entebbe, the paperback was in the stores and the film was a week away from release. What did this speed, the pace of reality transformed into fiction, do to the whole concept of history? Two weeks ago is now nostalgia? Earthquakes in China, floods in Denver—what a week. Can't wait for the movie.

The world was in a media trance. The thing about trances is that you don't know you're in one until you come out of it. Blink, and life slaps you in the face (Gurdjieff: "Remember yourself!"). But the CBS eye never blinks and I didn't think we'd ever come out of this one.

Finally, two days later, after two months on the road, we arrived at our final destination: The Boarding House in San Francisco. The first night at the club, Curley set himself on fire. He was standing at the bar smoking a cigarette and chatting up a girl when an ash dropped into his cuff. His pants started smoking, he looked down, freaked out and ran into the bathroom. He must have stuck his whole leg into the toilet, because when he came out he had a sheepish grin and his leg was soaked up to the knee.

From *The San Francisco Examiner*:

"The Boarding House has slipped in a three-day sleeper on their schedule this week. Chris Hillman and his seven piece Southern California countryrock band are sharing the bill with Ben Sidran's electric rock-jazz quintet. No one who is enthusiastic about the sounds of contemporary popular music should miss this engagement. And those who are just curious about musical directions in the mid-1970s ought to drop by too.

Hillman's presentation is somewhat more predictable than Sidran's and not as devastating. A veteran of the Byrds, associate of most of the country-folk oriented California bands and composer of some fine material, Hillman has made his mark in the Bay Area as much as anywhere else.... The strength of Hillman's performance was especially remarkable after the astonishing non-stop 50 minutes that Sidran and band presented.

Sidran uses tight boogie-blues meters, guided with relentless intensity from his piano keyboard, to drive woodwind player David Woodford and guitarist Curley Cooke—the band's front line.... The ensemble is so tight and sure that solos seem to spin-off in orbit. I seldom hear an audience cheer a solo while it is still being played—Sidran's band has that kind of excitement. In fact, Sidran, and then Hillman, are first-rate stuff, a chance of a lifetime to hear them together."

After the set, I felt totally destroyed. The tour was finally over and all my systems were shutting down. Friends and musicians came backstage to congratulate us, and the scene quickly took on a party atmosphere. There was Paul and Babe Pena, and there was Lonnie Turner from the Miller Band. Even some of the cats from The Tubes came backstage, including Quay Lewd, the roadie who had taken over the act and invented "white punks on dope." Talking to him reminded me how, as a posture, The Tubes were not that different from British theatricality, the "all the young dudes" pose, only they blew it way out into theatrical orbit, complete with primordial archetypes crawling around the stage. San Francisco always had that way of making the real unreal, and then marketing it to the rest of the world.

I was in this reverie, with my friends and my flowers and my cheese plate, when an old pal from the Midwest, Mike Kappus stopped by. Mike was now a booking agent in San Francsico, and after a few pleasantries, he said, somewhat hesitantly, "You know, Ben, ATI really hurt you."

I asked him what he meant.

He said, "You're being used as an example on the East Coast. Clubs are telling agents, 'I got Ben Sidran for $150 per night, why should I pay you more?'"

I looked around at the party in the dressing room. Suddenly, it was like watching somebody else's life on television. The eye that never blinks.

The next morning, the ground was visible 39,000 feet below as we flew over the Iowa flatlands. I was finally at peace. Down on the ground, the occasional small red dot represented a farm. Otherwise, there was nothing but the exquisite geometry of human handiwork, the fields and roads that confirmed the well-ordered life below. But up where we were, there were odd shaped clouds here and there with great flashes of heat lightening erupting within, like exploding puffballs of energy. Yet it was absolutely silent except for the white noise of the jet engines just outside the plastic window. It was like being suspended in one of those children's globes.

Two days later, I awoke in my own bed in Madison, rolled over and dialed "9" on the phone to get an outside line before I realized I was actually home.

I spent the next several weeks calculating the profit and loss from the tour. On the plus side, I had collected some good press. On the minus side, I was now much deeper in debt to the record company, and they did not seem to be working particularly hard to reduce it by selling my record. Everything was collateralized against my little royalty share — less than 10 percent of the retail price of the record — which meant that for every dollar of theirs that I spent, whether it went toward recording, touring or marketing, I needed to sell another record. Meanwhile, built into the cost of that record was a nice markup for them so that they collected three times over before I ever collected once. At the rate my record was selling, the point was moot; recoupment was not in my future.

The only thing to do was make another record. It was like going into a giant casino and pulling the handle on the slots one more time. Only to make this machine work required that I write ten new songs and do the dance for Clive Davis. Just like Tennessee Ernie Ford used to sing, "You load sixteen tons and what do you get?" I was becoming indebted to the company store.

I began playing a regular gig in a little club in Madison called La Creperie. I showed up every Wednesday and Thursday night to keep my hands together and generate new material for the next record. I agreed to play for the door and I also guaranteed to pay Clyde and bass player Dennis Oliver $50 a night each. That meant that occasionally, especially when the weather was bad or the competition was stiff, I lost money playing the gig. Several weeks, I even flew back to Madison from L.A. or New York for the privilege of losing the money. It reminded me of a story pianist Dave Frishberg once told me:

A young piano player was hired by Lester Young to go on the road. On hearing what Lester would pay him per week, the young man said, "Prez, that's not very much money." Prez said, "Son, you have to save up to play jazz."

The gig at La Creperie was successful in other ways, however. I wrote the ten new songs and I got to hear great stories about the life and times of my good friend Clyde Stubblefield. For example, he told me about "the walking band." Back in Chattanooga, when he and his pals were just kids, they would play in "splo houses" on the edge of town. A "splo house" was a little shack in the woods where moonshine whiskey was sold. Clyde and the boys had no transportation, so they would have to walk to the gig, carrying their instruments on their backs. Sometimes, they would walk for miles. "We had matching jackets," Clyde said, "and every Friday night people would say, 'There goes that walking band...'" Years later, when he was laying down those endless funky grooves for James Brown, and James—who could wear out a drummer and put him up like a wet horse—would want to go harder, Clyde would just keep diggin' in, walking to the "splo house." That's how he became famous around the world as the "Original Funky Drummer." One foot in front of the other.

The image brought to mind an enigmatic note I had received from the media guru Marshall McLuhan a year or two before. I had sent him a copy of *Black Talk* and he liked it well enough to write me back. In the letter, he said:

"One of the matters I have worked on is the relation of music to language and how jazz and Rock appear to me to be transformations of urban technological noise via the medium of language. i.e., the humanization of technological horror by reducing the human scale and experience of language...another thing I have discovered is that English is the only language in the world that has feet. All other languages, so far as I can discover, have only symbols. It would seem that the advantage of feet in incorporating dance rhythms, as well as speech rhythms, is decisive for the power of jazz and Rock to impose their assumptions upon the entire world."

Clyde's nickname was "sugar foot."

That September, Judy and I began Lamaze classes. We sat in a large room with other expectant parents and learned how to breathe in and blow out. I could tell from the outset that I was going to be precious little help in case there was a real problem, but it created the illusion that there was a role for me. The autumn leaves were turning, and gradually, the dust of the road was being washed away in the rain of a warm Indian summer and great expectations.

To pay the rent, I had been working on two special programs for television station WTTW in Chicago. The previous spring I had contacted producer Ken Ehrlich about developing some jazz programming for his "Soundstage" series. It was the only live music performance show on the air at that time and, while it had become very successful with pop, folk and rock, it had never featured jazz. So when I approached Ken with a couple of ideas — one was a show based on "Dizzy Gillespie's Bebop Reunion," bringing together Dizzy with the living members of his 1947 band, and the other was "Sing Me a Jazz Song," bringing together Jon Hendricks, Annie Ross, Eddie Jefferson and Leon Thomas, the premier first generation of jazz singers — Ken hired me to go forward with both of them, and they were now coming to fruition.

The first one we taped was the program with Dizzy. I had been talking to him for several months, calling him from pay phones and motels across the country, and everything seemed to be in order. The last week of September, we all gathered in Chicago and Dizzy arrived from his home in New Jersey in good spirits. That afternoon, we sat together at a table in the cafeteria at the WTTW studios, and Dizzy slowly turned the pages of a book called *A Pictorial History of Jazz*, which I had brought along to jog his memory. Looking at what he called "a bunch of dead guys," he said, "Oh look, there's Pete Johnson...I knew him. And there's Charlie Parker. Didn't he look good!" Just as we came across some classic photographs of Dizzy himself, one in Earl Hines' band, another in 1947 leading a big band with Ray Brown and Milt Jackson, suddenly the door opened and into the cafeteria walked Ray Brown and Milt Jackson in person, followed by Joe Carroll, James Moody and Kenny Clarke. The cafeteria came alive with bebop jive. "Hey," Dizzy shouted, "here comes the Preservation Hall Bebop Band!"

Rehearsals got under way slowly and dragged through the usual delays, an hour to replace a set of drums, another hour to figure out an arrangement on "Round Midnight." Gradually it became obvious that Dizzy was having a serious problem. He seemed to be in pain every time he blew his horn. He repeatedly wiped his mouth with a handkerchief and looked at his horn as if trying to figure out some new way to play it. Then I noticed what appeared to be a nasty, dime-sized cyst on his upper lip, smack in the middle of his embrasure.

After the session, we convinced him to go to a hospital, where a doctor told him his lip required surgery. The cyst that was growing there was probably noncancerous, but they would have to remove it in order to discover just how serious it really was. In any case, there was no chance he could play the next night and there was also the implied threat that he would never play again. At the time, Dizzy was fifty-nine years old.

The next morning, Dizzy said the growth had been there for six weeks, but he had left it alone, hoping it would disappear. While the rest of the musicians gathered at the studio to rehearse for that night's performance, Dizzy and I drove out to the Bahai center in nearby Wilmette. The premise was that we were going to tape background interviews for the show, but clearly it was also a way for Dizzy to seek some solace. He had been a member of the Bahai faith for ten years, because, as he told me, "There's no justice in this system. Everything's dedicated to the protection of the strong. The Bahais are dedicated to the protection of the weak."

When we had set up for the interview, I asked him if, in the early days, when he and Charlie Parker were the architects of bebop, he had been aware that they were changing the course of history. He said, "Our music operates the same as religion operates. We have messengers to the music who come and change the outlook. But there's one thing that they all must do. They must stick to fundamentals. So there's no difference between my playing and Louis Armstrong's playing. But my articulation makes the difference. We didn't create a new music. We embellished what had gone down before." Style, then, for Dizzy, was in the re-articulation of history.

We went into the huge chapel of the Bahai center and Dizzy sat on a bench for a long time and just let his focus go soft. After nearly an hour, he got up, said, "Let's hit it," and we drove back to the television studio. The director of the show was frantic by the time we arrived. He had learned the previous day that trying to block shots in advance with these musicians was like trying to arrange a rendezvous with fish in the ocean. And now the star of the show was out of commission. The audience was milling about, so there was nothing to do but open the doors and see what would happen. The big question, of course, was how Dizzy was going to explain why he wasn't carrying a horn.

It turned out, he didn't. In fact, he carried on so much, dancing, joking, scat singing, banging his rhythm stick, that most of the audience probably didn't even notice he never played. It was a virtuoso performance. He did Flip Wilson through a Lord Buckley filter. He told stories and introduced James Moody like this; "Moody's what you call hard of seeing. Yeah, he's a token out there in Las Vegas. That means he represents the five of us they're supposed to hire." He got the audience clapping some offbeat thing and he did a "shim-shim-shimmy," a shuffle dance with some scatting thrown in. The crowd went nuts. Dizzy turned to Moody and told him, "It looks exciting but it ain't nothing. It's just what you call show business."

Six weeks later, when Dizzy had recovered from surgery, he called me. I answered the phone in Madison and the operator said, "I have a collect call from Dizzy Gillespie, will you accept the charges." I said, "Absolutely," and the unmistakable voice of Dizzy came through and said, "Yeah, I would too if I was you."

He was at a pay phone in an airport, and he had called to thank me for the good work. It was another virtuoso Gillespie performance.

The next month, in October 1976, Judy and I returned to Chicago to tape "Sing Me a Jazz Song." By now, Judy was very pregnant, and all the musicians were very solicitous of her, offering her chairs to sit on and inquiring as to when she was due. I think some of them were concerned that they might be present at the blessed event. The afternoon of our arrival, Judy and I and all the singers went into a small room for a rehearsal. I sat on the floor and Judy sat on the only chair in the room while Jon Hendricks, Eddie Jefferson, Annie Ross and Leon Thomas got together for the first time in their lives and jammed on the song "Cloudburst." It was the hottest jazz singing I have ever heard, and it was one of the songs that, twenty years earlier, had propelled me out of Racine and into the jazz life. I was alone in the room, except for a blissfully pregnant Judy, my memories and my favorite singers. They were indeed present at the blessed event.

Leo was born November 27. Judy's labor was very difficult, more than twelve hours. It was like being skyjacked by a terrorist. Once it got underway, there was very little any of the Lamaze training could do to affect change in a positive way. Finally, Leo arrived at 11:45 A.M. Outside, a frigid wind blew off the frozen lake, but inside the delivery room, it was warm and dark and time stood still.

He arrived suddenly. The room was crowded with attendants, while Judy was hooked up to several machines and intravenous drips. There was starting to be talk of surgery. One minute, it was a crisis, the next minute, there he was. It was the highest high I have ever experienced. My heart leaped into my mouth, and the taste in the back of my throat was exactly the same as I remember from taking LSD, only this time it was truly euphoric, with no fear in my heart or alien buzzing in my ears.

Leo was beautiful. Incredibly, after an intense, twelve-hour journey, he was very pretty. The nurse bathed him, wrapped him in a blanket and handed him to me while the doctor stitched up Judy. Leo looked so familiar to me. It was like looking into the face of my ancestors. I told him, "Everything's okay now, you're here with us, and your name is Leo. And you're just the one we wanted." When the doctor told Judy it was a boy, her first words were, "But what am I going to do with a boy?" Clearly, she had been certain she was having a girl.

Several days later, we brought Leo home in a little car seat, set him on the dining room table and looked at each other. Now what do we do? I, for one, got busier than I'd ever been before. Within a month, I had sold the Porsche and bought a Ford. Funny how a growing family will re-calibrate one's priorities. I awoke every morning with a fresh list of phone calls to make and projects to hustle. I was like a squirrel running around the woods at the first whiff of winter.

For every idea that I was able to make happen, there were at least ten others that went nowhere. There was the idea for a *Rolling Stone* TV show ("Put Hunter on camera," I told Jann, "that's all you got to do..."). There was the "Monk Funk" album, an all-star project that proposed bringing together great jazz and R&B players to record the music of Thelonious Monk. Even my friends in the business thought it was a non-starter. Who would be interested in dancing to Monk? Well, Monk for one, but that's another story. There was the "Paperback Jazz" series, a proposal I put to several major labels as a way of re-cycling their back catalogs. This was before jazz labels, even Blue Note, had an active re-issue program, and my idea was to present the classics at a mid-line price, making them, and the vast history that languished in vaults across the country, available to students. Nope. I even spent several months researching and writing a story on "Women in the Record Business" for *Rolling Stone* — it was not a pretty picture of an old boys club — and in the end, I was given a kill fee not to publish it.

I formed the American Jazz Foundation, a non-profit corporation to document the music through filmed interviews, and I submitted applications to the Guggenheim Foundation and the National Endowment for the Arts. No go. And there was the "Jazz Tour USA" project, a city-by-city proposal to capture our great musicians in their native habitat — a kind of Frank Buck, bring-em-back-alive concept showing the music in context with the rest of the local culture: the food, the art, the architecture. I was, as Henry Miller once so eloquently put it, working feverishly to "beat my anguish into product."

I took these ideas and many more to anyone and everyone who would listen. I not only submitted them to foundations and organizations but also to friends I felt might be interested. I remember particularly a conversation I had with Charlie Watts about "Jazz Tour USA." I said, "You're a great collector of art, and you're a great lover of American jazz. Here's your chance to put your passions together. Imagine what these documents might be worth in ten years. In twenty years. In fifty years." Charlie said the timing was bad for him, but I suspect it was also difficult for him to envision jazz as a long-term investment. As in the rest of the world, jazz existed as a kind of cultural stepchild, halfway between a personal passion and a lost cause, but almost never as an economic opportunity.

The metaphor I learned to love during this period was "building a snowman." Making these projects happen was like trying to build a snowman one flake at a time. When you finally had a handful of them together, you had to carefully roll them into a little ball, and then gradually let the ball's momentum gather in still more flakes. You wanted the gravity of the situation to start working for you, like a little planet collecting its own moons. You continued this until you had a big ball (call it the concept), and then repeated the process two or three times (for the budget, the artists, the crew, etc.). In the end, you added a nice carrot for the nose and maybe some coal for the eyes, and there you were, you had your snowman. However, *first* you had to learn how to make it snow.

At year's end, I had one more mission to accomplish.

Following the 1976 presidential election, it seemed that the two big issues which had marginalized so many young people during the sixties — the Vietnam war and marijuana — might possibly be resolved. Jimmy Carter let it be known that he would be granting amnesty to those who had refused service in Vietnam, and he also hinted that he was willing to explore the decriminalization of marijuana.

It was an historic moment, a chance for the country to heal itself in several ways. Bringing the protesters home was a generous and necessary move, and decriminalizing marijuana was not simply about substance abuse; we had all seen much more damage being caused by alcohol than by pot. On the surface, perhaps it was about inefficient public policy, wasting taxpayer's money by warehousing people who were no threat to others. But down deeper, the issue was about an individual's right to control his or her own inner territory.

It was just a basic issue of personal freedom, as American as apple pie, and supported by the Judeo-Christian doctrine, "You shall know the truth and the truth shall make you free." Over the years, I had often expanded my conception of the world through this herb, and, like millions of other Americans, I resented the self-righteous, anti-pot crowd that continued to lie about its effects and to define my actions as criminal.

I approached Ben Fong-Torres at *Rolling Stone* about covering the Fifth Annual N.O.R.M.L. conference, which was to be held at the end of December in Washington, D.C., but he told me, "We gave enough space to N.O.R.M.L. in the paraphernalia issue." There was that old economic bias again, go with the advertisers and call it the news. I remembered what Keith Stroup, the N.O.R.M.L. director, told me the previous summer about America's elite: they acted as if pot was already legal, while many of the less fortunate were languishing in jail. I decided to attend the conference anyway, if only for my own enlightenment.

So on a cold day in December, I arrived at National Airport and took a cab directly to the house of Stuart Mott, a multi-millionaire supporter of N.O.R.M.L. Poetically, he lived directly across the street from the Supreme Court Building. In front of the place, I saw Hunter Thompson with Bill Dixon of the Carter transition staff. Hunter said he too was on the "transition team," and I said, "That's an interesting turn of phrase. You know, 'transition' is the stage of childbirth most likened to crisis." Obviously, I was still in my Lamaze head.

Inside the house, I met Andrew Weil. I had read his book *The Natural Mind*, in which he put forward the idea that we are all born with the drive to experience "episodes of altered consciousness." I asked him what had brought him here; pot was not really his issue, homeopathic healing was. He said, "Pot is a special case of a special case. It can be useful to some people for a wide range of cures, while to others, it is not useful at all, but rather is unpleasant. There seems to be a pot proclivity and a marijuana metaphobia."

I said, "So getting high is like jazz — it's kind of nice to know that not everybody can dig it. " Andrew said, "Well, consider the solar eclipse. Around the world, natives of so-called primitive cultures applaud the sun and the sky. Here, the federal government sent out a 'Warning! Impending eclipse of the sun!' pamphlet calling the event extremely dangerous, and advising citizens to put a cardboard box over their head and view it through a pin hole in reverse."

"I think," he said, "there is a kind of unconscious sense in people who imagine themselves to be in positions of control that something like the eclipse of the sun, something out of the range of the ordinary, is in some way threatening to their authority, and that therefore you have to try and stop it in some way. And its very interesting that in our day and age, their way of doing it is to use a medical rationale. That is, to say that this is dangerous to your health. I think that's a phenomenon we should think about, because it suggests to me that what we're concerned about here goes much farther than issues of marijuana or decriminalization. Marijuana is a special case of all drugs, and all drugs is a special case of something else. That we can get high in an infinite number of ways, many of which have nothing to do with drugs. And the problem is that in our culture, it is the business of getting high itself which is threatening to people."

Moments later, in a back room at the top of the stairs, I joined several people who were gathered to smoke the *High Times* playmate of the month, a saucy Colombian with a nasty after bite. On the other side of the door, on the first-floor landing, a couple of black pimps were explaining to their girls, "Yeah, these people are trying to make pot legal...No shit?...yeah," and the girls were looking around for some action. It felt like a Laugh-In set party.

I went outside and grabbed a ride to the Hyatt Regency with an unknown source, and when we arrived, searchlights were scouring the hotel from a police helicopter. I walked into the hotel lobby and a bellhop asked, "N.O.R.M.L?" Was it that obvious?

After checking in, I went downstairs to the banquet hall for the opening dinner. Keith Stroup stood at the podium, proclaiming, "We're on the verge!" Then he introduced Hunter, the "keynote speaker," a dangerous turn of phrase. I think Keith maybe made a mistake introducing Hunter as the "chief spokesman for the drug culture." Hunter took umbrage at being "a respectable dope fiend." He listed his credentials somewhat, said he had left his pot in a film can in the little plastic tray with his change and cigarette lighter back at the Chicago airport, and that he was worried that there was no pot at the conference, that the whole decriminalization thing was a sham if there was no dope here. Hunter was flapping about on the podium like a great wounded stork, slapping the ash off his spiked cigarette, trying to rip the microphone cluster into working, and preying on the issue that he couldn't get high. All the while, he was visibly stoned to the teeth.

As if in response, somebody passed around a joint, and I took a hit and passed it on. The guy next to me said, "Put that out. We're worried about the press." I said, "It's cool. I'm a musician." What I meant to say was that the stigma of being high in public is reversed with musicians; people expected their shamans to expose their inner turmoil to one and all. Besides, I felt there was strength in numbers. I took another hit of the fine Thai Stick and almost passed out.

Not a deep, cold pass out where you fall to the floor with your head ringing in the great eternal bell. No, a subtle, phase-shifting pass out, all mid-range and present tense. The lights in the room became very bright, and my mouth got very dry. I focused on Hunter up at the dais, the big bird of Paradise with a broken wing, and Keith, the Good Samaritan, the real Ralph Nader of the Inner Territories. This was the ultimate issue: who was going to control the psychic territory of ordinary people? Would the economic law of supply and demand dominate just as it did in the material world? Could this be the new battlefield, as Andrew Weil had implied?

Hunter was raving on. "My being here is bizarre on its face...standing here with all these crystal chandeliers, as a respectable dope addict...we're all respectable now. It's been about a ten-year war, active combat. At the end of these ten years it looks like we're sitting on the verge of some sort of victory. And I have no weed! That's a very disturbing fact. And the recent issue of *High Times* says it's gonna be a permanent fact. So it's really a hollow victory for me. And if I don't have any weed, we're all in trouble. Because I have a lot of access to weed if I want it...I have a feeling we might be deluding ourselves here. Weed is becoming a connoisseur's drug, like cocaine. I watch *The Untouchables* every night. That and the 'Gong Show'. Yeah, there's a place for geeks in the world. I was gonna go on the 'Gong Show', gonna write a letter and offer to suck a dog's brains out. There are these Brazilians who kill their victims by sucking its brains out...you laugh but go down the Amazon..."

It was a classic, bizarre Thompson rant, which, at its heart, expressed some very real issues. Hunter feared that when the tobacco companies took over production, we would all experience a "really ugly decline in the quality of the weed and certainly a tremendous loss of the whole mystique that has carried us for a long time. It will be like booze, where people who grow their own will be prosecuted like moonshiners. Seriously, how is the government gonna control it?"

In the guerrilla war for the psychic territory, Hunter's main fear was that when they grew grass on Georgia peanut farms, would it still have the Siam kick of good Thai Stick? Visions of American mediocrity haunted all reasonable men. What if they made grass legal but outlawed getting high?

The other subtext here was that a lot of people didn't really want to be dealt with as if they were "normal," and perhaps this was at the core of much of the behavior during the sixties. It went right to the heart of the question of "deviancy," which established the tenor of those times.

After dinner, I went to Hunter's room to talk to him about this, but I found him watching television, with Bill Dixon on the phone to room service. Bill, a masterful political operative with years of room service experience, was saying, "You got any beer? Okay, I'll start with an easier question. What hotel is this? Okay, you got any beer?" A soft-core porn flick was on the tube and Hunter was staring at it, muttering, "Got to get a grip. Focus, concentrate, concentrate, it's cool, right? Just watching a little TV here. What is this we're watching? Jesus! Did you hear that? Somebody get the door..."

He was holding a bottle with a nasty looking root in it. He said, "It's the elixir," and that he'd been working on it for weeks. To a cute, young girl standing off to the side, he said, "I'll drink as much as you will....You go first," and she looked around, flustered, hoping somebody would give her guidance. Seeing none, she said, "Well, I've been working hard all week so I might as well go for it." But she wanted to know what was in it. Hunter told her that it contained, among other things, "twenty-nine hits of windowpane acid," and that it would drive her out of her skull within moments. "Here," he said, "drink this capful." And she did.

The room went quiet. In Hunter's presence, the real and the unreal, the true and the make-believe were mutated. He was an alchemist. There was no telling what was really in the bottle. It could just as easily have been water and an old rutabaga. It didn't matter. It was what you believed was in the bottle that determined your outlook. Hunter forced people to redefine their reality on the spot, to make a new commitment to reality.

Hunter's point was that we should be worried about what would happen if the government regulated the *quality* of our excesses. And, while the average human is nothing more than 98 cents worth of chemicals, some water and a spark of life, Hunter clearly had an extra couple of dollars worth of chemicals onboard that night. But his main fear was that if pot was "decriminalized," and the focus shifted from cops and robbers to lawyers and accountants, we would all lose something essential in our collective soul. And wasn't this Andrew Weil's issue as well: that we lived in a society that was hell-bent on controlling our inner space?

December 31st, 1976, I was playing at a little club in Rockford, Illinois called Charlotte's Web. New Year's Eve is traditionally every musician's biggest pay-check, and even though I hated the idea of not being with Judy and Leo, I could-n't pass up the chance to work. The weather that night was awful and the drive from Madison, which normally takes a little more than an hour, took nearly two. We played the three sets, as agreed, ending at 1 A.M., and I went to find the club owner to get paid. I finally found her in the kitchen, arguing with the staff.

When she saw me, she said, "The crowd doesn't want to leave. Go play another set and I'll pay you another $500."

I said "No thanks, I want to go home to my family."

She said "You have two choices: you can play another set and make the extra money or you can leave right now and not get paid at all."

Out of nowhere, I went quietly berserk. Slowly, I picked up a chair and said, "How about I get my money right now," and was about to pitch it into a huge stack of china and glassware when she held up her hands and said, "Okay, okay, I'll get your money."

She went into a back room, leaving me standing with the chair in my hands in a steaming kitchen full of dirty dishes, foul-smelling garbage and a couple of stunned employees. Nobody said a word. Then she came out and handed me a check.

I said, "What is this? The contract said cash."

She said, "You want cash? Wait around another hour and I'll cash it for you."

I turned and left, told the band the gig was over and got in my car. After a harrowing drive through blinding snow and glazed roads, I finally pulled into my driveway at about 3:30 A.M. I crawled into bed without waking Judy and lay there listening to the small steady breathing coming from the next room.

That year was over.

~~~ Chapter Five

> *"Forms and rhythms in music never change without producing changes in the most important political forms and ways...the new style insinuates itself into manners and customs and from there issues a greater force...goes on to attack laws and institutions displaying the utmost impudence, until it ends by overthrowing everything both in public and in private."*

> —PLATO

1977

In January, I began recording another album for Arista, starting in New York, with Richard Davis on bass and Tony Williams on drums. I had pretty much decided, given the state of radio play and the past performance of my attempts to "cross over," to go "back to the future," acoustic jazz with an attitude. The first song we recorded was Horace Silver's "Silver's Serenade." Tony played with a big, splashy open high hat, and Richard's penchant for placing the beat in the holes rather than on the obvious points created a huge, loopy groove that made my own piano playing seem exotic. I was swimming in a whole new ocean.

After a few more sessions in Los Angeles with Phil Upchurch on bass, Larry Carlton on guitar, John Guerin on drums and, of course, Blue Mitchell on trumpet, I delivered the album, *The Doctor Is In* to Arista. It was March and time to book yet another summer tour. By the first week of May, I was back in New York to meet with Clive Davis on the subject of my career. The meeting was set for the morning of May 10.

At 10 A.M., I was in his outer office, kidding around with his secretary Rose. a warm, family person who made fantastic needlepoints that she had framed and hung on the walls all around her desk. We were chatting away when the buzzer went off and I was ushered into Clive's office.

Unlike the folksy craftwork surrounding Rose's desk, the walls of Clive's inner sanctum were hung with larger-than-life portraits of himself and superstars from his past (Janis Joplin, Miles Davis). His desk seemed elevated slightly so that one was always looking up, half-squinting into the light that came through the windows behind where he sat. It was hard to focus on the man or the legend.

Clive asked me, "How's it going?," but before I could answer, he was on the phone to London with Bob Buziak, his main man there, poo-pooing "punk rock." "It bombed at CBGBs," Clive was saying into the phone, "but you set it up for a night and I'll get as punk as you want." He turned and asked again how my tour was coming. This time I passed the route sheet across the desk to him, but before he could look at it, the phone rang again. He took the call. When he hung up, I just started talking. I said we needed to talk about career "development" and about his being more involved because I felt the company had lost my record last time around. Suddenly, he went very quiet.

I said, first of all, I needed his help to put together a decent tour, "like Warners did for Michael Franks." He looked at me for a long moment, and in his most seductive voice, he said, "Ben, why don't you call up Boz Scaggs and ask him if you can open for him? You know, like Jackson Browne called Joni Mitchell."

I said, "Boz is my friend. If I call him, I'll ask him how his son is and he'll ask me how my son is. Why don't you call up Irving Azoff (Boz's manager) and ask him if I can open for Boz and tell him that you will support it with some money and some promotion?"

He paused for another moment, and said, "Well, then perhaps you should find two or three other people with big names, you know, and form a supergroup, where your writing and playing would stand out more...."

I became exasperated. I said, "That's exactly how to bury myself." I said I was doing everything I could to heighten my musical profile on this new record. ("Yes," he mused, "it's very musical, very musical.") And, in any case, developing my own music was my only chance to further my career, which was, after all, the motto of his company, "Arista, where careers are launched." I said, "Let's put together some kind of plan. Let's do it now. Wouldn't that be more efficient than constantly playing catch up?"

That seemed to push his button. In a quiet, theatrical way, Clive went ballistic. His voice got tight. Whereas, in passing, I had put my hand down on his desk once or twice to emphasize a point while talking, he now banged his hand on the desk four times, each time louder than the last. "You have to *believe* you're a star," he said. "I have *never* worked with someone who doesn't believe that. I don't know *how* to work with someone who doesn't believe that. It means *nothing* that you work hard, that you are respectful. You are naive. I am as powerless as you are to do anything for you. The pieces aren't there. There is no outside person — a critic, a manager — proclaiming that you are the new sensation. That you are '*super*.' Any other adjective won't do. If, in this case, radio stations don't take up your cause, we're helpless."

I was stunned. He had turned so quickly. Perhaps because I had meditated earlier that morning and some of the Delta state was hanging around, I felt a kind of epiphany. I had a sudden clearing of vision, and I heard myself say to Clive, "I don't want to be a star. I just want keep growing as a musician and as a person. I've been working for six years to establish my identity and I'm gonna keep working for sixteen more if that's what it takes." Then, kind of offhand, I said, "There's nothing wrong with being a gourmet item. Look at Danon Yogurt."

He cracked a small smile. He said "Well, you better do some serious self-examination, because that might be your whole problem. Nobody who doesn't want to be a star can make it in this business. Everybody I ever worked with wanted to be a star more than anything, Even your friend Boz." I said, "Not me," and that was the end of the meeting.

Leaving his office, it was clear to me that Clive Davis himself wanted more than anything to be a huge star, and he couldn't understand anybody who didn't want to be like him. He was telling me that I think too small, that the name of the game is size, the bigger the better, bigger-than-life being the goal. My whole person seemed to be out of scale with his attitude; to me, the only thing bigger than life was death. But why was I at all surprised by the direction the meeting had taken? Hadn't my *Rolling Stone* piece virtually predicted the entire conversation?

Walking down the hallway, thinking, "Don't blame the messenger for the message," I ran into Miroslav Vitous, a great bass player who had also signed to Arista back when they were acquiring jazz. He blurted out that Clive had just told him to form a "supergroup." I said, "You're kidding! That's exactly what he told me." He said, "Whatever happened to style? Man, the difference between a real group and super group is the difference between one of Miles' great bands and a jam session."

I said, "It's the end of an era." We shook hands and went our separate ways.

As I walked out into the bright sunlight on 57th Street, I passed a beatup 1966 Chevy and a young black dude leaned out of the passenger's window and said, "Hey, yo, excuse me. Come here. Hey, I'm from the mid-town Self-development Corporation and we're looking for young men like yourself who want to better their position. Do you want to be more successful?"

I walked away laughing. "No man," I said over my shoulder "You got the wrong guy. I want to be less successful."

When you're given a straight line like that, how can you doubt that the play is being directed by a great comic mind?

Released in May, my album, *The Doctor Is In*, had one track that began getting a lot of airplay. It was called "Song for a Sucker Like You," and to help the hype, Arista sent me on a radio promotion tour. I showed up at various stations around the country, along with the local Arista promo man, and we pretended we just happened to be in the neighborhood and dropped by because we all really liked each other. The trip started on a warm June day in Cincinnati. There I met with Bill Scull, the local Arista man, who explained the lay of the land, and, after several drinks in the Holiday Inn bar, decided to level with me.

Stubbing out his cigarette, Bill turned and said, "Look, here's how it really works. Distribution is based on airplay. These days, the life of a record is down to six weeks. Without airplay, the record's maybe gone in two to three. But, if we don't actually monitor the stations, and we *don't*, we don't actually know how much airplay we're getting. When an LP first comes out, everybody at the company at the same time makes a push, calls in favors, and so all the stations who are gonna play it, or at least *report* it to the tip sheets, are hustled. The promo people hype the stations and the stations hype the tip sheets. They report that they're playing a record, but of course, there's no telling if they really are. So we're just really hyping ourselves. And then of course, when the record doesn't sell, cause maybe it's not really getting the airplay everybody says it is, the company turns around and tells the artist, 'Well, we're getting you airplay, but the product just isn't selling; sorry, it ain't in the grooves.' But more than likely none of it's true."

I said, "Why are you telling me this now?"

He said, "Because you should know what you're getting into. See, everybody at the company knows it's hype. But as long as this whole thing is taken as the sign of me doing my job, I'm not gonna argue. Bottom line: only if your record breaks by itself — one track is picked up, for novelty reasons, say — do you have a shot."

I said, "But if people don't get to hear the thing on the radio, how can they ever decide if they like it?"

"Well, that is a paradox, isn't it?" said Bill and lit another cigarette. "They can't. And you can't get played unless you get played. And companies really have to commit themselves out front to an artist or a record or nothing happens. Like right now, here's the truth: Arista is spending a fortune on Alan Parsons, so to be honest, they're not gonna give Ben Sidran too much consideration. Besides which, I hear they're not into you for enough money. They don't have to work too hard to get their money out of you, you know? If somebody at the company doesn't make this thing a personal vendetta, a torch, call it what you will, nothing's gonna go anywhere."

I was feeling the wind go out of the sails when Scull revealed his secret idea. "We need a marketing device," he said and he knew just the item we needed: hemostats. A hemostat is a medical tool that looks like a scissors but has a clamp at the end instead of sharp points, and locks shut. "It's perfect for *The Doctor Is In*," he said. "The programmers love getting swag, little free promotional items. And they'll love this because it's really a roach clip, see, but it has your name on it, too, so every time they get high, they'll be thinking of Ben Sidran and the new album." He delivered this last line like a magician revealing the rabbit. Then he said, "Promise you'll hit on Clive for them."

I'm sitting in the bar of a Holiday Inn with a regional promo man and I'm hearing that all the hard work that went into the album — writing the songs, playing the bad gigs, dragging myself from town to town — might all just come down to hemostats? "Yeah," said Bill, "and we're gonna need a couple of hundred of them within the next couple of weeks or forget it."

Ultimately, of course, radio doesn't exist to deliver programs to the listener, but to deliver listeners to the sponsor. And so by the mid-seventies, record companies had become pawns in the ad-men's game, and "the numbers" they relied on (the Arbitron Ratings, *Billboard Charts*, and Gavin Radio Tipsheets) became skewed by this false world of hypothetical radio exposure. It wasn't actual airplay that mattered but reports of airplay to the trade journals. The illusion of airplay could leverage the funds for things like the hemostats.

Who were the ultimate winners in this scam? Well, booking agents, who wanted and received their commissions; record companies, who wanted and got their cash flow; audiences, who wanted and got what they were told they wanted; radio stations, who wanted and got to glean the biggest harvest (numbers meant dollars); and ad men, who wanted and got to sell their clients' products. They all had a piece of the "win." And who were the losers? Well, at the bottom of this huge pile of "wants," there was the musician, left to survive as best he could. Statistically, less then 5% of all records released "broke even."

All that month, as I went from one station to another with Bill Scull and his colleagues, I heard pretty much the same thing from deejays and program directors across the country. Humble Harv, a local jock at some god-forsaken 20,000-watt radio station, said it best: "I love your music, man, and I play it at home all the time, but it's just too hard to segue with the rock group Kansas, you know?" When I looked at him without saying anything, he just looked away and said, "Ah, what can you do? The people, they're just sheep."

We never did get the hemostats.

Later that summer, I went up to Minneapolis to check out some musicians I had heard about from my friend Dave Rivkin. Dave had been a struggling song-

writer out in L.A. back when Judy and I were living there, and now he was working as a recording engineer in the Twin Cities. I had this idea for cutting bebop
tracks with a half-time shuffle — kind of a follow-up to my Louis Jordan idea —
and I was trying to find players who could go both ways, funk and jazz. Dave
said he knew some guys who might work, and I arranged to come up and meet
them. He himself was recording that week in a studio called Sound Eighty, cutting a demo for some local musician, but he arranged for me to record in the
room across the hall.

I showed up and met bass player Billy Peterson, saxophone player Bob
Rockwell and drummer Paul Lagos, and we spent the afternoon cutting various versions of Charlie Parker's "Moose the Mooche," just trying out different
approaches. At the end of the day, I went across the hall to thank David for hooking me up with these terrific players and he introduced me to the musician he
was working with, a skinny young black kid who was sitting behind the control
board. He was so shy he barely looked up. His name was Prince, and within a
year, the demo they were cutting would be sold to Warner Brothers, David
Rivkin would become "David Z" ("it just sounded better"), his brother Bobby
(now "Bobby Z") would be Prince's drummer, and Prince himself would be
wearing fishnet stockings and a jockstrap on the outside of his pants.

In early November, I left for Europe in a driving snowstorm. There was snow in
Madison, snow in Chicago, snow in New York, and landing in London the next
morning, it was starting to snow there, too. Arista had sent a Rolls to take me to
the office where I did interviews well into the afternoon. The last journalist to
interview me was a Japanese fellow named Angelo Suzuki, a very relaxed yet
focussed young writer who said he would be glad to translate *Black Talk* into
Japanese, and then he gave me the card of his friend, Nobu Yoshinari, a music
publisher in Tokyo. He said Nobu was a great fan of my music and had introduced it to many people in Japan. He suggested I get in touch with Nobu. In
time, I did, and it was the start of a wonderful friendship. Eventually, we even
started a record label together. But at the end of this cold London day, exhausted,
I barely made it back to the hotel and threw Nobu's card into my suitcase, before
I collapsed into a deep sleep.

The next morning, the sky clear and the sun bright, I called a cab to take me
to Glyn Johns' place in the country. The driver got lost on the way but the ride
through the Sussex downs was beautiful. Glyn's new estate was palatial, with gardens, horses, barns, and, in the Tudor mansion, an oversized snooker table. That
afternoon, Jerry Moss of A&M Records and Peter Townsend of The Who came
over, and the conversation, for some reason, turned to drug addiction and to what
extent the record business was responsible for the growing drug problem among

kids. Jerry copped to it immediately, saying, "We have a hand in this, no doubt, and we have a responsibility to do something." I said I thought people basically did what they wanted to do and that the record industry probably had greater culpabilities than this one. Peter looked kind of far away and then, out of nowhere, he said "Eric Clapton was cured of his heroin addiction by this new system where electrodes were attached to his ear lobes and a current was dialed in until he said he felt like he was wrapped in cotton. He said this feeling lasted even after the electrodes were removed." I guess it was meant to provide some context or solace for the conversation: perhaps technology could undo some of the misery that it helped to bring about.

Soon, lunch was announced and everybody stood to go to the dining room, but I had to excuse myself, as I had made a previous engagement. The look on Peter's face when we said good-bye seemed more than a little sad, like a man trapped, wanting out.

I took the taxi back to London, where I was having dinner with an old friend from Sussex. His name was Al Gowan, and he was a fine piano player who now lived in a cold-water flat in a rough part of town. Arriving there was a stark contrast to Glyn's opulent mansion. Instead of luxurious oriental rugs, there was ripped linoleum; instead of beautifully framed oil paintings, the walls held a few photos of musicians, including several of Al on stage. We sat down to a dinner of spaghetti and Guinness (Glyn was having duckling and rare wine). After dinner, Al and I played four-handed piano together, and it felt like old times. Finally, at the end of a long night, I stood at the front door to take my leave and it was then that Al told me he had been diagnosed with brain cancer. We just looked at each other, saying little. What was there to say? And then I went out into the night, in search of a taxi to take me back to my adventure.

The following night was the first gig of the tour, held at a club called Dingwalls. A big, nasty room in an industrial neighborhood, it was a fashionable venue for alternative bands. The band I had brought over from the States was ready to deliver the nonstop groove music we had perfected in the Madison clubs, and the room was stacked with avid fans. Where had all these true believers come from? Before I went up, one guy told me he had paid 30 quid (almost $60) for a copy of my first record, *Feel Your Groove*. Another guy said he had come all the way from Australia. "Even though it's not Friday night," he said, "keep those candles burning. I've waited five years, traveled 12,000 miles to tell you that. And every mile was worth it...." The gig itself was a success and the whole Arista crew was there to see it. Could this be a turning point in my British acceptance?

But, as I read the music press the next day, the answer became all too apparent. There was no mention of our gig but an enormous amount of hype surrounding the so-called "Punk Rock" movement. It seemed to me that the media was promoting it way out of proportion to its musical impact or commercial success. The papers (*Melody Maker, New Musical Express, ZigZag*) were falling over each other to praise unknown groups as the next big thing. The reason for this seemed obvious: "Punk Rock" was the only indigenous British music in years that hadn't been created by the record companies, and hence, was being labeled as a legitimate, ground-swell phenomenon. I saw that my chances of breaking through here were limited.

The next day, we flew to Amsterdam and were met by a young kid who worked for Arista. Riding through town, there was a kind of brooding heaviness in this, the so-called freest of countries. Hash and heroin were openly for sale in the clubs, but I could feel how it would be possible for George Brown to be gathered up off the sidewalk and put on a plane without the chance to go home for a change of clothes. There was, said our Arista guide, a growing connection with Germany, particularly over the issue of terrorism. The Baader-Meinhoff Gang was allegedly using Holland as their base. "The conditions," said the kid, "are reminiscent of Germany in the thirties."

Before I went on stage that night at the Paradiso, the owner, in an offhand way, said, "The people come to hear you sing, I think, not play. It is your voice that people love." It was the first time anybody had said that to me but it was something I would hear often throughout the trip: Europeans loved the *sound* of my voice, the untrained, human aspect of it, even if they sometimes didn't understand the words. That night, I came out talking and the crowd immediately leaned in. It started out hot and got hotter. The stage was "in the round" with kids piled on top of tables and chairs on all sides of us, and once we got them on their feet, we never let them sit down. We delivered dance music and conversation and bebop and after a ninety minute set that ended with a long stamping call for yet another encore, I left the stage feeling exhilarated and wired. The "human aspect" of the music, so often disregarded in America's search for "bigger and better," meant a lot here.

After the gig about a dozen of us went to a restaurant where we ate steaks and smoked hash and talked the night away. At the table were several journalists, and one of them, a very sharp, correct reporter from the major morning paper, the *Telegraff*, let slip that he had recently talked at length with both Steve Miller and Boz Scaggs. He said he wanted to tell me "a secret":

I said, "What is that?"

He said, "They both wondered why somebody like you, who is so smart and has such a grasp of things, is so naïve when it came to the music business. They both found it curious that you are playing in small clubs rather than going for the big record." And then he asked me, "Do you feel bitter?"

I said, "First of all, there's no formula for selling out. If there was a line to stand in, I might be standing in it tomorrow. But it's every man for himself out here, and I'm just doing what I know how to do. And second of all, your question is really just a sign of a deeper issue: why are Steve and Boz and I communicating with each other through a reporter? This is one of the things I hate most about so-called stardom. It separates people, from each other, and from real life." He nodded and wrote down my answer and I felt like I'd been setup.

The next day we flew to Brussels. People in Belgium seemed to be living very well; even those on unemployment, I came to understand, were being paid more than $100 per week. This was because Brussels was the arms capitol of the world, and Antwerp was the diamond center. If there was a problem getting the diamonds out of an embargoed South Africa, I was told, "There is always a way around it. People here between the ages of 35 and 45 are very hypocritical. They all claim not to know what's going on. But they all know why it is they are able to live so well."

The concert too was a bit odd. The crowd was absolutely silent between songs, very attentive, but in a way that I didn't understand. Too polite, really. Yet there was big applause after each number and a call for an encore after an hour-and-a-half set. After the gig, the radio interviewer said "Well, they need to be prodded and they are used to being prodded very hard. You and Tom Waits and Randy Newman, they don't really understand." But Mick Cater, our British tour manager, just shrugged and said, "Well mate, it's Belgium, isn't it?"

Twenty-four hours later, we arrived in Stockholm. It was a Friday afternoon and we were scheduled to do a television show that evening, which turned out to be a kids show, starring kids and run by kids. The host was a very young, very pretty boy who was also a well-known drag queen. After our rehearsal, the director of the show, a chain-smoking woman in her forties, pulled me aside and said, "The engineers like you very much — not like these so called progressive bands that write political lyrics mostly very bad and play very loud, also very bad."

Playing the show felt like doing a *Monty Python* sketch, perhaps "The Ministry of Ridiculous Jazz Venues." After surviving the taping, we returned to the hotel, and went to the bar where we were scheduled to play in a couple of days. We were not heartened to discover the sign over the stage that lit up when the band played over 90db (it said "you are playing too loud"). The bartender said, "Ya, in some clubs, if the sound is too loud, the power is simply cut off to the stage. This can help sometimes." Apparently volume was the issue here as well.

On our day off, we wandered around the streets and saw that many of the young people, like elsewhere in Western Europe, seemed lost, with no direction, no spirit and no work. The preconditions of Punk Rock were rampant, and volume, self-mutilation, and hostile indifference — a kind of aggressive malaise — was everywhere. This was born out on Monday, the night of our gig. The crowd came drunk and got drunker by the minute; they constantly grabbed, pushed and bumped into each other for no apparent reason. Very young people, thirteen, fourteen years old, blasted out of their heads on alcohol, acting thick as bricks. They leapt up and down and called it dancing. They even leapt up and down when the deejay played "Song for a Sucker Like You," but when we played it live around midnight, they just looked at us like we were a painting. Nothing in their eyes. I thought to myself, "Perhaps Ingmar Bergman was a documentarian." Very scary.

Two days later, flying to Hamburg after a nice gig in Oslo, was even scarier. The flight was routed through Copenhagen, but the Lufthansa 737 from Copenhagen to Hamburg was surrounded by German troops with rifles and machine guns and we were delayed in leaving. First, we were required to identify our luggage, which was spread out on the tarmac, before they would load it on the plane. Then we filed one at a time past the stone-faced soldiers. As we prepared for takeoff, everybody paid attention to the life-preserver demonstration. Apparently that morning, the Baader-Meinhof gang had threatened to blow random Lufthansa flights out of the sky with SAM missiles, and so this plane was not even a tenth full.

Landing in Germany, everything seemed very clean, very tight, with an incredible police presence. We were met by a kid with long hair, who told me, "I have been sent to take you to your rooms," in a Colonel Klink accent. As we drove to town, four jets roared directly over our heads, not 200 feet off the ground. "We're very close to East Germany," the kid explained. As we drove, I couldn't help thinking that every man over the age of fifty looked to me like a potential camp guard, every young person like a possible Hitler youth. I thought to myself "Ah, people are just people," but I was obviously spooked. Only thirty-five years earlier, I would not have been riding in this car, a musician on the way to a gig; I would have been riding on a freight train. "Things are very bad in Germany now," the kid was muttering to himself, and he stepped on the gas.

It started to rain and the kid started driving faster, as if to prove he was not afraid of conditions. The speedometer crept past 160 kph. He was going on about some ex-Nazi who still owned 85 percent of all the newspapers in Germany—"Last month," he said, "they passed a law within two days making it possible to detain so-called political suspects for six weeks without lawyers. Now everywhere there is fear." I said it sounded like 35 years ago. He said "Yes, that's not so very wrong."

The speed of the car and the topic of conversation made me nauseous. To distract myself, I reached into the glove box and found a road atlas. Paging through it I noticed detailed maps of Poland and Belarus as well. I found Warsaw. I looked for Drohiczyn, the city of my father's birth. Yes, there it was, very close to the Polish / Russian border. The car lurched and as I grabbed at the atlas my eye fell on a small dot just north of Drohiczyn. It did not appear to be connected by a road at all, just a speck out in the Polish wilderness: next to it was written the word "Sidra."

I felt a chill: perhaps a Sidransky was just somebody who came from Sidra. Somebody who made it to Drohiczyn, and then to Warsaw, and then to Russia, and then walking through China, to San Francisco and finally to Centerville, Iowa, where he sent for his children, who came to him under the cover of night, surviving only because their mother had blue eyes. Perhaps this was where the journey had begun. I wondered what my family's real name might have been.

The kid was railing on now, roaring through the rain-soaked afternoon. He was giving a history lesson. He said that the big difference between Germany and other European countries was that Germany was originally made up of many decentralized, strong states. "Can you imagine," he said over the slap of the wipers, "one thousand separate kingdoms, all worried about defense? This is why everybody here takes so naturally to the militaristic notion. It is cultural." I tried to make a joke. I said, "Perhaps that explains German disco; it's all just marching music." He did not laugh. The huge Mercedes windscreen wiper slapped back and forth, like a metronome, marking disco time.

No, there was not much laughing going on in Germany. Even in Belgium the jokes had been understood. But that night, at the Romer club, a very artsy little club in Bremen, I thought perhaps there was a language barrier. Yet, when I went into the audience after the gig, they all spoke to me in perfect English. They understand the words, but perhaps not the humor behind them.

Leaving Germany was another grizzly scene, right out of a bad World War II movie. Guards with machine guns examined every piece of baggage, bodies were searched, and passports were photocopied and stored in a computer. On the wall, there were posters of terrorists with a huge X through the dead ones. As we walked to the plane, we were surrounded by guards and there was even a small police tank. Hard to believe that it was 1977, but of course, in 1939, it was probably equally hard to believe. People have a hard time believing that history, which is written by the survivors, is actually being lived daily, by us all.

Back in London, I had one night before returning to the States. That night, I had a very vivid nightmare, a dream of terror, of science fiction desperation. There were specific details and information of a time and place that I didn't remember knowing. For example, there was a group of terrorists who had a vat of noxious chemicals which, when released into the air, would spread a pneumonia-like virus, the smallest amount of which could infect the body with a special sinister man-made disease that had a life of its own. I remember in my dream thinking that I was peeking into some distorted vision of the future, and that nobody would be safe then, not even in Madison.

Throughout this time of perpetual traveling, Madison had become the ground for me; everything else was up in the air. In the winter, if I was at home, I shoveled the snow; in the autumn, I raked the leaves. I used to tell Judy that our house was like a beautiful Bed and Breakfast, the nicest stop in my endless wanderings.

Outside observers must have thought that my being gone so often was hard on our marriage, but, in many ways, it was just the opposite. Just as Madison remained a respite for me, a place where I could be myself and which helped me define myself, it was also a place where Judy could grow into the person she wanted to be. Coming home from a three-week tour, flattened by the routines of the road or inspired by the people I had met, I would often find Judy in a state of activity and joy. She too loved her work, she loved her friends, and she loved the freedom to come and go as she pleased. Madison contributed to the success of our marriage, just as my constant traveling did.

Or, as we always said around the house, "How can I miss you if you won't go away?"

1978

In January, I went back to Los Angeles to record yet another album for Arista (*A Little Kiss in the Night*). I was determined, if nothing else, to find a new way to combine bebop and dance music. At the time, it just wasn't being done. There was so-called "fusion" music, which was essentially rock and roll with extended "jazzy" solos. But I was after something else entirely. I wanted to maintain the bebop forms from the forties and fifties but come up under them with a kind of R&B groove.

So that year, I went into Cherokee Studios with Abe Laboriel on bass and Bill Meeker on drums, and using standard bebop changes as a premise, I set up a vamp for Abe and myself and had Bill play a half-time shuffle. This laid the backbeat on the "4" so that the front of each bar opened up. Without thinking, I started talking to them through their headphones, just a goofy rap off the top of my head, something to distract them so that the groove kept going without too much premeditation. I began improvising a story:

"This is a story about a young man whose true love was blind
    So he was crying all the time
Thought he would find a new love in Paris, France
    He's gonna do the Paris dance
But when he got to town, all he found was he couldn't speak French
    So he was sitting on a bench
All alone, child, not to mention embarrassed.
But music is the language of love, play on play on
    Bud Powell was in town
So he thought he'd make down to the Chat Qui Peche
    And order a round of the rarest
    —wine that is —
But as so often happens in this world of travail and cheap wine
    The ridiculous becomes sublime
And your final reward is down at the end of the line
Because just then someone put a side on the box
And Bird flew by, chasing the fox..."

And then, on a visual cue, we broke into a burning 4/4, quoting Charlie Parker's "Moose The Mooche" and I sang Jon Hendricks' lyrics, "Bird fluttered by and sang a hipper melody from the sky, bebop, bebop...."

Listening to the playback, I knew this was the thing I had been searching for, the Louis Jordan connection, a new way to reinterpret a lot of my favorite jazz standards. It was swinging and funky, and it also reminded me of the little jazz dance Blue Mitchell used to do. He would put his hands in his pockets, hitch up his pants, and execute a little time step, kind of tip-toeing up to the edge of some unseen precipice to peer over, as if looking into the future of the music. This day, I found myself leaning into the track, like Blue, and when the playback ended, I reached for the phone to give him a call.

There was no answer. For the next few days I kept trying but still no answer. And then, driving down Sunset Blvd., I heard a record that changed my plans. Listening to a pop station, I heard a beautiful jazz saxophone solo and I knew immediately it was Phil Woods, but I had no idea who the singer was. The song was called "Just the Way You Are," and of course it turned out to be Billy Joel, the same guy who had come down to hear us at the Other End the year before. Returning to the studio, I made some more calls and discovered that, by coincidence, Phil was in L.A.

One week later, I was sitting in the control room when Phil and two other characters walked in. Wearing his trademark leather cap and his big smile, Phil unpacked his horn and went right to work. "Hey, baby," he said, "What are we doing today?" He listened to just a few moments of the track and then went into the studio. I turned to John Mills, the engineer and said, "Record it, whatever it is."

In the studio, Phil took out his horn, put on the earphones and as the track played down, just ripped off a series of phrases and then a solo that was fully formed and completely integrated with the music. He was flying blind, but he made continuous, infinitesimally small adjustments so that his playing felt as if he had been there, live in the studio when the track was recorded. It was inspired, completely unpredictable, and, in my experience, unprecedented, the way he was able to anticipate a musical terrain he had never transited before. At times he even seemed to set up what was pre-recorded, which, of course, was impossible; he had no foreknowledge of the arrangement or other changes. When his final notes died off, there was a kind of stunned silence in the control room. One of the guys who had walked in with Phil said "Yeah, baby!" Phil said, "What do you think?"

I had never heard such a completely inspired first take on an overdub before. Usually musicians, like Blue Mitchell, took their time, made several passes before finding the right way in, through and out of a previously recorded track. But Phil had just stepped out onto the wing and executed a ballet so graceful, so humorous and so hip that the entire flight became something much greater than it had been before he arrived.

I said, "Yeah, Phil. That was fantastic. Do you want to do another pass?" He said, "Whatever you want, baby."

We rolled tape again and put his next take on a different track. He played great, but it didn't have the transcendency of the first one. We tried a third pass, and it was even less inspired. Phil was starting to think about what he was playing; you could hear his thought process. He was starting to play himself rather than what came into his head. I said, "Come on in," and turned to the engineer and said, "We'll keep the first pass." Lesson learned: when you're dealing with a jazz master, roll tape on the rehearsal. You want to record him when he plays what he *doesn't* know rather than what he does know.

Phil put his horn back in the case, smiled, said "Thanks, baby," and he and the boys split just the way they came. The whole thing had taken less than an hour.

That July, a group of musicians — including Randy and Michael Brecker, Mike Mainieri, Muhal Richard Abrams, Pharoah Sanders, Steve Khan, Steve Jordan and myself — gathered in New York City to catch a flight to Switzerland to perform at the Montreux Jazz Festival. It was to be my first live recording and I had prepared several new pieces, including a song called "You Got to Eat It" that I had written with Tony Williams. I also had an idea for a backbeat version of "Someday My Prince Will Come" and Mike Mainieri, a great arranger as well as a brilliant vibraphone player, had written out some charts. We planned to rehearse once we got to Montreux.

Arriving in New York to catch the international flight, I was suffering from what I thought to be a bad cold, but gradually, it degenerated into something much worse. A nasty lung congestion cleared up, then flared into a mean cough and sore throat. The day we got on the plane to leave, I knew the throat was gone. We landed in Switzerland, took the picturesque ride through the Alps to the city on the edge of Lake Geneva and checked into an elegant old hotel, the Eden Au Lac. That night, the cough got worse, and the next morning I awoke feeling like a small animal had clawed the inside of my throat. I took all sorts of medicine but nothing touched the pain or put out the fire. I tried to relax, but the truth was nibbling at the edges of my awareness like the creature itself: I was very sick and getting sicker.

That afternoon, the Brecker Brothers and Mike Mainieri recorded their set at the Casino, a large open room filled with hundreds of happy kids who had been camping outside the building for nights, and the set was electric. I listened in the control room, and everyone, even saxophonist Stan Getz, who was hanging around that day, was visibly knocked out. After the set, there was a big press conference where everybody said how happy they were to be at Montreux, and then we were scheduled to rehearse my music. But it never happened.

Everybody was too high on the day's performance, so the rehearsal was canceled. To cover myself, I cornered Mike and Randy Brecker and asked, "You guys know 'Someday My Prince Will Come' in F, right? Well, we're going to do it with a half time backbeat. How about 'I Remember Clifford' in E-flat? Cool." That was the rehearsal. Later, seeing my anxiety, Mike Mainieri told me not to worry, everything would work out, but that night, after watching a spectacular sunset over Lake Geneva, I collapsed on the bed, sinking faster than the sun. I couldn't stop the pain in my throat or the fear that I was going to my doom the next day with no voice and no plan.

In the morning, I woke to find that we were all being thrown out of the hotel. There had been some mix-up with the Festival Office and we were told to pack up and move across town. From that point on, the rest of the day became a kind of religious blur. Partly out of the fever that induced semi-hallucinations, partly out of a kind of gallows humor that engulfed me, something inside just let go. I stopped fighting and let the river flow. By mid afternoon, I had begun to spit blood, but I looked at it impassively, as if it was happening to somebody else. I just hoped I would not be hospitalized before the set. I was actually becoming fascinated with my situation. It was like watching a slow motion car crash; I wanted to know how it would end. I meditated into another sunset, and then quietly as possible, I went to meet my fate. Slowly, as in a dream, the evening unfolded.

Backstage, Mike Mainieri huddled with drummer Steve Jordan and bass player Tony Levin, talking them through the set. He told them chords, feelings, things to watch out for. They nodded, asked a few questions, laughed here and there, totally relaxed. Mike handed out some charts he had prepared and then, seeing me with a kind of fifty-meter stare on my face, he reached over and hugged me.

On stage, I sat down at the piano, and was pulled out of my reverie by the voice of promoter Claude Nobs saying, "Ladies and gentlemen, Ben Sidran," and then a great wave of applause broke on the shore of my consciousness. I looked up into the Casino and there were a thousand happy people, ready and waiting for something to happen. Before I had time to panic, or wonder how to get this machine off the ground, Steve Jordan counted out one bar and hit a groove. The band stepped into the first song, and from the start, the music was effortless. There was a great power coming from the stage; it was like handling the Porsche all over again, where one could step on the accelerator or pull hard to the left and the vehicle was one with the thought. Song after song, we read through Mainieri's charts, and one after another, Mike and Randy and Steve played solos that were uplifting, even soaring. Randy's extended cadenza on "I Remember Clifford" sent chills down my spine. It was like hearing Clifford himself.

The whole set had the feeling of gliding on great wings, sailing on Alpine thermals. Half way through, I realized I couldn't even feel my throat. Some jazz alchemy had taken place inside my body: I too was out on the edge of the wing, working without a net, secure in the knowledge that falling might be the best thing that could happen to me.

When I walked off stage, I shook a few hands, made my way back to the musician's lounge and fell into a kind of swoon. I was feverish and the voices of the people around me sounded like babbling water running down the distant mountainside. I had surrendered, I had survived, and in my fugue state, I understood perfectly how jazz players turned a potential disaster into a moment of triumph. The act of surrender, the art of recovery: what was jazz if not the revelation of transcendence within every mundane moment, the possibility that exists in every action for an even more profound reaction, an act of faith which lives in every minute of our life?

Two days later, I was back in Madison, diagnosed with walking pneumonia and put to bed for three weeks. One morning, while lying there under my covers, I remembered a conversation I had had on the plane ride home. In my fever, I had gone up to Pharaoh Sanders and asked him, "Man, whatever happened to that hat with the mirror on the inside?" He looked at me with those soulful eyes and said, "I lost it. At Slugs." And in remembering the moment, I understood that along with the hat, we had all lost so much since the late sixties.

Two jokes I think of as being about the record business:

A man walks into a bar. Under his arm he's carrying a three-legged pig. The man grabs a stool at the end of the bar and puts the pig down on the stool next to him. The man orders a mango daiquiri, the pig orders a whiskey shot straight up.

The bar tender says, "That's incredible, a talking pig!"

The man says, "That's nothing. This pig is so smart, he's actually working on a cure for cancer. Not only that, he's singularly brave. Why only last month, during the big flood, he jumped into the swirling waters and dragged two children to safety."

The bartender is flabbergasted to be in the presence of such a great pig. "By the way," he asks the man, "How did he lose his leg?"

"A pig this smart," says the man, "you don't eat him all at once."

A man walks into a bar. He sees a spectacularly beautiful woman and, approaching her delicately, says, "You are a dream come true. I wonder if you would be interested in coming with me to Paris. We'll fly on the Concord, stay at the George Cinq, eat caviar, drink Champagne, and later that night, floating down the Seine, we'll make tender, passionate love."

The woman says, "That sounds great."

The man then says, "Well then, how about if I give you five bucks and you step outside and give me a blow job?"

The woman is outraged. She says, "What kind of woman do you take me for?"

He says, "We've already established that. Now we're just negotiating the price."

1979

B y February 1979, I was off of Arista and had signed with Horizon Records, an adventurous record label being run by my friend Tommy LiPuma. Tommy had also signed Dr. John, among others, and was in the process of trying to sign a whacked out singer named Rickie Lee Jones. Clearly, he was revisiting the spirit of Blue Thumb Records, where artists found a home because of, rather than in spite of, their individual quirks.

I had written lyrics to semi-obscure jazz songs and was going to record them in a contemporary R&B vein. An offshoot of my "Monk Funk" concept, I didn't want to cover jazz "hits" but, rather, take insider's songs — like Gigi Gryce's "Minority," Thelonious Monk's "Ask Me Now" and Randy Westin's "Hi Fly" — and make them sound like they were somehow part of today's popular vocabulary. Tommy put at my disposal all the technology money could buy. If it worked, it would be a musical sleight of hand that delivered the essence of bebop to a whole new generation in a whole new way. I even knew the title: *The Cat and the Hat*, a tribute to Monk, who always wore a lid.

I began gathering together the material, one song at a time. One song led me directly into the den of a show business lion. Like many jazz fans, I had long adored the melody of Neil Hefti's "Girl Talk," but found Bobby Troup's original lyrics so outrageously sexist that there was no way to sing them. I had written some new lyrics, replacing the old lines about how women just chatter away over "inconsequential things" with lyrics about the risk of falling in love, but I needed permission from Bobby to record them. I got Bobby on the phone and plunged ahead.

He said, "Yeah, a lot of people want to write new lyrics for that song. I don't see what the problem is with my lyrics."

Instead of going into detail about why the swinger sentiment of the late fifties was no longer apropos, I said, "Bobby, can I just sing you my lyrics now and you can decide for yourself?"

He said, "Sure, kid, take your shot." Over the phone, from two thousand miles away, I sang Bobby Troup my words to "Girl Talk":

"You take your chances when you fall for a girl like that
You pay your money and take your chance with love and that's a fact
Then later on you maybe wonder why you hung your hat
But later on it's later on and there's no looking back
She bats her eye, you want to cry, she sighs her sigh you want to fly
Run don't walk, that's just girl talk...."

When I was done, there was a moment of silence. And then Bobby said, "Okay, I like them. You can record them. But you can never seek the money." I agreed, and to this day, even though several other people have recorded my lyrics to the song, Bobby Troup's estate collects the royalties.

Writing the lyrics for the other songs was a challenge, and I thought often of what Jon Hendricks had told me about internalizing the music rather than trying to fit the words into the melodies "like a jeweler places stones in a setting."

The song that proved the most difficult was Frank Rosolino's "Blue Daniel." Frank was a legend in Los Angeles, a wild, happy-go-lucky guy who sat in the trombone section of Johnny Carson's "Tonight Show" band for years. They called him the "Silver Fox" because of his rich, white mane and his dapper appearance. He loved to sail and play golf, and he enjoyed a lot of friends, a lovely wife and two beautiful kids. All in all, he was on top of the world, leading the ideal jazz life. He had written "Blue Daniel" in the fifties, and I had first heard Cannonball Adderley's recording of it back in Racine. It was a simple, wistful melody, and when I met Frank back in 1973 and told him I wanted to write lyrics and wondered if the title meant anything in particular, he said, "It's just a waltz. Like the Blue Danube. But feel free."

Since then, I had made several attempts but always came up short; my tries seemed too inconsequential for the underlying elegance of Frank's simple little theme. Then one night in 1979 I got a phone call from a friend in L.A. Had I heard about Frank? No, I said, what about Frank? Apparently, he had come home earlier that same day with a gun and, without explanation, shot his wife, his children and then killed himself.

There was a long silence. I couldn't say anything. My mind went blank. I was sitting at the piano, so after I hung up, I started playing "Blue Daniel." And as if from out of thin air, the following lyrics arrived in my head:

"Life's a lesson, you can fail it
You can set your spirit free or jail it
But setting it free is no guarantee it's gonna fly when you sail it.
The object is to ride it,
But setting it free while you're sitting astride it
Isn't easy
You can learn a lot by going crazy,
You can fail it, you can set your spirit free or jail it.
But setting it free is no guarantee it's gonna fly when you sail it.
And if you feel like you're in prison
And no one is coming to talk or to listen,
Take it easy, know that no one ever has it easy,
No one ever learns to fly by freezing,
Life's a lesson you can pass or fail."

These lyrics, eventually titled, "Life's a Lesson," were as close as I've ever come to receiving dictation from a higher authority.

From the first note to the last, *The Cat and the Hat* sessions were something special. Drummer Steve Gadd in particular was an inspiration to work with. When we cut Monk's "Ask Me Now," the first take felt so great that there was talk about perhaps not even cutting a second one. I wanted the security of having a backup so, from the vocal booth I said, "Well, I missed a few phrases and I could probably get it right the next time." And in my earphones I heard Steve say, "Ben, nobody cares if you get it right. They just want you to feel good. And it's not gonna feel any better than that one felt." And that was it. We only cut the one take.

Another masterpiece of the session was the Miles Davis / Victor Feldman song "Seven Steps to Heaven." I had written some very simple lyrics — "One, two, three, four, five, six, seven, steps to heaven" — and Mike Mainieri, my co-producer, had come up with a chart featuring Steve playing a Latin clave pattern against a straight-ahead 4/4. There were several intricate time shifts and section changes, and the chart was eight pages long. Steve taped his copy around the inside walls of the drum booth so he could read it down from left to right. I was playing electric piano, facing the drum booth, and watched him do this. Mike counted off the song and Gadd sounded like three guys playing at once. He was reading the chart down flawlessly, top to bottom, and when the song was over, he jumped up from behind the drums and ran into the hallway. I walked out there and I heard him on the pay-phone, talking to his manager, saying, "I just recorded something and it's exactly the way I want my own record to sound." In fact, a transcription of his playing on "Seven Steps to Heaven" found its way into drum magazines, and to this day, the recording is considered one of Gadd's finest performances.

To ice the cake, saxophonist Joe Henderson came in to the play the solo on "Seven Steps." Watching him work was also a revelation. He had a huge recorded sound, but his secret was in the fact that he played very softly and let the microphone do the work. As Glyn had taught me years before, in the world of technology, reality often stands on its head, and small is big, soft is loud and what you get is rarely what you see.

The finished project really was a first-class example of bebop songs captured with a funk attitude — the marriage of the past and the present, of classic jazz and contemporary dance grooves — and musicians began talking about the record even before it was released. The buzz was fantastic.

Before leaving L.A., I went to see photographer Barry Feinstein, who was going to shoot and design the cover. I told him the title and said that it was "all about the spirit of jazz in New York during the fifties, captured with the attitude and technology of the seventies."

Barry said, "Well, we'll have to shoot the cover in black and white, that's for sure. Jazz was always in black and white back then. We can shoot it on the Warner Brother's lot, they got a New York street there, solid brownstones. We'll do it at 6 A.M. to get the right lighting. Very East Coast. No California sun. Oh yeah, and we'll need a midget."

"A midget?"

"Yeah, he'll be the cat in the hat. We need a midget wearing a hat, like a cool jazz lid from the fifties."

"A midget?"

"Yeah, you know, midgets have always been on the jazz scene. Like what's his name, the little cat at Birdland?"

"Pee Wee Marquette..."

"Yeah, Pee Wee...."

The next day I was standing at Nick's hot-dog stand on the corner of Hollywood and Vine, telling a friend about my conversation with Barry. As I was saying, "We need a midget..." my friend, who was looking over my shoulder, suddenly went pale and said, "Well, here he comes now." I turned around and saw a dapper little fellow wearing a hip New York lid walking right towards me.

I stepped directly into his path and said, "Excuse me, you don't know me, but..." and he stopped me right there. He said, "You don't have to know me to say hello." He had a gravely Brooklyn accent, a real street kind of guy, and I just relaxed and told him my whole story, concluding with, "So the photographer says we need a midget wearing a hat just like the one you're wearing."

He reached into his pocket and handed me his card, which simply read "Billy Curtis" and a phone number. "Have your man call me," he said. Only in L.A.: a professional midget! I couldn't place his face but it sure looked familiar. A couple of days later, as he and I sat on the steps of a faux brownstone on the Warner Brothers backlot while Barry Feinstein, snapped our picture, I found out why. Billy Curtis had been one of the chief Munchkins in the *Wizard of Oz*. Sitting on the stoop, he told me the whole story of when the little people rioted.

"I was hired to do the *Wizard of Oz* along with a lot of other little people," he said. "And you know, it was the first time we ever got together, so many of us. We were all staying at this hotel and one night a bunch of us guys were having a few drinks in the bar. And you know, these straights walk in. A couple of guys and a couple of nice looking women. And some of the little people, they started hitting on the chicks. Normally, it wouldn't have happened. But we had put up with a lot of shit on that movie and we were feeling good that night. And the women seemed to dig it. I mean a lot of straight chicks really dig getting it on with a little guy. So these straight guys, they didn't know what to do. They don't like it and some words get exchanged, and the next thing you know, a fight breaks out. Now these straights, they can't bring themselves to hit a little person. You know, psychologically. But we got no problem. And pretty soon it turns into a brawl. I mean we're kicking their ass and then the police came in and saved 'em. Yeah," Billy said, "they were some good looking women." He was The Cat.

The final act in the saga of *The Cat and the Hat* was the phone call I received from Tommy LiPuma in September, one week before the scheduled release date. "I don't know how to tell you this," he said, and I already knew what was coming.

The demise of Horizon Records and *The Cat and the Hat* ("It got shipped over a cliff," Tommy told me later) was just one of the many portents that year reminding me that life is what happens while you're making other plans. The previous spring, I had gone to New York to attend Blue Mitchell's wake at the Village Gate. He had died of brain cancer in June, even as we were finishing *The Cat and the Hat,* and walking through the echoing hall of the old jazz club, I felt a real loss knowing that the sound of his horn had been silenced. "Baby boy," he had called me.

Also that fall, Eddie Jefferson had come through Madison. I hadn't seen or talked to him since we taped *Sing Me a Jazz Song* three years earlier. I went to see him at the hotel lounge where he was working, and after the first set, he introduced me to his saxophonist, Richie Cole. Richie said, "Yeah, we met before." I said, "We did?". He said, "Yeah, I was there with Phil Woods the afternoon he played on your record. I was there when you asked him to do a second take, and he looked at me like 'Who is this cat?' We were all real glad when you decided to keep the first take."

That night, Eddie talked about a disagreement he was having with Jon Hendricks. Along with Jon, Eddie was one of the masters of vocalese, a self-taught musician with a great physical presence and a strong spiritual side. The disagreement with Jon had something to do with money. Eddie wasn't specific, but he kept alluding to Jon's interest in the material side of things. "This music is not about the money," Eddie said, stating the obvious. "You come to this music like you come to God. This music is about the spirit of man."

Two weeks later, Eddie, too, was dead, murdered on the streets of Detroit.

One day not long thereafter, I was in L.A. at the A&M lot to help Tommy and his secretary clean out the Horizon offices. We took Tommy's gold records off the walls and placed them in boxes. We gathered up the promotional items and the Rollodex and stored them away for another day. Tommy was dispirited and angry, but he was moving to Warner Brothers Records, where he would eventually produce million-selling albums for a string of artists. He might not be happy at how the business was treating him, but he was still comfortable as a player in the industry. For me, it was more of a watershed moment. I had thought *The Cat and the Hat* would be the album that finally broke through for me. We had had the resources, the ideas, the musicians and the marketing machinery in place. In many ways, it had been the culmination of all my work during the seventies, traveling with a band, doing the promotion, searching for an original way to combine bebop, funk and pop production. Losing this record was losing a lot more than just another sales opportunity. It really felt like I was being delivered a message and I was trying hard to read it.

A&M Records had ostensibly dropped the Horizon label because of the economic and spiritual depression of 1979. Americans were being held hostage in Iran, interest rates were nearing 17 percent and the country seemed to suddenly go rudderless in a psychic storm. Like many other areas of the economy, record sales experienced a strong and cathartic "correction." In the current economic squall, the first thing overboard was jazz. In the past, as John Hammond had pointed out, the record business accommodated the cyclical nature of things and continued to invest in the future of its roster, but by the eighties, when the quarterly report had become the most distant horizon to which businesses looked, this was simply seen as foolhardy.

Why did Horizon go out of business? In part, it was sacrificed to fashion: country music was becoming the latest thing, and jazz was failing to sell the way the corporations had hoped it would. Jazz stations around the country were going country. It seemed clear that the economic climate was trying to tell us something. It's like the joke about the boy who wanted to grow up and be a jazz musician. His mother tells him, "You have to chose one; you can't do both."

When we had put the last framed picture in the last cardboard box, Tommy turned to me and said, "Ben, there's nothing worse than when a record company gets disappointed. Once they fail to sell something, it becomes anathema — an artist, an idiom, whatever. The trend is to move away from failures rather than remain committed in principle and re-examine what's going on. When the fuck is off, the fuck is off!"

Or, as we like to say, when you come to a fork in the road, take it.

≋ Chapter Six

"I recognize an individual when I see his contribution; and when I know a man's sound, well, to me, that's him, that's the man..."

— JOHN COLTRANE

1980

O ne night, in the deep freeze of the February winter, I sat in Leo's room, reading him a bedtime story.
"In the great green room
There was a red balloon
And a telephone
And a picture of..."
I heard the soft flip-flipping of the clock radio, the even breathing from under the quilt, the smell of a wet thumb, the utter stillness outside.

When he finally fell asleep, I went outside to go to a gig. The car wouldn't start. It was frozen solid, as was everything outside that night. The key practically stuck to my naked fingers as I inserted it in the ignition. It turned, but there was dead silence. Not even a groan. For a moment, the thought occurred to me to just sit there and freeze: it's not such a bad way to go. Just slow down into silence. Directly overhead, a soft glow shone behind the drawn shade. Inside the room, the clock softly whirred, the breathing was peaceful, and there was the smell of a wet thumb. Tears started to form in the corners of my eyes, and immediately froze, pulling my cheeks tight. What would make the next step possible? When would I open the car door and stand up in the cold, move this body toward its appointed rounds? Suddenly I was standing, moving down the street, toward another car, another gig.

Inside the club, the walls were sweating and the groove from the juke box was pounding; it was a swamp of fur, rubber, tobacco and spilled beer. There was potential here, something could happen. Indeed, if everybody kept drinking for the next several hours, something would surely happen. Around 9 P.M., there was a lifting in the room, show time, a kind of gesture toward the shrinking bubble that wrapped us all tighter and tighter together on nights like this. I loved the line, "Lightning strikes at nine." It appeared in a song from Jamaica, the island where they make music by chanting to a Jewish god of black history.

I went on stage and started playing. The yoga of the blues is very old, very deep. The tension in the groove, the grasping toward release, is really just democracy in action. For without opposing points of view — tension and release — there can be no democratic process. And nothing in nature flows one way only, because then the vessel would ultimately empty out, and nature abhors a vacuum; Nature loves being full of herself. Playing the blues, in a way, was simply having intercourse with Mother Nature.

At the end of the night, after the last drunk boys and girls had spilled out into the freezing cold, I waited, along with the rest of the band to get paid, to divide up the small wet rags that smelled of smoke and passed for currency. "You should be grateful," a friend once told me, "that anybody, even just one person, would pay to see you play music. Never be so arrogant about what you do that you lose sight of that one person paying to hear you." It gave me something to think about every time I saw those smoky wet dollars being counted out and pushed toward me across a bar. And, yes, I was grateful. I was grateful for the opportunity to feel this feeling, to know what so many others before me had felt, to have intercourse with Mother Nature. In the end there was always this last moment of grace, when the currency was passed from hand to hand, signaling the end of the ritual.

"I need something…." But what did I need? The thought was plaguing me again as I stood in the cold and looked down an emptying road, past the blinking red stop light to the receding tail lights of the party cars. How long would I stand here in the cold, believing that help was on the way? My life seemed to have become a metaphor. But for what? I had only to wait a little longer, I told myself, keep my mind at peace, and surely the answer would arrive, perhaps in the form of transportation, preheated, with the bass and drums pumping; a way out of this terrible not knowing. I didn't want to move, but I had to, because there seemed to be an imperative to get the feet moving. As I picked them up, I realized the toes were already numb and delicately painful with each step. Each step was a fanfare of vibrations to the nervous system, a chord of sensation, enharmonically registering as hurt somewhere deep inside my leg.

When you are young, these gigs are a way out — out of town, out of your situation, out of your mind. Eventually, they became just a delivery system to get you from one motel to another, one small facet of the great parking lot that covers the land in a pattern that, as Vonnegut once suggested, probably spells out to an advanced civilization, "send help!" Like maybe send a bass player who can read. The thought made me laugh. Ah, there's life in the old boy yet.

Judy says having Leo softened me. Certainly, I became less interested in being hip and more open to just sitting on the floor in a pile of Legos and small things with wheels. We made it a point to let Leo know that he was an equal partner along with Judy and myself in the ongoing family circus. That meant he had certain responsibilities, like remaining affable at dinner parties. In return, on those occasions when I was on the phone making a pitch to somebody in Los Angeles or New York, and he wandered in with a broken toy, I would fix it and include the process in my phone call. It was an unspoken deal that we both kept to. There is something about a young child's sense of dignity and fair play — an elemental belief in the world as a basically honorable place — that I found very moving. Being with Leo often reminded me of that elemental feeling I got when I first heard jazz. There is a rightness and peacefulness at the center of this music. As Dizzy Gillespie once told me, "Jazz musicians are just naturally peaceful people, because there's so much on their mind trying to figure this music out that they don't have time to be evil."

Leo loved music, all kinds of music, and it was all around him from the moment of his conception. When he was three, I tried to give him piano lessons, but I soon discovered one had to choose between being a teacher and being a father. I decided on the latter and simply made available to him whatever information he wanted. Often, we would spend time together at the piano, making up little songs about fishes that talked or about Snoopy's friend Woodstock. One day he asked if he could play drums with such a serious disposition, that, for his fourth birthday, I bought him a small set. Within three weeks, he could keep time well enough that we could play together.

He obviously liked being part of the band. In fact, one night, when I was playing a small club with Richie Cole, Leo talked his way onto the stage. Actually, I think Richie put him up to it. Earlier that evening, unbeknownst to me, Richie had shown Leo how to hold a clarinet and blow through it to make a sound, and later, when we were on stage, just as I was about to play my first note, this aggressive bleating sound came from somewhere in the wings. I turned around to see Leo walking out, holding a horn which was as long as he was tall, blaring out a loud C sharp while I tried to play in the key of F. (It's as "wrong" a note as he could have chosen.) The crowd loved it, and Leo got a big hand. And then, of course, he refused to leave the stage. He seemed to think his next number would be even more successful. I had to get "the hook" and drag him off. Knowing when to quit is one of the first lessons for any jazzman.

That February, there was a grand event for the opening of the new Civic Center in Madison. I put together a special "people's night," to counter-balance the standard symphony offering of the night before. Our program started with saxophonist Bunky Green, Richard Davis on bass, a great local drummer we jokingly referred to as "free pizza," named Wendell Bond, and myself. The show then segued into Betty Carter and her trio, and concluded with Muddy Waters and his band. It was a night of raw, get-down music. Betty was transcendent in her vocals, imperious in her style, and by the time Muddy hit the stage brooding and moody, calling out "I'm a man. That's M...A...N," the crowd was standing on the brand new seats, applauding. I would like to say that after the show, we had one of the greatest cast parties ever, with Muddy and Richard and Bunky all trading war stories about Chicago, but it didn't happen that way. After the show, everybody just packed up and went home.

I was reminded of the fact that toward the end of their lives, bluesmen Sonny Terry and Brownie McGee, one of the longest lasting duos in the history of the music, didn't even drive to the gigs in the same car. They met there, played, got paid, and split the way they had come. The music is still very much alive but the living, breathing context, that was another story. It was as if we had all arrived at the end without ever going through the middle.

In early May, Richie Cole and I booked a nice little tour that started in Minneapolis and gradually wound its way West, concluding in Los Angeles at the end of the month. The rhythm section included a couple of great New York musicians, bass player Ron McClure and drummer Jimmy Madison. It was a funny, off-the-wall month, with a bizarre cast of characters. Jimmy, for example, was a rock climber and sometimes when we checked into a Holiday Inn, he would disappear around the corner, and when we finally found him, he was halfway up the side of the building, searching for another finger hold. But it was Ron McClure, a mordantly funny philosopher with a great spontaneous wit and many wonderful stories about his days with Wynton Kelly, Charles Lloyd, and Thelonious Monk, who was the revelation for me. Once, when I asked him what he got from playing with Monk, he said, "What you stumble on is usually better than what you're looking for."

On the road, Richie Cole and I carried on long, rambling conversations. I especially loved hearing about his travels as a young man with Buddy Rich and, later, with Eddie Jefferson. This was participating in the oral tradition the way it was meant to be, the way it had gone down for generations: great jazz stories being passed down from sideman to sideman as the countryside rolled by. All in all, it was as close to the old days as I could ever get, or the way I imagined the old days to have been: seemingly endless drives with self-invented cats, going from town to town, burning the club down and moving on to the next bonfire. We played longform music, just a few songs per set, open, classic bebop tunes for which I had written lyrics. I was stretching both musically and physically. At the end of the gig each night, whether the club had been full or empty, I was ready to get back in the car and roll.

We got to Phoenix at the end of the month, four hipsters stumbling out of a van wearing shades and looking for a meal. I was shocked to discover the club packed with young kids who had come to hear my "hit song." I didn't even know I had a hit song, but, apparently, the year before, a deejay on the local rock station had fallen for my "Song for a Sucker Like You" and played it to death. Now all these kids thought they were coming to a pop concert. Catching the mood, Richie styled through the club keeping his shades on, Alto Madness gone Hollywood, and after a quick meal of tacos and enchiladas, we played the "hit" song first, and then just burned away with our twisted bebop.

The crowd went wild for the whole thing, which just proves that hit music is most often in the ear of the beholder, and afterward, we were all treated like stars. Or, as I reminded Ron McClure the next day, after pounding on his motel room door for a half-hour before finally separating him from a very attractive new friend, "What you stumble on, Ron, is usually better than what you're looking for, right?"

A few days later, after we finally had made our way to L.A, I found myself walking through the endless, fern-draped, redwood-paneled corridors of Warner Brothers Records in Burbank, California. I knew enough not to admit I was lost: if you kept your shades on and made enough turns, you eventually got where you were going, but if you stopped to ask directions, they could always send you back where you came from.

As I passed the little cubicles, each with its ultra hip New Wave poster, a little island of control in the onrushing flow of American pop culture, I was reminded of how much trouble the record industry was in: all these beautiful bodies...in the service of what? Today, every 13-year-old who plugs in a guitar has a vision of a recording contract planted firmly between his eyes. The only music left to record and promote was this year's reaction to last year's hype. The people doing the actual work, slogging through the miles and miles of spooling tape, were generally creative with good ears. But they were "fattening frogs for snakes," as the old blues lyric went, working for the bean counters. Ultimately, the numbers guys, to whom the bottom line is both the starting and the finishing line, decided what music got recorded and promoted, hence what music lived and what music died. The frustration in the cubicles was palpable.

I was looking for my friend Ron Goldstein, an A&R man of the old-school, a former promotion man and a guy now responsible for manufacturing musical life in the test tube of the recording studio.

As I rounded one final corner, I found him and several other A&R men in the midst of a flap. "You won't believe this," Ron said to me, "but there's this New Wave band that's been in the studio for months. They can't figure out how to end the record. We've already spent over a quarter of a million on the project and there doesn't seem to be any end in sight."

"Sounds to me like you need a new producer," I ventured.

"No, you don't understand. Last night, we had six producers in the studio with them. You should have seen it. One says, 'more bass,' one says 'no bass,' one's on the phone. It was a mess."

"How did it end?"

"The six decided to try and find a seventh guy who could deliver it."

Everybody laughed. New Wave music was just a new name for what was yet again being hyped as the latest fashion come to return rock and roll to its street roots, a stripped-down sound so raw, so basic, that to capture its essence one only needed to put the band in the studio for a few days (or bring some microphones into the garage for a few nights) and, presto! A cash outlay of a few thousand bucks should net a few million. But, of course, as soon as the concept became studied and refined, it no longer held true. Soon every big label was rushing to sign a dozen or so of these so-called New Wave bands. In the record business, one often bought in large lots, not only to prove one's commitment to the future, but also to spread the risk around, so that no one executive would suffer unduly when the whole thing tanked or six or seven bands turned out to be stiffs. And all of this was promoted as something wild and natural.

So New Wave had become just as much a product of the recording studios as it was a reaction against the worst indulgences of the period. Hence, the six producers and the quarter of a million. In the good old days, stripped down rock and roll was an authentic expression of something, and it didn't have to be invented in the recording studio to exist. It might have been cheap, but at least it was cheap.

Into the midst of the laughing A&R men stepped Bob Krasnow. Bob was now working for Warner Brothers and had recently made millions of dollars riding the waves of popular taste; he was wearing what appeared to be one-ounce gold coins as cufflinks.

"What's so funny?" Bob asked. "Don't you know business is bad?"

"Well, that ought to be good for you," said Ron. "Pretty soon business will be so bad that you'll be able to buy this whole company outright."

"I used to wish that were true," Bob said, "But now I'm glad I don't own it. How's that New Wave project coming?"

Ron didn't miss a beat. "Terrible," he reported, "but it's going to be great. Maybe even the biggest ever."

That summer, on July 5th, I played at Carnegie Hall as part of a tribute to Eddie Jefferson. The cast included Dizzy Gillespie, James Moody, Jon Hendricks, Bobby McFerrin, the Manhattan Transfer, Richie Cole and myself. We all met in New York City three days in advance to rehearse. Each group was scheduled to do a set—The Transfer, Dizzy with Moody, Jon Hendricks and Bobby McFerrin, me and Richie—and, in addition, there were some special features: for one, I would sing the Dave Lambert / Buddy Stewart duet "What's This," with Tim Hauser of the Manhattan Transfer. This song had been the first vocalese hit from the forties, a real piece of bebop history. And then, at the end of the concert, the entire cast would assemble on stage to perform Dizzy's "Oo Pa Pa Da," another bebop vocal classic.

The rehearsals were funny, relaxed and historically riveting. For example, Jon and Dizzy spent the better part of an hour debating the correct way to sing the answer phrase on "Oo Pa Pa Da." Dizzy, the author of the song, tried to explain to Jon that the phrase was "blee ah ba da ah, blee blee ah." Jon said, "Really? I've always heard it as "bee ah be da ah, be blee da." It was like watching two Sanskrit scholars parsing some ancient text.

"No," said Dizzy, "One must be very careful with this point. Pay attention…" And he demonstrated it once again, "blee ah ba da ah, blee blee ah." Only this time, he shifted the emphasis a little, so the phrase started to mutate a bit.

"I see," said Jon and turned to the rest of us to demonstrate how we should be singing it. He, too, took some small liberties with the phrase. By now, it was even less clear what the correct phrase was. Janis Siegel of the Manhattan Transfer and I were standing next to James Moody, and Moody, looking professorial in his three-piece suit and horn-rimmed glasses, said to us out of the side of his mouth, "Pay no attention to these gentlemen. What we want to be singing is 'blee ah ba da bah, blee be dah'. Repeat after me."

By now little pockets of resistance and interpretation were breaking out along the line of singers. Richie Cole and Dizzy, Bobby McFerrin and Jon Hendricks, me and Moody and Janis, it was hysterically funny but nobody laughed because, first of all, it was impossible to tell whether Dizzy was being serious and Jon was actually paying attention, or whether this was the continuation of some long-running joke between the two of them, or, perhaps, we were all just the victims of a vicious riff being perpetrated at that very moment.

The rehearsal ended without a definitive version being agreed upon. Yet that night, at the dry run of the show, which we performed at the club Seventh Ave. South, the song came off without a hitch.

The following evening, Richie and I were backstage at Carnegie Hall in our dressing room, waiting for our quartet set to begin, reminiscing about Eddie Jefferson. Suddenly Richie launched into a tirade about how Eddie never got the recognition he deserved, and now his memory was being absorbed into this vague tribute to jazz singing. Just then, in the middle of Richie's rant, the insane disheveled visage of Professor Irwin Corey popped into the room. The Professor, who was not a professor at all but a jazz comic with a gift for hip double-talk, had been a friend of Eddie's. He and Richie greeted each other warmly. The Professor looked very much like his stage persona—a small man with a Groucho walk and wild wisps of fly-away gray hair—and after he introduced us to the young Puerto Rican girl in hot pants who was his traveling companion, he said, "Now what we need here, in honor of our dear departed friend, is the proper introduction."

Something in the proposition seemed to relieve Richie's anxiety.

"That's it!" said Richie, "The Professor will introduce us. Eddie would have wanted it that way."

Cheers went up from the rhythm section. "Yeah. The Professor will introduce us...."

Just then, Art Weiner, the promoter, arrived in the dressing room to tell us we were on in five minutes. Richie told him the new plan: the Professor had agreed to introduce us. Art said, "Absolutely not."

"Then we don't go on," said Richie.

I'm sitting backstage at Carnegie Hall and I'm hearing that I don't go on unless Professor Irwin Corey introduces us. This really was getting insane. Also, I couldn't find my shoes. I had brought some black shoes to wear on stage, and somehow they had gone missing.

"There is no way I'm letting him on that stage," Art said. "Because there's no way to get him off." Apparently, Art had worked with the Professor in the past and knew about his penchant for getting lost in his own mental labyrinth.

"Be reasonable," said the Professor. "Just a few words about Eddie and the boys in the band. I can be brief."

Art turned to the Professor and said, "Okay, here's the deal. You got two minutes. If you're not off that stage in two minutes, we're carrying you off."

"No need, no need," said the Professor. "Let me collect my thoughts."

Standing in the wings, waiting to go on stage in my brown shoes, I saw the Professor walk out. Looking past him, into the vaulted grandeur of Carnegie Hall, into a sea of expectant faces, I had a vague sense of déjà vu. Where had I seen this before? Gradually, it dawned on me — it was that magic place I had seen in my mind's eye when, as a kid, my mother told me the bedtime stories about a huge domed space filled with beautiful lights and people and music, where anything was possible. "What do you want, Benny?" she had asked me. Now what was it that I had wanted?

"This next band," the Professor was saying, "well, first of all, they're all white guys..." And off he went, into some mad tangential rap that only touched on me or Richie or Eddie Jefferson in the most peripheral way, and then, blessedly, from out of the opposite wings, came Art Weiner and an assistant. They marched up to the Professor, grabbed him under the arms, picked him up and hauled him off stage. Just before they disappeared into the wings, he shouted, "Ben Sidran and Richie Cole!" The crowd loved it.

Our set went by in a flash. The fact that we were in Carnegie Hall didn't really occur to me until later, when I had gone back on stage to sing "What's This" with Tim, and became painfully aware, as the band hit the tempo, that this would be the first time I ever sang in public without sitting behind a piano. I was about to recreate Buddy Stewart's intricate vocal part in a duet with a real jazz singer, a guy who had won several Grammy awards: would he notice that I wasn't a "real" singer? It was like the Gary Larson cartoon of the elephant who is on stage at the piano, thinking to himself, "What am I doing here? I'm a flute player." What was I doing here?

I felt completely exposed, "in the nude," as Art Blakey would say. I looked over at Tim, and he was grinning from ear to ear, obviously having a great time, totally comfortable. I turned back to the house, imagined Judy sitting out there somewhere, and just sang it to her. Soon, it was time for the grand finale, and I took my place in the group on stage singing Dizzy's "Oo Pa Pa Da." Standing next to Tim again, singing the nonsense lyrics we had "rehearsed," there was no more fear, no more tension, and I had a moment of intense clarity. This was the top of the hill, as good as it gets: on stage at Carnegie Hall, singing with Dizzy Gillespie and the others, with my wife and friends in the audience. I took a kind of mental inventory. How did I feel?

I didn't feel anything. I was not joyous. I was not scared. I was not happy. I was not unhappy. And then gradually, I became aware of this gnawing again at the edges of my mind. "I need something...I *need* something." What was missing?

"Dear Ben," the note read. "I don't know if you already have word of Bill Evans' death; but if not, I thought you might want to see the NY *Times* notice. Though by now I should be inured to the passing of one or another who has meant something to my cultural and psychological being. But each such happening only widens that lake of emptiness that resides somewhere in my spirit.... it's just very sad that we can't know what else Powell or Mingus or Evans might have had up their sleeves. Thank heavens, then, for you and your embattled, diminishing breed."

It was signed "Affectionately," Harvey Goldberg.

On New Year's Eve, December 31, 1980, I was the New York anchor for National Public Radio's live, coast-to-coast *Jazz Alive!* broadcast. *Jazz Alive!* had become the most important jazz program in the country, in part because commercial radio had virtually stopped programming the music, and in part because NPR was still funded by the government and the National Endowment for the Arts, and was mandated to go where commercial radio would not.

Normally, *Jazz Alive!* was a weekly, one-hour program broadcast over three hundred NPR stations and hosted by the great jazz pianist Dr. Billy Taylor. Over the years, this generous, personable man had helped make jazz more acceptable to the arts police, and his campaign to have jazz considered "America's classical music" was clearly targeted to secure more funding. Broadcasting live (on tape) concerts each week, *Jazz Alive!* established that the art form was not only still vital but was thriving in your own hometown. This special New Year's Eve program, however, would be a *Jazz Alive!* first: a four-hour trip across the country, with actual live concerts taking place in each time zone. I was hosting the kick-off event in New York City with a concert by the Brecker Brothers, and then I would pass it along to Chicago, Denver and finally, we would all arrive in L.A. where Billy Taylor was holding court.

At ten minutes to 11 P.M., Eastern Standard Time, I was in place in the broadcast booth set up at the rear of the club, with producer Fred Bork talking to me through the earphones and Randy Brecker sitting next to me, ready for the pre-game interview. Fred said, "Focus on the air of anticipation...build the excitement!" I looked over at Randy, who is like a big Basset Hound, diffident at best and resorting to dourness under pressure, and said, "So Randy, I guess you're really excited about this New Year's Eve?"

Randy took a long pause, like lifting his horn to his lips before beginning a ballad, and said, "Yeah.... Well, you know, man...."

And we both started laughing. It was so out of context. I said, "Well, fantastic, the air of anticipation is really starting to build here in New York City and we'll be right back with the Brecker Brothers, live from Seventh Avenue South!" I was still laughing as I handed it off to the Chicago host, and I thought to myself, "This is gonna be fun."

And it was. Live radio has a great sense of freedom about it. The audience is with you and can forgive just about anything because they are listening, in part, just in case the unexpected happens. It's very close to the feeling one gets talking to an audience from the stage. They've already paid their money so you know they're interested in whatever kind of fool thing you might have to say. You relax, they relax, and everybody has fun. The hour flew by, and when the Brecker Brothers had finished playing their funky version of "Auld Lang Syne," I hated to hand the broadcast off to Chicago. Taking off the earphones, I knew I would be back.

1981

In January, I got a letter from Alex Campbell's in Pennsylvania. They were the biggest dealer in "cut out" records in the United States, and they were writing to let me know that they had in stock hundreds (and in one case, thousands) of copies of my various Arista albums which had been dumped by the company. They were giving me the first chance to buy them for $.50 apiece before offering them to the retail chains. I was not only in debt to the company but was being offered the chance to pay for my work again. I sent a check.

That spring, Dan Zelisco, the promoter who had brought us to Phoenix the previous summer, called to say he was booking the Gamage Center, a beautiful Frank Lloyd Wright-designed auditorium in Scottsdale, to feature me and comic Rodney Dangerfield. "It will be great," he said. "You can open the show, people here know your music, and then you can play for Rodney. He uses musicians in his act. If this works, you can tour with him. This is a great opportunity."

Rodney Dangerfield was already famous for his Miller Lite beer commercials. But Danny figured he was still basically a Vegas comedian and would draw an older crowd, and since the Vegas crowd liked jazz, well, I was the perfect opening act. His motives were excellent, but he couldn't have been more wrong.

I flew into Phoenix with bassist Billy Peterson. An hour before the show, Rodney still hadn't arrived and Danny was getting a little nervous. In the two months since he had first announced the concert, Rodney's career had taken off in an unanticipated direction. "The cover of *Rolling Stone* did it," Danny said. Rodney had just been in the film *Caddy Shack*, and he was now a favorite of the younger set. Tonight, he was flying in on a private jet, and the hall was filling with drunk sixteen-year-old boys.

A half-hour before show time, Rodney finally showed up with two Las Vegas hookers. As they walked in, one of them was whining, "Rodney, you promised to take me somewhere nice...." Rodney went into his dressing room, closed the door, and emerged a minute later in a silk bathrobe and slippers. Passing me, he said, "Hi ya kid, how ya doing?"

Danny said, "Rodney, this is Ben Sidran. He's opening the show." Rodney focused on the Jewishness of my last name and said something to me in Yiddish. I didn't get it, so I just smiled, and he shook his head and said, "Ah, what can you do?" Like, "We're all Jews lost out here in the desert, but at least you could learn the mother tongue," and then he padded off to his dressing room again.

Billy and I went on stage. After our introduction, the crowd settled in for a moment, and we started to play the first song. A minute into it, it was as if the floor opened up and, gradually, we descended into a huge pit filled with the howling of the damned. It started slowly, with a couple of kids clapping, then whistling, then calling out, "We want Rodney!" A chant formed: "Rodney! Rodney!" I looked at Billy and he looked at me. We still had a half-hour to go.

By the second song, it felt like we were playing in the face of a hurricane. The chanting got louder: "Rodney! Rodney!" I looked down and saw blood on the keys, a little drop on the G, a smear on the E, and I became aware that I had been trying to hold back the crowd by playing harder. Some primal instinct had taken over. Just then, the sound equipment failed and the monitor speakers started feeding back. I looked into the wings and there was Danny, shrugging, "What can you do?" This was becoming the theme of the evening.

Suddenly, stepping out over the abyss, we seemed to go weightless. The music became some arcane ritual, meaningless now, being acted out in the face of primitive elements, Mother Nature's baser self. I remembered the story about John Sebastian opening a show for Steve Martin and facing a sea of heads with arrows through them, and I thought, "He was lucky." Much later, I heard that Andy Kaufman opened for Rodney and they had to erect a screen to stop the missiles; Andy probably dug it.

But we left the stage after the fourth song, defeated. I thought to myself, "Now I know how the hostages in Iran felt, living their life in the face of an organized, chanting mob." Passing me in the hallway, Rodney said, 'I'm sorry, kid. I don't attract a better class of people."

But the evening was still young and about to become even more surreal. Because after a brief interval, Billy and I went back on stage with Rodney, and he introduced us as his band. He called me "Skids" and referred to Billy as "Styles Bitchly." And then he proceeded to do his latest record album, verbatim. Same jokes, same order, same everything. And the kids had it memorized. They were throwing him the straight lines and howling when he delivered the meat.

"I grew up in a tough neighborhood... (How tough was it?) I'll tell you how tough. The sign in the library said 'shut the fuck up!'" (Big cheer.)

No respect. No respect. "I got a dog to pick up chicks. Dog was smarter than I was. He used me to pick up dogs." Wild applause. "First time I had sex I was really scared. (Everybody says it with him) I was alone."

Half way into the set, we did this little specialty number with him, and then it was question and answer time.

Somebody shouted, "What about Lite Beer?" He said, "My contract runs out in June. After that, drink whatever the fuck you want." A girl called out, "What is Johnny Carson like when the lights go down?" Rodney said, "He plays with himself." (Big cheer.)

Then somebody shouted, "What's your real name?" He said "Percival Sweetboater. I changed it for show biz. Whaddaya think? I'm a lousy Jew bastard. If I told you my real name would you let me join your club?" (Big cheer.) A kid called out, "What do you do for a living?" "Find guys for your mother." (Big cheer.)

Every gesture was his 10,000th delivery of a joke designed to sell the image of the tough Jewish schlemiel who gets no respect. They were shouting the straight lines at him and cheering when he did the pay off. It let them feel like they were smart enough to remember the jokes and cool enough to come to the gig. I was in Rome opening for the Jew as he got thrown to the lions.

"I was so ugly my father used to show people the picture of the kid that comes in the wallet. When my father wanted sex, my mother would hold up my picture. I made friends with a fly. I opened the window, he left me for some horse shit."

We came off stage and Rodney said, "What can I tell you? I'm just telling them what they want to hear." One of the hookers said, "Yeah, Rodney, that at least they ain't you." And Rodney said, "Yeah, it could be worse. You could be me."

Waiting outside Danny's office to get paid at the end of the night, I sat reading the book I had brought with me, John Updike's *Beck*, and I came across this wonderful image of Hollywood: "one of history's great love stories, the mutually profitable romance between Jewish Hollywood and bohunk America, conducted almost entirely in the dark, a tapping of fervent messages through the wall of the San Gabriel Range, whereby Jewish brains gave a formless land dreams and even a kind of conscience." I was on the edge of the San Gabriel Range, and I knew about the dreams and the bohunks, but what had become of the conscience? The door opened and I saw Rodney and Danny finishing up their negotiations. Rodney closed his briefcase, which was presumably filled with cash, and walked out the door. The last thing he said to me was, "Yeah, kid, I got the party rollin'. I only hope I live through it." And then he and the girls were gone.

Throughout the winter, even as I continued to play gigs, I spent as much time at home with Leo as possible. It not only broadened my horizons—which children will do if you actually listen to them—but it gave me relief from the constant casting of bread upon the waters. By now I had tossed several loaves to the currents and was awaiting the arrival of the first cheese sandwich. I had worked up a film treatment based on the true story of the most famous jazz "groupie" of all time. Nobody bit. I rewrote the *Blue Angel*, recasting the old professor as an aging sixties radical and the girl as a punk singer, setting the action at a small university sometime in the late seventies. Nobody bit. I pitched another series of jazz-based videos. Finally somebody bit. My lawyer, Emily Shenkin, called to say a man named Howard Boris had walked into her Beverly Hills office with a pile of Japanese money from Pioneer Laserdisc, a deadline to deliver a lot of music programming, and no idea where to begin. "I don't know anything about this guy," she said, "but it could be a way for you to get your jazz video project off the ground."

I called him and her take had been correct; he had no idea that the Japanese loved jazz, but said if I could draw up a list of artists and a rough budget, he would run it by them. It didn't take long for me to propose a series called *The Jazz Life*, six one-hour performance videos, captured live in New York at the Village Vanguard, featuring the bands of Johnny Griffin, Nat Adderley, Chico Hamilton, Art Blakey (with Wynton and Branford Marsalis), Mike Mainieri and Richie Cole. It didn't take long for Pioneer to agree to the series. Suddenly, I was a television producer. The first programs were scheduled for June.

Until then, I kept gigging to pay the rent. In the spring, I booked another tour with Richie Cole. Coincidentally, I had received a phone call from George Brown saying he was back in Grand Rapids, Michigan, that he was straight and clean and that he needed a gig. George sounded a little anxious, kind of over-selling the product a bit, but I was glad that he was no longer on the run in Europe and being home might be the medicine he needed. I said I would try to help. I ran the idea by Richie. "Yeah, I know George," Richie said. "How's he doing?" It sounded like Richie did know him; he asked the question with a kind of jaundiced tone. I said "He sounds fine," maybe stretching the truth a bit. Richie said "Okay," and I called George back and arranged to fly him to Madison. Billy Peterson was driving down from Minneapolis to play bass, and the plan was to hit the road after two days of rehearsals in Madison. We had a nice month booked all over the territory.

The day arrived when I went to the airport to pick up George, and he got off the plane looking sharp and dangerous in a charcoal gray suit and black shades. We hugged—we hadn't seen each other in years—and on the way into town we caught up. He told me he had been thrown out of Europe again and said it was all because of racism and the failure of the greed system to understand his way of life. I was becoming a little concerned as his rant escalated, but when he said he needed to make a quick stop, and then directed me to a liquor store, I knew we were in trouble. He came back with a pint of cheap vodka. When we got to the house, I introduced him to Leo and Billy and Richie, showed him to the gue- stroom and hoped for the best. He put his things away, came downstairs, and hung out, laughing and listening to music, like his old self.

The next day, rehearsals went well enough and soon we were off, driving toward Ames, Iowa. The first gig was in a little club called the Maintenance Shop, and by the time we set up and sound-checked, we barely had time to go to the motel and change. George seemed fine through it all, until, strangely, when we got on the stand that night and started to play, he began drifting in and out of the music, thrashing from time to time as if fighting to get back inside his body. It was terrible to watch, this man who had once been among the most gifted drummers in jazz, now struggling to do something he could have done in his sleep. At one point, he got lost inside a triplet and the time seemed to expand dangerously, and then suddenly snap closed, making the music lurch and grab for the rails. He still had brilliant technique but now, on occasion, it seemed to be connected to a random events generator rather than to a human heart.

We survived the set and I said nothing. The second set was the same. After the gig, backstage, I told George we needed to talk. We went into a small room and closed the door. I said, "George, something is very wrong. I don't know what it is. But it could be your drinking. This music is not complicated, and you're not making it."

He said, "What are you talking about?" He still wore his black shades and I couldn't see his eyes but I could feel them on me.

I said, "You know what I'm talking about. You told me you were clean and I put myself on the line to get you this gig, and you're not cutting it."

He just looked at me, emotionless. "Okay," he said, "Give me my money."

"I'll pay you for tonight and tomorrow but I got to find a sub for Chicago."

"I want my money. All four weeks."

I said, "Look, I'll pay you for one week and fly you home but that's it. I got to find another drummer for tomorrow."

There was a long silence, and then George said, "Ben, you should fear me."

"What?"

"You should fear me," he said, and pulled out a switchblade knife.

I looked at him and the knife and went totally off. "You motherfucker! After everything we've been through and all the bread I sent you and all your fucking talk about music and brotherhood and you pull a knife on me!" He was completely emotionless, holding the knife in his right hand, not moving.

Just then, the door opened and Richie Cole walked into the room. I didn't see him but I heard him say, "Ben, I need to talk to you for a minute." He put his arm around my shoulder and walked me into the hall. I was breathing hard.

He said, "Man, that is not your friend George Brown in there. That is somebody else. Your friend George Brown is gone. You better be very careful."

I caught my breath and saw that he was right. My friend George, along with a big chunk of my past, was really gone for good. And I was still living as if there was something permanent about the old days. I walked back in the room. I told George I would pay him for the week and left. That was it. It was the last time I saw George Brown until many years later, in Paris. By then, it was as if two old strangers were meeting, rather than two old friends.

On our drive to Chicago, nobody in the car wanted to talk about George. It was such a tragedy, a great waste. Perhaps one of the scariest things for a jazz musician is to watch a friend, a teacher, a pioneer leave the scene in a bad way. It hits too close to home. Everybody puts up with a lot of bad behavior in jazz for the sake of the art, in part, because we all know, "There but for the grace of God…" Anybody who's lost a brother to the war, and George was a great warrior in his day, knows there is an injustice larger than the loss of a single soldier.

Billy Peterson, who is also a great speed skater, got on the subject of sports. He started talking about "the threshold of surrender." He said, "Most people get to a point in their training when they have to surrender. They reach their limit of oxygen uptake, and their muscles simply stop working. But then there are some athletes who can train beyond the threshold of surrender. Eric Heiden was like that. That's how he won five gold medals at the Olympics. Because when every part of him wanted to quit, he could still reach down inside himself and keep going."

"Yeah," I said, "It's always about the spirit. If you lose that, the body is gone for good."

In Chicago, we met Gordy Knudtson, our new drummer, and did a quick sound-check at the club. Then we went across the street for a fast pizza. I was sitting across the table from Richie, who was facing the door, when I saw a stricken look come over his face. Following his gaze, I turned and saw two people walking into the place, one a pleasant looking woman, the other a striking teenage girl. There was something about the girl — and then, wham!, it hit me. She looked just like Richie.

Richie jumped up and brought them back to the table. It turned out the woman was someone Richie had met fifteen years before, when he was on tour with the Buddy Rich band. It had been a one-night stand in Buffalo in more ways than one. Amy, the charming young redhead, was the result, a daughter he had never met. On this night, her mother, now living in Chicago, had decided that the time was right. Richie was beside himself, glowing; he took them back to the club and sat them down in the dressing room. Sitting next to his daughter with his scrapbook open, he started turning the pages. "See, that's Sonny Stitt. There's Eddie Jefferson. Look, that's me and Phil Woods." It was as if he was trying to get her caught up on her own extended family. That night, he played transported.

In June, we taped the first four programs for the *Jazz Life* Pioneer Laserdisc series. In the three months since I had proposed the series to Howard Boris, I had enlisted my friend Ken Yagoda as a producer and hired the best crew in New York City, guys who were hungry to shoot creative music instead of commercials, along with director Stan Dorfman, a pioneer in music television. I had negotiated with Max Gordon, the owner of the Village Vanguard, to use his club, and had arranged with Johnny Griffin, Nat Adderley, Art Blakey, and Chico Hamilton to be the first guests of honor.

We were shooting two shows a day for two days, and by 9 A.M. the morning of the first shoot, we had three huge trucks lined up outside the club on Seventh Avenue, with miles of cable snakes running everywhere. Guys were carrying lights and cameras down the narrow stairs and into the dim recesses of this jazz institution. Max Gordon, who was already well into his seventies and had been running the place for forty years, simply sat in the kitchen smoking his cigar, nonplussed, watching the action unfold. From time to time, I would chat with him about the old days. I asked him, "What was it like when Coltrane played here?" He said, "Business was good." But just outside the kitchen, not all was sweetness and light.

Boris had brought with him from L.A. a production lackey named Steve Altman to "beat people up," as he so eloquently put it to me that morning. "Like if some guy says he wants 250 bucks for something," said Altman, "We give him two hundred cash and say 'take it or leave it'. And you know what? They usually take it." What was this low rent hustler doing in the middle of my production? It was too late to do anything. I just had to try and keep him away from anybody and everybody, the musicians most of all. At the time, I had a bigger problem: Johnny Griffin, who was scheduled to go on first, was late. Boris and Altman pulled me aside by a pile of dishes.

"What are you gonna do?" Steve asked.

"You gotta fine him, " said Boris

"Yeah, how much are we paying him anyway?"

I said, "Twenty-five hundred dollars." He knew full well how much it was.

He pretended to be shocked, outraged. "We're paying him twenty-five hundred bucks for one hour? Are you crazy? You gotta beat him up!"

I looked at these two L.A. hustlers with their Japanese money and their cheap cigars and I actually started to feel sick. I said to them, as quietly as I could, "We are not paying him twenty-five hundred bucks for one hour of work. We are paying him twenty-five hundred bucks for the fifty-five years of his life that lead up to this one-hour. We are paying him peanuts." And I turned and walked out of the kitchen.

I met Johnny Griffin coming down the stairs. He had a wide smile on his face. I told him I was happy to see him, and he said, "I bet you are." His band set up quickly and by 3 P.M. the invited audience filed in and we were taping, right on schedule. After the opening number, Johnny stepped up to the microphone and said, "Jazz music! Your music! Our music!" The crowd applauded madly, lovingly, happy to be in the presence of a healer, and Johnny said, "This music is made *by* and *for* people who have chosen to feel good *in spite of* conditions," and I started clapping and screaming right along with the rest.

As we all know, to paraphrase the great cartoonist Gilbert Shelton, jazz will get you through times of no money better than money will get you through times of no jazz.

On August 4th, the *Jazz Alive!* radio program was doing another special, this time live from The Chicago Jazz Festival in Grant Park. Tim Owens, the producer, once again called on me to be part of the team. My job was to wander through the festival grounds and do the local "color," reporting on the fans' reaction to the music, interviewing musicians and finding ways to fill time in a musical manner. Billy Taylor was again the host, and, as usual he was very generous with me. He made it a point to take me backstage and introduce me to Ella Fitzgerald and Count Basie. When Billy told Basie I was a piano player, Basie just looked up from his little motorized golf cart (he had recently suffered a stroke and was using it to get around) and said, "Well, man, you keep playing. It just keeps getting better."

That evening, I was wandering through the festival grounds when I heard the director in my earphones say, "Ben, we need you to fill a few minutes. What have you got?"

I said, "Well, I see a guy selling glow-in-the-dark necklaces..."

"Okay, we're coming to you in 30 seconds..."

I walked up to the man, extended my microphone, and in my nicest roving reporter's voice said, "Excuse me sir, what makes those necklaces glow in the dark?"

He turned to me and said, for all the world to hear, "Go fuck yourself!"

I started backpedaling fast. I said, "Thank you very much. Well, back to you Billy...."

But the man had turned and begun chasing me, pursuing me back across the grounds. "You want some more?" he said, "I got some more for you."

By the time I got to the production truck, Tim and the others were sitting there laughing with tears streaming down their faces. "Well," Tim said, "You definitely made the NPR Christmas party reel this year."

In September, I began to think about the Jewish High Holy Days. Leo was about to turn five, and I wanted him to have some sense of being Jewish, something he could feel on his pulse just as I had felt the spiritual energy of those old men back in Racine. I know now that I was also trying to reconnect to my own beginnings. As fate would have it, I happened to wander into a little Madison synagogue called the Gates of Heaven on the day that Hannah Rosenthal was leading her Rosh Hashana service. The building was the oldest free standing synagogue in the Midwest, built in 1864, but over the years, it had fallen in and out of hard times, and was now a local landmark owned by the city. Hannah had rented it for the occasion, thrown open the doors, and just started davening, It was wonderful, very "heimish" (down to earth), with a text and an atmosphere that nimmed the heart. One of the first prayers she read was,

> "The Gods we worship write their names on our faces, be sure of that
> And a person will worship something, have no doubt of that either
> One may think that tribute is paid in secret
> In the dark recesses of his or her heart, but it is not
> That which dominates imagination and thoughts will determine life and
>   character
> Therefore, it behooves us to be careful what we are worshipping
> For what we are worshipping, we are becoming."

It caught me up short. What was I worshipping? What was written on my face? And if, as the text said, man is capable of change, indeed, obligated to change, was it time for me to change, and if so, what should I be doing that I wasn't doing? In Hannah's service, which she had written herself, drawn from sources both liturgical and literary, God was not an old man or a removed omniscience, but a presence, the sum total of human experience, the knowable and the ineffable. And there was a kind of simplicity in her presentation that made me comfortable sitting among these people and thinking these thoughts. In the past, Jewish ritual was just that: the hollow scraping of reeds in the wind. Here, I found in the smallest of moments the largest of meanings.

Now I believe that everyone wants and needs to think these thoughts. Who are we? Where did we come from? Why are we here? And, even if there is no retribution or justice on Earth, what is the right way for us to walk the path, from the first step to the last? Further, I am part of that generation that is determined to unify the whole of life into one long learning experience — to become the information, as I said, rather than just define and dispense with things. Particularly in this culture of planned obsolescence, which extends way beyond the material objects of our lives to the very thoughts in our heads — and especially to someone like myself, steeped in the jazz life, where tradition is either a living, breathing thing or we are all just wandering through a vast museum of yesterday's artifacts — these are vital questions to be asking.

What was of particular interest to me, however, was the music. The service was full of songs I found I remembered from childhood but hadn't thought of since. Children's songs that were so unremarkable that they would normally have passed without notice. And yet in the context of this service, they provoked powerful feelings in me. Feelings not of awe or transcendence, but rather a kind of visceral memory of what it felt like thirty-five years earlier in that old synagogue back in Racine, swaying with a minion of refugees to the chanting of an impenetrable liturgy. Those moments had led me into the jazz life, because of the rhythm and the vocalized physicality of the room, but also because of the unspoken belief that there is something meaningful in the gathering of people, some larger purpose to our travail than the constant social squirm (saxophonist Ornette Coleman's phrase) that passes for real life. And perhaps there are some things that cannot and should not be "known" at all. As opposed to the way modern life strives to reduce all our experience to answers that can be scanned on a test sheet or digitized on a computer. Perhaps to experience the truly important moments, one must not try to define them, but rather, to simply feel one's heart beating, hear the in and out of the breath, with an open heart.

At the end of the service, I went up and thanked Hannah and said that I had really enjoyed myself. But there was just one thing. "No offense," I said very softly, "but your guitar playing and singing is a little distracting. Would it be possible for me to help with the music?" And so the path branched again.

Beginning that year, and every year thereafter, as Leo grew from five to six, and then six to seven, and then seven to eight, I prepared and played the music for Hannah's High Holy Day services at the Gates of Heaven. The night before the services, she would come by the house and worry me through all the songs. They were so simple — "Avinu Malchenu," "Oseh Shalom," "Mode Ani" — that I sometimes lost my way while playing them. Bruce Paulson, a trombone player on the "Tonight Show" band during Johnny Carson's reign, once told me, "I played Johnny's theme song every night for twenty years and I had to read the music every night. I never could memorize it. I can't tell you why." I think I can. It has something to do with ritual, and how it replaces normal consciousness, for better or for worse, with an alternative state. If it's a living ritual, this lapse can be soothing, renewing. If it's a hollow ritual, one just falls asleep.

Every year, I encouraged Leo to sit next to me on the piano bench so he would pay more attention to the service. And every year, as his feet got progressively closer to the floor, he played the music along with me, improvising on the keys at the top of the piano while I played those at the bottom. The same year his shoes actually touched the old wooden floor, Hannah asked me to include the song "Life's a Lesson" in the service. I rarely performed the song in public after I had recorded it, but she had heard me sing it quite by accident and remembered it. "It helps me to understand the Kaddish," she said. "You'll play it right before we read the prayer for the dead."

It took years for me to understand why Hannah associated this song with the Kaddish, a prayer that is said in remembrance of the dead and yet does not even mention the subject of our mortality. This prayer, which is basically in praise of God, is itself a kind of mystery to Jews, and the lyrics to "Life's a Lesson" say that there is a purpose to life, that it resides in the striving for freedom, that freedom is often out of our grasp but we must strive for it anyway, that we all go a little crazy from the effort, which is part of the teaching, and the teaching is that we are not alone. In short, it describes the human condition, a gift from God.

At noon, Monday, September 8, 1981, the same week I wandered into the Gates of Heaven, the week of Rosh Hashana, New York City lost its only commercial jazz radio station.

Being from out of town, I didn't find out until the next day, when I called a concert promoter to ask about a show we were planning. "Obviously, you haven't heard what's going on here," he said. "Sunday night, New York went to bed listening to jazz on WRVR. Monday morning we woke up to Loretta Lynn."

I thought he was joking. He said, "No, when the deejays came in Monday morning, they were told that the management had decided to go country that very day. They didn't even tell the jocks beforehand." I could guess what was coming next. "The new WRVR sure isn't gonna play your records anymore," he said. "And in fact, there's a whole lot of people who won't be heard on the radio in New York now. And since my concerts are aimed at that old WRVR audience, I'm kind of out of business at the moment. I just lost my conduit to the people. Your show is canceled."

How could the largest jazz market in the world go without a jazz station? I decided to call one of the deejays at the station to find out what happened. I reached Lois Gilbert in the control booth, as she was putting on a song called "Red Neck, White Socks and Blue Ribbon Beer." "It's like the Twilight Zone," she said. "It's Future Shock. When I came to work Monday morning, the general manager told us, 'I have great news! As you know, the trend in the country right now is toward country music. This is an exciting opportunity for us to become the only FM country station in New York. Of course, we expect some protest from some of you and from some of the audience, but it's not such a great transition. Jazz and country are related. They're both American music.'

"The black community is up in arms," she continued. "I told him that. He said, 'Yeah, well a lot of blacks like country music.'" When she came out of the meeting, there was a 40 foot truck hauling away all the jazz records from the library and another one unloading automated cart machines to play the country music tapes. "The last jazz record we played was 'Goodbye Pork Pie Hat,' a little after noon. The next record was Waylon Jennings, 'Are You Ready For Country.'

"People just thought there was something wrong with their radio."

During this period, jazz music was being marginalized on many fronts, and it seemed like the whole jazz life was becoming an anachronism. Only a decade earlier, jazz musicians had thought of themselves as gunslingers out on the fringes of the psychological territory. Charles Mingus even wrote a song called "Gunslinging Bird, Or, If Charlie Parker Was a Gunslinger, There Would Be a Whole Lot of Dead Copycats." But now Mingus himself was dead, and his last recording, his final legacy, was a collaboration with pop/folk singer Joni Mitchell. Mingus may have hoped she would bring his music to more people, but in the end, she simply inserted herself into his myth. Jazz was just more fodder for the killing machine.

Like cowboys when the Wild West was giving way to fences, jazz musicians now seemed to be left to talk about what it was like in the old days, when there was freedom and individuality. Jazz festivals were becoming like the Buffalo Bill shows—a few hot shots, showing off their skills for the rubes. The "Wild West" was gone. It remained only as a marketing concept, and the last cowboys were sitting around the final camp fires, even as the fences were going up right before their eyes. You could hear the sound of chomping getting closer, the sound of sheep, a lot of sheep, sheep eating the grass down to the roots, killing the very landscape that nourished them. In the cold night air, under the psychological "Big Sky," there weren't too many campfires springing up anymore.

That fall, Ron McClure and I toured as an opening act for singer Al Jarreau. We played large arenas (Al was doing well at the time) and were like the opening comic. We played mostly for the band. They hung out in the wings to dig our little set, which was performed as folks filed into the vast space. It occurred to me that I had been doing this my whole life, making my records and performing primarily for friends who were mostly musicians. Backstage, after our set, we stayed only long enough to grab a sandwich from catering and swap a joke or two with the cats, and then we were gone, waving goodbye to the other musicians who were tied to the caravan. Even Al sometimes watched us leave with a certain wistfulness as he was about to go on stage. All in all, it was a great trip.

While Al and his entourage traveled by private jet, Ron and I traveled in a station wagon, from Milwaukee to Ann Arbor, Rochester to Ithaca, and ultimately to a nice concert at Boston's Orchestra Hall. We were free to explore the blue line highways while the circus, with its trucks and roustabouts, labored down the main roads. True, Al had twin playboy bunnies for breakfast at the Marriott Hotel, while Ron and I were served greasy club sandwiches by a bored waitress down the road at the Embers, but even that was not without its moments.

"You're musicians huh?" asked the waitress, spotting Ron's instrument. "You play anything by the Bee Gees?" "No," Ron said without missing a beat, "But we use a lot of the same notes."

After the Jarreau tour ended, Ron and I continued on across the country with a quartet, arriving in San Francisco at the Keystone Corner on a double bill with Dave Liebman's group. The music was intense. Dave, who may be best known for his work with Miles Davis, is an intellectual, a teacher, and a groundbreaking musician, pushing the boundaries of swing and freedom every time he puts the horn in his mouth. Hanging for a week with these guys, feeling the intense rise and fall of the conjured spirit...well, given the choice of being huddled around this particular campfire or selling barbed wire to the rubes in the coliseums, there really was no choice at all.

Almost as if to confirm this, on returning home from San Francisco, I received a call from National Public Radio. Billy Taylor was leaving *Jazz Alive!* and Tim Owens, the program's producer, was calling to offer me the job of permanent host. "We need to do a better job of capturing what's going on around the country," Tim said. I thought to myself, yes, it's a terrific time to document a vanishing way of life.

At the same time, I had an idea for another album and for the first time, I decided to pay for it with my own money and then license it around the world. The idea was to record what I called *Old Songs for the New Depression*, classic material from the thirties, Depression era songs, updated for the "New Depression" we were all living through. I had been working out the arrangements on the live gigs, so that summer, I went in with Richie Cole, drummer Buddy Williams and bass player Marcus Miller and cut a collection of ten stripped down, reharmonized songs, such as "Let's Get Away from It All," "Old Folks," and a handful of originals. The second day, my friend Michael Cuscuna came down to listen to the playbacks. Sitting in the control room, he said, "What ever happened to that song you wrote about all the piano players?"

I had completely forgotten about it. Several months before, while on a phone call to Michael, I had sung him some lyrics based on the names of my favorite pianists. I couldn't imagine who would be interested in something like this but he said, "No, you should really record that," and so I got Buddy and Marcus and we walked into the studio and cut it, just like that. Over the years, it has become very popular, particularly among jazz musicians.

Piano Players

"They played piano and it went like this
They could swing as sweetly as an angel's kiss
I've been hearing George Shearing, running steady with Freddy Redd
Talk about piano players
In the past they really knew how to fly
They were a one way trip on a magic carpet ride
In the park with Sonny Clark, walking through the dark with Bud Powell
Won't you listen to them?
Walter Bishop, Walter Norris
Walter Davis, wall to wall explorers, like
Wynton Kelly and Art Tatum
Phineas, Thelonious, any way you rate 'em
The music that they made it's alive today
'Cause when you hear Cecil Taylor you hear Jelly Roll play
And nearing that clearing, you're hearing the real McCoy
Roll 'em Roy
Horace Silver, Horace Parlan
Barry Harris and don't forget Red Garland
Herbie Nichols, Harold Mabern
Flanagan, Ellington, Jay McShann, they burn
More brightly rightly today

Because nothing in the world's gonna take your breath away
Like Count Basie, Fats Waller
Pine Top , Erroll Garner
Hamp Hawes, Norman Simmons
Kenny Drew, Bobby Timmons
Duke Pearson, Duke Jordan
Hank Jones still recordin'
Oscar got the Grammy but
Bill Evans put the whammy on Miles..."

Six months later, when the record was released on the Island label, this song helped propel it to number one on the jazz charts.

With Jon Hendricks learning "Old Folks" (1975)

The Bicentennial Bebop Band (1976)
Gary Zappa, Ben, David Woodford, Curley Cooke, Richie Morales,
Vince Ohern (tour manager) and Bill Brown (roadie)

Judy, Jon Hendricks, Eddie Jefferson, Leon Thomas, Annie Ross (1976)

On stage in Montreux (1978)
Ben, Tony Levin, bass, Steve Jordan, drums,
Steve Khan, guitar, Mike Mainieri, vibes

"The Cat and the Hat" sessions (1979) L to R: Abe Laborielle,
Al Schmitt, Linda Tyler Lee Ritenour, Ben, Mike Mainieri,
Tommy LiPuma, Steve Gadd, Buzzy Feiten

Carnegie Hall (1980) with L to R: Tim Hauser, Ben,
Michelle Hendricks, Janis Siegel, Jon Hendricks, Dizzy Gillespie,
Cheryl Bentyne, Richie Cole, James Moody

Leo and the clarinet (1980)

With Al Jarreau (1981)

"Bopcity" sessions (1982) L to R: Phil Woods, Mike Mainieri, Peter Erskine, Ben, Eddie Gomez

Finishing the marathon with Henry (1982)

With Archie Shepp in "Survivors" (1984)

Interviewing Chick Corea for "Sidran on Record" (1985)

Part Three

ON THE RIM
OF THE WELL

Chapter Seven

"The smartest way to work is to not quite know what you're doing...If you keep changing occupations, you can attain a kind of incredible ecstasy of learning."

— TIBOR KALMAN

1982

At National Public Radio, I was given a small office with piles of tapes and told to listen to them, and if I found something I really liked, to arrange to put it on the air. Tim Owens was hoping I would move to Washington, D.C., but I preferred to take part of my paycheck and invest it in Northwest Airlines. I flew to Washington every Tuesday morning and returned to Madison on the last flight Thursday night. In D.C., I stayed at a hotel around the corner from the NPR offices and generally hung out at work for ten or twelve hours a day. I heard a lot of great music, some of it obscure, much of it inspired, and I talked to many musicians from around the country. I also read all the audience mail and answered as much of it as I could.

What became clear was that the stereotypical image of the jazz audience in America was inaccurate. It was not limited to small pockets of sophisticated connoisseurs in major urban areas. Jazz listeners were young and old, black and white, rural and urban, rich and not rich (you couldn't be poor if you had jazz). The people who loved this music came to it on a kind of personal pilgrimage, and took it with them throughout their entire lives, wherever they went. When Tim and I went over the listener surveys, it became clear that we could be doing a much better job of serving our audience and getting out the news that jazz remained a kind of people's music. After a decade of "fattening frogs for snakes" in the record business, it was a blessed relief.

Coincidentally, *Old Songs for the New Depression* was alive and well, despite having received a scathing review in *People* magazine. The unsigned review said, in part, "Ben Sidran is to music what a wrecking ball is to sculpture." I was in shock; I couldn't believe my songs could draw such an intense reaction from anybody, let alone an unidentified reviewer in a popular rag. But for a few days, I was profoundly depressed by the thought that every "straight" person I ever knew would see it. My close friends all called to say, "Ben, consider the source," but I remained despondent until the afternoon Henry Wilson came over to go running bearing a present. It was a T-shirt with the words "wrecking ball" emblazoned across the front. I put on the shirt and we ran nearly ten miles that day, singing "Easy Street" (life could be so sweet), one of the songs from the vilified album.

Henry Wilson and I had started running together sometime around 1974. I had stopped smoking the year before, and I remember clearly the first day Henry came by my house to get me. I put on some old sneakers, and we went out the front door, turned right, and set out to run to his house, one mile away. We got as far as the end of the block and I had to walk back home. It took me about a month to be able to run the mile to his house, and another month to be able to run the second mile back to mine. But once I could run two miles, it was all downhill.

Running with Henry was a breeze. He was a natural, and he ran effortlessly, as if his feet didn't actually strike the ground, but just kind of passed over it on their way back up into the air. When he ran, his thumbs and his index fingers naturally formed little circles, almost as if he were meditating. When you ran with Henry, you just naturally fell into his pace, your feet seemed to float like large feathers, and your hands just naturally formed perfect little mediation "O's."

We ran in all kinds of weather. I have pictures of us coming in from a run with every hair on my face caked in ice — it had been well below zero — and pictures of us sweating up steep hills deep into the August heat. When we ran, we talked about everything and everybody. We talked about jazz and about medicine and how they were one and the same.

Henry was my doctor. There was no question about this as soon as we met. He was an internist with a small practice in a local neighborhood center, but he was really on call all day every day. One night, when Judy sliced her finger making dinner, Henry came over and stitched her up as if it was part of the preparation. Henry demystified medicine. He treated the whole being. Once he had a patient, an older man, whose health was failing, and after spending some time with him, Henry determined his problem was that he had no job. So Henry found him a job.

You could ask Henry anything and he would tell you the straight dope. He told me to do three things: wear a seat belt, don't smoke cigarettes, and take an aspirin every day. This was back in 1973. He said if I did these three things, I was doing 80 percent of what was possible to preserve my life. The rest, I assumed, was connected to this running thing. Henry got me running to save my life.

So we ran. A few times a week. For years. As time passed, like so many fools of the day, we ran further and further. I'm sure we were hooked on the endorphins — we would run six, seven, ten miles at a good clip and then finish in a ferocious wind sprint — but we told each other we were getting stronger. We even fantasized that when we were old, the doctor would have to use special instruments to cut into us because our bodies would be so tough. Henry said not to worry about my health; he would tell me if it was ever time for me to worry. I gladly put my life in Henry's hands.

I even went flying with Henry. He loved his little plane as much as he loved his junky old VW Beetle. Flying was just a part of his life, so that when he got his pilot's license, I went up with him. My memory of this was like being five thousand feet up in his VW. The plane was small, loud and drafty, and we went rattling up into a beautiful spring day, when you could see miles of green corn fields and an endless blue sky. Not long thereafter, some pilot clipped a power line coming down and crashed into a field, and I asked Henry if he was worried about doing the same thing. He said, "No," that this guy had been a fool, flying beyond his abilities, and that virtually all the accidents that happened in small planes were caused by pilots who did stupid things. The implication, of course, was that he was no fool.

Eventually, in the winter of 1982, we decided we would run a marathon. We picked up the paper, saw the May 15th "Syttende Mai" run from Madison to Stoughton, and decided to train for it. By April, we were running from one side of the city to the other, up every hill and down every boulevard. We got to know Madison from the ground up. We were unbelievably strong. I remember the feeling of running with no effort at all. No pain. Actually, no sensation whatsoever. Just the feeling of moving through the wind, with Henry gliding along next to me.

The day of the big race, the temperature was unseasonably hot. We suffered terribly up long steep hills out in the treeless countryside. To keep our spirits up, we sang "Easy Street" and "Old Folks," the song Jon Hendricks had taught me. We made it to the finish line together, and I have a picture of us sprinting the last 100 yards. We were a couple of whipped dogs, but we were going to be hard to cut into.

After the race, I felt like a million bucks. I remember walking around the city and feeling no pain, no exhaustion, only the unbearable lightness of being.

A few months later, I also began to feel something unpleasant in my left knee. At first I tried running through it. It did not go away. Then I tried laying off of it, and it would quiet down. But at night, I would sometimes wake in screaming pain, the knee frozen in whatever position I had fallen asleep in. I would have to take my left leg in both hands and physically move it just to stop from crying out. Henry was working me through this when his plane crashed.

Leo says the first time he ever saw me cry was when I hung up the phone. Henry and I were supposed to play racquetball that afternoon, and in the morning, he had come by to say he was going flying and did I want to go with him. I declined so he decided to go up with a more experienced flier and practice some routines he was working on for his instrument rating. That day, the sky was blue, and I'm sure he could see the rolling green hills for miles.

I stopped running after Henry died and gradually the knee felt better on its own. It would act up if I pushed it. I dreamed of Henry sometimes. I was so angry with him, I would confront him in the dreams, saying, "You promised to take care of me. Now what am I gonna do?" I told Judy that I was so angry with him for dying that the next time I saw him, I was gonna kill him. We got older, but Henry didn't. He was forever 35 in our memories, and in the pictures of us crossing the finish line together.

That spring, *Jazz Alive!* went to New Orleans to cover the Jazz and Heritage Festival. It was my first chance to do the kind of location reporting that Tim and I had been talking about, capturing the feel of a whole jazz community, not just the music. I arranged to take an engineer and go on a car ride through the city with Mac Rebennack (a.k.a. Doctor John). Mac was in great spirits that day, having just survived a harrowing experience with his health. As the car sped through the Garden District on our way to one of his old haunts, Mac turned to me and said, "Man, your song 'Life's a Lesson' got me through some hard times in the hospital." I felt a chill. It was as if a note I had placed into a bottle on the ocean had come back to me with a kiss. I said, "Thanks, Mac, I just wrote what I heard in my head."

We drove through the streets and he talked about how the city had changed. He said, "Air conditioning. Before air conditioning, people would just sit on their front porch at night and everybody knew everything about everybody. Now people sit inside and nobody knows what's going on in the streets. Crime went way up." He told me how district attorney Jim Garrison had ruined the city's music scene in the early sixties by shutting down so many of the clubs under the pretense of controlling this new crime wave. It was a first-class example of the hidden agenda that comes along with every new technology.

Mac took me to the pool hall where the great "rhumbalerro" piano player Professor Longhair used to play. The old upright piano was still there. We sat together on the bench and Mac showed me how 'Fess used to kick the side of the piano when he played, creating the off-rhythms that so confounded musicians from out of town. Mac remains one of the last living repositories of this arcane technique. And, finally, he told us the story of how the character "Doctor John" was born. "I wasn't supposed to be Doctor John," he said. "I had somebody else in mind. I just wanted to make this record. But at the last minute, he flaked out, so I said, 'OK, I'll be the front man.'" What you stumble on....

That night, Mac was playing a gig on a riverboat called *The President*, an old stern wheeler that still made its rounds up and down the Mississippi. It was a double bill with Wynton Marsalis, who was performing in New Orleans for the first time since winning two Grammys for parallel jazz and classical recordings. The mayor had declared it "Wynton Marsalis Day," and *The President* was packed to the gunwales with three thousand happy fans a good hour before the whistle blew and we all slipped away from the levy.

Before the set, I interviewed Wynton for *Jazz Alive!*. I said, "It must be a great feeling to return home to 'Wynton Marsalis Day' and to be able to carry the banner of jazz back to its birthplace." Wynton, still in his early twenties, said, "Aw man, it ain't nothing. You know, New Orleans has never been much of a jazz town. These people are just here because they were told they were supposed to come. It's a fashion thing. If they really listened to my music, it would change their lives."

I knew what he meant, but I couldn't believe he had said it. Was it possible he was so indifferent to his extraordinary good luck and great recognition, even knowing how many musicians, including his father Ellis, had received so little? Years later, it became clear that his issues were much more complicated than that, driven in part by the massive balloon of hype that was lifting him higher, and he was feeling the hot breath of history on his neck, the pressure to be both the leader of the black "young lions" and a paragon of classical Western virtue. At the time, he was still a very young man, struggling to find his own musical voice, and he was clearly uncomfortable about having to make his mistakes in the spotlight.

As he told me a few years later, "You listen to recordings of Clifford Brown, I mean Clifford Brown plays ten times more trumpet than me or anybody I've heard. But when Clifford Brown came into the music, he was playing a *type* of music. He wasn't responsible for providing an *environment* of music. I'm sorry. He just didn't have to do that... He played inside of the body of the music, to learn the craft of the music. You see what I'm saying? I mean, if all these great musicians didn't do that, how am I going to come out, and I have to provide an environment and learn how to play, too? Come on, man, I can't do that."

After his set, which was received with sincere enthusiasm, Dr. John came out and just ripped up the crowd on *The President*.

All through the spring and summer, I toured to keep the spirit of *Old Songs* alive. Starting in Chicago on June 1, I headed west. through Phoenix, Los Angeles, San Francisco, Seattle, Anchorage, then across the Pacific to Honolulu, then over to Sydney and Auckland, finally arriving back home in late July, in time for Judy's thirty-fifth birthday party. After a few days rest, I began my commute to Washington, D.C. again, helping to turn out two hours of *Jazz Alive!* each week and reaching out to as many musicians around the country as I could, encouraging them to send us tapes, to use NPR as their contact to the heart of America's heartland.

Except for a brief trip in November to Germany, London and Paris, I spent the rest of the year commuting between my little office on N Street and my house in Madison. Leo was always waiting with Judy at the airport when I returned on Thursday nights, and I always brought him a Twix candy bar that I had grabbed from the World Club before the plane took off. Walking down the jetway to the terminal in Madison, I would see this little blond curly head jumping up and down with excitement. "You have something for me?" he would ask knowingly as I came through security. Another meaningful ritual established. To this day, a Twix is a magical thing.

In mid December, I had lunch with NPR's Susan Stamberg, one of the key reporters on the "All Things Considered" news program. When I first arrived at NPR, I had gone looking for her. Her seductive way with words, and the disarming style she used when interviewing even the toughest guests, made her one of my favorite radio journalists. Over the months, I had several opportunities to watch her work, but I really wanted to know how she did what she did. It seemed so effortless, yet I knew that like all good technique, hers was invisible by design.

As we sat down, she asked me, "How are you getting on?"

"Good," I said, "but I'm struggling to find my voice reading scripts. I feel wooden. I'm not sure who to be."

"Look, they hired you because you are a musician, not because you are a professional radio voice. Be yourself. Tell it to a friend." I pictured Henry Wilson's face. Yes, I could just talk to Henry.

"I think of it like music," she said. "If my voice goes up in one part of the line, I make sure to match it with a descending line further on. It's like you have to sing it as you go."

I said, "So when you write the script, you can hear this internal melody?"

"Yes. And Ben, you have to do more interviews. You're good at it. You should get a whole segment where you talk to the musicians. You bring them out, and nobody is giving them a chance to be heard. It's a natural for you."

"It's not up to me," I said.

"Yes it is," she said. "Fight for it."

1983

We continued to expand the *Jazz Alive!* format with live remotes. In April 1983, we went to Los Angeles to paint an aural portrait of that city. We were still basically a performance show, airing as much live music as possible, but we included verities and tricks borrowed from news production, making radio programs for the mind as well as for the ears. We used live standups in historical backgrounds to create a living picture of jazz. In a way, we were fighting a holding action, because at the same time, the assault on the jazz life continued on all fronts. The economics of the nightclub business, the record business, even the radio business, resulted in a reduced jazz presence in most American cities. But hard times never killed jazz. Like a wildflower, it continued to sprout through the concrete of adversity and indifference, and the music blossomed when and wherever it was watered with a little kindness.

In May, I went into the studio to record a follow-up to *Old Songs*. The experience of paying for it myself and licensing it to the world was working. That is, I wasn't selling fewer records than before, and now, I owned my work "in perpetuity." *Bop City* was another small format recording, captured in a balanced environment with earphones optional. What you played was what you got. Again, I had written lyrics to jazz classics, including Miles Davis' "Nardis" (my last name backwards), Freddie Hubbard's "Up Jumped Spring," Charlie Rouse's "Little Sherry" and Thelonious Monk's "Monk's Mood." Along with Mike Mainieri, drummer Peter

Erskine, bass player Eddie Gomez and saxophonist Phil Woods, I took the *Jazz Alive!* ethos with me into the studio: anybody could be creative with a lot of time and money, but it took a special group to pull it off with very little of either.

Before we cut the title song, an original called "Bop City," I sketched the arrangement to Phil Woods. He stood by the piano watching as I played the melody, saying nothing. When I finished, he said, "Cool," and pulled out a small wooden pipe. "Time to get in touch with my true feelings," he said, and lit the pipe, took a long pull on the contents, and then offered it to me. Wisely, I refused. (Later, I discovered it to be some of the most insane weed I have ever smoked.) Peter counted off a burning tempo and Phil seemed to leap out of his horn, attacking the melody and then launching into a ferocious solo that built in dizzying loops, ultimately landing precisely on the downbeat of the interlude that took us back to the head. One take was clearly all that was required. It was not a question of whether you could step into the same stream twice, but, with these guys, could you dare to step into it once. It was all about getting your feet wet.

Two days of recording ended with Mike and I performing a Monk ballad — "Monk's Mood" — as a duet. I had written lyrics capturing the last days of two people who have been together a long time. The lyrics were dedicated to Monk and his wife Nellie, of course, but I was also thinking about Judy and me. It is a difficult melody to sing, and I tried not to force the sentiment or the notes in any way. It felt like I was standing on a precipice. As Mike counted it off, I just took a deep breath and jumped.

Monks Mood

"You and I together
Ever a brave new start
As we grow old, dear
Songs that we hold dear
Play for the day we part
You and I forever
So sweetly we play our part
Time doesn't pass, it's wine in our glass
Let's drink now to dying's last art.
And when we're gone
Who will carry on
Who will remember today
Those who are strong
Will carry us on
And music will show them the way
You and I completely

So sweetly we play our part
Turning the page and
Crossing the stage
We bow once to life and we depart."

Listening to the playback, I loved the dark spontaneity; clearly, I no longer cared about my shortcomings. I was simply proud to have been part of the moment. Several months later, when Mose Allison heard it, he said, "Man, that's the one. That's your contribution."

Throughout that spring and summer I continued to play concerts, notably a series of duo gigs with bass player Richard Davis — one concert was recorded and later released as the album *Live at the Elvehjem Museum* — but mostly, my activities were focused on *Jazz Alive!*

So it was a blow to arrive at the NPR offices one afternoon in September and learn that Frank Mankowitz, then president of NPR, had somehow misplaced a couple of million dollars. The immediate and practical effect was that many programs had to be jettisoned. The jazz programming went first. Even though *Jazz Alive!* had won the prestigious Peabody Award that year and was the single most popular program on the NPR cultural programming service, it was being thrown overboard. Jazz has always been among the first to get the news, whatever it is. That's why jazz musicians are like canaries in the coal mine: when they stop singing, you better stop digging and run.

The shock waves spread quickly beyond the NPR offices. It was just the latest in a series of economic hits for the jazz community, and within months, many record companies were again rethinking their commitment to the music. In a year-end summary, *Billboard* magazine captured the tenor of the times:

"From a business standpoint, the picture remained bleak, darkened considerably by further attrition in the available avenues for mass exposure and the continuing retreat of major record companies from the jazz arena... Explaining the branch firms' (major labels) reluctance, at least in part, was the turmoil seen in radio. With formal commercial jazz formats nearly extinct, jazz artists had come to rely upon the national reach of National Public Radio stations, but NPR financial problems led to the cancellation of the network's influential "Jazz Alive!" series and curtailment of its satellite-fed jazz programming blocks. Meanwhile, live jazz, like live music in other genres, faced the encroachment of recorded entertainment..."

That week, when I returned home from Washington, Leo and Judy were there to meet me as usual, but Leo wasn't jumping up and down at the gate. When I came through security and said to him, "Here's your Twix," he took it and looked away. In the car on the way home, he said nothing. But that night, when I put him to bed, he said, "Are you gonna be okay?"

"What do you mean?"

"You lost your job...."

I had always looked at NPR as a chance, a party with a purpose, a continued graduate education, a way to do some good, to leave the planet a little better off than when I found it. But a job? I guess it had never occurred to me. I had finally had a job, like everybody else, the first one since we left England more than a decade before, but it had to end for me to realize it even existed.

"Don't worry, Leo," I told him. "Tomorrow I'll get a new job."

Susan Stamberg was on the phone to me. "How would you like to be our new jazz correspondent? We don't really cover jazz on *All Things Considered,* and I think we should. You pick out a record or a musician or a story each week and you and I will do it as a conversation." It was a wonderful idea, making jazz a part of the flagship NPR news program. For more than a year, Susan and I held these weekly, on-air conversations about the music and the people who played it, ranging from a feature on a little known jazz whistler named Ron McCroby to a tribute to Frank Sinatra ("the chairman of the bored").

These segments were almost more powerful than *Jazz Alive!* had been for exposing the music, because they placed jazz — "America's only native art form" — squarely in the context of the news of the day. We are accustomed to hearing about sports and the weather on the news, but rarely the arts. By regularly including jazz on *All Things Considered,* we were bringing the people's music back to a lot of people who had no other way of finding it, or who perhaps didn't even know what they were missing. This is still the most viable way for jazz to survive: either it becomes part of the news or it's just history.

1984

One cold January night, I was lined up against the back wall of Wallebsky's saloon, a funky joint down an icy Minneapolis side street.

I was standing with blues singer Nick Gravenitis, saxophonist Archie Shepp and Doctor John. Nobody was talking. We were fixated on the stage where blues-master John Lee Hooker was ten minutes into one of his hypnotic one-chord chants. "Go back to school little girl. Go ahead, go ahead. Back to school. You fine and good looking. You're too young, you're too young. Don't look at me the way you do. Don't look at me, don't look at me. The way you do. I just might forget. I'll be your man one day. Wait for you. You turn twenty-one. Wait for you. Gonna be, be your man one day...."

The room was packed with sweating, twisting bodies. It was hot and sticky as only a Midwestern bar in the dead of winter can be, and right down front, not three feet from where John Lee was singing, right in his face, a very sexy young girl was just grinding away, smiling up at him. You knew John Lee was not gonna let this groove go anytime soon. It was a fantastic example of cause and effect, although it couldn't be said just who was which.

We were at Wallebsky's, along with a few dozen other musicians and a few hundred fans, to participate in a film called *Survivors*. Produced by Cork Marcheschi, a neon artist turned music entrepreneur, it was three days of blues and beer. Archie and I were scheduled to play a duet later that afternoon, and we had rehearsed the night before. That is, I had gone to his hotel room and hung out for a couple of hours, talking politics, race, music, travel, food, education, friends, everything but our performance. Since neither one of us knew what to expect at the gig the next day, there was no point in rehearsing the future.

We had arrived earlier that day, me from Madison, Archie from Massachusetts, where he was teaching, and you could tell he was glad to get out of town. We hung pretty hard that night, and when he asked about George Brown—Archie and George had known each other back in the day of John Coltrane—all I could say was, "I think he's back in Paris now." I felt a terrible loss. George had once been a connection to the center of the musical universe, a powerful, spiritual world of black music, of striving to push the boundaries of the known a little further each day. And now this whole scene was scattered to the four corners of the earth. Not only George Brown but all the George Browns, all the warriors who had set off in search of the Holy Grail, the transcendent moment, the lost chord. Many, like Archie, had taken shelter in rural universities, giving out three credits to kids who couldn't possibly have any idea about the potency of their music. Many more, like George, were holed up in cold water flats or selling instruments in music stores or, worse, were simply gone. Archie was unpacking his tenor, talking about this "motherfucker" and that "motherfucker," and I was thinking, we're all fucked. We're here doing a blues archive show. We're being called survivors.

When we got to the club, Archie wearing his three-piece Harris Tweed suit, me in a sweater and dress slacks, we were confronted with this seething crowd of young white kids in T-shirts and jeans, just grooved to the teeth on the three-chord shuffle. Many of them had been hanging out for all three days and by now, it was just one long boogie to them. When John Lee Hooker finally came off the stage, there was a brief set change and then Cork was at the microphone saying, "They're gonna do it a little different now folks. Please welcome Dr. Ben Sidran and Dr. Archie Shepp."

We walked up and looked out into the sea of faces and Archie immediately broke a sweat. It was 110 degrees on stage, and he was wearing a wool suit. He just looked at me and nodded, and I started singing the opening verse to the blues song "Going Down Slow:" "Well I have had my fun if I don't get well no more...." Never had it seemed more appropriate.

We played for about an hour, and Archie never even unbuttoned his vest. When we came off the stage, sweat still pouring down Archie's face and his expression resolutely impassive, Cork put a microphone in front of him and asked about the blues in America. Archie said, "America has put a lot of unusual phenomena together. I think here we have a possibility to do things that have never been done before. Culturally, racially, socially, to evolve in the sense that the South American countries have done. Because ultimately, for America to survive, we have to dispel with the question of race. And I think black music is an important part of this process." Listening to Archie roll on, I thought, "All the hot air and high hopes in the world won't keep this balloon afloat. It's going down slow."

That April, I went to Boulder, Colorado to attend the annual Conference on World Affairs. Every year since the late forties, a distinguished if somewhat motley collection of intellectuals and practitioners, thinkers and doers, locals and visitors, got together for a week under the auspices of the University of Colorado, to hold endless panel discussions, talk and eat and scheme and generally make merry. Hence the Conference's inside sobriquet, a twist on Veblen: "The Leisure of the Theory Class." My panels attempted to confront the issue of how technology mutates human relationships, and I shared several of these with an earnest young scholar named Langdon Winner, at the time a professor at U.C. Santa Cruz.

Langdon was interested in the distinction between popular culture and what's popular, and, talking about the impact of today's mega stores, he said, "They create the illusion of freedom of choice, but in fact, they produce market glut, which ultimately reduces volume because the overabundance of choice becomes paralyzing." Market segmentation, dividing up the audience into ever-thinner segments, is the main way the music business attempts to make the "too big" smaller. The result, of course, is a new kind of segregation, as well as a new level of super-abundance. This is one basis for the argument that the music marketing system today is inherently racist. It is also a reason why blues and jazz are often sold to folks as entirely different things, when in fact, and in history, they share they same root.

Talking on the phone to Susan Stamberg, I told her about an idea I had for a radio show. "It's called 'On The Record,'" I said. "I'd interview a different jazz musician each week, and we'd listen to records together. It's a great way to walk through somebody's career."

Susan said, "Good idea. But the name of the program is 'Sidran on Record.'"

"Really?"

"Absolutely. You're presenting a lot more than chat and records. It's about your relationship to these people and to this music."

1985

The pilot program for *Sidran on Record* was recorded in July with David Sanborn. On the way to meet him at his hotel, I ran into drummer Buddy Williams, whom I hadn't seen since we recorded *Old Songs* a few years earlier. I asked him how things were going, and he said, "I feel like John Henry, just keeping one step in front of the machine." He was talking about the drum machine, a device that had come into fashion and which, along with synthesizers, would soon put a lot of studio musicians out of work. But he was also tapping into a much deeper vein. Man-versus-machine would be the story of the music business for the rest of the century.

When the pilot program was completed, we sent it out over the NPR satellite. By September, we had commitments from over one hundred stations to carry the show for a minimum of thirteen weeks. This was the critical mass needed for NPR to distribute the program. I got to work arranging the interviews at a small recording studio on lower Broadway in New York City. Starting that October, and continuing approximately once a month for the next five years, I rode the elevator at 648 Broadway up to Roxy Recorders on the third floor and continued my musical and spiritual education. Abdullah Ibrahim, Art Blakey, Gil Evans, Pepper Adams, McCoy Tyner, Barry Harris, Sonny Rollins, Bob Moses, John Scofield, Donald Fagen, Steve Gadd, David Murray, Charlie Rouse, Carla Bley, Phil Woods, Freddie Hubbard, Bobby McFerrin, Jack DeJohnette, Frank Morgan, Max Roach, Miles Davis, Jackie McLean, Jon Hendricks, Tony Williams, Grover Washington, Horace Silver, Keith Jarrett, Paul Motian, Steve Lacy, Betty Carter...the list is long, and, sadly, it is often a reminder of just how many we have lost.

The program quickly became a full-time job. Each week, I was scripting and editing one show, mixing and voicing another, and booking several more for the future. This too was a lot like trying to stay one step ahead of the train. Once you were on the tracks, you couldn't stop running because of the weekly commitment to ship the programs to Washington. The initial thirteen shows extended to twenty-six shows, and then thirty-nine, and then to the following year. In the end, I managed to produce more than one hundred episodes before I ran out of steam.

Over the years, people have asked me which interviews were my favorites. Perhaps it makes more sense to ask which were my favorite teachings, because each of the conversations, whether they lasted one hour or, in the case of Miles Davis, all day long, was a lesson in how a person chose to live his or her life. The music is a vehicle, a passion, a log in the flood, a visitation from on high, whatever, but the message is always in the life that's lead. You live it as you play it; you find your voice and you simultaneously find your story.

Over the years, I asked virtually every guest on the program where their sound (their voice) came from and nobody could answer the question. Miles came the closest, "Your sound," he said, "see, that's like your sweat!" But everybody agreed that your sound was your most important contribution. I ultimately came to believe that jazz music must be proof of some higher power, because this voice is visited upon such a broad range of the most unlikely people.

The following are a few of my favorite teachings.

- **Art Blakey: You are, in fact, you're in the nude.**
  Art Blakey was already a senior citizen and had just fathered a new baby boy when we spent the afternoon together. More to the point, he had been a spiritual mentor and father figure to several generations of players. When I asked him how he always managed to find such gifted young musicians, he said, "A lot of musicians I hear I'd like to have in the band, but they won't fit. Their personalities won't fit. You have to find out about their backgrounds and their dislikes to bring about cohesion in the band, and in the music, you know? Because if it's up there and it's a dislike among the different personalities on the bandstand, it cer-

tainly comes through the music. I teach musicians to look at it this way. You are, in fact, you're in the nude. You're in your birthday suit. People can see clean through you."

- **Jon Hendricks: Everything you do can swing.**

Jon Hendricks said, "I always try to swing, whatever I do. I think that's what I got most from singing with good jazz musicians. You don't just have to swing on the bandstand. Everything you do can swing. The way you relate to your fellow man, you know, that can swing. The way you pick up your little child, and bounce him, there's a swing to that. Everything can swing. I think everything in nature does swing."

- **Sonny Rollins: Can any of us ever really hear ourselves?**

Sonny Rollins, one of the most celebrated saxophonists for over a half a century, said in a quiet, almost sad voice, "When I got out of high school, I used to be very much interested in art. I used to love to do cartooning. And at that time, that was sort of my first love. And I sort of felt that this was what I would like to do. But I guess the main thing that I should say is that I didn't have a lot of confidence that I was good enough to really make it, you know...I never really thought I was good enough to play with some of these guys and make this music." At the time, Sonny, just out of high school, was being courted by both Miles Davis and Thelonious Monk, and, as the recorded evidence from the period shows, his playing was logical, inspired and fully formed. Can any of us ever really hear ourselves? Do we ever really know what our own voice sounds like?

- **Max Roach: Jazz doesn't just come from musicians.**

Max Roach, the premier drummer of the bebop period, was telling me how he was influenced by the tap dancers who used to open shows for jazz musicians in the forties. He was saying jazz doesn't just come from musicians, it comes from musicians hearing the world. He remembered clearly how, "When I was traveling back and forth from Brooklyn to the Manhattan School of Music, and riding the subways, a lot of ideas came out of the rattles of those wheels on those trains. I mean, it's unbelievable the rhythms that the subway creates. When you're interested in percussion, you know. I'd sit down and close my eyes and just swoon."

- **David Murray: If I can't have fun, get me off the stage.**

David Murray, the avant garde saxophonist, loved to take the air out of people who took "serious" music too seriously. "My whole thing," he said, "is to do it on a high level of art, *and* to have some fun. If I can't have fun, get me off the stage. I could be mundane at home, you know. But when I'm on the stage, I want to have fun. I think that's why people, probably like to see me, 'cause when I'm playing, I'm having a ball. I don't feel like I'm working, I'm just enjoying myself. It's like in football players, those cats get out there and they get pumped up and they just want to hit somebody. They're having fun. They're getting paid a lot of money for it, but, when it comes down to it, they're having fun."

- **Phil Woods: They had a passion about the life.**

Phil Woods talked about the importance of the road to the education of young musicians. In the lore of jazz, the bus was where the oral tradition was passed down from sideman to sideman, from the elders to the initiates. It was more than learning the music, it was learning how to live the life. "My first real bus," Phil said, "was the Birdland Allstar tour of '56. It was Basie's band, Sarah Vaughan, Al Hibbler, Bud Powell, Lester Young. I was with a group with Al Cohn, Conte Candoli, Kenny Dorham. I mean, you got on a bus with these guys, and you learned so much. These cats, they knew how to laugh to pass the time. There was never this agonizing artist stuff, you know, like, 'God, what a rotten President,' 'Oh, life is terrible...check the stock reports.' You know what I mean? They had a passion about the life. No phony bitching. And everybody knew what was happening. But within the confines of the bus. You'd leave that stuff off the bandstand, man."

- **Keith Jarrett: It's the only state from which to make music of any value.**

Keith Jarrett described his piano technique to me as "drowning." I asked him if he could demonstrate it at the piano. He said, "Well, you want me to drown for a little while?" I said, "Okay, I withdraw the request." He went on to say, "All through each day, every day, I am aware of that place. It's like a state. And it's the only state from which to make music of any value to you or anyone else. It's also a gift. I mean, it isn't as though we'd have to have this state available to us. And I would never have been able to invent it. I consider it a sacred thing, not to be fooled with, or played with, you know." I said I did.

- **Benny Golson: You're always just a half step away.**

We were walking down the street following the official interview when Benny turned to me and said, "Don Byas once told me that there are no wrong notes in jazz because you're always just a half step away from the right note." And then he laughed. But the joke contained solid information. Byas, an original saxophone master from the thirties, was passing along the simple truth of jazz improvisation — no mistakes, only opportunities — and Benny was passing it on to me. A moment later, as we were waiting for the light to change, Benny again absent-mindedly turned and said, "You know, they say necessity is the mother of invention, but opportunity is often the midwife." And he went on to tell me the story of how bass player Larry Graham — who worked with Sly Stone in the sixties and is credited with inventing the highly imitated "popping" sound — came up with his style: "he was working in a lounge act that had no drummer, so he had to be both drummer and bass player. The popping on the bass was just him playing the drums!" Walking with Benny Golson was like that: you were always just a half step away...from history.

- **Gil Evans: A certified fair share.**

Gil Evans walked into the studio one afternoon, dressed like a teenager in faded jeans and a T-shirt. He looked lean and fit and when I said he looked half his seventy-five years, he said, "Of course the only time I know how old I am is when I look in the mirror, right? When I don't look in the mirror, I never think of that. But the mirror has to remind me." He had survived three quarters of a century without the recognition that he deserved. "I'm so used to living from hand to mouth," he said, and even though he had just received a commission to do a film soundtrack, he was still hoping to finally receive "a certified fair share." "It's so rare," he said. "Most all the time, you're either gonna get fucked or you're gonna have to fuck somebody, right?" I told him I had recently talked to Mose Allison who told me "In business, it all comes down to somebody's money versus somebody else's life." He sighed, looked away and said, "That's right." Gil died not long after we spoke. And when the film came out a few months later, his music was not in it. He had been written out of his own history again.

- **Dizzy Gillespie: You have to know how to pack.**

Dizzy Gillespie was staying in the penthouse of a hotel on Chicago's "Gold Coast," "the reet suite on the sweet street," he called it as he welcomed me at the door. The suite was enormous, there were television sets blaring in various rooms, and Dizzy was smoking a big joint. I remember we were laughing a lot, and at one point I asked him how he managed to stay on the road so long. He got very serious, in that mock serious way he had where you never knew if he was clowning or not, and he said, "You have to know how to pack." And he took me into the bedroom, where yet another television was blaring, and showed me how he had organized his suitcase. It was a masterpiece of efficiency. He said, "You see, I have everything I need and I know where everything is." We laughed and smoked for what seemed like hours, and as I was leaving, he got quiet for a moment and then, out of nowhere, said, "Ben, you keep your heart right, you'll be all right."

- **Miles Davis: Now that you have so many records and cassettes, it's not about sound.**

I asked Miles about his magical voice on the instrument. He said, "It's just a 'sound.' And it's popular. You know, like years ago, composers...the reason you read about Beethoven was because he was the one they could understand. The other ones, you know, that they couldn't understand, they didn't get mentioned. So my tone must be the easiest for somebody to hear. You know, like Louis Armstrong, that kind of sound." And then he said, "Lester Young had his sound. Coleman Hawkins, Clifford Brown, Fats. You know, there's no more 'sound' today. During those days when you didn't hear anybody to copy, guys got their own sound. But now that you have so many records and cassettes, it's not about sound, you know what I mean?"

As usual, Miles had put his finger directly on the pulse of the program, the inverse relationship between a person's "sound" (their voice, their unique style) and the spread of technology. Miles' point was that the more one learns from documents (artifacts) rather than real life, the less likely one is to develop a distinctive voice.

"So," I said, "before there was such widespread distribution of recordings, people were forced to develop their own sounds?"

Miles said, "*Forced* to play without...they didn't have anything to listen to, you know? But you would *watch* guys play an instrument, and you would like the *attitude*, the *concept*, the way it looks, the way they hold it, the way they dress. But nowadays, they have..." and here he drifted for a moment, then said, "I saw maybe three trumpet players in Lionel Hampton's band...they all sound alike."

At the end of a long day, I asked Miles one final question. "The song 'Nardis'," I said, "How did you happen to name it?."

"I can't remember," Miles said. "I think I just liked the name. What does it mean?"

I said, "I don't know, but it's my last name backwards."

"No kidding?" said Miles," I don't know, but that's a nice name, man."

- **Rudy Van Gelder: The problem of recording jazz music**

Unlike the other guests on *Sidran on Record* who were musicians, Rudy Van Gelder is a recording engineer who was present at the birth of many great jazz records. More than most others, he was aware of how advances in technology shaped the music.

We talked at length about what he called the "problem" of recording jazz music. The problem, he said, was that a musician never hears himself the way the listener or, for that matter, the microphone hears him. For example, a trumpet player is behind the instrument, and the sound is going "out." But on the recording, it is going "in," into the microphone and into the tape machine. "And that's usually, to his own mind, different from what he thinks he should sound like." So the very process of recording, of documenting the music, distorts the music from the performer's point of view.

But the problem becomes further complicated by the process of multi-track recording, which began in the sixties. Up until then, what you played was what you got. That ended with multi-track machines. Multi-track machines allowed you to record each musician on a separate track (and on a separate day if you chose to) and to rebalance, or even replace them later (an "overdub"). In addition, because of these possibilities, multi-tracking meant musicians were often literally separated by portable walls and baffles, so that the sound of one instrument wouldn't "leak" into the microphone of another. Players became isolated in their own little worlds. "It was my philosophy at the time," Rudy said, "that this thing is really great. I thought, 'Now I'm gonna have a second chance at this.' And if I miss an entrance of a solo, or something like that, I'm going to be able to fix it later."

"But it didn't work out like that," he said, "because musicians were just as aware of this as I was. And it ended up that they wanted to overdub. And therefore,

once you got into an overdub situation, they had to have earphones. And everyone had to hear what was on the tape. And a generation of musicians developed
that relied on that, and expected to be able to use that as a way to make records."

"That's an interesting point," I said. "The use of earphones was a radical
departure."

"Right, that's right. Now each musician has his own feeling about what he
wants to hear. That didn't exist in the earlier time period."

"So what made the earlier recordings special was that people were having to
make live adjustments in order to get the music down."

"Absolutely..."

"And these days, we're talking about ways of removing each individual from
the live process."

"That's exactly right," Rudy said. "It's almost as if you wanted to think of
a way to inhibit creativity in jazz music, I would come up with a multi-track
machine. A 24-track recorder that you could overdub on...It's a machine of
mass destruction."

During this period, I came to recognize that technology had its own agenda. It
brought repeatability and the means to fix things, but just because it is possible
to "fix" something doesn't mean it's always a good idea. In many ways, perfection
is the enemy of intuition. If intuition is the heart of one's style, then "fixing it" is
often erasing one's personality. The overuse of technology is one of the main reasons why style, as we used to know it, is dying out.

In his book *Songlines*, the author Bruce Chatwin tells a marvelous story about
an aborigine who is riding in a car through the Australian outback. The man is the
repository of the "song" of his people, and the song, which has been updated and
passed down by all those who have sung it before him, describes the actual landscape,
down to the smallest detail, as one would see it while walking across the countryside.
Driving through his homeland, this man attempts to sing his song, but of course the
car is moving too fast for him to articulate the words, to describe the geography as it's
passing, and so his song is essentially useless. Less than useless, because in destroying
the value of the song, the automobile also removes his continuity with his ancestors.
The technology literally strips him of his history and rips him up by the roots.

In the U.S.A., we throw away our treasures so easily. Like children, we
become enchanted with the box and discard the contents without a second
thought. Indeed, we become fascinated with the act of disposing; it gives us a
sense of power, of progress, and we become obsessed with each fancier and
newer package that we can dispose of. In the end, all that remains is this gesture
of dismissal. And it is this that we Americans are known for.

Whereas recording technology was originally the means of disseminating a piece of living culture, by the end of the century it had rendered the actual act of playing music together "old school" or "irrelevant." It's as if Heisenberg's Uncertainty Principle had come home to roost on yet another perch: we cannot perfect the documentation of culture through technology without fundamentally altering that culture. This is how the recording business has come to alter the music forever, to change the people who made the music, and, finally, to trivialize the documenting process itself. A textbook study of men and women who learned their lessons too well.

By the late 1990s, kids considered a sampled four-bar loop from a classic jazz record to be some kind of tribute to the past, a way of keeping it alive. In fact, by making it fodder for the technological abattoir, it was killing the entire concept of the past as surely as the car in the aborigine's tale was making him homeless.

In 1985, I made my synthesizer album, *On the Cool Side*. In part, it was a result of a trip to Japan. One day, while riding on the bullet train from Tokyo to Osaka with my friend Nobu Yoshinari, I asked him to tell me something I might not know about the Japanese. He said, "Do you know about the Mitsubishi Boy?"

I said, "No, what is a Mitsubishi Boy?"

"It's like a company man, only more intense."

"What would a Mitsubishi Boy say?"

"Anything, just not to be a failure."

That afternoon, I wrote the song "Mitsubishi Boy," chronicling what I saw out the window.

Mitsubishi Boy

"They grow up outside of Nagoya where the houses are old
And the graves are carefully tended
In the ancient fields, they grow power lines and neon signs
And the word Mitsubishi floats like freedom
And the smoke rises from the fires
Where they burn their desires
And they say anything
Not to be a failure
They grow up outside of Sapporo where the houses are new
And the graves are carefully tended

They wear the mask, pump the gas, stand in line, drink the wine
Hang up the washing in the rain to dry out on the line
And the smoke rises from the fires
Where they burn their desires
And they say anything
Not to be a failure
Mitsubishi Boy, Mitsubishi Boy
The haiku of fast food, the rain and the smoke
The sky is crying and nobody gets the joke
The train moves too fast to make out the face in the window
The train moves so fast, it's just one long window, faceless.
And the smoke rises from the fires
Where they burn their desires
And they say anything
Not to be a failure
Mitsubishi Boy, Mitsubishi Boy"

The song was a perfect vehicle for the new technology. Later, working at Paragon studios in Chicago, I got my hands on a Lynn drum machine and programmed the rhythm and used a DX7 keyboard to sound like a Fender Rhodes, and played the bass parts on yet another synthesizer. I found the process tedious and I wasn't really very good at it. But talking to Billy Peterson about it several days later, I discovered he had two younger brothers, Ricky and Paul, who were masters of the art. So I headed for Minneapolis again.

Billy was living at a place we jokingly referred to as "The Portland Arms," a run-down apartment house on the edge of the Minneapolis ghetto. In his first-floor apartment, there was a Hammond B3 organ, a seven-foot Yamaha grand piano, a drum kit, a talking bird, usually one or two guys sitting around watching an oversized television and somebody else crashed in one of the bedrooms. Billy's own little room in the back contained a single bed and a closet full of weights, pulleys, inner tubes and other workout gear. Billy was serious about his music and his physical training. Everything else was up for grabs.

His younger brother Ricky had just moved into the apartment, and the three of us spent a week living in this bachelor rubble, creating grooved arrangements of standards like "Lover Man" and "Heat Wave," along with originals like "Mitsubishi Boy." I wanted to somehow get back to dance music, back to the hypnotic groove.

The problem with drum machines, and music computers in general, is that even though you can react to them, they will not react back to you. It's a one-way conversation. And if jazz is the art of surprise, it's pretty hard to be surprised by something you have just programmed. The finished record has some nice moments, but to my ear it has always seemed devoid of air, existing in an atmosphere like pure nitrogen, where everything can be seen, but nothing can be believed. Recordings made this way tend to get dated very quickly. A few years later, you hear the synth programs and the samples and the waveforms and you know exactly what year it was made and what gear was used. Hearing *On the Cool Side* today, only the title song has meaning for me. And that is because it brought Steve Miller back into my life.

1986

I had been touring with my band that spring, a West Coast junket that started in Los Angeles and got as far north as Anchorage, Alaska—where we played at Mr. Whitekeys' "Fly By Nightclub," a roadhouse that served both Spam and Chateau Lafite Rothschild, and where Whitekeys himself occasionally came out of the kitchen wearing a paper mache salmon on his head to introduce the band. At one point, as we were settling into a two-week run in Seattle at the Jazz Alley, Steve showed up. He had moved to Seattle a few years earlier, in 1982, after touring behind his last big hit "Abracadabra." Even though he had had the number one single in the country at the time, he was not playing to full houses, so one day, he simply walked off the stage, handed his guitar to his roadie and said, "That's it." He hung it up, left the road, and moved into a large house on Mercer Island.

The first night we played at Jazz Alley, Steve was there. He came back a couple of times that week and listened to the band. During the day, I hung out at his place, listening to music and telling war stories. By the second week, Steve brought his guitar and a little amp down to the club and was playing some blues and shuffles with us. A couple of times during the week, we cruised Lake Washington on his yacht, the *Abracadabra*, and on one such afternoon, as we were listening to rough mixes of the song "On the Cool Side," Steve started singing along with it. He sounded great as usual. I asked him if he would add a vocal part to the master and he agreed. The result is

Steve at his best, a hip R&B vocal arrangement on top of a pop track with philosophical lyrics:

On the Cool Side

"You know sometimes it seems like all the good times are gone
But you got to keep pushing, you got to keep on keeping on
For example take me sitting up here today
I wouldn't be with you if I believed the things that the people say
You got to keep on searching (Keep it on the cool side)
Keep on keeping on
You got to keep on searching (Keep it on the cool side)
Keep on keeping on
For example, they say you won't find water digging in the sand
But you keep right on digging you might find your own lemonade stand
They say you won't find your dinner looking up in the sky
But you keep right on searching and all four courses might fly by
You got to keep on searching (Keep it on the cool side)
Keep on keeping on
And when you get a little tired and you can't find a place to rest
And what used to come easy is now some kind of test
Just remember there ain't no substitute for life
You wouldn't even know you were living if it weren't for all this pain
and strife.
You got to keep on searching (Keep it on the cool side)
Keep on keeping on"

That winter, I went to Australia. Time moves so slowly Down Under, three weeks felt like three months. It began in Sydney with Barry Ward, the promoter, who introduced me to "No worries, mate." First we went to the racetrack where he masterfully picked six winners. Walking through the paddocks with him, watching him exchange tips with the jockeys and the punters, it was obvious that this was not his first trip to the ponies. He said, "Just do what I do," and I did. After the track, we went back to his office at the Bronte RSL (Returned Serviceman's League) and listened to music. At one point, he put on a tape of a swinging big band featuring a very hip singer. I said, "Who is that?" and he said, "Georgie Fame." I made Barry play it three times in a row as the sun set behind Bondi Beach. It was a name I wouldn't forget.

After a week playing at The Basement in Sydney, Barry and I started to travel the jazz outback, picking up sidemen as we went and playing little clubs here and there. When we got to Melbourne, we caught a cab from the train station to the club. The taxi pulled up in front of a run-down strip joint and Barry said, "Now this gig doesn't look like much from the outside, but it's not bad." We walked up a dark flight of rickety wooden stairs and at the top we found a large room littered with broken chairs and, in the middle, a battered upright piano. "No worries, mate," Barry said, "It's cool. Mose Allison played here." My heart broke. Months later, when I told Mose the story, he said, "Man, you don't have to go all the way to Australia, you can just go to West Texas and find the same thing."

Back in the States, I had booked a big concert at the Ordway Theater in St. Paul. The Ordway is a large, modern hall that holds a couple of thousand people, and, since a local radio station was promoting it, I knew it would sell out. Along with my band, I had Phil Woods playing with us, and then, when Steve Miller heard about the gig, he said he would like to play, too. It would be his first time back on stage since he had walked off in 1982. I decided to videotape the event—some kind of history was sure to be made—and I hired my friend Ethan Russell to direct it. For a month, we had our hands full with budgets, lighting, audio, trucks, cameras, transportation, after-market rights, above the line, below the line, per diems and post production. And then, on March 22, 1986, the day of the show arrived.

The rehearsals went fine, Steve was wearing his killer black shades and was loose and laughing; Ricky, Billy and Gordy didn't really need to rehearse. There was one glitch, however. By mid-afternoon, Phil Woods still hadn't shown up. Two o'clock became three o'clock, and then four o'clock, and still no Phil. I was getting wrapped up pretty tight, trying not to freak out in the midst of all the cameras and cables and microphones and people, but by five o'clock when Phil still hadn't arrived, I called a dinner break and retreated to my dressing room to stew. Steve walked back with me, took me inside and shut the door. He said, "From here on out, you are not the producer of this concert anymore. You are the artist. You don't answer the door, you don't answer the phone. If people want to talk to you they have to get through me." And suddenly everything got very quiet. Steve had created a classic cone of silence, as only a rock star can. I felt I was in good hands.

Just then, the door opened and in walked Phil. "Hey, baby," he said. "Hope I'm not late."

"Phil," I said, "you are always way ahead of everybody else."

1987

One rainy evening, I was sitting in the living room of Steve Miller's rambling house on Lake Washington. Leo was splashing around in the indoor swimming pool, Judy was in the kitchen with Steve's wife, Kim (third wife, second Kim), and Steve and I were listening to a tape of some tracks from a record I had started to make in Minneapolis. The first song we heard was a reharmonized arrangement of "Zip A Dee Do Da" and Steve started singing along with it. Next was an arrangement of Billie Holiday's "God Bless the Child," and Steve started singing along with that too. He sounded a little like Chet Baker, cool with no vibrato, and I said, "You know, we really could make a jazz record together. We could reharmonize the standards and some R&B tunes, and all you'd have to do is be yourself." I could see he liked the idea.

Earlier, we had been talking about how he still owed Capitol one more album, and he didn't know what to do about it. He wasn't writing original songs anymore, and if he didn't deliver something, they could tie him up indefinitely. I said, "Man, let's make a record your father would dig and you can split from the label." And that seemed to do it.

Steve's father, a prominent doctor, first in Milwaukee and then in Dallas, was a jazz and blues fan and a personal friend of guitar greats T-Bone Walker and Les Paul. (There is a famous tape of Steve at age seven or eight playing a song on guitar for Les, and saying over and over, "Hey, Les. Hey, Les..." trying to get the man's attention.) So his father loomed large in Steve's consciousness. But there was a darker side, which Steve was also candid about: his father sometimes drank to excess and could be abusive. So music connected Steve to both his father's love and his father's anger. It was a powerful motivator. And, finally, his father had recently been diagnosed with a serious illness. By the time dinner was ready, we had outlined the project.

Originally, it was planned to be "our" record, using my band and a lot of the songs I had been working on ("When Sunny Gets Blue," "Willow Weep for Me," "Ya, Ya") and both of us sharing the vocals. As soon as we got down to business, however, it was clear that it would have to be a Steve Miller record. We would produce it together, using my band, but it would be delivered to Capitol Records as the final album due on his contract. Steve was basically retired, hadn't played a gig in several years, and his dislike for the record industry was legendary. Several generations of Capitol executives had their own scary stories about encounters with Steve. His general message to them was "You are a bunch of clowns who don't know what you're doing, and it's my job to straighten you out, the sooner the better." I said, "This project could be a great way for you to say goodnight to this business." I was thinking of the prestige for him of doing a real "musicians album" instead of a pop record. He might have been thinking of something else, but he said, "Okay, let's do it."

A week later, I went back to Minneapolis and told Billy, Gordy and Ricky, "Boys, I've got good news and bad news. The good news is that Steve just heard the tracks we've been working on, and he wants them for his own next record. The bad news is that Steve just heard the tracks we're working on and he wants them for his own next record." I explained that the road we were about to go down was uncharted, that parts of it may be paved with gold but that nothing came for free, and there would probably be a price to pay somewhere down the line. On the other hand, if we kept our eyes open, possibly nobody would get hurt, and we could have some fun. I said, "It's all about money and fun. Usually the more you have of one, the less there is of the other."

A week in the life:

On March 23rd, Richard Davis and I went to the women's maximum-security prison at Taycheeda, Wisconsin to play a concert for the inmates. I was hoping to catch a peek at Barbara Hoffman, the "Playboy Bunny killer," but I didn't see her, or anybody that looked like they might have been a former resident of Heffner's hutch. Richard was magnificent as usual. By the end of the hour, he had all the women scat singing and clapping on two and four.

On March 29th, Leo and I went to Chicago, where he recorded one of his own songs in a full-blown recording studio. He played all the instruments, as he did in his studio at home, and completely took charge when it came to the vocals and the mixing. Marty Feldman, the owner of Paragon Studios, said to me, "We could make some money with this kid." I said, "Yeah, but maybe we should wait a few years before we permanently screw him up."

On March 31st, I talked to my congressman, Bob Kastenmeier, about HR 1195. I had been playing benefits and fundraisers for Bob since 1962, and he was now the chair of the House Judiciary Committee. I had called this extraordinary, reasoned man, because the record industry was making one of its periodic attempts to collect a tax on blank tape. Their position was that creators like myself were being robbed of our rights, and they were the natural parties to protect our work and collect this money on our behalf. I said to Bob, "These are the same crooks who haven't paid me in years. Who's going to protect me from my protectors?"

Then, on the first of April, I flew with my band to Seattle to record the tracks for Steve's album. It took three days. Gordy, as usual, was the drill sergeant, while Billy and I reharmonized the songs and cut them so they felt fresh. After Gordy and Billy went back to Minneapolis, Steve and I began to work on his vocals and guitar solos. Like a lot of good musicians who came of age in the age of the recording studio, Steve has learned to distrust his intuition and is reluctant to accept his first takes, or for that matter, his fourth or fifth takes. He prefers to "fix" everything and make it "perfect," and the process can take months. After a few days of this, I had to leave, so we prepared multi-track "slaves" of all the masters, giving Steve an additional twenty-four tracks to fill with vocals and another twenty-four tracks to play around with guitars.

I flew from Seattle directly to Washington D.C. to perform at the "Freedom Seder," a gathering of Jewish musicians and politicians from around the country, celebrating Passover together and, at the same time, helping to bring attention to the plight of the Russian Jews. The watchword of the event was "Let my people go," and I played "Eliyahu," a song dedicated to the prophet Elijah, who, the Torah tells us, will return to Earth, and on that day, that the lion shall lie down with the lamb.

From Washington, I flew to Boulder, Colorado, for the next annual Conference on World Affairs. This year, the music contingent was expanded to include jazz writer Leonard Feather and the brilliant arranger Johnny Mandel. We all stayed at the house of Betty Weems, an architect and jazz fan, who also housed various odd-men-out, including astronaut Rusty Schweikert. Coming back to the house late one night, I found Rusty showing his "home movies," only they weren't pictures of him at home, they were shots of him floating in a space capsule. A can of soda languidly drifted across the screen as Rusty waved and the Earth grandly rotated in the window behind him. "Escape velocity is the only time you're just looking," Rusty said. "After that, you're actually pretty busy."

For me, the highlight of the conference was seeing Hank Ballard and the Midnighters at a roadhouse on the edge of town. The band wore tight, black, three-button blazers. They played one opening number and then Hank came out wearing an even tighter, four-button blazer. He dropped his hand, the band hit "Work with Me Annie," and the place just went nuts. Next to me, Molly Ivins and Jonathan Broder launched into some kind of sixties soul dance, and I slid next to Zev Chafets, the Detroit homeboy, to sing back-up on the line, "Annie had a baby, she can't work no more!" Hank Ballard was one of Steve Miller's early heroes, and "Work with Me Annie" was one of the first songs he ever taught me. The synergy wrapped itself around me like Rusty's G forces, and I thought for a moment I too might reach my own escape velocity.

Early that May, I went to New York to produce a record with Mose Allison. It was to be his first for Blue Note Records, and he had written a typically acerbic collection of new songs, among them, the title track, "Ever Since the World Ended (I Don't Get Out As Much)." Producing Mose was more than a dream come true for me. It was a lesson in musical dignity. He knew what he wanted or, at least, he always knew exactly what he didn't want. Beyond that, the sessions were a joy because, instead of spending hours and hours overdubbing and editing on masters and slaves — even these technical terms speak volumes about the process — Mose sang and played it live. What you got was what you saw. And while he was clear that his music was not autobiographical — "If I could live that life," he once told me, "I wouldn't have to write about it" — his songs all contained powerful connections to moments of everyday experience, the dark undercurrents backlit with humor and delivered with the narrative sense of Celine. Plus, his songs all had an historical perspective. "If I was selling fantasy," he sang, "I'd be a millionaire. But I'm not discouraged. I'm not discouraged, no I'm not discouraged, but I'm getting there...."

We started Mose's album on May 10. On May 11, it was finished.

I stayed on in New York for a few days to do some promotion for my album *On The Cool Side*, including hosting VH-1's New Visions program. New Visions was the television show that aired at 11 P.M. Sunday nights, a great ghetto time-slot to feature jazz videos and live performances. Each week a different musician acted as host, and when I finished taping my segments, which included a few improvised introductions and a live performance, Mike Simon, the producer, said, "Let's go get a drink." At the bar, he asked, "Have you done this before? Because you're really good at it."

"I have a lot of experience getting in front of a microphone and just letting my mouth run."

"We're thinking of a permanent host for the show. Would you be interested?"

"Sure," I said, "As long as I don't have to live in New York."

That night, as the plane circled Madison, I saw the lights of the state capitol emerging out of the corn fields like a beacon, and I really felt that the whole city was my home, not just the small house on the small street in which I actually lived, but the place itself, Madison, Wisconsin. It was May 15.

On May 20, Harvey Goldberg died. Two days before, I had gone to see him at University Hospital. I wandered through the hallways for a while, from the

E Tower to the F Concourse, and suddenly there in a nondescript room on the third floor, I found him lying on a gurney. He was wearing a standard issue hospital gown with one skinny leg sticking out from beneath a thin white sheet.

"Harvey," I said, "It's Ben."

"Ben, call the nurse. My knee hurts."

"Your knee?"

"My knee hurts. I think they may have to operate. She said she was going to bring me something...."

"Okay," I said, and I went into the hallway. There was nobody to call. I came back into the room. There was a call button next to the bed, and I pushed it.

"Is the nurse coming?" he asked.

"I rang for her...." Just then, a nurse came in the room with a small paper cup on a plastic tray. Inside the cup was a pill. I said to the nurse, "He's in a lot of pain. Can you tell his doctor?"

She looked at me and smiled that nurse's smile and said, "He knows." Turning to Harvey, she said, "Here you go professor," and gave Harvey the cup. Harvey swallowed the pill with a little water and lay back down. After she left, he started talking about his knee again, about how they were going to fix it. It made no sense to me, so I changed the subject. I asked him if a lot of people were coming to visit him. He didn't seem to want to talk about it. He was not at all delirious, but he seemed strangely focused on fixing his knee; strange because clearly the rest of him was in much worse shape.

I said, "Is there anything I can do for you Harvey?" He closed his eyes and his breathing got easier. He didn't say anything.

"Harvey," I said, "I just want to tell you how much you've meant to me. You really saved my life and I will never forget you." I stood there for a few moments just watching him breathe. And then I left.

Everybody knew that Harvey had not been well for several years, and there had been rumors, but we were all caught off guard by his death when it came. He was an institution, like a building on the hill you couldn't imagine being gone. I should have suspected something back in September, when he called and came by the house with an armload of record albums. It was his Smithsonian collection of jazz, and he wanted me to have them. "I'm cleaning house," was all he said. We had made plans to have dinner, but I was traveling, and he was busy, and in the end, we never saw each other again until that afternoon in the hospital. Like James Brown sings in "It May Be the Last Time," "Turn around and shake hands with your best friend, you might never never never see them again."

I felt like there was so much more to say. But maybe if you haven't said it up until then, no amount of saying it at the end will get you over. The devil is in the details. Maybe Harvey's knee was just his way of saying, "Ben, pay attention to your life." If so, it would have been prescient advice, indeed, but of course at the time, one couldn't have known that.

The next month, my quartet played a solid five weeks, starting in New York, going to San Francisco for a week, then to Seattle for two weeks, and, finally, we went to Japan. Judy and Leo came to New York—Leo even got up and sang a blues with the band at Fat Tuesday's—and they also came out to Seattle where we all had a week hanging out at Steve's house. Steve and Leo spent hours having races in the swimming pool. Steve kept winning, even though he gave Leo a head start, and Leo kept swimming, even though he got frustrated. At the end of the week, Judy couldn't make the Japan trip, but Leo wanted to keep traveling, so we made him our road manager and took him along. He was just twelve years old, but we gave him plenty to do.

When we got to Tokyo, where we were playing at Sadao Watanabe's Kirin Club, we introduced Leo to the sound man and the stage manager and explained that he was in charge of our sound check and making sure we had whatever we needed on stage. The house manager at the Kirin Club looked at him very seriously and took Leo off to show him the club. Apparently they had quite a long conversation because when they returned, Leo said, "He wants me to sing." I asked him how this came up, and Leo said, "I told him I sang in New York and he wanted to know if I was going to sing here." Leo was becoming one of the band, or as Billy Peterson said to me later that night, "Ben, he's got the curse."

After several years of playing together and a month of steady work, the band sounded great. Everything felt fresh, and we played songs we didn't even know. We actually had so much confidence and humor about what we were doing that somebody would start playing a theme, a fragment, a melodic line, and everybody would pick it up. Our ears were so big that in a minute or two, a little arrangement was born. One could see how the music had come together back in the thirties, on Basie's band, and how it had evolved, night after night in the bebop era, when groups routinely played three and four sets a night, six nights a week. Inevitably, a group sound would emerge, a telepathy developed. Hence Art Blakey's advice about hiring not just great musicians but musicians who "can fit in" with the band. The band becomes a living organism, with a mind and a spirit of its own, and this communal presence is what jazz is all about. Surrendering to something larger than yourself, staying in the moment, finding your voice. The jazz teaching is clear on these points. But without the gigs, there is just no way to arrive at the solution.

The last night in Tokyo, the house manager came to me and said in a shy way that he and his co-workers were wondering if Leo would be singing that night. Apparently, during the week, Leo had made friends with many of the staff. I said if the night went well, he could come out for the encore. That night, the band was absolutely burning, and at the end of the second set, we brought Leo up. It was a tough moment to walk into, but he came out of the wings, wearing a coat and tie and sang:

"Everyday, Every day I have the blues...
Everyday, Every day I have the blues...
You see me worry baby, well it's you I hate to lose..."

It was the blues he had learned from Steve Miller back at the Ordway Theater. He even had the growl in his voice in the same places Steve did. He was dead-on serious and dead-on pitch. The audience loved it, and, at the end of the night, after everybody but the band and the staff had left the club, the employees all formed two long lines. As we passed between them, they all applauded. Leo was in road dog heaven.

In July, the Steve Miller Band was honored with a star on Hollywood Boulevard's "Walk of Fame," and Steve invited all the past band members to come out for the ceremony. Tim Davis came from Las Vegas, where he had moved after suffering debilitating diabetes. He was still the same old Tim, upbeat and crazy, and walked around on his prosthetic legs as if it was the most natural thing to do. Leo was all over the scene by now, mugging for photographs, doing the splits, and Steve was his best pal. At this stage of their relationship, Steve was using him for a foil (all the goofy poses, being the eccentric benevolent uncle) and Leo was using Steve for a straightman (after Prince, Leo's favorite recording artist at the time was Mel Brooks).

Steve had the band's star placed on the sidewalk directly in front of Capitol Records just to rub their faces in his success. He openly disdained the people who worked there. Knowing they would have to step over his name every day was a great source of pleasure for him. I asked him how he had arranged this whole thing, and he told me it was easy. To arrange a star on the "Walk of Fame," assuming you had enough notoriety, all you had to do was pay Johnny Grant, the "honorary mayor" of Hollywood, $3000. "It's the same old story," he said. "You have to throw yourself the party and then send yourself the flowers."

In August, I went to Minneapolis to begin my next record. Each morning around 11 A.M., Billy Peterson and I would meet at Creation Audio and sit together at the piano. I would play the song of the day for him and Billy would say something like, "Okay, but what if instead of playing those chords, we use these altered ones instead..." and off he would go, showing me a string of alternative chord voicings. I would let him wander through the harmonic fields until I heard something I could use and then I'd say, "That's it, don't move your hands." By 1 P.M., we would be ready for Gordy and Bobby to come in, and spent an hour or two cutting the track. We recorded ten songs in ten days at this leisurely pace. Bob Malach's saxophone solos were inspiring. Especially his playing on the standard "Everything Happens to Me." He had the lyrical ease and absolute etched-in-stone authority that we all search for but seldom achieve. Several months later, after the album *Too Hot To Touch* had been released, I got a call from Matt Dennis, the writer of the song. "I love what you did with it," he said, "and tell the saxophone player he sings it as good as anybody."

The band was running like a well-oiled machine and each of the tracks on the album, especially the dark narrative, "Enivre D'Amour," had the offhand intimacy of a group that had survived some serious road miles together. But perhaps we did push the boundaries of foxhole humor a little too far on the last day of recording.

That day, I had been telling Gordy about a conversation I had had with the great saxophone player Pepper Adams just before he died. Pepper had been telling me about how the critics had savaged him throughout his career, and, especially, following a concert he had done with Thelonious Monk back in the sixties. Pepper was still despondent at the end of his life over the fact that this one review had cost him the chance to work with Monk again. I told Gordy I was thinking of writing a song about critics, dedicated to Pepper, and I even had the hook: "Critics, they can't even float, they just stand on the shore and wave at the boat." Gordy said, "Let's do it. Right now." And so fifteen minutes later, he and Billy were in the studio laying down a "devolved" groove (shades of Tony Williams: Billy even de-tuned his bass to make the track as raw as possible), while I retired to the lounge to complete the lyrics.

Critics

"Critics, can't even float
Just stand on the shore and wave at the boat...
I once knew a critic
Blind as he could be
He could hear the surf he could taste the salt
He couldn't even find the sea
Convinced of his wisdom
Unfettered with the facts
He finally solved his problem
He took the ocean off of his maps

Why's that? He's just a Critic!
Can't even float
Just stand on the shore and wave at the boat...(3X)
Nobody would pay a quarter
To hear that critic sing
Hey, if you hung him from a good hook
He couldn't even swing
They never pay the cover
They never buy the drink
But they hang around for hours
Just to tell you what they think (who's that?)
Critics
Can't even float
Just stand on the shore and wave at the boat...(3X)
They did it to Charlie Parker
They said he was playing junk
They did it to Trane, did it to Miles
They saved the best for Monk
They did it to Pepper Adams
They broke his heart all right
Call up your local critic
See where Pepper is playing tonight, that's right
Critics, can't even float
Just stand on the shore and wave at the boat...(3X)
So when you meet the critic, face to face
If he's got one, or two, or several all over the place
I know you might be tempted
To rearrange his head
Just because he took your dough
And baked it in his bread
Remember brothers and sisters
He's living here in sin
He's getting fat on you this time
But next time, he's coming back thin
As a snake, named Jake..."

And then, as the band vamped out, I may have stepped over the line.
Because the day before, Michael Cuscuna had told me the following joke:
A rabbit runs into a snake out in the jungle. They're both blind, you understand. The rabbit says to the snake, "Say, I'm blind, could you tell me what
kind of animal I am?" The snake licked him all over and said, "Well, you have

long furry ears and a soft furry tail, you have got to be a bunny rabbit. But by the way, Mr. Bunny Rabbit, I, too, am blind. I wonder if you could sniff me up and down and tell me what kind of animal I am?" The bunny rabbit sniffs him up and down and says, "Well, you're kind of slimy, you got no ears, you must be an A&R man."

It was a typically dark, self-deprecating music business joke. Even A&R men could laugh at it. I however changed the punch line to "you must be a critic!" and told the joke as "Critics" faded out. At the very end of the song, you heard the voice of Pepper Adams saying, "Thank you Ben, it's been a great pleasure."

When the album was released, this track got all the attention. *Billboard* magazine mentioned it in an editorial, Leonard Feather referred to it in the *Los Angeles Times* and Mike Zwerin devoted the entire back page of the *International Herald Tribune* to the song. None of the critics were amused. I couldn't believe that these guys, who had been dishing it out for years, couldn't take it, even in the form of a funky dance track. And, as I told Mike Zwerin, an excellent trombone player in his own right, "You understand that I make a distinction here between a journalist, an historian, a writer like yourself, who is trying to put the music in context, and a critic, who is basically telling me who I am *not* as opposed to who I *am*." Mike was still not amused. In short, the song took on a life of its own. Musicians dug it, of course — both Mike Brecker and Herbie Hancock went out of their way to say so — but the press was universally scathing. This one song overshadowed all the other tracks on the album, and, ultimately, the label that released it, Windham Hill, couldn't take the heat and chose to stop distributing my records altogether.

Gordy told me he was really sorry if he had caused me any problems. I said, "Aw man, it was something that had to be done...once!"

Starting that September, I also began working on Steve Miller's album at Creation Audio in Minneapolis. Steve had sent the slave tapes with his guitar and vocal parts, and along with engineer Steve Wiese, I began the tedious process of logging and "comping" the various alternate takes. It took almost a month, but when it was done, every vocal and every guitar solo was pristine. I called Steve when we had finished and told him we had just given him the best haircut of his life. I spent another couple of weeks flying the tapes around the country, doing string overdubs in L.A. and miscellaneous solos with Milt Jackson and Phil Woods in New York. By December, after a month of mixing, the album was finished.

Born to be Blue, the result, is really a lovely album that captures the best of what we had to offer at the time: Steve's super-cool vocals and pop sensibility, the harmonic concept that Billy and I had been working on for years, Gordy's absolute precision when it comes to studio drumming, Ricky's molten synthesizer overdubs, and Bob Malach's solos, all overlaid with a deep jazz sensibility. The album had a sonic landscape that was modern and hip, and it captured a side of Steve Miller that had never been heard before. The songs stretched from jazz and blues to ballads, from Horace Silver's "Filthy McNasty" to Ray Charles' "Mary Anne" to the old chestnut "Willow Weep for Me." And, in the end, it was a record that Steve's father loved.

It was like a survey of Americana seen through the eyes of a couple of kids who came of age in the sixties. In that sense, it was as true a project as we had ever done. Or, in Professor Ragsdale's phrase, it was "a lie that tells the truth." What did it in, however, was success. Steve Miller's success. But that would be almost another year in the telling.

In late October, I went to the VH-1 offices in New York to meet with Mike Simon and his boss Eamon Harrington, and we agreed on the terms for my becoming the permanent host of the New Visions program. They would pay me next to nothing and in return I would come to New York a couple times a month, hang out on the set with the musicians and keep things moving on camera. It seemed fair to me.

Immediately following the meeting, I grabbed a cab to Kennedy airport to catch a flight to Barcelona. A French producer named Victor Mitz, who had a love for musicians who sang, had contacted me the year before. He said his dream was to start a record label and record these musicians, myself included, in historical settings. His first project had been with Bob Dorough and Clark Terry in Paris. He called to ask me if I was interested in working with Johnny Griffin in Barcelona. I said, "What's it gonna cost me?"

Of course I had known Johnny for almost a decade, but knowing him and recording with him were two different things. Johnny's nickname is "The Little Giant" because of his diminutive stature, his towering musical talent and his reputation for taking all comers to the woodshed. He could simply out-play, out-hang, out-party and out-talk a dozen men half his age. It was a musical education not to be missed. And at this stage of my career, if something sent a shiver of fear up my spine, I had trained myself to go toward it. An opportunity like this, to step off the highest peak in the jazz mountain range and tempt fate, was almost too good to be true. I gathered up a handful of standards, many of them from the 1930s and 1940s, and a few originals, and got on the plane for Spain.

Victor had also booked drummer Ben Riley, best known for playing with Thelonious Monk in the sixties and seventies, and bass player Jimmy Woode, an expatriate American who had traveled for many years with Duke Ellington's orchestra. Arriving in Barcelona around noon, I went to the hotel, dropped off my bags and then went directly to the recording studio. I felt like I had been running all the way from New York City, but at the studio, I found a very relaxed scene. The studio itself was primitive by American standards, with a cramped control room, a rudimentary mixing console and a slightly out-of-tune piano. I felt like I was back in the fifties. Musicians were standing around chatting, the engineers were in no hurry, and there was a general air of *laissez faire*.

Johnny Griffin immediately put me at ease by calling out "Hey, homeboy," making reference to the fact that we were both born in Chicago. Ben and Jimmy came over to say hi, and, without ceremony, we were off.

We only had a couple of days booked, so the conversation before each take was as meaningful as any of the arrangements I had brought with me. While recording "Lullaby in Rhythm," for example, Johnny and Jimmy Woode got into a discussion about how Jimmy Lunceford would have done the introduction. Then Griffin phrased the melody in the style of Ben Webster, reminiscing about how he had first heard him play the song. That segued into a long shaggy-dog story about Ben Webster that had as its punch line Ben taking a swing at Phil Woods and then passing out. By the time we actually got around to recording the song, the arrangement had shifted to accommodate these historical references, and more. Griffin phrased the melody with an old-school strut, something out of the thirties using a triplet feel instead of the standard dotted eighths, and Ben Riley swung the whole thing closer to Monk than to either Lunceford or Webster. I felt like I was riding in the Baroness's Bentley.

After the first night of recording, as we walked out on the Ramblas, past the cages of exotic birds and the street mimes and the Algerian hustlers, I asked Johnny how he liked living in Europe. He had moved to the South of France in the sixties and now only returned to the States once or twice a year. "I left New York running like on a tread mill," he said. "You know, from the club to the record company back to the booking agency, back to the club. Everything's in a rush. Never taking my time. But in France, everybody's coolin' it. You know, they teach you how to wait a minute. Take your time, have a nice glass of some good Bordeaux and relax." That night, we shared several bottles of good wine, and by the next afternoon at the studio, my tempos were definitely more relaxed. For the moment, I was living on Johnny Griffin time.

1988

B ack home, I continued the commute to New York for VH-1 or NPR, spending hours every day talking to musicians or about musicians, preparing for the conversations or ruminating about them. Often, individual days became kaleidoscopic in their variety and refractory nature. One day, it might be conversations with Mose Allison and Wayne Shorter; the next day, Jay McShann and Lou Reed; or Ken Nordine and Michel Petrucciani; or Donald Fagen and Sun Ra. I was still producing records and playing gigs, which meant that during the course of a single day, I might step in and out of a variety of roles several times. I might be calling a musician to hire him for a date, arranging an interview for VH-1 or getting some practical advice on how to play a particular passage.

So in April 1988, I was looking forward to returning to the Conference on World Affairs in Boulder and hoping to spend a week with folks from other parts of the cultural zeitgeist, people who were not necessarily in the music business. When I arrived, however, I discovered I would be rooming with trombonist Al Gray, a veteran of multiple musical campaigns, and Gene Lees, a writer of sensitivity and depth. It turned out to be one of the best vacations I ever had.

Al, who passed away in 2000, had a huge smile that contrasted magnificently with the omnipresent satchels under his eyes, as if he were constantly fighting sleep because he was just having too much fun at the party. The three of us stayed in a small cottage on the property of Betty Weems, who again housed the musicians, including Johnny Mandel, Dave Grusin and the great pianist Les McCann. Breakfast was a circus not to be missed, with Betty's boyfriend, Spike Robinson, having his ceremonial cigarette and can of beer, and Les McCann entertaining the troops with stories of L.A. back in the sixties. But the moments with Al are what stay with me most.

Al called me "roomy," and he told me and Gene Lees stories about riding on old buses so raggedy that you had to get out and push them up the hills, playing in the big bands of Benny Carter, Jimmy Lunceford, Dizzy Gillespie, Count Basie and Lionel Hampton. Hampton's band was a great collection of musicians who were often forced to clown around to entertain the audience. Al told us, "coming from Lunceford to clapping your hands with the white gloves, I really just didn't think that that had anything to do with the music...we had acrobats who would go out in the audience playing their saxophones and walk the edges of the seats, jump from the balconies on the stage, and all like this. And, yes, Lionel Hampton had them standing in line waiting to get in." It was a lesson in show business that really gave me some perspective as the year progressed.

Late in June I went to L.A. to deliver the Steve Miller masters to Capitol Records. Walking through the halls of the Capitol Tower always brought back memories, memories of going to the studio with Glyn Johns back in the early seventies, memories of having to scramble to make a few bucks with Jessie Davis' band, memories of that fateful lunch with Art Mogul. They were all gone, of course, moved on to greener pastures, and now label president David Berman occupied the office where Art Mogul once held court.

David, a genuinely nice man with a reputation as a tough lawyer, had inherited the presidency of Capitol Records and had received a phone call from Steve a few days before I arrived. It had not gone smoothly. Steve had demanded to know how many albums Capitol would be pressing, and when David said he didn't know, Steve got aggressive. "He demanded we press a minimum of one million copies," David told me, "and when I said I couldn't commit to that, he called me an asshole." David was smiling as he told me the story—we both knew this sort of thing came with the territory—but you could see that he was not looking forward to the next few months. I told him I thought I could help smooth things out with Steve—I was still naive about what drove Steve's wheels—and I went to talk to Jean Riggens, the product manager in charge of *Born to be Blue*. She was also the woman who had been instrumental in Steve's previous success, and she was very straightforward. She said, "If Steve doesn't want to work with us, there's nothing we can do. This is not a pop record and it's going to take some time. Will Steve tour?"

I had talked to Steve about this before going to California. He said he hated touring. "It was like putting a circus on the road," and the worst part was dealing with the rock and roll press. They didn't respect him and were "mostly fools." I said, "It doesn't have to be like that. We can go out and play good music at nice theaters. You can talk to the jazz press about why you finally made this record and it could be a lot of fun." He said, "You don't understand."

I told Jean, "I think Steve will tour."

The rest of that summer, I did my own touring with Billy, Gordy and Bobby. (Judy said it sounded like a bunch of kids staying out late: "Where's Ben? He's out playing with Billy, Gordy and Bobby....")

We opened in New York at the Blue Note on a double bill with Horace Silver. I had met Horace once or twice before, and knew what a sweet, gentle man he was, but I was not prepared for how nervous I would be as his opening act. Horace had been my first hero, and it was Horace's music, his phrases, his musical voice, that had resonated in my consciousness as a boy. How could I sit there, night after night, and play my little derivative licks in front of the master? It was a big lump to swallow. It took me back to those days of surrender, back to England, when I had stopped playing altogether and had to accept myself for being as small and frail as I was before I could even sit down at the piano again.

Every night at the Blue Note, I approached the stage with humility, determined to carry the message forward: if you're not having fun, you're doing it wrong. A lot of friends and musicians came to the club that week—Tommy LiPuma, Ricky Peterson, Nobu Yoshinari, Al Gray, Bruce Lundvall, Michael Cuscuna, Herbie Hancock, Chic Corea, Junior Cook, Milt Jackson, even the actor Michael Keaton, who sent a note asking me to play "Girl Talk"—and at the end of the engagement, I felt years, not days, older. Horace was particularly generous with his comments, and I felt I had finally passed my oral exams. I had graduated.

From New York, we went to Paris to play at the Theatre de Ville, then to Vienne, where we played at a lovely Roman amphitheater, and then on to the North Sea Festival which, as always, was held in a crowded Casino in The Hague. Finally, we arrived at a little club in Brussels, where pianist Michel Petrucciani showed up with drummer Roy Haynes, sat right behind me and called out, "play that song about all the piano players!" It was, as the saying goes, about as much fun as you can have with your clothes on.

We returned to the States and continued gigging up and down the country until August, when we finally ended the tour on a muggy August afternoon in my home town, Racine. It was my first time back since my army physical in '68. I had no idea what to expect. That afternoon, as Billy and I drove around my old neighborhood and I showed him the house where I used to live, and the house across the street where my girlfriend Terry had lived, and the corner where I would wait to "skitch" on passing cars, everything looked better than I had remembered it. There was not the pall, the pockets of gloom that always colored my memory of the place. In fact, the old neighborhood looked rather cheery and prosperous in a wholesome, Midwestern way. Could this be the Racine of my memory?

The gig was at the Zoo, a place I had gone often as a kid to look into the deep pit and watch the turtles do nothing, or walk past the lion cages and watch the old moth-eaten cats do nothing, or go to the monkey house and let them watch me do nothing. For my return, a bandstand had been erected facing Lake Michigan. The Racine *Journal Times* had even done a front-page story, listing my recent whereabouts and welcoming me home. It was bizarre to say the least. I was waiting to run into myself riding on the Little League float.

And then I did. After the concert, as I was coming off the stand, a middle aged woman came up to me and said, "Ben, I was your fourth grade teacher." It was Miss Nelson, and I remembered fourth grade well. It had been a horrible year. A long, boring, frustrating year. It was the beginning of my descent into loneliness. "You were my favorite student," she said. "You know, you weren't even supposed to be in my class. You were supposed to be in the accelerated class. But I enjoyed having you so much, I kept you behind." And then she smiled at me as if I would be happy to hear the news.

There was the Racine I remembered.

Born to be Blue was released in September and Steve agreed to do a promotional tour beginning in November. It would be a low-key affair, played out at small theaters with the band — essentially my quartet augmented by Ricky Peterson and his younger brother Paul — dressed in dark suits and shades. The repertoire was a combination of jazz and blues, things like "All Blues," "God Bless the Child" and "Born to be Blue," and Steve pulled out classics like "C.C. Rider" and "Just a Little Bit." We even put together a new version of "Space Cowboy" in the style of Weather Report, a very modern and funky arrangement, and Steve taught the band Johnny Guitar Watson's "The Gangster of Love" and a few of his hits, like "Fly Like an Eagle," "Rockin' Me," "The Joker" and, of course, "Jet Airliner." We rehearsed for a few days at Paisley Park in Minneapolis and then flew east. Steve had rented Arlo Guthrie's old tour bus and we all piled in and headed for the first gig in Binghamton, New York. Steve seemed truly happy and relaxed, and not at all in his record-business mode.

The concert was at the State University of New York, and we anticipated a house full of intelligent, college-educated listeners. At the soundcheck, we were told the gig was sold out. However, when the lights went down and we walked on stage, we were stunned by the roar from the kids. This was not a jazz or blues audience. This was a room full of party animals, chanting the name of one of Steve's past hits, "Jungle Love! Jungle Love!"

We opened with another of Steve's hits, "Rockin' Me," and they went crazy. We almost couldn't hear ourselves because the crowd was singing so loud. They got quieter when we played some of the blues things. They got real quiet when we played some of the jazz things. Not disrespectful, just lying in wait. And they went nuts again when we played "Jet Airliner." We had a two-hour program planned with a half-hour intermission, and in the break I asked Steve what was going on. He said, "You got me," but he was grinning from ear to ear. He was back.

What was going on was that these kids, mostly eighteen-to-twenty-year-olds, had been twelve and thirteen when Steve first retired. In the interim, Capitol Records, impatient for Steve's next release, had put out *Steve Miller's Greatest Hits*, a compilation of his most popular songs, at a cheap price so that young kids could afford it. At the same time, the "Classic Rock" radio format had taken off across the country and had begun featuring the hits of the seventies, putting Steve squarely in the middle of play lists from coast to coast. While Steve had been cruising Lake Washington on his yacht, he had quietly been selling more CDs (approximately 25,000 per month) and receiving more airplay than most of the bands that were out on the road, working non-stop. Now all these kids couldn't wait to party along with the Steve Miller Band. Steve had left the scene as an aging pop artist with leftist/ecological leanings and returned as a teenage icon.

In some ways, it was his dream come true. He now had the biggest party band in the country. Like the Ardells back in the sixties, only on a national scale. The only fly in the ointment was that we had made a respectful little jazz record, and he was now in his late forties and had stopped partying years ago.

They say you must be careful what you wish for because it could come true. As the tour progressed, the kids didn't want to hear any of the adult stuff. They got bored quickly, bringing an MTV mentality to our show. They just wanted to hear the ten songs from the "Greatest Hits" CD, and if we would have played each of them three times in a row, that would have made them happier still. "Fly Like an Eagle," a song about feeding the poor and shoeing the shoeless, was fast on its way to becoming the theme for the U.S. Post Office. Steve had obviously been right when he told me I didn't understand. He, too, got frustrated and a little nervous when we would take a break from playing the hits and the crowd would get quiet and restless. Each night, we would try a different set list, but the running order was not the problem. The problem was that the "Greatest Hits" CD was larger than life.

Steve Miller is only one of many musicians who had become eclipsed by their own artifacts, imprisoned in their own product. It's the nature of the "star system" after all. But in Steve's case, it was a little eerie. He could even walk out into the parking lot before the concert, where thousands of kids were preparing for the big party, and no one would recognize him. It wasn't him, per se, or his talent that was being honored. It was, as he had told me before, the fact that he was "throwing the party and sending himself the flowers." And ironically, he had stopped drinking years before. His audience was now nothing at all like he was. He was a captive of his own past and there was virtually nothing he could do to be reborn except walk away from the money. And that was one thing that was clearly not going to happen.

We continued to have our own party on the road, and along with the dwindling chance to play any serious music came a kind of giddiness that translated into occasional choreography on stage and the constant hope that in the next town—Boston, New York, Philadelphia—the crowd would be hipper, more mature, ready to listen. This didn't often happen, but, from time to time, particularly when Bob Malach dug into one of his magical, twenty-four bar solos, or when we were able to stretch out on the blues, the music could be transcendent. In general, Steve played and sang great, and was clearly enjoying the adulation.

The day before Thanksgiving, we pulled into Toronto where we were sched-uled to play at Massy Hall after a day off. My sister Maxine was living there, and she came over to the hotel where the band was staying so I could buy her a nice meal. Over the years, we had grown closer together, like survivors of some small natural disaster, and between us, perhaps to honor the memory of our departed father, we adhered to a strict no-bullshit rule.

I told her that the tour was going well but that we were slipping into a kind of musical irrelevancy: what had started out about the music was now all about screaming kids and repetitive motion. "But," I said, "playing at Massy Hall tomor-row night should be great, because one of the most historically important jazz records of all time was recorded there, back in 1953." I told her how *Jazz at Massy Hall* was the only document of Charles Mingus, Dizzy Gillespie, Bud Powell, Max Roach and Charlie Parker playing together, and I said, "Max, when we walk out on that stage tomorrow night, and I get to play my little Dizzy Gillespie lick on 'Space Cowboy,' it will be like bringing a single coal back to Newcastle."

Later that night, however, I was with Steve in his suite when he casually dropped a small bomb. His father had just died. Knowing how powerful a force his father had been, I said I was sorry, that it couldn't be easy for him. He kind of brushed it off.

I asked, "When are you leaving?"

He said, "I'm not."

I said, "You're not going home?"

"Nope," he said, "I saw him a month ago. I said goodbye."

I wanted to say something more, but all I managed to say was, "Hey, it's only a gig."

The next night the show went on as scheduled. And when we walked onto that hallowed stage, it seemed so much smaller than it had appeared in the pic-tures of that legendary night back in '53. And when we played "Space Cowboy," after the usual string of sing-alongs and screaming kids, it felt like nothing at all. There was no fire in Newcastle. It *was* only a gig.

By the time we got to Los Angeles, after winding through Cleveland, Ann Arbor, Chicago, Milwaukee, Madison, Atlanta, Miami, Lakeland, Gainsville, Houston, Austin, Dallas, Phoenix and San Diego, Steve was in full rock-star mode. He and I went to the Capitol Tower to discuss the album's promotion with David Berman, and it took Steve less than five minutes to walk across the room, lean over David's desk, put his finger in David's face and deliver his famous, "The trouble with you people..." speech. He had been making this same speech to various Capitol executives for years. When we left David's office, there was no further question about the album's promo-tion. Steve was virtually off the label, which had probably been his objective all along.

⟨⟨≋⟩ Chapter Eight

> *"Not only does democracy make every man forget his ances-*
> *tors, but it hides his descendants and separates his contempo-*
> *raries from him; it throws him back forever upon himself*
> *alone, and threatens in the end to confine him entirely within*
> *the solitude of his own heart."*

> —ALEXIS DE TOCQUEVILLE

1989

"The show is in the Green Room. Forget what's happening on the set. It's all staged. Put the cameras in the Green Room, that's where the good stuff goes down."

I was in Mike Simon's office trying to convince him that the best way to do jazz on television was invisibly, leaving in the rough edges, capturing the attitude and letting the viewers see the real deal. As the producer of New Visions, Mike was always interested in pushing the boundaries a bit. But the lighting guys would tell him there wasn't enough light to shoot in the Green Room, and he was afraid that there was no way to control the action. Which, of course, was exactly my point.

"Turn it loose! Let's let the musicians be themselves."

Weekly, the scene in the green room was like another world. VH-1 had few resources at the time, and the green room was just a fifteen by fifteen foot cubicle with cold cuts, coffee and Mike's assistant, Susan, sitting at her desk by the door making phone calls. On taping days, a variety of musicians would be hanging out, watching the taping on a monitor, talking, reminiscing, hitting on Susan, meeting each other for the first time. It was wonderful. Who wouldn't want to be a fly on the wall the day Robert Cray and David Byrne and Wynton Marsalis were forced to interact? It really gave some insight into their music.

"It doesn't have to be the whole show," I was saying. "We can still do the interviews and the performances on the set. How about if just we cut away to the green room from time to time?"

Mike laughed and said, "Put it in a memo," I said, "Yeah, when you want my opinion, you'll give it to me."

Of course he was a professional and I was an agitator. My role, as I saw it, was to step up and take a swing at whatever the pitch, and from time to time, to swing for the fences, to make a little history. The evening Dr. John and Leon Redbone and I sang Christmas Carols, that was some kind of history. And the day I convinced Mike that it would be a good idea to have Sun Ra and Don Cherry on the show will live in television infamy.

I knew that they probably would not fit into the little three-minute boxes Mike would need to put them in, but I thought, what the heck, it could be good television, and it would be good for our show. On the evening of the performance, they started playing a ballad and wouldn't stop when the floor manager gave them the cue to wrap it up. Mike was screaming at me "Get them to wrap it up! For Chrissake, it's been five minutes already!" I said, "Mike, I'll give them any sign you want but it won't matter. They're gonna play until they're through." I was laughing and he had no choice but to go to a commercial, and when he came out of it, Sun Ra and Don Cherry were still playing. This went on for the better part of a half-hour.

There was also the program where Paul Shaffer and I sang the doo-wop song, "Tears on My Pillow." Some things will never die no matter how hard we try to put them out of their misery. But the rough edges of the show were what made it special and, ultimately, why musicians liked coming around. Carlos Santana came on to talk about John Coltrane and found a sympathetic ear. Harry Connick's first national television appearance was on "New Visions." Bill Cosby came on, conducted a band and acted like one of the guys. From time to time, it's true, the edges got a little too rough. Like the afternoon we wired a bass player with a microphone and a battery pack and told him to wait in the green room until we were ready for him. Instead, he went out of the building and into the street, where he proceeded to do a drug deal in a parked limo. Unfortunately, he forgot he was wired, and everybody in the control room heard every word. This was reality TV before it became popular.

The quarters at VH-1 were cramped. I shared a miniscule dressing room with Rosie O'Donnell who was a veejay. She would usually tape in the mornings before we started the jazz marathon, and since she was doing "stand ups," just looking into the camera and introducing videos, it didn't take her long. Rosie was all business. She'd kid around with the crew but when she wasn't on camera, she was on the phone, fighting to get out of the dives in New Jersey or wherever it was she was working at the time. "I don't care what the fuck he told you," she would say, "I'm not going back there for that money!" She had her one rack of clothes and I had my few things on hangers at the end of it. It didn't seem to bother her that, from time to time, guys like the World Saxophone Ensemble would be knocking on her door.

Television is labor intensive compared to radio. You spend a lot of time eating donuts, drinking coffee and waiting. By the time the lights are set and the cameras are rehearsed and the floor manager counts "four, three, two, one" and then points at you, you have no idea how a real person would react in the situation. How can you possibly be natural in such an unnatural environment? Of course this doesn't matter most of the time because television isn't about real people or natural environments. But jazz is. This is part of the reason jazz fares so badly on television. Another reason is that it is always boring to see some artsy close-up of a musician's fingers running up and down the keys. This shot has nothing to do with jazz. In fact, if you look at the one film that exists of Charlie Parker, the striking thing is how little he moved at all. Close your eyes and the world is coming to an end. Open them and there is a chubby, angelic-faced cat calmly blowing into a brass tube. How different is that from the histrionics you see young players going through today, just trying to look like they're doing something?

I kept goading Mike to break down the walls of the show. He countered with building a new set and throwing a party in my hotel room. That night, I staggered in tired and beat from a long NPR recording session, only to find ten people in my room, ordering room service and making long distance calls. Mike, stuffing his face with shrimp, was the one on the phone. I loved him for the gesture but threw his ass out pronto.

I didn't need to get loose. I wanted to find a way to get the musicians loose. Hugh Masakela, Philip Glass, Al Jarreau, Grover Washington, Jack DeJohnette, Lester Bowie, they kept coming and the show kept rolling, but it was still just a glimmer of what it could become. It was a cartoon show when we had a chance to do something important, a document of contemporary jazz. But, of course, television hates long form, and so it works against the essential nature of jazz. Sun Ra and Don Cherry proved it pretty well.

It is a great irony that so often success ensures the demise of a jazz program, and, sadly, New Visions too was cut short by its own achievements. This would not be the first nor the last time that recognition begat ambition and ambition brought on ruin.

By the end of the year, our programming had been so consistent that in January 1990, "New Visions" was awarded the Ace Award for best music series on Cable Television. This prompted the folks at VH1 to expand out of the

Sunday night 11 P.M. jazz ghetto and program New Visions five nights a week—"New Visions World Music" on Monday, "New Visions Rock" on Tuesdays, "New Visions Country" on Wednesday. If they had a chance, they would have done a New Visions "Rap" as well. Obviously, this expansion had little to do with the jazz show we were running on Sunday nights, the program that won the Ace Award.

In record time, the network found itself pouring a lot of money down this New Visions hole. Our ratings on Sunday were essentially the same as always (virtually non-existent) but the rest of the week, nobody was watching either, and with this glaring lack of an audience, VH1 pulled the plug on the whole New Visions series. Within a year of winning the Ace award, there was no more jazz on Sunday nights. Voila!

In March, I took my quartet to Rome to perform on the "International Doc Club," a television show that was a combination of "Saturday Night Live" and the "Tonight Show." Each weeknight, there were comedy skits and live music, an on-set audience populated by gorgeous international models and hipsters of every stripe, and a young host named Gege Telesforo, a fantastic scat singer in the tradition of Jon Hendricks. Each week there were two musical guests, and we shared the stage with blues singer Koko Taylor. For five days, we spent an hour rehearsing, another hour taping the show, and then for the rest of the day we were free to explore the city.

Billy Peterson and I took long walks, across the Tiber, through Trastevere, the ancient quarter, past the old Jewish synagogue surrounded by soldiers with machine guns (because of terrorist threats), and finally, into the Vatican. We spent one whole afternoon in the catacombs, viewing the tombs of the Popes and wandering through the endless rooms of golden crowns, bejeweled scepters and the various trinkets representing a minute fraction of the Church's astronomical wealth. Perusing the Vatican is one of the most humbling experiences one can have. The message to the individual seems to be, "You are nothing, the church is everything, submit!" I couldn't help but think of all the people through all the ages who did just that.

After the week was over, the band flew home, and I flew to Costa Rica where I met Judy and Leo for spring vacation. We traveled the bumpy roads in a rented car and spent a gloriously haunted night in the La Selva rain forest, sleeping in a cabin and listening to the exotic sounds that God put on the Earth. The next morning, walking through the dense growth, we saw monkeys swinging in the trees and ants as big as your thumb and a great hog crashing through the underbrush.

On our way back to San Jose we stopped in a little town to watch a parade. It was a religious procession in honor of a local saint, and a long line of folks walked slowly up a hill behind a young man dragging a large wooden cross. There was also another group of men carrying a float symbolizing the Virgin Mary and some other icons I didn't recognize. All the children were dressed in their finest clothes, even the ones who had no shoes. The girls wore freshly starched white dresses, the boys white shirts and clean pants; the women all wore festive bright shawls, and the men had on their best suits. There was none of the somber, black-hooded religiosity I had seen at the Vatican. Instead, these folks were celebrating daily life as a community, perhaps looking forward to a big meal at the end of the day. Watching them climb the hill bearing the wooden cross, I thought of the Vatican overflowing with gold and jewels, tithed by people just like these, and wondered which was the more difficult cross to bear.

Summer, 1989, encouraged by the multitude of kids that had come to see us the previous autumn, Steve Miller booked a tour of the "sheds," the outdoor amphitheaters that are so popular around the country. Some of them can hold up to 20,000 people, and there is serious money to be made. Steve was very enthusiastic about the band and about the tour; he had booked a solid two months all across the country, beginning June 1, and had leased two big new buses. The hip little jazz / blues stage of the previous year was replaced with a giant flying horse logo and a bunch of expensive "vari lights." Rock and roll was back.

We still kept a couple of the jazz songs in the act, and sometimes I opened the show with "Mitsubishi Boy," which Steve loved to play. But it was obvious that these songs were just markers. The crowd was young and had generally been drinking since early afternoon and was looking to party. The various members of the band dealt with the reality of this new situation in different ways. Of course Steve was in rock and roll heaven, having a vast young audience reconfirming his popularity. Billy, being young at heart, got right into it and enjoyed the rock and roll trip as well. Gordy, a consummate professional, took the opportunity to perfect his craft, playing along with the electronic click and guiding the band through its paces. Bob Malach, the most inspired musician of the lot, kept his humor as best he could and practiced on the bus during the day. As the set evolved, he had less and less to do, until, ultimately, he was reduced to playing a few unison lines and two solos. That meant he spent most of the two-hour show pretending to play or hitting a cowbell. It was like hiring a brain surgeon to pass out condoms. And then there was me.

I spent a lot of time that summer talking with Steve about life and the choices we had made. He was obviously imprisoned by his past, the hits that drew the kids in. They didn't want to hear anything new from him, and at the same time, Steve was determined to make a "come back," to be bigger than ever. His goal was to play coliseums, but as a forty-seven-year-old man, he had very little in common with the seventeen-year-old boys and girls who were at the heart of his new audience. The hunger for success, the same drive that had gotten him where he was, wouldn't leave him alone. He couldn't simply enjoy having beaten the system more than once already. It was ironic that while Steve liked to think of himself as a voice for progressive music, his overriding drive for success had proscribed his ability to write any music at all. He hadn't written a song in years. On the stage, he continued to talk about "saving the planet," but in the dressing room, the conversation always turned to being "bigger than the Beatles."

On the other hand, I simply looked forward to the times when my friends brought their kids to the show, and I could take them backstage at the circus. Here is the man who takes care of the elephants, there is the crew that puts up the tent, here's the dancing bear, and there is the ring master who will give you his autograph. They were always thrilled. Leo came out and rode the bus for a couple of weeks that summer before going to camp. Watching the rock and roll circus through the eyes of a thirteen-year-old made it infinitely more interesting. It reminded me of why it worked at all: because kids believed the dream.

Leo loved sleeping on the bus as it sped through the summer nights, and, arriving at the venue, he would spend afternoons out at the mixing console or backstage running the monitors. He was in and out of everything, and he hung out with Steve a lot. The two of them would show up wearing funny noses or carrying squirt guns. They were pals, and since he was closer in age to Steve's audience than Steve was, in some ways, he was a bridge. When he left for camp, we all missed him.

In truth, there was very little to do. The music was so simple that I actually had been teaching Leo to play my parts, and by the time he left, he was capable of taking my place at the sound checks. Although I flew back to New York every couple of weeks to tape New Visions, the tour was becoming less about having fun and more about making the money. On July 10, Judy and I celebrated our twentieth wedding anniversary in a dusty field on the edge of Oklahoma City. Porta-sans and a bad Caesar salad. When I reminded Steve of our wedding day back in San Francisco two decades ago, he said, "Yeah, well I guess you guys knew what you were doing."

That September, with the aid and encouragement of my friend Nobu Yoshinari, I formed Go Jazz Records, a company to record and distribute my own music, along with the music of a few others. This move would signal a sea change in my work habits, gradually pulling me away from radio and television production and marking the start of a decade in which I virtually lived in the recording studio.

From the beginning, Go Jazz was all about hanging out with my friends; it was a chance to make the calls without having to make the call, to be wrong or to be right but to be able to write the check and move on. To begin, I went to Minneapolis with my band and cut *Cool Paradise*, my own next record, and from the first note, the sound of the music, the modern harmonies, the heartbeat of the ensemble, the abstraction of the lyrics, all seemed to suggest a new future. I was finally working for myself. The following year *Cool Paradise* was released as Go Jazz Records LP 001.

On November 4, Leo had his Bar Mitzvah at the Gates of Heaven, the little stone synagogue down by the lake in Madison, and all our friends and relatives came to watch him roll out the first major performance of his adult career. He was, as usual, serious and funny at the same time. He even provided the opening act, playing a song on the piano, and he read his favorite passage from Hannah's High Holy Days services.

"We live at any moment with our total past.
We hate with all our past hatreds
We love with all our past loves.
Every sunset we have ever seen has formed our sense of the beautiful.
Every bar of music we have listened to is included in our response
      to the melody which now rings in our ears.
This is why it is so important that we be cautious in what we make of
      each day.
      It will be with us always."

In his speech, he thanked Judy for making such a warm and wonderful home and thanked me for exposing him to the "finer things in life." The congregation laughed, and then I placed a beautiful old tallis around his neck and said,

"This tallis comes to you by way of my father, your grandfather. He wore it at his Bar Mitzvah, and then I wore it at my Bar Mitzvah. So it is as close as we have to a family heirloom. And I remember my Bar Mitzvah, and I remember my father at my Bar Mitzvah, and I remember thinking back then that he had all the answers. And I know I got angry at him later on when I found out that he didn't have all the answers. And I hope you will spare me that. And right now, I can really identify with my father. I'm him. I'm at my son's Bar Mitzvah, and I know it's not possible to have all the answers. I know it's really hard just to know what the questions are. Leo, as your Torah portion says, the world is crazy. But I think the world has gone crazier, faster than any of us could have imagined. And yet there are people like you in it. You're young and honest and intelligent, not to mention good looking, and I think to myself if there are more people in the world and the world is a lot more crowded, well then there are probably a lot more people like you in the world. And that's a great cause for hope. The world is getting a little better at the same time it's obviously getting worse. I won't lie to you, Leo, it's a jungle out here, but it's a wonderful jungle and I know you're going to leave your mark on it, and even more important, I know you're going to leave it better than when you found it. We love you."

Then Leo stepped up to the bima and read his Torah portion, just as millions of young men before him had read it, chanting the ancient mellismas in a kid's voice, promising to take his place in the long line of Jews who revered the word and in the community that kept the word, and, as tradition dictates, there were tears of joy when he had finished. And also a few tears of grief for his grandfather, who did not live to see it.

December 4 I landed in New Orleans in a flood of near biblical proportions and met Mose Allison at the baggage claim. The idea of recording Mose in New Orleans popped up during one of our phone conversations almost a year before. We had been talking about some of his favorite drummers around the country, and Mose mentioned "a guy down there named John Vidacovich who can really play my music the way it should be played." Even though Mose has lived on the East Coast since the fifties, he was born in Mississippi and has always been thought of as a voice of the South. So it was a natural leap to suggest we record in "the home of the blues." Admittedly, he was less than enthusiastic, almost rueful, implying that in the South, you never knew what you're going to get. He called it "the quagmire."

It started with the rains, the kind of deluge that makes you wonder where all that water can possibly go in a city that is itself several feet below sea level. We drove through great puddles to the French Quarter where we checked into a small hotel and prepared for the next day's recording. In the morning, we rose to thunder and more pounding rain, and, driving through the flooded streets, we arrived at the studio to discover that it was "being remodeled." In fact, it was a disaster: the walls and ceilings were caverns of studs and insulation, and the floor reeked of tile sealer. In the middle of this mess was a grand piano and a patch of carpeting for the drums. "Where would you like the piano?" asked the engineer. "Manhattan," said Mose. We spent the rest of the day looking for an alternate place to record. Welcome to the quagmire.

When the recording finally got underway, the sessions with John Vidacovich and the others went smoothly. John understood Mose's approach to rhythm perfectly — no backbeats, no high hat on the "2" and "4" — and everybody was thrilled to be working with Mose, who was, of course, a Southern legend. But outside of the studio, when we went to Chez Paul for dinner or Café du Monde for breakfast, Mose seemed uncomfortable, even agitated. One night, driving back to the hotel, he talked a little about his earliest trips to the city, back when he was a young man on military leave. One of his good friends in New Orleans had been saxophonist Brew Moore, a soulful tenor player and something of an intellectual, who died after living a life of obscurity remarkable even for a jazz musician. Mose said, "You know, he never got the recognition. His picture was never on the cover of any jazz magazine..." Somehow, Mose's sadness as he remembered his friend seemed connected to his whole memory of New Orleans and the cloistered South.

In fact, Brew's story was even more disturbing and, perhaps, somewhat apocryphal. After years of kicking around the States with little success and a penchant for heavy drinking, he had moved to Denmark. It was there that his legend took a bizarre turn. He unexpectedly inherited a large sum of money, and, to celebrate his good fortune, he threw himself a big party at the Tivoli Gardens, the palatial amusement park in downtown Copenhagen. The night of the party, he invited all his friends, bought everybody lots of drinks and had a great time. And then, at the end of the evening, on his way to the bathroom, he slipped and fell down a long flight of concrete stairs. And that's how he died: rich, obscure and thousands of miles from home. It was tragic in its jazz symmetry.

As we pulled into the hotel parking lot, almost as an afterthought, Mose said, "If I ever write my autobiography, I'm gonna call it 'Too Much, Too Late.'" I laughed; Mose did not. He was uneasy in the Big Easy.

It rained for three days straight, and for three days the songs just kept rolling out, like the Mississippi itself. Some of the songs were nostalgic, like "Was," a waltz Mose wrote about how he might be remembered when he's gone. Or "Big Brother," a song he had written back when he was fresh out of college, around the time he was running with Brew. On our last night, after we had packed up the tapes and said goodnight to all the musicians, Mose turned to me and asked, "Say man, did you ever hear of the 'Bo Hog Grind'?"

I said no, what is it?

He said, "It's something I heard when I was a kid back in Tippo, Mississippi. I've been searching for it ever since. I don't know, but I think it's what all this music comes down to in the end."

I said that I guessed I'd been searching for it too. I just hadn't known what to call it.

1990

Every year, in January, the MIDEM organization runs an international music industry convention in Cannes, on the French Riviera. It's a marketplace for music publishers and record distributors from around the world, with rows of trade-show booths and endless dinners, and, because of the exotic location, it's always well attended. MIDEM also presents several nights of gala music performances in the main theater, the Palais des Festival, and in 1989, my quartet did a performance there. That evening, following our set, the producer of the event asked if I would be interested in presenting two nights the following year. One night would be dedicated to the music of Charlie Parker, and for the other, they wanted me to mount a Johnny Otis-style review of rhythm and blues. For the first time, the performances would also be televised live to the rest of France.

The jazz evening would be easy, like old home week. I made a few calls — to Frank Morgan, Phil Woods, Red Rodney, Roy Haynes and several others — and it was arranged. However, my idea for the rhythm and blues program was more problematic. I called it "Back to Stax," and I wanted to reunite the best of the Memphis sound, which was created at the Stax record label back in the 1960s. I rounded up Booker T and the MGs, The Memphis Horns, Carla Thomas, Sam Moore (of Sam and Dave) and Eddie Floyd. It wasn't easy to find some of them. I found Booker T, the great organ player and arranger, selling real estate in Los Angeles. Carla Thomas, the daughter of the irrepressible Rufus Thomas, was teaching school back in Memphis. The Memphis Horns were on tour with the Blues Brothers band, and Sam Moore, who kept touring after his partner Dave had died, was maintaining a somewhat low profile. The MIDEM show would be the first time they had all performed together in Europe since their wildly successful tour with Otis Redding back in 1967.

By the end of January 1990, we were rehearsing in Cannes. Booker T was all business. Along with guitarist Steve Cropper and Duck Dunne, he had recorded virtually every hit on the Stax label and had arrived in Cannes with that knowledge very much intact. After some initial backslapping and comments about how good everybody looked, Booker got down to business, running the groups through their paces. Within the first half-hour, however, a major disagreement broke out over the right way to play "Sitting on the Dock of the Bay," which would be the big closing number. Even though these were some of the same people who wrote and recorded the song 30 years before, there still seemed to be some question about the finer points. Eddie Floyd thought it went one way, Sam Moore said it went the other. The conversation got heated. Eventually, we had to stop the rehearsal for half an hour to let these guys cool down, during which time I was made to understand that Eddie and Sam had been having a simmering competition going on for many years, and that the current situation had almost nothing to do with this particular song. Rather, both men wanted to claim the crown left by Otis Redding, the King of the Soul Men, and neither would give an inch to the other.

The evening of the Stax reunion, the Palais des Festival was packed with the world's most difficult audience, industry types full of food, wine and themselves. Looking out from the wings, I asked Booker T if he still felt a rush before going on stage. He smiled and said, "You know man, I had no idea this music would ever get outside the city limits of Memphis. I thought it was local music. Every time is a rush for me."

When the lights went down, I walked out and announced, "Ladies and Gentleman, Booker T and the MGs!" and the crowd gave them a standing ovation. They walked out grinning and played "Green Onions," then brought out the Memphis Horns for a number. And then the band hit, "Hold On I'm Coming," now known everywhere as the Blues Brothers theme, and slowly, as if he was a king acknowledging his subjects, Sam Moore strolled out of the wings, deadpan, surveying the house. He went to the microphone and sang, "I know you're down, you got a problem, you're about to drown. Well hold on! I'm coming!" — the song that launched John Belushi into a thousand back flips — but Sam was cool as Sinatra, in total control. "Reach out to me for satisfaction, call out my name for quick reaction..."

It was all a pose but the Palais was loving it. Next, he sang a hokey ballad, and I wondered why he chose to do this when suddenly the band launched into some gospel breaks, and, by the second verse, Sam was sweating that sanctified sweat. The band went into a slow 6/8 stroll, the kind of groove that James Brown would hit and then shout "wait a minute," and fall to the floor, to be covered by a cape. Sam appeared to be crying actual tears, calling out, "I wonder do you know what I'm talking about?" The band was like a precision funk machine, a lesson in operational tactics. They were underrehearsed but like a green beret search-and-destroy team that had been on furlough for a couple of decades, they still remembered how to fan out and hold the territory. The song ended with wild applause.

Then, as Sam started to walk toward the audience, Carla Thomas magically appeared from the wings, taking the words out of his mouth, singing the opening phrase to the soul classic, "When Something Is Wrong with My Baby." Carla, luminous in a white gown, reached her arms wide to the crowd. Sam too was extending his hand to the people at the front of the stage and, perhaps to distract the crowd from the roughness of his performance, he suddenly cued the band to break down and he and Carla went into a raw, gospel call and response.

These were some Memphis folks playing by some Memphis rules; they were selling it so big that nobody could possibly focus on the missed notes. As Carla told me earlier that afternoon, "This sound was just pulled from the gospel roots and the blues roots, speeding up the tempo, putting the big brass with it, putting in the bridges and things like that...and they tagged it 'soul music' 'cause people just stood and sang from their guts, you know, whatever they felt, they just let it come out."

The fourth song was the rocking "I Take What I Want," a real roadrunner, with Sam pacing the stage, shouting, "Let's get busy...do you feel it? Do you feel it?" He was doing a gospel strut—that sanctified, one foot slide across the stage, churching up and down, the bad man being redeemed. "I feel it," he said, "I feel it in my hands. Do you feel it?" Then he said, "I want everybody to get up out of your seat. Get on up! Put your hands together and your arms together too." And as the band slipped into the theme, "I'm a Soul Man," he became the conquering hero and the crowd was screaming out his name. Sam had just arranged his own standing ovation.

It was a masterful performance. At the end, he looked down at the audience from the height of the stage with royal disdain, complete arrogance. He stepped back, as if trying to decide whether their tribute was sufficient for him to do yet another song. He wandered the stage, in apparent confusion, appearing troubled. "Do you feel it?" he asked again and again, pointing at the crowd. Before they could answer, he stepped off the stage and into the house. The band continued the sanctified vamp, and he pushed deeper into the crowd as if in the throes of a holy visitation. The spotlight followed him as he chanted "Do you feel it," and a conga line began to form behind him. He shouted, "Why don't you dance?" and some guy ripped off his shirt. He was doing that sideways, head down, ear cupped, happiness skip from the holiness church, and suddenly he said, "Aw, I gotta leave this song alone!" and ran back on stage, arriving stage center with his arms over his head like Mohammed Ali just as the song ended. In a flash, I was at the microphone calling out, "Sam Moore, ladies and gentlemen, the great Sam Moore!" I felt like Bobby Byrd, James Brown's m.c. I was in soul heaven. Off in the wings, however, I could see that Eddie Floyd was not amused.

As Sam passed me, ringing wet and grinning, he said, "You got to do the songs that got you here!" And he was gone.

In a flash, Eddie Floyd ran out and hit the crowd with "Raise Your Hands," another burning churchy groove. No warm up, nothing. He immediately started prowling the stage. In five minutes, he too had two thousand people pogo-ing up and down in ecstasy. "I want everybody to stand up in the name of soul!" he shouted and got his own standing ovation on the first tune. Now he was driving the band like a teenager pushing a '57 Chevy down a dirt road, four wheel sliding, throwing up gravel, "Aw yeah! raise your hands!" Fifteen minutes into the song, he was downshifting, upshifting, double-clutching. "I come in the name of soul!" he shouted. "Do you feel all right?" You could feel the room becoming hypnotized by this spirit, this vision of sixties soul. "Yeah," Eddie shouted, "have you got it? Everybody raise your hands!"

The horns started moaning that Memphis moan, and then the moan became the introduction to "Knock on Wood." Eddie and Steve Cropper had originally written the song for Otis Redding, but when Otis didn't want to record it, Eddie made it a hit himself. "Its like thunder, lightning, the way you love me is frightening. I guess I better knock //// on wood." Eddie was the goods. There was no posing, no theatrics. He just called the spirit down. "Hey, I feel all right!" and you knew he did. By the time Sam and Carla came back out for the big "Sitting on the Dock of the Bay" finale, the audience was tranced out. If you asked me who had won the title that night, Sam or Eddie, it was Eddie Floyd, hands down.

The next night was the tribute to Charlie Parker. It featured trumpeter Red Rodney, who as a Jewish teenager played in Bird's band for three years, drummer Roy Haynes, who took Max Roach's place in the same ensemble, and saxophonist Frank Morgan, who as a child had fallen in love with Bird's sound ("I heard the voice that I wanted to be my own"). They began with the theme, "Ornithology," and I was immediately struck by the high level of seriousness of this music, the artistic conception. Both soul music and jazz are serious black forms, of course, but the goal of jazz is so much higher. It is an elegant, transcendent expression of the human spirit that at times seems to rotate before your eyes like a multifaceted crystal, splitting the beams of intuition and reason into multiple shards of brilliance. This is sacred music. The way Frank Morgan played the opening phrase of Monk's "Round Midnight" was like davening; he was cantorial in his anguish.

At the rehearsal that afternoon, Red Rodney had said, "Bird would never rehearse. But he would instruct. When a new thing came in, if we didn't know it, he would turn around and gently look at you, play it to you once or twice. If you didn't have it by the third time, he would turn all the way around fast and fiercely play it to you, and you better have it then." Roy Haynes nodded and said, "And Bird would never count a song off. I don't remember him ever saying, 'One, two, three, four,' anything like that. He would just pat his foot, I would just follow his body motions and his feeling." That evening, all the players seemed to be following the feeling of Bird.

Then Frank Morgan played "Parker's Mood" with that same tortured junkie soul Bird had. Roy's drumming in particular seemed "etched in stone," every stroke, every hit placed exactly where it was supposed to be. This, too, was the real deal, the spirit of Bird. "Play it like you mean it." Bass player Rufus Reid was watching Frank closely, almost as if to see if he was going to be okay; Frank sounded so sad, he was crying his story out, nursing it, "come with me to Kansas City...." It was so sweet to hurt like this. Pianist Monte Alexander slipped in a chromatic II - V substitution at the turn-around, and the whole band just lifted and went into a double-time shuffle, hands in the pockets, holes in the shoes, kicking the tin can down at 12th and Vine. It was poetic.

They played another Parker blues, then Phil Woods took the stage. He stood in front of the microphone twisting, eyes closed, head cocked, neck fully inflated, looking for an updraft, teasing every ounce of lift out of the rhythm section, going to the next chorus. On the breast pocket of his blue blazer, he wore the medal given to him the year before by the French Minister of Culture, when he had been named a Chevalier of the French people for his service to the arts. Phil wore this medal with the dignity of a soldier who has survived many a great campaign, and perhaps in memory of all those who were left behind.

The rhythm section departed and Phil's own quartet took the stage. This band was Phil's pride and joy, and he had fought valiantly to keep it together for decades, in the face of economic hardships and the indifference of the recording industry. They played without monitors, completely acoustic, balanced in the space, the old-fashioned way. The four of them were like one living organism. "Hell," Phil once told me, "I even hate to use microphones when I record!"

They played "My Old Flame," one of Bird's favorite ballads and Phil's tone was like a Stradivarius. He was moaning through the well-worn melody, singing a whole world into being. Years before, when I had commented to him on the extraordinary expressiveness of his playing, he said, "Yeah, well when you play 'Harlem Nocturne' five times a night at the Nut Club, where they pass out hammers as you come in, you gotta sing, baby, or those strippers will kill you. Expressiveness. I know nothing but expressiveness...."

A decorated survivor of the jazz wars, Phil was playing every note as if his life depended on it, and, in fact, it probably did. He couldn't half-step, even in front of this audience of cynical record industry types. He was singing about love and truth and about something higher, a beautiful ass-shaking mystery, human intelligence, passion, romance, a joke, a great cosmic joke. He, too, was walking down the dirt road of life, wearing his medal proudly. His last notes, at the end of a roaring set, were the opening six notes of the song "Harlem Nocturne." No matter how far he may roam, he never forgot where he started from: he was one of Bird's children.

After the show, Phil said. "Bird was like a meteor. I don't think he was meant to stay around too long. He just came here and turned the whole universe around and left."

A jazz joke:

A sax player falls out of the 13th floor window and lives. His pal says, "you must be the luckiest sax player alive." "No," he says, "Kenny G is."

To build the Go Jazz catalog, I naturally turned to musicians I felt closest to. There is nothing quite as fine as being in a recording studio with good friends and great players and knowing that lunch is on the way.

Saxophonist Bob Malach was the first person I asked to record for Go Jazz. Bob is somebody who played with The O'Jays as a teenager in Philadelphia and then went on to work with Horace Silver, Stevie Wonder and Joe Zawinul among others, so he is well schooled in the classic traditions. Every note he plays comes from the Blues. That January, on the way to MIDEM, my band had played a week in Paris, and afterwards, Bob and I stayed over for a few extra days to record some duets with pianist Michel Petrucciani. Michel was a French gypsy all of three feet tall, having been born with a rare disease called osteogenesis imperfecta, or "glass bones." He literally had to be carried around in the arms of a friend, like a package of groceries, and he lived with the possibility of death at any moment—he ultimately died of pneumonia in 1999. But Michel was anything but fragile emotionally. In fact, living with this disease only seemed to make him more fearless. He was notorious for grabbing life with both hands. Plus his hands, and his head (and, reportedly, one other organ) were larger than normal. Michel and Bob had been great friends since the day, several years before, drummer Aldo Romano first carried him into Bob's New York apartment.

"Hey, baby, what's happening," was Michel's greeting in perfect street English as he arrived in the control room. Within moments, the room was full of talk about old friends and young women, and the session became a rollicking, historic afternoon. Then, a month later, Bob and I went into Skyline Studios in Manhattan with drummers Steve Gadd and Vinny Colaiuta, guitarist Robben Ford, Russ Ferrrante on keyboards and Will Lee on bass. On the last day of recording, Dr. John came in and sang a couple of things, including the old Screaming Jay Hawkins hit 'I Put a Spell on You." Collectively, these sessions were released on the *Mood Swing* album later in the year.

The next Go Jazz project grew out of a tour of Australia. I was back down under for three weeks when I wound up in Perth. After flying the five or six hours from Melbourne, over endless stretches of wasteland, no roads, no cities, nothing, I arrived in this modern city on the edge of the Indian Ocean. I was scheduled to play at the Perth Jazz Festival the next day, so I went over to the venue where the festival was going on to check it out. As I walked into the lobby, I heard a great jazz singer working with a tight horn band. It was Georgie Fame, the voice I had heard on the tape at Barry Ward's office a couple of years before. That night, Georgie and I got as tight as only a couple of jazz fiends from different corners of the world can get, huddled together at the end of the earth, drinking fine wine and exchanging classic lyrics from the past. By the time we had said good-bye, Georgie had agreed to join Bob Malach and me as the third Go Jazz artist.

The fourth Go Jazz artist was Ricky Peterson, Billy's kid brother. I had been encouraging Tommy LiPuma to sign Ricky to Warner Brothers Records for almost a year. Finally, I arranged for Tommy to come to Minneapolis to meet Ricky in his natural habitat. The day we arrived, it was a typically muddy spring afternoon, and Tommy was a good sport about dodging the puddles in his five hundred-dollar shoes.

At the time, Ricky was still living at "The Portland Arms," the tumbled down house on the edge of the ghetto, and when we pulled up in front of the building it was even more of a disaster than I had remembered. The front porch had collapsed, or was being rebuilt, but either way, it didn't exist. We had to climb over a pile of rubble to bang on a front door situated three feet off the ground. At this point, Tommy, who has a game leg and is not a sportsman under the best of circumstances, was clearly not having fun. When my pounding on the door went unanswered, I said, "You have to understand, things here might appear to be a little bit loose…" And we both cracked up. Loose didn't begin to describe the scene.

The front door finally opened and a stranger in his underwear let us in. He said he didn't know if Ricky was there but to come on in anyway. The shades were all drawn, and in the center of the dimly lit room was a huge cage with a mynah bird shouting "hello" and screeching like a monkey. Around the corner, in the kitchen, there was another guy sitting by the telephone, playing back messages on the answering machine and laughing. I didn't recognize either one of them. By this time, Tommy was almost enjoying himself. He has that wonderfully perverse sense of humor that is generally a result of living the jazz life. I finally dragged Ricky out of bed and introduced the two of them, and we went off for breakfast and a tour of the city.

That night, after Tommy heard Ricky play, all was forgiven. He signed Ricky to Warner Brothers, and the two of us co-produced Ricky's album, *Nightwatch*. It was a first-rate album, and it went nowhere fast when Tommy left Warner

Brothers right after its release. Ricky was dropped from the label and that's when he became Go Jazz artist number four.

At Go Jazz, our motto became "Let History Decide!"

That May, the Steve Miller touring machine cranked up again. Steve was still determined to be bigger than ever and had booked a sprawling two-and-a-half month caravan across the United States. Although the band was still my original guys plus Ricky and Paul, Steve had reduced the music to its bare essentials. The set was now devoid of jazz tunes. The program started with three chords in the key of B and progressed to three more chords in the key of D, and no playing of sevenths or jazz licks allowed. Or jamming at the sound checks. Or doing anything that resembled being loose and doing what you felt. Like dancing on stage. Or having fun. This was the army, and we were playing the marching music.

Okay, one might ask, why was I there? Fair enough. Certainly I was there for the money. I was being paid more *not* to play for two hours a night than I could possibly make playing six nights a week in a jazz club. And I was there for the band. We were still working together throughout the rest of year, and I had this kind of bunker mentality, that we were in this together. But mostly, I was there for Leo. He was now fourteen years old and was about to spend his summer vacation on a tour bus with a rock and roll band. How cool was that?

However, something happens to you when you do it for the money, especially when you get paid *not* to play, not to be yourself. Somehow, it denies your existence even as it ensures it. It calls into question the things you love exactly because doing those things pays so precious little. This particular brand of self-doubt doesn't usually rear its head until you happen to find yourself making large amounts of money to do practically nothing. If, as Lester Young said, "You have to save up to play jazz," what happens when the act of "saving up" undermines the place your inspiration comes from? The whole process shakes your faith. At least it was shaking mine that summer.

Leo got to choose the bunk he wanted on the bus and naturally he took a top one, so I took the one right below. Often, around four or five in the morning, I would wake with a start and realize I had just heard the huge bus wheels veer off the blacktop and onto the gravel shoulder, roaring by just inches below my ear at eighty miles an hour.

Sometimes I went to the front of the bus to check on the driver. He was a red-neck from Wisconsin and was in full bus driver mode. He would tell stories with asides like "she was hotter than a half fucked fox in a forest fire," and "that mosquito was so big it could stand flat footed and fuck a turkey." He was also a first cousin of Wisconsin's Governor Tommy Thompson, so I spent some time pumping him for dirt on the governor. I got stories about them raising a lot of hell back in the Elroy woods, chasing women and being wild, but nothing to equal the mouth on this character. He was a racist, an anti-Semite and a good ol' boy, but heck, he could drive a bus. After the first week, he was told not to go near Leo or Billy's daughter, Theresa, who was also out for the ride.

If nights were spent racing from venue to venue, days were spent sitting around doing practically nothing. Generally speaking, we were virtual prisoners in a pitched camp at the edge of some godforsaken field, surrounded by a vast blacktop sea full of teenagers getting juiced. Steve had agreed to hand out a little stage-written rap about "saving the environment," which was printed on recycled paper. There was always a crew of college kids around to pass them out. I would talk to these kids from time to time, nice earnest young people who felt they were making progress. One's dad was a sixties survivor, and the way he talked about his father and the sixties was the way I might have talked about the twenties when I was his age. It was striking how the perception of money, hipness, and good works was changing. Back in the sixties, the talk ran from saving our souls to stopping the war, but we tended to live the life we sang about; that is, the war was about to happen to us personally. Now kids were talking about saving the whales and writing about it using biodegradable ink but at the same time, they were racing four wheel drive vehicles through a fragile ecology. Not to mention the whole issue of noise pollution.

In Michigan, I climbed a large hill. In the distance, you could see the Great Lake as it ran for miles, shimmering behind the rolling dunes. There was a long line of kids coming to the concert like ants to honey, called by the volume of our soundcheck. The rising clouds of dust as they drove through the field made the sunset glow red. It was a beautiful setting, openly desecrated by the excruciating high-end squawks being fed through our p.a. system. Everything was thriving, the kids in particular. They were partying like it was the fall of Rome, and, all around us, their all-terrain vehicles were ripping up the soft rolling dunes.

That night, as we left the venue, a car with four, fat teen-aged girls roared past the bus, and all the girls waved their environmental books at us and then lifted their shirts to show us their tits. Big nipples in the Michigan breeze. One T-shirt said, "If I'm Not Wasted, the Day Is."

On the tour bus that summer, I came to think of the road as a metaphor for the oldest of human struggles, that of Cain and Abel. Cain was a farmer and a vegetarian, and he killed Abel, a nomad and a carnivore, because, some say, civilization required it. The Bible, then, can be seen as the story of the war between those who travel and those who erect fences. This helped explain the popularity of rock and roll bands; every kid wanted to ride with Jesse James.

The road was also a metaphor for Einstein's theory of relativity, where one stays younger by moving faster. It's so American, this arrested development, this delayed adolescence, this worshipping of speed. It is the triumph of institutionalized democracy, proof of H. L. Mencken's dictum that you will never go broke underestimating the intelligence of the American people. On the road you never have to grow up, until you do. Hard is soft, dark is light and what worked when you were twenty still works, until it doesn't.

And finally, I saw that the road is literally endless. There are not many roads. There is only one road, infinitely connected, always leading away from home and back toward home at the same time.

By the end of July, the tour buses pulled into Manhattan, and Steve, Leo and I went to Manny's Music Store to buy Leo his first guitar. Steve had been showing Leo how to play guitar all summer long, and now he was going to show Leo how to chose the perfect instrument. After an hour of playing every guitar they could get their hands on, Steve left with a new Steinberger and Leo had a Hohner knock-off.

Later that day, Billy and I took Leo on a walk through the Village. On a street corner near Bleecker and Seventh Avenue, a funky cat named Jay was playing a washtub bass and singing "Lullaby of Birdland" for spare change. He said he was going to tour Europe in the fall, and he swung so hard, a homeless cat threw in 35 cents and offered me some beer. He heard Jay telling Billy about the washtub bass and turned to me and said, "That's a half-million dollars worth of information he's giving away for free, right there...."

Around the corner four cats — two black, two white — sang doo-wop to two seventeen-year-old girls on a stoop and the girls were going for it. The attitude on the street was literally fantastic, a theater of the absurd. We saw a wino panhandle a baby in a stroller, some terrible reflex that couldn't be stopped. A homeless drunk walked by the pizza parlor and said, "choose to be happy" and kept walking. One block away, a black beggar solicited for the "United Negro Pizza Fund." The style, the groove, the insult, the struggle of the streets was like a medieval fair. Leo was trying to relate to all the hustling. Clearly you couldn't give money to everybody. "Let's give money to the funny ones or the really sad ones," he said, establishing a hierarchy in the human condition that I can still live with. First comes comedy, then tragedy.

The tour buses kept rolling, through New Jersey, through Connecticut, through Maine —where the insects were so unrelenting that I went to an army surplus store and bought a beekeeping hat to wear on stage. Not to be outdone, Paul Peterson invented an outfit wearing black panties on the outside of his red tights and a pair of high top black work boots. The level of artistic seriousness was now completely out the window. We were like a bunch of aging strippers on stage, and somehow the kids didn't see past the smoke and mirrors. Huge video screens projected our image forty feet high on each side of the stage, but the larger we loomed, the less real we became. Which was the point, after all.

Leo settled down to writing songs on his new guitar and mastering the portable recording studio that Steve had installed on the bus. Of all of us, he was the only one who took advantage of the road to be creative. The rest of us were just holding on, but Leo was in full swing. You could always find him there, over-dubbing a vocal or a guitar part. If Steve wanted to use the studio, he had to ask Leo to engineer for him. Leo was the only one who knew how to run it. He had paid attention to how Steve's songs worked. They didn't have to be complicated. In fact, the simpler the better. Three chords was plenty. You needed a hook and Leo was throwing out more hooks than a fly fisherman in a Montana stream. One day, he came up to me in the dressing room and said, "Ben, how come *your* songs don't have any hooks?" I just looked at him.

We rolled through Rochester, Pittsburgh, Nashville, Birmingham, where a huge bolt of lightning hit the stage just as we were going on, and as we retreated to the mobile home that served as our dressing room, ten thousand drunk kids cheered and wallowed in the mud. When we got to Atlanta, where Leo would be leaving us —he was going to camp for a month —Steve asked him if he wanted to come on stage for the encore. Leo had never actually confronted this roiling sea of hormones head on, even though he had spent a lot of time on stage during the sound checks, and by this time he could play most of the songs.

When the encore came, Leo walked back on stage with the band. I picked up a tambourine, slid next to Bobby Malach and let Leo get behind the keyboard as Gordy counted off the hit, "Jet Airliner." Leo was all smiles and the audience was howling louder than a 747. You could just see his smile freeze as he understood the impossibility of actually playing music while standing in front of this blast of energy. The next day, he got on a jet airliner of his own and went to be a kid in the Wisconsin woods.

But we kept on rolling, through Orlando, Miami, Ft. Lauderdale, Houston and Dallas, Memphis, St. Louis, Kansas City and Denver. They were all the same, "sheds" that accommodated ten to fifteen thousand kids separated by miles of highway and featuring, at the end of the day, a bad Caesar salad and the same three chords. Bobby Malach was hunkered down with his horn, practicing as much as six hours a day. Gordy smoked his pipe and got the nickname "grampa" because he was never part of the hilarity. Billy and his brothers pulled workouts in the parking lot and started drinking before dinner. Steve was locked in the celebrity dressing room with his toys, the computers, cameras, guitars, clothes. And I read books, made phone calls, and flew back to New York or Madison every chance I got.

The first week of August we had several days off in Los Angeles and Steve wanted to go into a recording studio. As he had written no songs of his own, the five songs he planned to record were all written by Leo. Which made a lot of sense since Leo had been the only one to write on the road, and his songs really reflected the mood of Steve's audience, loose, happy, boy meets girl, boy loses girl, boy gets girl back. Leo broke out of camp for a few days and flew out to Ocean Way Studios in L.A.

It was a strange scene to say the least. There was Leo in the control room, a kid who could barely see over the mixing desk, watching while the rest of us cut his songs. From time to time, he would get on the "talk back" and crack a joke or comment on how we were doing. Steve and the band made his little three-chord anthems sound like the real deal. You could just see how Steve's great vocal ability and natural guitar playing had propelled him to the top. He was like a pop-song machine. Whatever you put in came out sounding like Top Forty radio.

Stranger still, Glyn Johns was also working at Ocean Way that week, recording with his own son, Ethan, a talented singer and guitar player. It was touching to see them working together. I remembered when Ethan was born and had watched him grow up in this world of instruments and recording gear, just like Leo. Glyn seemed softened by working with Ethan. There was none of the brusque bravura he usually brought with him into the studio. Leo and I spent time each day in the studio with Glyn, not just because it was nostalgic for me, remembering the sixties when Glyn first introduced me to the world of recording, but it also gave me a sense that what we were doing was a craft that could be passed on to our children.

When the band pulled up stakes and got back on the bus, Leo flew back to camp with a cassette tape of his songs. Later, he told me he didn't play the tape for many of the kids at camp. "I didn't think they would understand," he said. Irvine, Santa Barbara, San Francisco, Vancouver, Salem, Seattle, on we rolled, until finally, on a hot dusty August afternoon, the bus pulled off the main road and drove down a rutted track for several miles. At the end, we came to the Gorge at George. We had arrived at our last stop, a huge field on the edge of a deep canyon not far from Yakima, Washington. This was where we had been heading for two and half months. Nowhere.

On September 4, I was invited out to Taliesin, the original home and studio of architect Frank Lloyd Wright in Spring Green, Wisconsin, to speak with the apprentices about the relationship between Mr. Wright's theory of "unit structures" and jazz improvisation.

The cliché is that Wright called architecture "frozen music." In fact, the words were not his, but I used the image to consider jazz music as "thawed architecture." Before the lecture, which took place in the lovely little theater Wright had designed and decorated with quotes by Thoreau and Whitman, Judy and I had dinner with the students and their teachers. Our meal was served by Wes Peters, a hunched over man in his eighties who was one of Mr. Wright's early apprentices, now a master architect and still part of the Taliesin Fellowship, which required that everyone do daily chores on an equal basis. There were no stars at Taliesin. There was only the work that needed to be done, a discipline left over from the days when Wright was a devotee of Gurdjieff, and those who remained in the Fellowship were dedicated to the work.

The first line of my little talk that night was, "You cannot imagine how good it is to be here among you, a fellowship of equals."

That year, September 20 marked the beginning of the Jewish High Holy Days.

One of the keys to Hannah Rosenthal's service is that it is the same every year. And yet every year it is subtly different. Every year we repeat the reading of the same prayers and sing the same songs in the same order. (It's amazing that, after twenty years, she still comes over to the house the night before so that we can "rehearse.") But each year, one finds something new on every page, in the simplest lines. "The Gods we worship write their names on our faces..." And there is a shifting of mood from year to year, as the children grow up and leave, as old friends return or go missing. The circumstances of our lives spiral around the central, immovable fact of these Rosh Hashana and Yom Kippur services. In this way, they have become a living tradition. They live on in the lives of our children and our friends.

Of course, if tradition isn't living, it isn't really tradition. It's just ritual. Or as Bob Dylan put it, "Those who are not busy being born are busy dying." After a few years, I got a chill one night as I started to sing "Life's a Lesson," and, as I sang the opening line, "Life's a lesson..." I heard several small voices join in, "you can fail it..." My little song had taken on a life of its own, inserting itself like a virus into the minds of the youngest of our little ad hoc congregation. And so tradition replicates itself and its message moves down through the generations. And that is why, as the service says, it is so important to be careful what we are worshipping, because what we are worshipping we are becoming. And so often, music is the way that history travels best.

I have always thought of Thelonious Monk's song, "Ruby My Dear," especially the version with John Coltrane, as a piece of sacred music. Or Charles Mingus' "Goodbye Pork Pie Hat," or Horace Silver's "Moon Rays," and, of course, all of Miles Davis' *Kind of Blue* album. There is no shortage of sacred jazz music. But why, I wondered, sitting there at the Gates of Heaven, wasn't the music that was supposed to be sacred — the Hebrew liturgical music — being treated better and more often? Why didn't the recordings of it feel "spiritual?"

African-American jazz musicians have often recorded Gospel-related songs or albums, but to my knowledge, no Jewish jazz musicians had ever recorded the liturgical music of their people. One could suppose that this was due, in part, to the fact that when the black jazzman plays, he is in a way staking out his cultural territory, while the Jewish jazzman is often in the process of fleeing his own. But why were the recordings of Jewish liturgical music always so flat? They sounded slapdash and thrown together, poorly recorded with out-dated equipment. Or, on the other hand, the recordings of the great cantorial voices were often so over the top with all their g'shrying and pyrotechnics that it had very little to do with the price of milk. It was no longer presented as a part of our everyday lives.

So when year after year, the people leaving the Gates of Heaven Synagogue said to me, "You should record this music," I knew I would have to do it, and, after twenty years of producing records, I knew it would not be easy.

First of all, there was the question of how to raise the money. So often the record business reminded me of the fable of the Little Red Hen. The Hen asks all the animals of the barnyard, "Who will help me plant the corn?" and of course, nobody volunteers. After the corn is planted, she asks, "Who will help me harvest the corn?" and again, no takers. When the corn is harvested, she seeks help grinding the flour, and still no help. The same for baking the bread. But when she finally asks "And who will help me eat the bread?" suddenly the table is teaming with wildlife. I knew there was no chance that anybody at a major record label would be interested in financing this kind of recording. At the same time, I was producing the Go Jazz series in concert with the Japanese, and I had an active distribution partner in Germany. Whereas the American record companies were already deep into their love affair with Gangster Rap, the Japanese and the Europeans were still enthusiastic about the jazz and social commentary albums I was making. I had also just started working on the music for a film called *Hoop Dreams*, which no American label would fund; I had taken it to my foreign partners, and they had agreed to help.

So, in the spring of 1990, just before the Miller tour took off, I called a meeting of my partners at a nondescript hotel just outside the international airport in Minneapolis. We discussed the usual business, and then, at the end of the day, I asked Nobu Yoshinari, my partner from Japan, what he thought about an album sung in Hebrew and including famous Jewish jazz musicians performing liturgical music. In his wonderful, reasonable way, he said, "I think that would be interesting." I turned to Vera Brandes, the German distributor, and asked how she thought their market would react. "It will be well received," she said. The axis powers had just agreed to help finance the Jewish record.

Following the High Holy Days services that September, I went into a recording studio in Minneapolis to begin. First, I recorded all the songs with just myself on the keyboards and Lynette Margulies, who sang at our services, on the Hebrew vocals. Then, for the next three years, I traveled the world with tapes under my arm. I would call up a friend, or perhaps just a musician who I knew had Jewish roots, and make my pitch. Like the call I made to saxophonist Josh Redman, who has an African-America father (the avant garde musician Dewey Redman) and a Jewish mother.

"Josh," I said, "I'm doing an album of Hebrew liturgical music and I've got you down for 'Oseh Shalom.' Are you interested?" He laughed and said, "Seriously, what are you planning?" I repeated myself. It took a couple of tries, but invariably, it worked. They came, they played, and they left with a tape for their mother. Twenty of America's finest Jewish performers played like angels on songs they hadn't heard nor thought of since they were kids. What was so striking was the similarity of the stories they told me. "I was born Jewish," Randy Brecker said, "But I'm not religious...." "I know," I reassured him, "Me too. Just come down and try it, and if you don't like it, we won't use it." He, too, left with a tape for his mother.

There was some deep, almost primitive, connection being made in the studio as the music unfolded. I included only two songs in English — a song I wrote for my sister called "Face Your Fears" and, of course, "Life's a Lesson" — and the sound of Lynette's soaring Hebrew filled room after room in city after city, as I traveled the circuit documenting our communal jazz childhood. In our day, each of us had stood as a child in a temple somewhere, swaying and hypnotized by the language and the hope that there was justice in the world.

As the word was getting out in the jazz community that I was making this record, I started receiving phone calls from musicians, some quite famous, saying things like, "Ben, you can't record 'Avinu Malchenu' without me. That's my song." It was as if, to become jazz musicians, we had all taken a fork in the road and now we wanted to revisit that territory.

Perhaps the most striking of these phone calls was the one from Mike Mainieri. He said, "Hey man, I hear you're making this record of Jewish music. I'd like to play on it." I said, "Yeah, Mike, but it's just for the brothers, you know?" Because I knew he was raised Catholic, and I was taking a lot of pleasure in assembling this Jewish team. Even the engineer, James Farber, was wearing a yarmulke in the studios. "No," Mike said, "we've got to talk about this." And so several days later, we met at the Mayflower Hotel in New York City. Mike immediately placed a large, coffee table book in front of me. It was titled *Jews in the Renaissance* and it was opened to a page with the biography of a painter named Daniellie. It was his distant relative, who had changed his name and converted to avoid persecution. Mike said his grandmother was Jewish too. In Italy, many of his family had converted to Catholicism. His father had told him, "Don't ever bring this up; it will come back to haunt you." It was clear that Mike had been waiting his whole life to come out of this particular closet.

I said, "Okay, Mike, you're on. You can represent all those folks whose relatives converted but who still feel connected."

Why should it matter if it happened a couple of years ago or a couple of hundred years ago? And if Mike felt that the Jewish part of him was still significant, it raised an interesting question in my mind: who is a Jew? We know that according to Israel's law of return, your mother must be Jewish. But this is only one interpretation. I myself know several people who have neither a Jewish mother nor a Jewish father who are clearly quite Jewish themselves. And one can always convert. So what does it mean to be a Jew? Mike came into the studio later that week and played on the song "Life's a Lesson," which I sang as a duet with Carole King.

If making this record opened up deep philosophical questions for me, it also opened up urgently practical ones. I got it finished. I got it paid for. I arranged to license Marc Chagall's "Praying Jew" from the Art Institute of Chicago for the cover. I saw to it that the record was distributed in Japan and throughout Europe, where the reviews were very positive. But in the United States, I couldn't get distribution.

It's not that I didn't try. I had come to know most of the men who ran the record business. As the cliché would have it, many of them were Jews, some quite active in the Jewish community and well known for their philanthropy. Several had even received the B'nai Brith humanitarian award for their good deeds. So originally, I felt confident that one of these gentlemen would see the beauty and the logic in this recording and at least make it available in his home country, to his own people. I sent copies to a dozen of these top recording executives. To a man, they were complimentary about the music. Likewise, to a man, they turned it down. Clive Davis at Arista let me know that it didn't fit his roster. Ron Goldstein, who was at Private Music, told me it was an "heroic effort" but there was no way he could distribute it. Larry Rosen at GRP, after asking for two extra copies for his wife's family, let me know he wouldn't be helping me out, either.

At one point, I was telling this saga to an older black musician, a long-time friend and someone whose career I had been helping along. When I got to the part about being unable to get distribution in the U.S., he was simply incredulous. He finally spit it out: "But man, everybody knows you got to have a Jew in this business." I felt a double chill; first of all, I had never heard the expression before, and, second of all, it was obvious—I had been *his* Jew. My inability to get the Jewish record distributed made *him* feel vulnerable.

Finally, Bob Krasnow, who was then chairman of Elektra Records, said, "I'm going to tell you the truth, Ben. Nobody is going to put this record out. The reason is simple. We don't believe it can sell."

I tried to reason with him. I said, "Bob, you put out tons of awful rap records that don't sell. Why not put out something you can be proud of?"

"You don't understand," he told me. "It doesn't matter whether those records sell. It matters that I *believe* they can sell. And I don't believe this one can." Dayenu, as the Jews say. It's enough.

Since then, I've had a lot of time to reflect on why the business rejected this obviously righteous project. At the time, I had to wonder if it wasn't because of the classic self-hating-Jew syndrome, but with the passage of time, I've come to believe that this wasn't necessarily the story. It was mostly about the money: god the father, god the son, god the almighty dollar. These men just didn't want to go into a marketing meeting with a bunch of guys about to hit the streets on behalf of their latest product and expose their Jewishness in this way: "Let's see, we got the Ghetto Boys rap group, which we think is gonna do great in Philly, we got Black Death, a heavy metal group breaking big in Atlanta, and, oh yes, there's this little Jewish thing I'd like you to work that could really catch on big around Passover." Their hearts might have been in it, but their budgets were no longer connected to their beliefs. At bottom, the record business had become a business without a moral compass. As Krasnow had so succinctly put it years before, "Money; that's the philosophy of every business." There was simply no longer room for human scale music. And this music is not larger than life, it *is* life.

It would take a few more years for *Life's a Lesson* to finally surface in America, but when it did, it would bring with it one of the great teachings of my life.

1991

I continued to build the Go Jazz catalog.

That spring, Georgie Fame was touring the States with Van Morrison, and we arranged to record his first Go Jazz album in New York at the conclusion of the tour. The rhythm section I had booked for the date — Steve Gadd, Will Lee,

Richard Tee and Robben Ford—was as good as they come, and the *Cool Cat Blues* album was recorded totally live. I sat in the control room and felt like I was at the nightclub, enjoying one great performance after another. This must have been what it felt like in the studio thirty-five years ago, before multi-tracking made everything possible (and some things impossible).

Willie Dixon's classic "I Love the Life I Live" came screaming onto the tape in one take. When it was over, I found that I was on my feet and I didn't remember getting out of my chair. When the guys casually strolled into the control room to hear the playback, Robben, grinning like a kid, turned to me and said, "I just love the blues, it's like one big playground."

Spending time with Georgie was a lesson in surviving gracefully. He had been a legend a lot longer than most of today's rock stars have been alive. He started young as a professional in London, and by the middle sixties, he was already a hero to some of today's biggest pop stars. In 1963, when he was leading a house band called The Blue Flames at the Flamingo club, he had his first hit record, singing Jon Hendrick's lyrics to the Mongo Santamaria instrumental, "Yeh Yeh." It changed everything for him. Up until then, he had been an insider's musician. Suddenly, he was everybody's favorite. A string of top ten singles followed, and The Beatles and The Rolling Stones were calling him.

But Georgie did the remarkable thing. He began to pursue in earnest his interest in jazz, eventually touring Europe with Count Basie's band. Pianist Blossom Dearie paid him the ultimate jazz tribute when she wrote the song "Sweet Georgie Fame" for him. And while the song introduced his name to thousands of jazz fans, many of them, to this day, still have no idea whether "Georgie Fame" is a man or a myth. But in New York, all the musicians knew his work and everybody dug recording with him. A year later, when we came back to record the follow-up album, *The Blues and Me*, Paul Shaffer, David Letterman's partner on television, thanked me for letting him play organ on the session, thus making him "A Blue Flame for a day." Working with Georgie Fame was a walk into history.

Next it came time to record Ricky Peterson for Go Jazz. Actually, Ricky produced *Smile Blue* himself and I just ordered lunch. One historic moment I do remember quite clearly, however, is the day I brought Johnny Griffin in to play a solo on the old Benny Goodman theme "Goodbye." Ricky had done an ultra-hip reharmonizing of the chord changes over a particularly interesting funk groove, and there was a spot in the middle that we thought would be perfect for Johnny. The idea occurred to us because Griffin was working in Minneapolis at a small club at the time, and we were recording in Minneapolis at Paisley Park, Prince's sprawling sixty-million-dollar recording enclave.

That night, we went to hear Griffin, and he played a burning two-hour set, talking, joking and chiding the audience. He took a cassette tape away from one fan, telling him "records come out from tapes like this," and then he told the audience he loved them, that they "made the music with him, truly," even though they probably didn't believe this. He went on to say he hated recording studios and microphones and loved being in the club with them. It was a masterful performance. When he came off stage, he seemed ten feet tall.

The next morning, I picked him up at his hotel and took him out to Paisley Park Studios. He walked through the lobby looking at the odd ritualistic symbols that Prince had painted all over and just shook his head. I took him on a tour of the place, with the soundstage that's as big as an airplane hanger, and he seemed to get smaller and smaller as the tour continued. (It reminded me a little of walking through the Vatican with Billy.) When we finally got into the studio, we played the pre-recorded track for him and he said, "Yeah, that's pretty." He went out and put his earphones on and took a pass at the solo. It didn't sound like Johnny Griffin. It sounded tentative and fragmented. He took another pass, and then another. Finally, he threw down his earphones and came back into the control room and said, "I never got shot down like that before. I never looked inside and found nothing. I always thought 'Music, bring it on!' And the music was pretty. But...I don't know, man. It was like romancing a ghost." Johnny Griffin wasn't going to play John Henry. If the machine wouldn't respond to him, he wouldn't respond to the machine.

All too soon, it was time for the next Steve Miller Band tour. My motivation for getting on the bus was growing pretty thin. By now, I was spending more time in the studio and less on the road, and the band was clearly looking to Steve for life support. I no longer felt the obligation to hang in there with them. And the money was no longer as much an issue for me. It's amazing how quickly you can become jaded.

This time, the only real motivation was Leo. He had been writing a lot of songs, really good songs, and I could hear Steve singing them. It was a perfect match. Leo had gone to school on Steve's hits, the band, the rehearsals, he knew the audience, in fact he now *was* the audience demographically. And Steve was determined to release a new album this year and still hadn't written any songs of his own. With this in mind, and with Steve telling Leo, "Kid, you're an important part of the organization," I got on board. It was only a month long.

Steve had added his old pal Norton Buffalo on harmonica and replaced Ricky Peterson with Byron Alred, the synth programmer who had invented the "spacy" sounds on the song "Fly Like an Eagle." Every evening, Byron pretended to play these sounds as the spotlight shone down on him. In reality, the effects were pre-taped and triggered, but Byron loved his moment of posing in the spotlight. All the guys in the band thought it was ridiculous, so we posed right along with him. It made him angry, which was part of the fun. One night, just as we were about to go on stage, Byron came up to me and said, "Look, man, just don't pretend to play when *I'm* pretending to play, Okay?" That was it. Time to get off the bus.

My diary for the entire month is blank, which says something, except for one entry dated August 6, 1991.

Miles Davis was sick and dying in a New York hospital. In his room, he had all his things around him, his horn, a boom box, tapes of his music. One night he called Tommy LiPuma.

"Tommy," he said, "I got something I want to play for you."

"Okay, Miles," Tommy said. "I'll come right over."

When Tommy arrived, Miles slipped a tape into the boombox and out came a song he had been working on. Tommy listened to it and said, "Yeah, Miles, that's nice. I like it. Maybe you should..."

Miles cut him off. He said, "Tommy, I don't want to know what you *think* about it. I just wanted to play it for you."

The further adventures of Go Jazz:

I had wanted to make a record called *Whatever Happened to the Blues* for some time, and finally decided to build it around guitarist Phil Upchurch. The idea was to create an authentic, contemporary blues ensemble, with great singers and great players, and to use all the different blues forms, twelve bars, thirty-two bars, 6/8 vamps, whatever, to create an antidote to all the super-slick smooth jazz that was being recorded. Some of my favorite blues singers were Pops & Mavis Staples, Les McCann and Chaka Khan, and they were all friends of Phil's. And there is no more authentic blues guitarist than Phil Upchurch, who grew up on the streets of Chicago in the fifties and sixties and became a local legend. Or, as Mavis Staples once told Phil's son, "Boy, I could have been your mama."

For Phil's sessions, I brought in Prince's drummer Michael Bland and James Brown's drummer Clyde Stubblefield, and I had them play together. Maceo Parker and the JB horns came in, and for good measure, I had a phenomenal gospel group, the Steeles, along with organ player Jack McDuff and Chicago jazz poet, Oscar Brown Jr. We were going to prove that the blues were alive and well.

We went into Studio B at Paisley Park the second week of October. At the time, Prince was rehearsing his "Diamonds and Pearls" tour on the soundstage. Starting in the early evening and running long into the night, you could sit on the couch and watch them road test this enormous phallic experience. The set had huge modular pillars that suggested genitalia, while Prince and a couple of girls rode in a flying bed above a nest of musicians, rappers and semi-naked women who were writhing below in a nasty Caligula dance. Once Leo found this scene, it was pretty tough to get him off that couch. One afternoon, Jevetta Steele introduced him to Prince, who apparently said, "Hey, we're having a party tonight if you want to come." Leo asked me if he could go to the party. Prince's parties usually started around 2 A.M. and featured gangsters and strippers from all over the Twin Cities. I said absolutely not.

"Why not?"

I said, "I'm not even going to dignify that with an answer." I think maybe he was a little relieved.

It was an unusual cast of characters running through the halls of Paisley Park that week: Prince and his crew, Phil and our crew. Oscar Brown Jr. had flown in from the West Coast where he appeared to be living—it wasn't clear, even to him—and proved to be as mystical and down to earth as his songs. Over dinner one night he said, "Everything is energy. You're either giving it or taking it, feeding or being eaten. And money is just the means, the way the energy travels." It reminded me of Mose Allison's dictum: everything comes down to somebody's money vs. somebody else's life.

The highlight of Phil's sessions was a little song he had written one night in the hotel when he couldn't sleep. It was a catchy figure, eight bars on one chord with a release, which he composed while sitting on the toilet, slapping his bare feet on the tile floor. We decided that the only way we were going to recreate the feeling was to record him playing barefoot on a marble floor, so we set him up in the drum booth and recorded his feet as well as his guitar. I wrote some lyrics with J.D. Steele, and when Pops and Mavis sang "The Tide Keeps Lifting Me," it sounded like something off the Stoval plantation.

Phil Upchurch had the bad luck of being both a great blues guitarist and an extraordinary jazz improviser. As far back is the mid-sixties, he recorded with Philly Joe Jones, Paul Chambers, and Wynton Kelly (Miles Davis' rhythm section) and with Jimmy Reed, Little Milton and B.B. King. So he's too hip for the blues crowd and too funky for the smooth jazzers.

A year later, when we recorded his follow up album, *Love Is Strange*, there was one track, called "B's Blues," that started to get a lot of attention. In fact, it was doing so well at radio stations that Broadcast Architecture, the top consulting company, was considering adding it to their playlist, which would have meant a lot of airtime for Phil at urban radio stations around the country. There was just this one little problem. Broadcast Architecture did its research by hooking folks up to buzzers, playing them smooth jazz tracks, and then instructing them to push the buzzer whenever anything got their attention. Not when they liked or disliked a passage, but when they actually paid attention to what they heard. Those moments were considered inconsistent with the "Smooth Jazz" format. (Musicians refer to it as "wallpaper music.") The problem was that on the fade of Phil's song, people had pressed their buzzers.

I was told that if we would remove some of the notes from Phil's solo on the fade of the song, make it simpler, they would add it to their play list. I immediately thought of Mozart's response to the king in the film *Amadeus*, and asked which notes they would like me to take out. The answer came back, "Any notes." There it is, as the king would say. They didn't even get the joke, let alone the irony. When I told Phil what had happened, he went nuts.

"That's censorship!" he said.

"You're right," I said.

"They can't do that," he said.

"You're wrong," I said. "That's exactly what they do, all the time."

"I thought music was supposed to make you feel something."

"Yeah, well, music can do what it wants and so can they."

We did not remove the notes and we did not get the airplay. In time, it all just got added to the sack of blues that Phil Upchurch carries around with him all the time.

1992

The film *Hoop Dreams* originally started out as a half-hour television program to encourage kids to stay in school. It was called "Higher Goals" then, and Peter Gilbert, the producer / director called to ask if I would compose the music. "Donate" the music was more like it. They had no money. Being of the jazz world, this was part of my normal operating procedure. So I remixed various Go Jazz tracks for "Higher Goals," including something I had recorded with Oscar Brown Jr. but never released.

After "Higher Goals" won an Emmy and the MacArthur Foundation came up with some additional resources, Peter and his partners pushed on with the feature film, and I expanded the music to include rap, blues and jazz, with an eye toward making the soundtrack album part of the Go Jazz catalog. For a while, I had been interested in the confluence of these street-corner musics, where people met and informed one another of the distant places and the disparate truths that bind us together. Even dyed-in-the-wool beboppers like Max Roach had talked to me about the connection of rap and bebop. Since both forms grew up on the streets of Brooklyn and Harlem, he said, "Where art, music and dance were taken out of the educational system, so people had to invent it themselves," one could see them both as the flowering of a similar spirit. At the same time, Peter was delivering fantastic footage that played off the power of basketball against the pathos of everyday life. *Hoop Dreams* was obviously a great premise to make the statement that these various corners are all connected in some fundamental way.

I began at Paisley Park in Minneapolis with Ricky Peterson; just the two of us locked in a small room with drum machines, synths and almost no budget. I paid Prince's "loop doctor," a mad scientist whom Ricky called Poindexter, to deliver a half-dozen pounds of fresh loops, multi-layered drum beats invented inside the computer and capturing the madness of the moment. We arbitrarily spread these grooves out for six or eight minutes each and then began throwing bass and keyboard parts on top. I told Ricky that since we had no money, we were going to do it fast. First take on everything, chord changes, solos, whatever. If we stumbled onto a great hook, we would go with it, no second thoughts. "Play the stuff that got you thrown out of school," I told him. Within a couple of days, we had six fairly ripe tracks to work with.

One of them became the title song, "Hoop Dreams," and Tony M, Prince's lead rapper, contributed the narrative. Another became known as "The Original Lesson" after Shock G. put the lyric concept together. Shock, a.k.a. Greg Jacobs, was at the center of an Oakland, California band called Digital Underground, and his alter ego, Humpty Hump, was one of the cleverest, funkiest personas in rap. When I got Greg on the phone to ask him to write some lyrics, he said, "Man, I've been a fan of yours for a long time. Let me ask you something. How come you and all the other jazz guys are out there scuffling, and we're doing these stupid things and making all this money?"

And I said, "Shock, if I could do the stupid things you do, I'd be doing it too." This cracked him up, and when we finally came to record his lyrics, I found he had inserted my name into them, which made me a big deal around the house for an afternoon. I told Leo, "Shock G. called my name!"

At the same time, I composed themes for the two young men whose lives were followed in the film. I recorded them in New York with bass player Rufus Reid, drummer Carl Allen and Bobby Malach. We spent a lazy afternoon improvising variations on the themes, some played by the quartet, some by the trio, and some I played as duets with Rufus or Bob. As an afterthought, I asked Bob to play the themes all by himself on saxophone. When it came time to use the music in the finished film, we mostly chose Bob's solo horn for the intimate family moments. It was magical, and astonishing, to see how much emotion is conveyed by just one saxophone playing a theme.

Hoop Dreams was a phenomenon that connected with a lot of people exactly because it was tangentially about the sport of basketball and essentially about the lives of ordinary people, the story of two mothers trying to keep their families together and of two boys trying to find their way out of a terrible predicament, carrying with them the hopes and dreams of their community. These were things everybody could understand. Watching *Hoop Dreams*, it was clear that every life on the planet is a powerful story, if only one can find the words and music with which to tell it.

In the summer of 1992, Michael Franks asked me to produce part of his album *Dragonfly Summer*. One song, a duet with singer Dan Hicks, was easy. Dan knew what he wanted to do and stepped up to the microphone and did it. He and Michael sounded like two pals sitting around on bar stools late at night, talking about the girls they left at home.

The second song, a duet with Peggy Lee, was much more problematic. Miss Lee arrived at the studio wrapped in an elegant fur stole and accompanied by a very handsome, very young amanuensis. She was also in a wheelchair and traveling with an oxygen tank. Peggy Lee was American music royalty, and we were all thrilled to meet her and work with her, but she was also in such fragile health that she clearly could not sing the way she would have liked. But she was regal in her bearing, a triumph of the will given her circumstances, and she insisted that she wanted to sing the duet with Michael live. After we set her up in front of her favorite microphone and tried a few passes, I called a meeting with Michael and James Farber, the engineer, in the control room.

"Okay," I said, "This isn't working. We're going to have to spend a lot of time getting her parts right, and Michael, you can do yours later. So I'm going to go out there and tell her I have some technical problem in here and that it's not possible to do both vocals at once."

Which is what I did and for an hour, I said, "Miss Lee, that was lovely but could I ask you to sing that line again because we're still having problems in here." She was a real trooper and when it was over, we had the makings of a very poignant vocal track. I said, "Thank you, Miss Lee, that was superb," and bade her goodbye. The rest of us took a break for lunch, and when we came back, James and I spent the rest of the day sampling, tuning and editing each of her words, syllables and phonemes, taking extra care that none of the sutures would show, giving her finished vocal the greatest facelift known to man or woman. It was a prime example of what the technology was for: creating a new reality. It wasn't what any of us had wanted, but listening to the duet today, there is no sense that Peggy Lee was in desperate straits, and the interplay between the two of them on the little samba is tragic and bittersweet.

That fall, I went to Rome to produce Gege Telesforo for Go Jazz. He was the scat singer I had met the year before, and I wanted the label to have an international presence, to make the point that Jazz is a universal language, the mother tongue. Gege's musicality and attack is world-class. As Jon Hendricks said, "When you hear him, you know you're listening to a soul that's on the inside singing out, not on the outside looking in."

In Rome, Gege was connected to a circle of talented musicians, like saxophonist Stefano Di Battista, pianists Rita Marcotulli and Danilo Rea, drummer Roberto Gatto, trumpet player Marco Tamburini and guitarist Marco Rinalduzzi. More than that, everybody could sing. It was as if in order to graduate from grade school there one had to master solfeggio. In all my travels throughout Europe, I had never come across such deep, authentic musicality and swing from the local scene. I asked Gege why this was and he said, "Ben, you don't understand. In Italy, we are the blacks of Europe." And then I understood.

These sessions, which were released as *Gege and the Boparazzi*, produced classic renditions of Dizzy Gillespie's "He Beeped When He Should Have Bopped," "Oo Shoo Be Doo Be" and Clark Terry's "Mumbles." And also an intriguing version of Peggy Lee's "Fever," featuring a beautiful young singer named Giorgia. Today she is a very big star indeed, having recorded with Pavarotti and Sting, won the San Remo song festival, and sold a million records. But her very first recording was on Go Jazz, as one of Gege's Boparazzi.

After the sessions in Rome, Gege and I went to New York to finish up with Jon Hendricks and Clark Terry, who were booked to join Gege in a scat fest of international proportions. Clark was recovering from a serious illness at the time and was still quite fragile, and he came to the studio escorted by his old friend, Al Gray, my "roomie" from Boulder. Al drove an old, beat-up Chevy and he just naturally looked so road-weary that the kid in charge of letting folks into the recording studio balked at admitting the two of them. Al had to struggle to convince the kid to let them come up. After he had prevailed and had settled Clark into a chair in a control room, he turned to the rest of us and said with exasperation, "Man, I told that kid, 'You may not know who I am, but I've played for every president since Roosevelt!'"

That week, we also worked with percussionist Candido Camera, who had appeared on many sessions during the fifties and sixties. He came to the studio bearing a scrapbook with pictures of himself and all of the jazz greats he had ever worked with, including Charlie Parker, Sonny Rollins and Dizzy Gillespie. Candido was a fun-loving man, always telling jokes and laughing, and we all gathered around his scrapbook to hear his stories about the old days. But when I mentioned to him that the first song we were going to record that day was Dizzy Gillespie's, "He Beeped When He Should Have Bopped," he became very quiet, very serious. He said, "You know Dizzy is very sick. You should send him this song. It will make him feel good. You should do it very soon." After we finished the recording that day, I did make a tape for Dizzy and sent it right off, but he died not long thereafter. Like a giant redwood falling in the forest. It will take a thousand generations to produce anything close to his stature.

One day that autumn I was just walking through my house when the phone rang; I picked it up and a voice said, "Ben? This is Diana Ross."

I assumed it was a friend playing a joke and said, "Oh yeah? How you doing Diana?"

She said, "I want you to work with me. I'm doing a jazz concert and you've been recommended as the right person to produce the music."

There was no hint of humor in the voice, and it did sound like a voice that could be singing, "Baby love, my baby love..." I straightened up real quick.

"Tell me about it," I said.

She described the live, pay-per-view concert she was doing at the Roxy in New York in a few months. It would feature a big band and much of the repertoire from the film *Lady Sings the Blues*, the bio pic of Billie Holiday in which she had starred.

The call ended with my agreeing to meet her in New York. But first, I had to go to Berlin.

Bob Malach and I were scheduled to perform at the Berlin Jazz Festival the last week of November, and the news out of Germany was troubling. The wall was down and the anti-Semitism of the East was spilling over into the West. The week before we were to arrive, a rabbi had been killed and there was turmoil everywhere, agitation and anxiety as years of bottled up frustration came pouring out.

I had been recording the Hebrew liturgical song for *Life's a Lesson* and not only the music but the message of the music was very much on my mind. I had recently recorded "Eliyahu," with saxophonist Lee Konitz, which spoke of the prophet Elijah, who would return to earth to befriend the helpless and bring peace, and "Oseh Shalom," with saxophonist Josh Redman, a song that is actually part of the Kaddish prayer and is a serious affirmation of the belief in God, traditionally said when remembering those who have died. I told Bobby these songs would be part of our repertoire in Berlin.

The concert was held in an old theater that sat about six hundred people, and about eight hundred showed up. The place was packed to the walls, and backstage, before we went on, I looked at Bobby and realized that what we were about to do might be uncomfortable for him. I said, "How do you feel about where we're taking this?" He just said, "Yeah, man," eloquent as usual in his simplicity.

We went out, just the two of us, and I made a little speech. I said we would be including some music that spoke to the fact that there was more that joined us together than kept us apart. Then I quoted Martin Niemöller: "First they came for the communists and I didn't speak up because I wasn't a communist. Then they came for the Jews and I didn't speak up because I wasn't a Jew. Then they came for the trade unionists, and I didn't speak up because I wasn't a trade unionist. Then they came for the Catholics, and I didn't speak up because I was a Protestant. Then they came for me and by that time no-one was left to speak up." The room went dead quiet. I said, "It's important that we speak up, that we talk about what's happening." And then we played "Avinu Malchenu," which asks God to hear our prayers.

I had never sung this song outside of a synagogue before. To perform it as a piece in a jazz concert was wrenching. Context is such an important and powerful part of liturgical music, and one cannot just sing these words as "lyrics." They are a prayer, and so I was forced to consider this hall a sacred space and the people in it my brothers and sisters. Hearing the Hebrew rise up into the silence of hundreds of people, I became choked. Then we did "Eliyahu" and I called down peace. Finally, we played "Oseh Shalom," which I introduced as part of the prayer for the dead, and I mentioned the rabbi who had been killed. It was as if the air went out of the room.

After the concert, many people came backstage. None identified themselves to me as Jews, although several made reference to the experience as being quite powerful, and one woman said to me, "You wouldn't have been so quick to say what you said if you lived here. You are leaving and we are staying." And I realized I still didn't fully understand where I stood in this whole Jewish continuum.

The first week of December I flew to New York to work with Diana Ross. She was "Miss Ross" to most people, and having spent thirty years in the international spotlight, she was able to execute the "star turn" as well as anyone. One afternoon I watched her stride into a recording studio, slide the fur coat from her shoulders without looking back, and the coat never hit the floor. She knew she was covered at all times. She could make herself ten feet tall, especially on stage during a performance. In a tight fitting sequined gown, with her hair flowing in waves, it was impossible to take your eyes off her. But in a rehearsal room with some of the best jazz musicians in New York—Ron Carter, Barry Harris, Jon Faddis, Seldon Powell, Roy Hargrove and Slide Hampton—she was just Diana, and she was all music.

Clearly, she had a special place in her heart for jazz and for the men and women who made it. Her interpretation of Billie Holiday's repertoire was moving and dead-on. She had Billie's coyness, the tragic air of loss and disappointment, and even though she took a lot of heat when the film *Lady Sings the Blues* came out, watching her work through the songs of love gone wrong, returning to this well of bitter tears, it became obvious that on some level, Billie's story was her story too.

The concert at the Roxy was a triumph of technology, with three major recording trucks parked outside the venue all cabled together. There was the video truck, coordinating the cameras and lighting, the audio truck, where we had a forty-eight input board to cover the band, the audience and Diana wherever she went, and a satellite truck to uplink the show live to the pay-per-view audience. In the midst of this madness, Diana, as executive producer, kept calm, yet remarkably, at times, seemed to wear her heart on her sleeve.

During the final dress rehearsal, she seemed to take refuge with the musicians. Music was her way of staying connected to some essential part of herself, so she hung out, joking with the band, just one of the guys. Pianist Barry Harris, who remembered Diana from thirty years before, back in Detroit, told her, "Your vibrato, that's always been you. I can always recognize you by your vibrato," and she smiled at him as if he was her hip old uncle. When she walked away from the musicians, she was again "Miss Ross" and could be imperious and distant.

The night of the performance, the club was packed. When she stepped out on stage and sang, "My man don't love me, treats me oh so mean..." a scream went up from the room. She was luminous and riveting. "Thank you for being here," she said, "and thank you for giving me this opportunity to do a special intimate evening of jazz and blues, something I've dreamed of for a long time...We want it to be what jazz and blues is all about, which is really loose and free and mellow." And then she made love to the audience for an hour and a half.

A few days later, she and I sat in her apartment in the Sherry Netherlands Hotel, and she was again just Diana, barely 5'4" in a pair of jeans and a denim shirt, with chewed finger nails and no make up. An actual Nor'Easter had blown in the night before, and the wind was howling outside. Coming across the park from the Mayflower Hotel that morning, I had seen scenes of devastation, street lights out, trees blown down, and cabs stranded in rivers of water. The view from her apartment up 5th Avenue, however, was serene, a sea of blinking red lights and bright yellow taxis. "Let's watch the show together," she said.

We sat on the couch and went song by song through a video of the evening's performance. About a half-hour into it, as she was singing the song "Loverman," she blew a lyric. Suddenly, she stepped off the stage and walked into the audience. I stopped the tape and asked her what had made her do that. She said, "I don't know, when I get insecure, I just go into the people. I don't know why. I just feel secure with them." She stayed in the crowd for four songs; she kissed them, they touched her. Watching herself, she laughed and said, "Sometimes I do things and I would never do in real life." Like what, I asked? "Like this," she said and, stretching out her arms, shimmied her boobs.

Outside the storm was picking up; we could hear it pounding the windows. She was worrying about her kids in Connecticut. She had a house on the water, and the water was rising. She was afraid she wouldn't get home. We decided to call it. I told her about the mixing sessions I had booked in L.A. in a few weeks and asked if she wanted to fix anything before then. She thought for a moment, and then said, "Not unless you hear something you hate." I said I liked most everything I heard. She said, "I think in a live situation, it's okay. Let's just go with it." Her smile was brilliant and her confidence was completely unexpected. I had been prepared for a diva's insecurity, but she had a total jazz attitude. She basically gave me the tapes, her phone numbers in Switzerland and Austria and her schedule for the next two weeks and wished me luck. "Phone it in," she said.

1993

Diana did show up a few weeks later in Los Angeles for some of the mixing sessions. A large, chauffeured Rolls Royce with Connecticut plates pulled up to the studio (did she have it driven all the way to L.A.?), and she came in and hung out with me and engineer Al Schmitt for a while. She seemed very small and sad. She sipped brandy from a little silver flask that she carried in her purse and as she offered me a drink, I said, "What's the occasion?" She said, "It's my wedding anniversary." Her husband, a European financier, was out of the country, and on their anniversary, she was alone with us in a recording studio, listening to the playbacks of a night gone by. As the evening progressed, she became nostalgic. "One thing Berry Gordy taught me," she said, "was tape is cheap. Moments are expensive." Then she looked wistful. "You know, people say I slept with Berry Gordy and that's how I got ahead. Well, I wasn't the only one."

Immediately following the Diana Ross concert, I flew to Madison, picked up Leo and continued with him to Sun Valley, Idaho. There, in an elaborate barn made of the finest, hand-carved hardwoods from around the world, Steve Miller had built a recording studio. It was a quirky affair, with all the musicians placed in separate rooms, connected only by video monitors and earphones, but it had state-of-the-art technology, and Billy and Gordy were there to work on the new record as well.

Leo had brought with him the digital tapes of the songs he recorded in his own studio, a room put together with gear from Steve's bus and a few things purchased with his Bar Mitzvah money. Typically, Leo spent at least three or four hours a day after school in his studio, and on Saturdays, he would stumble up there in his bathrobe around noon and stumble back down around dinner time. The four songs he brought to Sun Valley included a pop ballad called "Lost in Her Eyes," a really funky track called "Conversation," a new wave pop thing called "Perfect World" and a silly dance track called "Walks Like a Lady."

When we got to the studio, Leo went right to work transferring the parts from his ADATs to Steve's big Sony digital machine. When that was done, he worked with Gordy and Billy to replace the bass and drum parts that he had originally played himself. Most of the guitar and keyboard parts he had played were left on the tape. Occasionally, he redid something and then moved on. When the songs were transferred and overdubbed, he left them with Steve and we went back to Madison. The process took two days.

Leo was sixteen years old.

A couple of months later, Leo got a call from Steve. Steve said the record was finished, the artwork was done and, "You're going to be really excited about this. I got your name right here on the credits, let's see..." and he began reading to Leo from the copy in front of him. "It says, Leo Sidran, guitar and keyboards and programming...let's see, 'Lost in Her Eyes' by Leo Sidran and Steve Miller, Sailor Music. 'Perfect World,' by Leo Sidran and Steve Miller, Sailor Music..." As Steve kept reading, it dawned on Leo that Steve had put his name on all the songs Leo had written and had taken all the publishing rights. When they hung up, he asked me about this and I immediately called Steve back.

"You can't put your name on his songs..."

Oh, yeah, Steve said, that must have been a mistake. A typo. He would see what he could do.

"And what about the publishing. We never talked about that. Why isn't it co-published with Leo?"

"If I record it, I own it."

"You don't have to do this."

"This is about business. I don't co-publish with anybody anymore."

I couldn't believe Steve was playing hardball with Leo. I said, "We'll call you back." I called Emily, my lawyer, and told her the story. She said she'd put in a call to Steve's manager, Herbie Herbert at Nightmare Productions. Herbie was a three-hundred pound promoter from San Francisco who liked to hang out on the band bus and trade blues licks with Steve. The next day, Leo got a phone call from Herbie.

Herbie said, "Look, the record is being manufactured right now and you and Steve never talked about this clearly. Now you can try to fight for the publishing and you could probably get it, but you should know that if you do, on the next printing of the record your songs won't appear, none of them will ever be released as a single, and essentially, your business relationship with Mr. Miller would be over." Leo put down the phone and said, "What should I do?"

There is a time-honored tradition in the music business whereby those with power take what is not rightfully theirs because they can. Miles Davis did it to Victor Feldman with the song "Seven Steps to Heaven." Victor told me that Miles changed one note in the bridge, just one note, and took not only the publishing but half of the writer's credit as well. Duke Ellington's business partner Irving Mills appears on the credits of a lot of Duke's songs, and Irving was not even a musician. And in the fifties, it was common for deejays like Alan Freed to take a writer's or publisher's credit on a song in return for playing the record on the radio. In this way, muscle has always insinuated itself into the sinew of a musician's life. But how to break the news to Leo, particularly when it was "Uncle Steve" doing the muscling?

The more I thought about it, the angrier I became. I was so angry at Steve, at the whole business, at Herbie, at everybody, that I could hardly speak. Why couldn't there be at least one transaction, one relationship, that didn't come down to "somebody's money versus somebody else's life?" And how could you do this to a kid and say it's just business? And for what? A few dollars in royalties.

I felt like this was the day that Leo truly became a man. This was his real Bar Mitzvah. Welcome to the jungle. I asked him, "What do you want to do?"

He said, "I think I want to work with Steve in the future."

A few weeks later, Leo and I and our lawyer went to court. Leo was a minor, so I had to certify that the deal he was entering into was fair by industry standards, and promise to keep the assets he received from his labors in trust until he turned eighteen. The judge in the case just happened to be Leo's old soccer coach. "Congratulations," he said to Leo when all the papers had been signed. "I hope this is the start of a long and happy career."

Steve's album, *Wide River*, was released in June of 1993 to universally negative reviews. One of the first reviews, in the *San Francisco Chronicle*, said, "The only original material worth the digital time was written or co-written by Leo Sidran...'Lost in Her Eyes' — a rock ballad with sweet vocal harmonies — sparkles. An uptempo new-wavy rocker 'Perfect World' is in the Miller 'Rock 'N Me' mode, but doesn't sound like a low-brow collage of catch phrases." Implying that the rest of the album did. That was pretty much the end of Leo and Steve's musical partnership.

The affair also brought to a close my own collaboration with Steve that had lasted over thirty years.

Coincidentally, the same afternoon we came home from Leo's court date, the phone rang and it was Lucy Scott, a producer at the CBS "Sunday Morning" television show. She was calling because she had heard about the Jewish record and about me, living a normal life in Madison and yet traveling the world, playing and recording so much different music with such a diverse group of artists. We talked and I agreed to let her and the crew follow me around.

Ultimately, they filmed me working with Diana Ross in New York, and with rapper Shock G in San Francisco. They captured me in the control room with Mose Allison, and performing live in Tokyo. And they kept coming back to me and seventy-five of my neighbors at the Gates of Heaven Synagogue, singing these little songs and following Hannah's service. They focused on this record that nobody would release. They even had a wonderfully revealing vignette where I am sitting in the office of George Butler, the man in charge of jazz at Sony Records, who is smiling at the camera and saying to me, yes, he'd love to release the record, only to be followed by footage of me trying to get him on the phone unsuccessfully a few days later. I look at the camera and say, "Sometimes, you almost wish they'd just hit you in the head with a board and get it over with."

In the fall, when this program aired, interest in the Jewish record exploded. I am always taken with the fact that this adventure, like so many others, started with my answering a simple phone call. It is almost as if a small twig on the path of life can hold within it the power to change everything, if only we know how to see it — to read the trees.

That spring I was invited to participate in a concert of Jewish music at Lincoln Center. Part of the JVC jazz festival, it was actually promoted as "The Jazz Connection: The Jewish & African-American Relationship," a subject about which volumes could be written. For example, it is well known that Louis Armstrong was very close as a boy to the Karnovskys, a Jewish family in New Orleans that took him in and gave him his first trumpet. But what is not so widely known is that Louis, who is credited with inventing "scat singing" on his 1925 recording of "Heebie Jeebies," actually had been practicing this form of vocal improvisation since he was little kid singing on street corners, and that the original source of his inspiration, as he told Cab Calloway years later, was "the Jews rockin'" (he meant davening). Louis never talked about this in public, he said, because "he didn't want people to think he was making fun of the Jews."

In fact, the real miracle of jazz is that whereas the world around it may be narrow and exclusionary, the music itself has always held its arms wide open. Blacks and whites, Baptists and Jews, each gave to the other throughout the music's history. Lester Young (black) took from Frank Trumbauer (white and native American) and then passed it along to both Stan Getz (white and Jewish) and Charlie Parker (black). Jazz is that rare and beautiful example of humanity coming together for a higher purpose; the world it has been played to, well that has always been out of our control.

So there were a lot of connections to explore, and it is a crucial subject. One of the greatest losses of the twentieth century, in my opinion, has been the loss of community between blacks and Jews. But none of this got explored that evening because there was no context at all to the program. A string of Jewish-influenced music and musicians rolled out, one after another, and the audience was left to its own devices to fathom the connections. They were ticket-holders, not participants, and they were generally confused as to what to expect and what, in fact, was happening.

At the end of the evening, as the closing act, I went on stage with Josh Redman, Rufus Reid, Carl Allen, Steve Kahn and Lynette Margulies and started to play "Avinu Malchenu." As soon as the first notes sailed off into the deep of Avery Fisher Hall, I knew that the exercise was futile. This music was not about jazz, as in a jazz concert; it was about jazz as in communal spirit. Trying to perform this music without being in a place where people came together for the purpose of experiencing that sense of community was just ridiculous. Worse — the notes not only mocked the intention behind the music, but also wasted its power and diminished its future.

Never play this music out of context. This was the message. Perhaps the greater message was never play *any* music out of context; context is where the power of all music comes from. It is the meaning behind the music. This is something we rarely think about. You get hired to perform, and you show up, whether it's at a concert hall or at a night club, and you do your bit and make your money. Generally, the performance is linked to some piece of plastic, some artifact of the recording industry, and that becomes the context: selling. Merchandising takes the place of community. But the true power of music is in the context of its performance — or as Archie Shepp once said, "When people get down, *where* they get down" — and I came away from Lincoln Center determined not to make this mistake again. Feeling and context, place and person, are inextricably interconnected. Every act of human communication has to come *from* somewhere. That is why, in this rootless world, it is so important to know not only where you stand, but also where you came from.

This point had been driven home earlier in the week. Prior to the Lincoln Center gig, we had been rehearsing at Studio Instrument Rentals, a huge facility in midtown Manhattan. Leaving the studio one afternoon, I noticed the Rolling Stones were rehearsing on the soundstage next door, so I left a note for Charlie Watts to give me a call if he wanted to go hear some jazz. The next day, while I was out, Charlie called and Leo picked up the phone. When I got back to the hotel, Leo said, "Charlie invited me to their rehearsal."

So later that day, we went back to the soundstage and there, set up at the far end of the vastness, was the most famous rock and roll band in the world. They were alone, no audience, no assistants, just the four members of the Stones and a bass player who was hoping to take Bill Wyman's place. We went over to them and I introduced Leo to Mick and Charlie and Keith. Mick said, "Nice to meetcha. Make yourself at home." About twenty feet away from the stage, there were several couches and tables set up with snacks and drinks and we sat down to watch the rehearsal. After a couple of numbers, the band took a break and, as I talked to Charlie about who was in town at the jazz clubs, remarkably, Mick came over to talk to Leo and asked him if he was comfortable, if he wanted something else to drink, etc. The band went back to playing and after another couple of songs, Leo and I looked at each other and we both said, "Let's go."

There wasn't much going on there. Why? Because even the greatest rock and roll band in the world, playing out of context, doesn't move a lot of air. Even though Mick couldn't help but conduct the band with his little chicken walk, and Charlie's groove was as strong as ever, it wasn't happening emotionally. When we left and went out onto the street, I think we were both a little surprised at how tame it had seemed. We had been prepared for something much grander. But we shouldn't have been. The context of rock and roll is the audience. Without it, it's just a lot of notes.

"Context" seemed to be the message of the week.

Earlier that year, forty-three interviews from the *Sidran on Record* radio series were published in a book called *Talking Jazz*. In May of 1993, I went on a book tour, reading excerpts from some of my favorite interviews and playing piano in the back of bookstores around the country. It made perfect sense, trying to convey the words and rhythms of Jon Hendricks, Miles Davis, Art Blakey, Frank Morgan and the others, and then playing some of the music they had instilled in me. Jazz in a bookstore seemed much more "in context" than jazz in a lot of other places.

For example, the previous fall, I had taken Georgie Fame and Ricky Peterson and Bobby Malach on a "Go Jazz Allstars" tour of the United States. After six weeks of gigs at jazz clubs from coast to coast, we eventually landed in San Diego, more than $10,000 in debt and with a pile of excuses from club owners, promoters and the record distributor as to why it hadn't gone better. The real reason was that it was out of context. Even jazz stars like Michael Brecker were getting off the road that year. Here in America, the clubs were all scuffling, and jazz was becoming strictly a "festival phenomenon." In Europe, however, even though festivals are quite popular, jazz clubs were still doing nicely, due to the European's greater sense of history. There, one could still set up in Paris or London or Rome, as American jazz musicians have been doing for almost a century, and play for a week or two, becoming part of the living history. I began turning my attention there as well. Book stores and European clubs were an historical context that began making a lot of sense to me.

In June, Leo, Judy and I went to see the Steve Miller Band at the Marcus Amphitheater in Milwaukee. Steve was out promoting the *Wide River* album, and we wanted to hear what Leo's songs sounded like in front of a crowd of screaming kids. The show seemed really corny, but it was a lot of fun to sit in the audience for a change and watch the band go through its paces. There was Gordy and Billy and Bobby and a new keyboard player up on stage, and Steve, in his sunglasses, saying the same old lines, "Welcome to our little rock and roll show..." The kids were jumping up and down as usual, and it really was heaven not to have to be part of it. I felt like I had escaped with my life. When they played Leo's song, "Perfect World," it sounded just like another one of Steve's hits, except that nobody sang along. The crowd still sat there waiting for the "Greatest Hits," as they had been doing for years.

I couldn't keep my eyes off Bobby Malach. This is one of the greatest, most dedicated jazz musicians I have ever met, a man who doesn't follow fashion, who has developed his own voice and pursued its perfection relentlessly. Watching him for the first time from the audience, and not from across the stage, I could see just how hard he had to work at not working. His evening was spent with cowbells and tambourines and playing a few notes here and there, trying to stay busy. He was in for a long hot summer.

That spring, Leo said he wanted to start playing in clubs. He was sixteen, and he had "the curse," as Billy had pointed out in Japan. At home, we played duets all the time, me on organ, him on drums, and that was more than enough for me. But he really wanted to play out. I, on the other hand, was burned out. After the disastrous Go Jazz Allstars tour, I didn't care if I ever played in a club again. The Miller gigs had almost ruined my sense of proportion about live music in general. The gig at Lincoln Center had been quite unsettling, in Johnny Griffin's lyrical phrase, like "romancing a ghost." I was confused in general as to why I was playing music in public at all in this "context of no context."

I was also gradually becoming aware that I rarely listened to music for pleasure anymore. When had I stopped? How long had it been since I was excited about putting on a new CD? Maybe I just knew too much about the business of music. Music was now a problem to be solved, a condition to be borne, no longer an emotion to be felt on the pulse. Like the old blues lyric said, "The nightlife ain't no good life, but it's my life..." I knew I was not alone in this. Many of my friends in the business were singing the same song, "everything's changed." Was it just "age appropriate"—were we all just getting old—or was the world really that different?

One night, sitting in my office, looking at the picture of my father in his army uniform that has hung on the wall for years, I remembered Saul Bellow's words to me—that we must be careful about the size and shape of our devotions. "If you love to read," he had said, "maybe you don't want to be a literature major." He could just as easily have said, "If you love to listen to music, maybe you don't want to make it your business." You can either "know" something or "have" something. And sometimes, the more you know, the more you don't want to know. Nothing is without its consequences. Sometimes it seems that to love at all is to love too much.

But I had wanted to make it my business. I had purposely set out to "become the information," to know what it felt like, and now I did. I still believed, as Jon Hendricks once told me, "that the language of the American jazz musician is the most functional and, in its way of expressing itself, the most beautiful of all languages. It's the greatest way to speak, ever!" I still loved the music and the people, like Jon, who made it. I never outgrew my sense of gratitude and awe for their contributions to my life. No, it wasn't the music or the musicians I found so troubling: it was the daily grind of show business, a "cruel and shallow money trench," as Hunter Thompson once observed, "a long plastic hallway where thieves and pimps run free, and good men die like dogs. There's also a negative side." Playing in a small club in Madison, Wisconsin was about the last thing on my mind.

But I loved being with Leo, and playing music with him had a special place in my heart. Not just because we had grown up together and had developed a kind of musical shorthand, an intuition, where we could just look at each other and know which way the music was going to go. Even more special was that when we played together, I was no longer the father, no longer the cop or the guy who was supposed to have all the answers. I was just the guy on the keyboard and he was just the guy on the drums and either it swung or it didn't. Music was the great leveler for us, a way to stand toe-to-toe and look each other in the eye. If, in Art Blakey's words, "The eyes are the windows of the soul," playing music with Leo always comforted me because when I looked at him, I saw my own heart. This was where I was *from*.

Coincidental to Leo's request, I had received a call from the proprietor of a funky little neighborhood bar in South Madison. It used to be known as Trotter's Tuxedo Lounge when I played there back in the sixties, doing six nights a week with an organ trio. Now it was called Mr. P's Place, and when Gene Parks called and asked me to play at his club, I told him I didn't think so. But after talking with Leo, I called Gene back and said, "Okay, if I can come in with Leo, I'll do it." He said, "I don't care how you come in here, just come in here." And so Leo and I got to work putting our repertoire together. Suddenly our fooling around in the attic took on a more serious edge. We wrote a song called "Mr. P's Shuffle" and rearranged some old standards, like "No Moon At All." Then, on a warm night in June, Leo and I slipped into Mr. P's.

The place was exactly as I remembered it. Nothing seemed to have changed in the thirty years since I last played there. The same red vinyl stools crowded around the circular wooden bar, the same neon beer signs hung in the windows, and the same crooked cues were racked by the old pool table. It was like coming home.

Gene had made a big pot of red beans and some barbecued ribs and laid out salad and bread, and anybody who showed up could eat for free. We set up in the window, just as we used to do so many lives ago, and at nine o'clock, Leo and I went up and launched into "Mr. P's Shuffle." I looked at Leo and he looked at me and we couldn't stop grinning. I was back.

Through Leo, I began to feel music again. Like the first drops of cool water down a parched throat, I began to remember what music felt like when I was his age, the first time it felt good, life-giving, sustaining. His desire became my desire, and I remembered myself at sixteen, felt the delicious trembling of the limbs before going on stage, the downhill rush as the music took off, the sense that you could soar on this feeling forever. Most of all, I realized that as one got older, as one became more aware of the "way things worked," life inevitably became more difficult, not less difficult. When you are young, the world is open, full of possibility. And this possibility, the belief in change, parallels desire, that which comes so hard later on in life.

In time, I stopped worrying about selling records; in fact, my Japanese partner in Go Jazz crashed and burned not long thereafter, taken down by the Japanese economic disaster, and it didn't really seem to affect me one way or the other. Soon, a new European partner, Christoph Diekmann, took up the slack, and we kept on making records for Go Jazz. And I stopped taking gigs I didn't want to play. I stopped doing a lot of things I used to do.

At the end of the summer, I spent some time in New York with Mose Allison making his next record. Over the years, Mose and I often talked about the books we were reading, and this time, he was in the midst of a book on the biological roots of thinking and emotion. He said it reminded him of a science fiction story he once read where, "There was an advanced civilization somewhere out in the galaxy, and they sent an emissary to Earth. When the emissary reported back and described life on this planet to his superiors, they were incredulous. They said, 'You mean you want us to believe in sentient meat?'" That cracked Mose up, the image of sentient meat, human suffering reduced to a bizarre conundrum. It fit well with the songs we were recording, especially the title track, *The Earth Wants You*: "You think nobody gives a damn about what you're going through, but one thing you can count on: the earth wants you." Coming from Mose, this too had a calming effect.

I returned from New York to prepare for the High Holy Days again. This year's service would be a little different, because the television crew would be there. September 15 was Rosh Hashana. On Sunday, September 19, our little service went national on the CBS "Sunday Morning" television program. That same day, my phone started to ring and it didn't stop for weeks. People from all over the United States wanted to know how they could get this record, *Life's a Lesson*. And, of course, they couldn't.

I still hadn't learned the lesson life was trying to teach me. I wanted so badly to give my work away, as I had done in the past, perhaps so that somebody else might be responsible for my failures. But in the United States I couldn't even give this record away, and because I had promised a few of the folks who called that if they left their names, I'd send them an album, I did what, for me, was a dramatic, last-ditch move. I actually contacted a factory and manufactured 500 copies of the album. Up until this time, I had lived my professional life by two guiding principles: do not have boxes of CDs in your basement and avoid the Jewish thing at all costs, only to wind up with boxes of Jewish CDs in my basement. Then I got it: we are always moving toward our fears; we just don't know it sometimes.

In November, I took the "Go Jazz Allstars" to Tokyo for a week and was surprised to find that the Jewish record had become celebrated there as well. The editor of *Swing Journal*, an important jazz magazine in Japan, had himself written a long article tracing the impact of Jews on jazz, going back to Benny Goodman, Artie Shaw and Buddy Rich, up to the present. His article claimed that *Life's a Lesson* was an historic event, the first of its kind, a homecoming for Jews and their Jewish roots in the jazz idiom. I was very surprised by how interested the Japanese were in the emotional context of this record, as there are virtually no Jews in Japan. But people there have a great feeling for the outsider's experience, if only because, as they say in Japan, "the nail that sticks up gets hammered down." There are so few outsiders in Japan that perhaps many people have this longing to understand, to face this particular fear of being "hammered down."

Returning home, the stories and interviews kept coming — in the *L.A. Times, Billboard, Jazziz, The International Herald Tribune, Moment, Jerusalem Report, Hadassah*. Eventually, the record sold and sold, more than 25,000 copies, out of the basement. And while not a hit record in the real world, it was the biggest selling Jewish record in many years. Eventually, I began to play the Jewish music all over the country, at the Simon Weisenthal Center in Los Angeles, at the JCC in Boston and Symphony Hall in Chicago; big venues, small venues, and I was careful so that each time we played this music, there was a real reason, a context, so that the audience became participants, and there was the real possibility of change in the air. Leo played drums with me at all these concerts, and sitting with him on stage, playing this music that we had played together on the small piano bench at the Gates of Heaven Synagogue for so many years, was an extraordinary feeling. It was as if the contemporary cliché, "Think globally but act locally," had been turned on its head.

In time, this small part of my life in Madison expanded exponentially. The music took me deeper and deeper into the world of contemporary Jewish culture, and I had hundreds of conversations about it; with people like Velvel from Whitestone who was now the biggest distributor of Judaica in America; like the European refugee who wanted to know how to come to Madison; like the hot shot L.A. lawyer who now wanted a piece of the action, and like the many ordinary folks who called from pay phones and car phones and home phones, and who, like the grandmother who called with tears in her voice, wanted to tell me that my record had reunited them with an estranged member of the family or some aspect of their past. Obviously, I had not been alone in feeling a pent-up need to integrate my past with my current life, to "keep my heart right" as Dizzy had advised me.

≈≋ Chapter Nine

*"How can we stop running from pain and reacting against it
in ways that destroy us as well as others? That's the kind of
teaching we need these days, that difficult circumstances can
be the path to liberation. That's news you can use."*

— PEMA CHODRIN

1994

In January, Siskel and Ebert called *Hoop Dreams* the best movie of the year, period. It hadn't even been released yet and suddenly, because I was already talking about the Hebrew album, I was doing interviews on the subject of blacks and Jews. What were the similarities between these two cultures? Where did they meet? My answer was that, aside from the common roots in North Africa and the obvious similarities in harmonic orientation (the "blue notes" that exist in the music of both), these two cultures understood the outsider's point of view, having been strangers in a strange land, and had long relied on humor and a strong woman to keep the family and the traditions alive. Historically, blacks and Jews both turned to music in good times and bad, and had used show business as a way to escape the ghetto. Beyond that, while the first ghettos were built for Jews in Europe and the newest ghettos for blacks in America, ultimately nobody would be free anywhere until there were no more ghettos for anybody. We are all one; every other story is a lie. Racism is not possible because we are all part of the human race. The rest is local color.

Throughout the year, Leo and I continued to play gigs at Mr. P's, inviting friends like Richie Cole and Richard Davis and Phil Upchurch to join us. Frank Morgan, the great alto-saxophonist who was so influenced by Charlie Parker as a young kid, had moved to Milwaukee, and he also came to Mr. P's. Those nights, Leo was taken to the old school by a master. Frank was on him like white on rice, calling all sorts of tempos, turning and glaring when he wanted double time or sticks instead of half time and brushes. This was the way the music had traditionally been passed along, trial by fire, the public ordeal. The legend of Charlie Parker itself includes a moment when Bird was so ill prepared as a kid that drummer Joe Jones threw a cymbal at him to call an end to an inept solo. Mr. P's was where this kind of experience happened.

There is no way to learn life's lessons without living the life. Classrooms can't present them and that's why you can't teach style. Style, as Miles said, is "like your sweat." First, you have to sweat. And without the physical place there is no heat, no trial by fire. That is why I became so fixated on context, being *from* someplace. That year, I made a record called *Mr. P's Shuffle*, featuring the whole gang, Phil and Richard, Clyde and Leo, Frank and Rosco Mitchell and Howard Levy and a couple of other local characters. The record was *from* the experience of this club, this city, this life. It had its origins in a place and a time and a community.

It seems to me that our lives have become so digitized that we often come to believe this is the ultimate goal; we value anything that can be reduced to a series of "1s" and "0s." But, in the words of Pat Frendreis, the director of the Adler Planetarium, "It's an analog universe. There's nothing digital about the way stars move through space." And even though, by the end of the twentieth century, the world's greatest music catalogs were owned by a virtual reality company (AOL, which controls Atlantic, Reprise, Elektra and Warner Records) and a European waste management company (Vivendi, which controls Verve, Impulse, MCA and Decca), this irony is about commerce, not creation. And while the Internet allows us to be everywhere simultaneously, it is nowhere physically. The digital universe is not a place, it is the absence of place.

In the age of the Internet, people are losing their sense of where things came from. So being culturally rooted, where you know and are known, is not only a virtue, it has become a kind of luxury. This came across on the CBS "Sunday Morning" program, where I was pictured in a small building surrounded by friends, and it was also dramatically revealed in the film *Hoop Dreams*. Both of these events tapped into a deep pool of longing to know not only *who* you are but also *where* you are from.

1995

Georgie Fame called to say that he and Van Morrison wanted to record a tribute album to Mose Allison, and would I like to join them. Georgie said, "Just pick your favorite Mose tunes, you know, maybe some of the 'cotton sack' stuff he won't sing any more, and you'll do a few and I'll do a few and Van will do a few." I went to work picking my favorite songs but couldn't narrow the list down below ten or twelve. When the time came to fly to Van's studio in England, I was the only one who had actually picked out any songs, so my little list became the repertoire.

The studio was in a great stone hall where, in previous times, sheep farmers had gathered to do their business, and Van had converted the building, as well as several others, into a recording room, a series of guestrooms, and a suite of offices for himself. We arrived the night before the sessions and, since I had worked with Mose regularly and had a knowledge of how his songs were constructed, I volunteered to write out the charts. That night, after a dinner of local vegetables, meats and fresh baked rolls served in front of a roaring fire, I sat down at a long wooden table and sketched out the music the way Mose would do it. I could actually hear Mose's music in my ear; it seemed like it had been there my whole life. I knew the piano phrases that set up his lyrics and I could recite his words as if taking dictation: "Look here, watcha think you're gonna be doing next year. No lie, how you know you're not gonna up and die..."

The next day, Georgie and I rehearsed the songs with Van's rhythm section, Ralph Salmins on drums and Alec Dankworth on bass. We set up as a band so that we could see and hear each other live in the small studio, me on piano, Georgie on B3 organ. There was a microphone hanging in the middle of the room for Van, who had still not arrived. We ran down the shape of the songs, all the ins and outs, the rhythm patterns, and were putting down a test recording when Van walked in. He listened to the playback in the control room and said, "Okay, Ben, you sing that one." And that was it. I sang the first song, "If You Live." After it was over, he called the second song from the list. It was then that I realized that Van was totally in the moment, that there would be no going back, no second takes unless there had been a train wreck, no shaving down the rough edges. What you sang, what you played, that's what you got. Of course that's the way Mose did it too, but I had not expected it from Van, perhaps because of the size of his celebrity; fame often drives people in the opposite direction, causing them to distrust their instincts. But Van is anything but typical.

The second song was "You Can Count on Me," and Van pulled out his harmonica and walked into the studio. Standing in front of the microphone, he played the intro as we hit the groove, no pretense, no self-doubt, and then launched into the lyrics. It was as close to playing a live gig as any recording session I have ever done. No hand wringing, no theatrics, just, "Okay, Georgie, you sing the next one." In one day, we recorded ten songs. The tempos and performances were remarkably relaxed, perhaps because we were all reacting to the moment, not trying to remember the "right" way or to avoid the "wrong" things. Georgie, masterful as usual, was the glue in the mix, delivering a poetic vocal on "City Home," the song that first got me out of Racine so many years before. At the end of the day, after the three of us sang "Benediction" together ("When push comes to shove, thank God for self love..."), we all went to dinner at the little pub down the road. A few months later, the result was released as *Tell Me Something, The Songs of Mose Allison*.

Van's admiration for Mose extends way beyond his writing and singing. To Van, Mose represents a way to live a life of artistic and personal integrity. Mose never sold out and continues to pursue the path he chose a half century ago; he has a private life and an unwavering sense of purpose. Van, too, is a kind of anti-celebrity, having walked away from the business more than once, only to return because of his love for the music. This tension is at the heart of his work, the push and pull between the call of the wild and the howling of the celebrity press.

One afternoon, sitting in his office behind the studio, we talked about the difficulty of walking one's chosen path in this business. Van said his original inspiration had come from what he called "Corner Boys," hanging out under a streetlight and singing with his pals when he was a very young man. For his whole life, he had been fighting to stay in touch with this impulse. I said that I thought it was a spiritual impulse.

He said, "Yeah, I suppose this is what drives me, whatever this thing is. It's like being in that pocket or that space — where you're just doing it and you're not thinking about it — it wipes out all the thinking I do the rest of the time. And all of the solemnization. It gets me into the other state where I'm not analyzing everything, you know?"

I said I did and that the problem has to do with trying to find a balance in your life and your dreams. We become driven, just as we are sometimes driven towards various addictions, to find this balance, to make ourselves whole.

"Yeah," he said, "I think that's it. To make yourself whole. I believe that's what it is."

"And the more successful we become, the more difficult it is to find this balance. I mean, here you are, you have all the king's horses at your disposal, and the hunger is still the same. You still feel essentially the same way you felt back then, as a kid."

"Probably more so," said Van. "There's more to fight now. There's more struggle."

Success can be like a noose that tightens around an artist's neck. One might think how great it would be to swing and suffer in front of millions, but like all nooses, once you put your head inside, it's a different story. It's all part of the risk, the gossip, the hype of a business where to be larger than life is the only thing. But as we know, the only thing that's "larger than life" is death. And so, success is a kind of little death. Norman Mailer once said that when he became famous, his work became infinitely more difficult precisely because he could no longer observe people; they were all watching him. Under these conditions, one can easily become isolated and trapped inside the persona that is being marketed until one is, in the words of Percy Mayfield, "a stranger in your own hometown."

Or, as Van himself once wrote, "I got what I wanted but I lost what I had…to be satisfied."

1996

One morning in April, down in Orlando, Florida, off a tacky strip of honky tonks and PayLess stores, I woke up plagued by thoughts of the Holocaust. It was the 50th anniversary and PBS and TNT were presenting nightly specials with images of dead Jews like so many sacks of skin and bone being dumped into pits as the town burghers looked on. Daniel Goldhagen's thesis, that ordinary Germans enjoyed torturing the Jews, was being debated everywhere. If there wasn't some truth to it, why didn't the Germans just kill their victims? Why shave their heads, why wake them in the middle of the night to beat them, why make them watch the deaths of their own children? Why have a band playing at the hangings, and then hang the band when it was over? These were ordinary people enjoying torturing others. And last night on television, there was Louis Farrakhan raving, "Where does it say in the Bible that the Jews can foster homosexuality on our children?"

It had been going on for weeks, these documentaries, articles, the crazies coming out of the woodwork, the debate about German identity, Jews, old and young, trying to make sense of the horror that happened to them, that continues to happen to them.

That morning, in this little compound of poor blacks, Hispanics and transients, I stepped out the front door to feel the fine, soft morning sun on my face, and I saw, on the phone wire across the street, a large black crow. Hissing and darting around it was a small, angry bird. The crow ignored the bird. Then it flew off languidly to the pond by my door.

Suddenly, it was flying towards me with something in its claws. It perched high in the tree just in front of me and placed its prey on the branch in front of it. I wondered if it had caught a fish. Then I saw these little feet, a leg. The crow bent down and slowly pulled tufts of feathers off its victim. One beak full at a time. Then it pitched the fluff to the wind. The little feet were motionless. I had to look away.

My mind was so full of death, torture, the cruelty of life. I kept coming back to look. Eventually a second crow arrived and the first one moved off. The second crow picked at the little thing. Then, "plop," dropped it from the branch, and it too flew off. There in front of me on the ground was a small baby duckling. I went to it. One little spot of its belly was plucked clean. One small bloody organ protruded from the hole. The duckling was still alive. It righted itself. It moved its mouth, tried to walk. There was no sense of pain or panic. Just a little motion. Then it fell over in a swoon and was quiet. It had been tortured, plain and simple. It was not needed for food, not sacrificed to a higher cause. Just another small flame snuffed out for no reason at all.

I looked at the pond. A mother duck and twelve little ducklings were swimming toward shore. Soon they were joined by a big father duck. I had been throwing bread to the ducks for the few days I was staying at the condo. Maybe they were coming for breakfast. The mother seemed unaware that one of her brood was missing. The squirrel that had come down from the tree to forage in the grass passed right by the duckling's corpse and ignored it. I went and got the remainder of my Grapenuts and tossed it out back. The mother, father and twelve baby ducklings gobbled it up. Happy, oblivious. I wondered if the father duck could have scared the predator away, or if he even had any feelings in him, like the little bird that had hissed at the crow in the tree.

Back on the phone wire, the crow just sat and surveyed the scene by the condo, the pond, the front yard, me.

I still believe we can live together. I still believe in the dream of Jerusalem.

1997

Asked to put together my "dream concert" by Michael Goldberg, the director of the University of Wisconsin's Union Theater, I went home and thought about my past.

I'd been running so hard for so long, I had never really stopped to look over my shoulder, to see, as Satchel Page had predicted, "somebody gaining on you." That somebody, of course, is you. It reminded me of the Charles Adams cartoon where a man is sitting in a barber's chair and the mirrors both front and back reflect the infinitely receding image of his own face. Except that about five reflections back, instead of his own face, he sees the face of a gargoyle. Maybe the somebody gaining on you is a face you haven't faced yet.

I decided to approach the concert like a retrospective of my own musical past, to check out all those receding reflections to see if anything interesting would pop up. I called Phil Upchurch and Phil Woods and Mike Mainieri and my friend Gege in Italy and I called Richard Davis and Lynette and my favorite drummer, Leo. The concert was booked for Saturday, May 3, 1997. On Thursday, the first of May, the team started arriving. Gege flew in from Rome. He and Judy immediately began preparing the pasta. Next came Mike Mainieri and Phil Woods from New York, and the eating began. Phil Upchurch never made his flight. When he did arrive the next day, he told us a long story that can be summed up by saying he stole his own car, but fortunately he found it again before the police found him. Instead of rehearsing, we kept enjoying ourselves around the fire of each other's company. The party continued well into Friday night.

Phil Woods had stopped drinking earlier that year, but in honor of the occasion, he started again. After two bottles of red wine, we went to the piano, and he began playing standards. He played "Lush Life" with the most gorgeous chord substitutions I have ever heard. He talked about the early fifties, when, as a teenager, he first arrived in New York City. His father had given him permission to leave home and study music. Money was scarce but friendship was plentiful. "It was easy to walk in and meet Coleman Hawkins and talk to him and get to know him," he said. "The clubs were small. The community was small. We were all over in that one spot, around 52nd street and Broadway. That whole area belonged to jazz musicians. If you needed a little help with the rent or something, people would chip in." He had been sixteen at the time. I said it sounded wonderful, like being raised by wolves.

Then he became very nostalgic. He talked about his family. Years later, he had married Charlie Parker's widow, Chan, and had taken on the job of being a father to Bird's children. I knew the story of how, one time, he had played Bird's horn in public, a bitter memory for him. The family was broke and needed money for groceries. He was so poor, he had to pawn his horn. Then at the last minute, he got a gig and as he had no instrument of his own, he used Bird's horn, a legendary instrument, with the name "Charlie Parker" engraved on the bell. "You know, " he said, "it's just a horn, without the original guy playing, it's not a holy receptacle or anything." But that night, as he was playing, trying to earn enough money to get his own horn out of hock, Charles Mingus walked into the club and, recognizing the horn, came right up to the bandstand and made a point of looking at Phil with total disdain. "I mean I'm just trying to feed the family. You love Charlie Parker so much. Well how come I got to scuffle to feed his kids?"

Phil started to cry. He said, "I haven't been such a great father." He talked about how he hadn't taken the time to provide the kind of guidance he felt the kids needed when they needed it most. He said he was always on a bus or a train or a plane, and even when he was home, he was working on his music. "I failed," he said. "I failed at that."

It was heartbreaking. I remembered my very first jazz record, *The Birdland Stars on Tour*, with Phil's fantastic playing, the hope that it had instilled in me, the sense of future. I said, "No Phil, you didn't fail. You were a great father. You were a great father to me." We are all Bird's children. I, too, was raised by the wolves.

The next day, we arrived at the theater hung over, wearing dark glasses and moving slowly. We were recording the show, and there was a lot of setup time for the engineers, a lot of waiting around, so we decided to bring some chairs onto the stage. That way, when we weren't actually rehearsing, we could crash. By the end of the afternoon, this area had evolved into a little lounge with rugs, plants, a couch and catering. We decided to keep it there for the concert, and we took to calling it "the celebrity lounge." All musicians love to perform for their peers and the celebrity lounge made it inevitable. That night, after the audience was seated, I myself sat down at the piano and sang, "Gonna take a sentimental journey, gonna put my mind at ease, gonna take a sentimental journey to renew old memories..." and for a couple of hours, the stage became my living room, and the party continued, no mistakes, only opportunities, *Live at the Celebrity Lounge*. Phil Woods in particular was transcendent.

September was the eighteenth year of Hannah's High Holy Day services, and, in part because the number eighteen represents "chai," or life, in the Jewish tradition, Hannah asked me to write a new piece of music to mark the passage of time. It was also the first year that Leo was not going to be there. Like many of the kids who started out with us as small children, he was now in college and had gone off to study in Spain. Sitting on the piano bench, I was profoundly aware of his absence, and the song I prepared, "In the Fullness of Time," was about just such passages. It was the first song I had written specifically for the services.

Fullness Of Time

We're here but for a minute
That's all the time that's in it
We're here but for an hour
Like a passing shower
We're here but for a day
And then we're on our way
We're gone before
We're here but for a minute
That's all the time that's in it
We're here but for a week
There's hardly time to speak
We're here but for a year
And nothing's very clear
We're gone before we're
Here
In the fullness of time
Fruit falls from the vine
And hope is restored
To those who've resigned
And the dreams of our days
Become memories sublime
In the fullness of time.
We're here but for a minute
In the fullness of time.
That's all the time that's in it
In the fullness of time.

November 9, 1938 is known as Kristallnacht, "the night of broken glass," the night the Nazis rampaged throughout the streets of Germany and Austria, breaking the windows of Jewish businesses and homes, burning synagogues and looting. When that night was over, more than one hundred synagogues and thousands of Jewish businesses had been destroyed. Kristallnacht was the beginning of the "final solution," the blood bath of the Holocaust. In 1997, because of the impact of *Life's a Lesson,* I was invited by the Jewish community of Vienna to perform at the Odeon Theater on the anniversary of Kristallnacht.

Once one of the grandest Jewish communities in the world, Vienna's Jews have been decimated, reduced to a few thousand people. And yet the Rabbi of

Vienna, whose own father had been the rabbi during the war, was determined not to let his people be defined by the horror. To do that, he said, would be to admit defeat. Instead, he started a day school and every day more children were coming. Seeing them in the classrooms, their art on the walls, their voices lifted in song, it was possible to believe that the Nazis couldn't kill us all precisely because the seeds of Judaism existed in the communal moments, in the teachings. The spirit was reborn every time the torah (the "tree of life") was opened. Yet the smallness of the community there, its fragility and the lack of a real Jewish presence in the city spoke volumes about those who were gone. Walking the narrow street of the old synagogue, I looked down at the cobblestones and thought of what those stones had witnessed. It was terribly sad.

Lynette was there, and Howard Levy and Steve Khan too. And Leo flew in from Seville to play drums. The Odeon Theater is an old grain distribution center and had surely been filled with Jews doing their business some sixty years before. Now it was converted into a large open performance space with stacked seating for about eight hundred people. That night, the room was full, and as there were not many Jews left in the city, we assumed that at least half of the audience was non-Jewish. As soon as we walked into the space and Lynette began singing the opening phrases of "Avinu Malchenu" ("Our guardian, our protector, hear our prayer...") my eyes filled with tears. The whole concert was like that. Singing "Life's a Lesson" in this space, for these people, Jews and non-Jews alike, was a sanctified moment. I heard my voice rise into the heights of the hall, and I felt a happiness and a sense of presence I had rarely known. Bringing this music back to where it belonged was nearly overpowering, the opposite of the experience we had had at Lincoln Center, where it was just another performance, a festival ticket, notes scattered in the air. This night, the music was an incantation, a terrible longing expressed, a sense that we had all, somehow, come home.

There seemed to be no end to where this music was taking me. Until, at last, it finally seemed to lead me to my own endgame of sorts. My whole life, I had been listening to jazz as if there was some way to unravel its message, to penetrate the ineffable and parse the mystery at its core. But perhaps this is the very purpose of this music. It speaks in ways that we otherwise cannot, without all the baggage of verbs and nouns, and it expresses, as the great African pianist Abdullah Ibrahim told me, "the heart's deepest desire." And isn't this what prayer is? The heart expressing its deepest desire. Hadn't I been praying all these years? Hadn't I been running toward, rather than away from, my own past?

It's well known that jazz is a means to transform grief into joy. (Hence the expression, "I love the blues, they hurt so nice.") When the jazz musician plays, he is in fact transforming himself. All those long hours he works not just to master the piece of metal or the ivory keys under his fingers, but to make himself the vessel, to learn to listen to the voice in his own head and to sing it to the world. Marshall McLuhan taught us that the medium is the message. In jazz, the musician himself is the medium, so his life becomes the message. The kind of vessel you become is determined by your heart's desire. I believe we all want to do something important, to be connected to something greater than ourselves. Isn't this at the root of the rampant fundamentalism in the world today? And jazz training, where you are forced to find your own voice, to accept yourself for what you truly are, to be yourself completely, is a kind of religious training.

Only it's more than that. It's eminently practical. It relieves you of the guilt of thinking there is a wrong way and a right way, because all roads lead to home. It keeps what has been called "the beginner's mind" open and fresh, even in the oldest players. It forces you to find your voice and to appreciate the differences between what you have to say and what the others are saying. And all one really has to do is learn how to listen to this music. That simple act keeps the tradition alive. The simple act of listening with an open heart is like watering the tree of life.

That night in Vienna, following a reception attended by the leaders of the Jewish community, I went back to the hotel and Leo went off with Steve Khan. Steve is the son of Sammy Cahn, the great American songwriter who wrote so many of Sinatra's hits, like "All the Way," "Three Coins in the Fountain," "High Hopes," "Call Me Irresponsible," "I Fall In Love Too Easily," "Teach Me Tonight"...the list is long indeed. Steve had changed the spelling of his last name years ago so that he could make it or break it on his own. And while he has been making it just fine, he is still struggling with his legacy. The next day, on our way to the airport, Leo told me they had talked long into the evening about how to define your identity in the shadow of a famous parent and a great tradition.

Leo and I flew into Spain together. When we landed, he went back to school, while I spent some time in Madrid. Arriving in Seville a few days later, I found him living in a cold, dark apartment down a Gothic alley just yards away from the great Cathedral. One could easily imagine ranks of black hooded men struggling under the weight of a great medieval Madonna, negotiating these narrow passageways and chanting in the flickering candlelight. This was really the first chance we had to talk since he left home.

He was in crisis. He felt lost. He had come to Spain to establish his own identity and had plunged headfirst into the world of Sevillanas. But he was "la mitad," in the middle, suspended between the Old World and the new. And there was a girl. I sat with him in his little room and listened as he played the songs he had written, felt his emotional pulse, felt the damp cold rise up from the stone floor. He told me of the crazies and the bohos and the flamencos and the beboppers and the university and hiding from exams in bed until noon and then until one or two o'clock, and finally, one day, not getting up at all. But he had discovered this music, had begun studying guitar with a flamenco, had found the recordings of Jorge Drexler, a beautifully poetic songwriter who spoke directly to his soul.

His life was very much being lived on the ground. He had been mugged. He had found a jazz club. He had put together a band. He had come to Spain to reinvent himself, and as the past fell away, the future, the neat plan he had been working on, had lost its focus as well. He was thrown back on the present. Hence staying in bed. Not a bad place to be on a cold November afternoon with no heat, the stone floors warmed only by a forty watt bulb and a few Coltrane CDs. I told him, "If you can't get out of bed in the morning, then that is what you're working on. That is your job for the day, and it is as good as any other. Don't ever feel you're wasting time if you're living your life. That's what your time is for. I love your songs. Let's go have a pizza."

Over pizza, I said, "Come to Granada with me." I was leaving the next day.

Sometimes when you travel, you find yourself in a hotel room, and you ask yourself "Why am I here?" The obvious and usual answers—I came to perform, to get paid, to get away, to seek my future—don't work, and the awful emptiness of your situation truly looms. But in those moments, if you persevere and pay attention, often a truer answer reveals itself. Perhaps the reason you are there, the real reason you came, is to meet the man who will interview you that day, an elegant, bookish fellow who starts talking about the spiritual nature of music in such a casual way that it is perfectly clear you came to share this hour or two with him, to take a blindfold test, with each choice a perfect incision into the emotional corpus of your life.

The reason you came reveals itself in these small mysterious ways. It is almost never about why you think you came. The booking is just a ruse. Invariably, some small interior moment, a spark of insight, is the true reward of the quest. Something to put into the magic bag we wear under our shirt, under our skin, and which we finally empty at the very last moments of our life, like one last Halloween eve, with all our candy spread out on the floor, the fruits of our long night's hunt.

The hope is that these little sparkling moments of insight will add up, take shape, reveal some larger sense of purpose, and so bring peace. The truth is probably that each sparkling moment works on the human heart in some small healing way, provides some brief relief to the daily dose of fear and sorrow, and so the end result is a warmer, calmer heart, rather than a heart transformed in one last incandescent flash. We all search for the quick fix: everybody wants to go to heaven but nobody wants to die.

Why did we come? We came to get well.

In the penthouse suite of the Granada Center Hotel, Angel Harguindey, the editor of *El Pais*, Spain's newspaper of record, was ordering room service. One of the three young women who attended him asked me if I would like something to eat. I said no, maybe just something to drink. In the background, music was playing. I recognized it as the record, *Solita*, which I had produced that year for the French singer Clementine. Leo had written the title song. I commented to Angel on his good taste. He smiled. One of the women remarked on the purity of Clementine's voice. I talked a little about making the record, how I tried to strike the balance between jazz and pop, to showcase Clementine's natural strengths. Just small talk.

The food and drink arrived and was distributed. The music changed. Now it was a Georgie Fame record. I smiled and talked to the woman next to me about the experience of working with Georgie. Angel spoke of the passion that's in the music. He said, "To me, your music is a sentimental shock." I said, "Often when one lacks the material resources, they do their best work." This went on for some time, the group eating, drinking and socializing. Nobody took notes, and yet when the article appeared in *El Pais* the following Sunday, it was filled with accurate, verbatim quotes. Angel had great ears. When it was time to go to the concert, I stood up and we all shook hands. One of the women kissed me on both cheeks. Her name was Laura Garcia Lorca and, in the end, it turned out that she was the real reason we had come.

That night, Georgie Fame was playing at the Jazz Festival of Granada with his two sons in the band, and Leo felt connected to the boys in part because, like Steve Khan, they, too, were dealing with this conundrum of how to break free and stay connected at the same time. After the concert, Leo and Georgie and Laura all wound up at a small bar where the intellectuals of Granada congregate. I was long asleep by the time they returned to the hotel. In the intervening hours, Leo and Laura had bonded over yet another conversation about legacy, the responsibility of carrying on a tradition. Laura is the niece of the great Spanish poet Federico Garcia Lorca, who had no children of his own, and so she too had been fighting this "heir apparent" tattoo her whole life. Raised in New York City, she had recently come to Granada to assume her role as director of the Huerta de San Vicente, the family home that was now a museum dedicated to Lorca's memory. She was determined to keep more than his memory alive.

Talking to Leo over breakfast the next morning, I found him changed, calmer, more at ease. He said, "Ever since Vienna, it's like I woke up to this part of myself that I've been forgetting about. Because everything here in Spain has been 'mine.' I came here, I found a place to live, I found a life that had nothing to do with you or home or anything else. And then suddenly, in Vienna, to go back and feel part of something that is bigger than that...it made me aware that these are thoughts that don't go away. If you are part of something larger, then that's who you are. And talking to Laura last night about being part of a family and a tradition, it just brought it all home to me. It's like I can't escape this. And maybe the ultimate act of rebellion is coming to terms with your own legacy. Accepting it and defending it."

Steve Khan had changed his last name and Laura Garcia Lorca had avoided using hers for years. And finally, they both had to come back to their own "Granada," to accept their history. I thought of my father, who had changed his name as well, and of my lifelong search to belong to something meaningful, something larger than myself. I said, "I know what you mean, Leo. I am trying to come home too."

1998

I n April, Judy and I returned to Seville for Feria, the grand pasado of horses and riders that culminates in a weeklong orgy of bullfights, drinking and flamenco. Every afternoon, the fairground was a sea of women in bright skirts, men in tight-fitting jackets, and carriages pulled by the finest Andalucian horses. We sat under a tent, drank Manzanilla and applauded the passing parade well into the night. Then one day we drove to Granada to see Laura. When we arrived, she said why didn't we all go to the sea, to her family's place in Nerja. And so along with Leo, the four of us drove through the Sierra to the Spanish coast. There, behind a nondescript doorway down a small beach road, we discovered Lorca's summer home. The house was filled with old books and artifacts, and in the dining room stood an ancient upright piano that had obviously been the center of family life.

Laura was on a special diet where she could drink nothing but rum, so we went on the diet with her. Late one night, we were sitting around the dining room table and Laura began talking about the celebration she was planning for the one hundredth anniversary of her uncle's birth. Federico Garcia Lorca had been murdered in 1936, one of the first victims of the Spanish Civil War. After Franco's death, his story and his work were resurrected. By the end of the century, Lorca was more alive in Spain than ever before. There were major tributes being planned all over the country, and Laura herself was organizing a series of concerts in Granada, speaking to the fact that Lorca's first love was music. She was working with Paco De Lucia and Patti Smith and Van Morrison and Bob Dylan and then she said, "Elvis Costello was scheduled to perform this June with the Brodsky Quartet, but it looks like he's not going to make it. He called to say he was having trouble getting it together."

I said I understood. The work was daunting. How would one go about putting together a tribute to Lorca in his own hometown?

"Ben," she said, "I wonder if you would you be interested in filling in for him?" Nothing specific about what to do or how to do it. Just a simple invitation to perform at the Huerta de San Vicente in six weeks.

The next day, Leo returned to Seville, and Judy and I returned to the States. Naturally, I had agreed to do the gig. Later that week, at a party back in Madison, I asked if anybody in the room might know somebody at the University who could provide me with a crash course on the writings, history and philosophy of Federico Garcia Lorca. My good friend Bob Skloot looked up and said, "I wrote my dissertation on Lorca." And so, the next day, he deposited a pile of books on my doorstep. I began by reading the philosophy of Miguel de Unamuno, Lorca's inspiration in "The Tragic Sense of Life." Six, eight hours a day, I devoured the poems, the essays, the biography. I was so immersed that I began dreaming Lorca, quoting long sections of his poetry in Spanish, and I don't even speak Spanish.

I needed to find some new forms. I wanted to be able to talk about the things that were important to Lorca in the context of jazz, to slip in and out of the music and weave Lorca's text within the larger story. I heard in my head a way to do this, but I didn't exactly know how to get there. I kept rereading the essays and the poems and then going to the piano to let my hands move as though by themselves, hoping they would divine the way. I thought about the difficulty of improvising and storytelling simultaneously. Lorca's themes were powerful, dramatic; he spoke of "duende," that "mysterious power which everyone senses and no one explains," a life and death struggle to be in the moment, on "the rim of the well," fighting hand to hand with your own mortality, a struggle out of which true art comes. To keep this spirit alive, I knew, context was key.

And then, on a hot afternoon in June, we were back in Granada. Remembering the day is like remembering a dream, the road winding up into the mountains and the city shimmering there in the heat of the afternoon. I missed a turn off the highway and passed a sign for Fuente Grande and a shiver went up my spine; this was the place of Lorca's last moments, the unmarked grave by the side of the road. Eventually, we found ourselves in the traffic of a modern city, and ended up at the edge of an old orchard, the Huerta de San Vicente, where Laura was waiting, smiling as always, welcoming us to the house of her uncle, of her grandfather, of her aunts and cousins.

Leo and I walked through the gardens to the whitewashed house, up the stairs, the same stairs down which the caretaker had been thrown by the fascists sixty-three years ago, the fascists who then came back the next night for Lorca himself. Now, they led up to a modest office housing a fax machine, a desk, a few chairs, and a window overlooking a large walnut tree in a simple gravel courtyard. A dream within a dream: we watched as Lorca's own piano was carried out of the house and positioned under the tree for the concert. This piano, which was once dismantled by the Falangists in a frantic search for a radio transmitter they believed Lorca was hiding, now appeared to be a humble antique.

Laura had insisted that we use it for the concert, causing something of a stir in the community. In Spain, Lorca's piano is an icon, a national treasure, and it is said to be haunted. As it was being moved into the garden, several people were visibly agitated, but Laura was serene. She said, "There's no reason not to play it. Either it gets used or it's just a museum piece." Essentially a parlor instrument, this was the first time in sixty-three years that the piano had left the house, and it seemed strangely out of place, liberated. But as Phil Woods had reminded me about Bird's horn, it is not the artifacts of life that are sacred, it is the message of the life; Laura too was very clear on this point. The message lives on or we are all just museum curators.

Laura's casual invitation to consider her uncle in a jazz context had led me down a path where history and poetry, tragedy and self-examination could come together and ignite for a few moments, spin like smoke in front of a small audience and then disappear again into the warm night air. We were not planning to record the concert so we would be playing these songs only once, tell this story and be gone. There was a wonderful sense of being in the moment. I felt a great gathering of forces inside of me.

By 10 P.M., the chairs in the courtyard were full, people were laughing and taking drinks from the bar and Leo and I were talking quietly in the doorway of the Huerta. We were both in a kind of ecstasy, for on the drive to Granada, we had talked about our lives, about how fate had cast us up together on this distant shore, and about the dark under side of Spain and about the beautiful, passionate side too. We were both feeling a tremendous bond; the concert had really brought us together, and the night seemed pregnant with possibility. Under a black sky, with pollen from the old tree floating like motes in the stage lights, we walked onto the platform to begin. And then something very odd happened.

Manuel Calleja, the bass player from Seville who had seemed so calm, so sympathetic the day before, suddenly went "flamenco." He disappeared from the stage and couldn't be found. After a minute or two, he reappeared from behind the stage with a pack of cigarettes in his hand. He was acting as if there was nothing more important than his personal comfort. Slowly, as three hundred people waited in some confusion, he pulled out a cigarette and asked me for a tuning note. It was a classic gypsy moment, an act of studied indifference, a thumb in the eye of society. It was caused by his own insecurity, of course, but it was a direct shot at everything I had been working toward. I looked into his face and hit the opening chord of the concert. For a moment, our eyes locked, and then we were off. He could come with us or not, as far as I was concerned, but this train was leaving the station.

I felt the tug of desire on the inertia of the moment. We want what we want, but we are given what we are given, and in this moment, I felt the "duende" descend into the bullring of life. I, too, was fighting hand to hand with my own mortality, dragging the weight of someone's indifference behind me like a stone. In that moment of struggle, I recognized that this was exactly Lorca's message. Manuel had inadvertently given me a great opportunity, something to push against. He had given me the living context I was searching for, a greater reason to care.

I felt the chords and rhythms settle into the horizon against which the story of Lorca's life could be told. I was no longer performing. I was in his garden, calling down his spirit, chanting his poetry, playing his piano, describing his death at the hands of the fascists, reminding those who had ears to hear, "To act in such a way as to make our annihilation an injustice, in such a way as to make our brothers, our sons, and our brother's sons and their daughters, feel that we ought not to have died...this is the way...to perform our occupation passionately, tragically if you like...this is the way...we are impelled to stamp others with our seal, to perpetuate ourselves in them and in their children....this is the way," I repeated the phrase, like a sanctified chant, rising into the night air, "this is the way we defeat death. This is the way death is defeated."

Everything that gets done in life gets done because at that moment it mattered more to someone than anything else. It's that simple. Ideas are as common as pollen in the air. The power is in the caring. If you care, the words and the music can be transformative. If you are going through the motions, it is just random notes, the hollow scraping of reeds. And one can't pretend to care, to slip it on and off as one does a sweater on a cool evening. Caring is a form of pregnancy. You either are or you aren't; you either care or you don't. This is where faith comes in, the faith that it's *worth it* to care. In the moment that you make that choice, to struggle against the odds rather than accept what's been given, to say what's in your heart rather than to remain silent, in that moment the "duende" is present and anything is possible.

At the end of the evening, after the last words of Lorca's lovely poem for his friend Margarita Xirgu had echoed through the garden,

Si me voy, te quiero mas
si me quedo, igual te quiero
If I leave, I love you more,
if I stay, I love you just the same

after Lorca's final salute to life had been remembered,

"Life is laughter among a rosary of deaths...
but look beyond the braying of man
to the love in the heart of the people,
to be the wind..."

after Unamuno's farewell blessing had been recalled,
"I hope dear friends, some time while our tragedy is still playing, in some interval between the acts, we shall meet again. And we shall recognize one another if we do. Until then, Que Dios te niegue la paz pero que te conceda la gloria, may God deny you peace, but grant you glory."

I walked offstage and Chema the soundman approached me with an out-stretched hand. "Perhaps," he said, "you would like to hear this," and he handed me a digital recording of *The Concert for Garcia Lorca*. Unbeknownst to me, the evening had been documented.

A few hours later, Leo and I sat in a small bar somewhere in the caves of Sacre Monte under a radiant Alhambra moon. At the table were musicians, historians, gypsies, fellow travelers, people of unknown profession and no questions asked. We ate and drank and talked about the adventure of this life and how it had brought us here together for this one night only. This is how we defeat death, this is how death is defeated: Garcia Lorca had become more than a subject, he had become a way of traveling.

Through the spring, summer and fall, I rode my bike around Madison, or around the lake, or around the 10K loop through the arboretum. In the winter, of course, I rode the "bike to nowhere," sitting in a health club trying to read the *New York Times* while the computer took me up and down imaginary hills. Not as much fun as running with Henry had been, but I was feeling good and the knee was only a small problem. Then in the summer of 1998, two things happened. First, I started practicing yoga aggressively. This, I know, is a contradiction in terms; one does not bring one's aggression to the practice of yoga. And yet I sat on my knees with such fervor that within six weeks, the left one was nicely swollen and starting to scream at night. Second, I passed out while riding my bike through the arboretum.

I felt it coming, a rising in the pit of my stomach as I crossed the little bridge into the woods, and I said to myself, "This doesn't feel right, perhaps it would be good to pull over," and the next thing I knew I heard a loud "thud," and it was my head hitting the pavement, and then I was coming to with my bike spinning next to me and a sense that something bad had just happened but I didn't know what it might be. It took me an hour to crawl the mile back home. I would stand up and use the bike for a kind of rolling crutch, half staggering a few yards before I would start to swoon again and have to rest. When I got home, I made some calls and the tests began.

I passed every test with flying colors. The stress test was a breeze — they practically had to pull me off of the treadmill. The Holter monitor showed no problem. The tilt table was inconclusive. The consults with the specialist got me nowhere. I kept saying things like, "I just feel like I'm coming apart. I feel fragile, like I could cry at any moment." One doctor told me, "If it happens again, lie down and put your feet up."

My knee was a more immediate problem. I was going to Europe for six weeks that November, and I was still having trouble walking. Eventually, I took anti-inflammatories and hobbled through London, Paris and Madrid. The dizziness gradually receded, and by the time I got to Rome, the knee was actually feeling kind of normal. So when I got home in mid-December, I decided if I couldn't deal with the dizziness, at least I would deal with the knee. After seventeen years (had Henry really been gone that long?) I would finally have the surgery to repair the cartilage tear. I went to the best knee man at the University Hospital, and after a workup, we scheduled the surgery for the following April. It was the soonest I would be able to stop traveling for the four-week recovery period.

1999

I went about my life. In February, we went to Hong Kong, where I played a week at the Jazz Club in Lan Kwai Fong with a swinging Indian drummer and a brilliant Chinese guitar player. It was a fantastic week, with unbelievably good food, great weather and nice people. The morning we were about to return to the States, I awoke at 5 A.M., got out of bed, and was staggered. I wasn't just dizzy; I felt my life was hanging in the balance, yet I was in no pain and I seemed to be breathing normally. It was like I was experiencing a profound crisis of confidence, but on such a grand scale as to make even walking the ten steps to the bathroom an insurmountable challenge. I knew I had to somehow get myself home.

For the next twenty-four hours, I clung to consciousness with every ounce of strength I had. In the insane, predawn taxi ride to the airport, while changing planes in various cities, through the landings and take offs, I focused on one breath at a time. I just didn't want to pass out and be taken to some foreign hospital or, worse, pass out in the plane and cause a forced landing.

Somehow, I got home, but the problem didn't go away. For the next three days, the waves of nausea and panic kept coming, sometimes every few minutes, other times not for hours. Just when everything seemed normal, the feeling would well up again from the pit of my stomach, and I knew my life was hanging by a thread. I wracked my brain to try and understand what was happening to me, although I suspected it was not something that could be "understood" in any conventional way. It felt too primitive, almost primordial. Rationales didn't seem to affect it. I was not calmed or reassured by any suppositions. It was the most powerful emotional experience I have ever faced. It kept coming and coming, waves of panic and fear, emotional waves rising and falling in my chest. I could almost taste the fear. It was my constant companion, like having the flu — a deep pool of nausea always lurking in the background.

I went to several doctors, but nothing could be found. For the following month, I lived on the verge of tears. I was coming apart; I felt that I was as fragile as an infant, completely unprotected. The *me* that had always been there to pull me through a crisis was no longer available. I was losing my persona. I was dying. When I would tell the doctor this, he would check my pulse and my blood pressure, and since it always seemed normal, I was eventually diagnosed with "neurocardiogenic syncope," meaning perhaps I had an arrhythmia but we didn't know why. As my symptoms mirrored those of panic attacks, I was given an anti-anxiety medication and sent on my way.

Within a few weeks, I was back to flying through the air in commercial planes, off to record in Minneapolis, to attend the World Affairs Conference in Boulder. True, sometimes I couldn't even summon the energy to walk across the room, and sometimes if I stood up too fast I got very lightheaded, but these were also symptoms of the medication I was taking. It's amazing how we can come to accept virtually any condition as "normal" if we are deeply enough in denial. We decided to wait and to watch. And so I decided to go ahead with the knee surgery as planned, to be proactive about something.

The period of waiting for the surgery was like living under water. I knew something very bad was happening to me and I was trying very hard to "live with it," to understand it and adapt. I found comfort in spending time with our dog, Peaches. We went on long car rides together, and I loved seeing that it made him happy. It was just motion to him, the rush of wind in his face. He had no idea that I was driving the car, or, indeed, that the car was being driven. He had no concept of "driving," and I realized that, like Peaches, I, too, was unaware of the many forces in my life, and that there was no way I could ever know what I couldn't know. I became acutely aware of small things, like the sunlight moving across the carpet. And then one day, in the midst of this ongoing descent into the unknown, driving nowhere with Peaches, I became profoundly happy.

We were stopped at a light, and as I watched the traffic passing in front of me, suddenly, it was clear to me that all the worrying I had been doing for so many years came to nothing. Like the fear of not having enough money, Did I have enough money to last three more months? Yes. Well, how did I know I was going to last three more months? Clearly, I did not. I thought of the old axiom, "If you have a problem and you can solve it, why worry? If you have a problem and you can't solve it, why worry?" I started laughing. Why worry indeed.

The extent to which we worry about the future makes it come true. There is no future except as it exists in our projections. Choosing to project a particular future causes it to come about because it solidifies the perception. All life is on the edge. On the "rim of the well," as Lorca had said. Retreat from the edge and you retreat from life itself. The thing to do is to find out as soon as possible what you do best (what you feel best doing), and do it every moment you can.

Why does the soul doubt itself so? Why must it be so blind to its own beauty and prefer the neurotic observances of others? Perhaps because it needs struggle to grow. That adversity is why we are here. And the soul will seek out adversity as a plant tropes to the sunlight. Perhaps only after an inner struggle can the soul give or accept love, unconditionally.

Over the years, more than a few well-intentioned people had given me the same heartfelt advice: stop trying to do so many different things and pick a "career" — be a piano player, be a producer, be a journalist, whatever — and focus on that. In the end, it turned out I wasn't exactly doing any of these things. I was working on self-transformation, and the playing, the writing, the producing, were just fueling the process, providing the means of transportation, providing cover.

I thought of all my daily frustrations, and I saw clearly that you should never be disappointed or have a low opinion of yourself just because you are not every-thing you hope to be. Otherwise, what are hopes for?

My whole life had been a search for "higher understanding," only to discover that there is no understanding higher than simply *being* and no greater way to be than a life in the music. For me, if life was a lesson, that was the teaching. Everything else, all the internal chatter — "I need something, I *need* something" — was just my way of trying to stave off the inevitable, to fill up the silences, to think my way past the unthinkable. Trying to avoid the fragility of life, in the end, I discovered that fragility was all there is.

Then the light changed, and with Peaches at my side, I drove on, floating like a bubble in the wind, feeling light and completely at peace.

The week before the scheduled knee surgery, I went in for the pre-op physical. They X-rayed the knee. They drew the blood. They did the ECG to check my heart. And the nurse said, "Do you feel okay?" By then, I didn't know what okay was, so I said "Sure, why?"

She told me very matter-of-factly, "Well, your pulse is awfully slow. Are you a runner?"

I guess I'd been waiting a long time for that question. I said, "Yes. Well, not now, but I used to be."

She said, "That might explain it." Then she gave me the ECG and told me to go to the anesthesiologist. When I left the room, I looked at the graph she had handed me. Across the top, it read "Abnormal ECG. Average pulse rate: 36." I immediately stepped into the first office I passed and asked the woman there to photocopy the paper for me. I went through the rest of the pre-op in a kind of daze. When I got home, I faxed the graph to Tom Ansfield, my cardiologist. I was in his office in a matter of hours.

The following day was Wednesday, and I was wired with a heart monitor. Because I was feeling so "normal" that day, I went out of my way to prove it. I rode the bike to nowhere for forty minutes, raked leaves, had a few drinks at the nightclub, hung out with Leo. I was going to prove I could make myself well. Two days later, on Friday, Judy, Leo and I were back in Tom's office. Leo thinks Tom has the aura of James Bond, and there is a kind of worldly nonchalance about him. As he showed us the results of the heart monitor, he was relaxed and offhand. My average pulse rate for the day had been 36. It had gone as low as 24: I had, he said, "a complete heart block." He reached into his pocket and threw something at me. It was a small titanium disc. I said, "I don't want to go there."

"I can do it on Monday," Tom said.

"We have some gigs in June," Leo said. "How about after then?"

"If you need some time," Tom said, "Thursday is also a possibility."

That night Judy and Leo and I had a meeting in our kitchen with my kitchen cabinet, Zorba Paster, our longtime family doctor, and Ken Robbins, our longtime family psychiatrist. Zorba took one look at the ECG and said, "You are a perfect candidate for a pacemaker."

I said, "I just don't know if I want to do it right now. Maybe I should try some alternatives first."

Ken said, "Ben, you are no longer driving this car. Sit back and let the driver drive." I looked down at Peaches. He was so happy that company was over that he was sitting in the middle of the floor licking himself. Life was a lot simpler than any of us knew.

Sunday night, Judy and Leo and I went out for Chinese food. At the end of the meal, I broke the cookie and my fortune read, " When skating on thin ice, your safety is in your speed." I swear to God. I said to Judy and Leo, "If anything happens to me, I want you to know I've had a great life and I love you both more than words can say."

On Monday, I showed up for surgery. I was extraordinarily weak. They took me directly to intensive care, exchanged my clothes for a backless gown and hooked me up to computers and monitors. As the nurse was attempting to start an IV, I heard alarms going off and was aware of people rushing into the room. I looked over and saw the lines on the monitor sinking. Then I saw Judy and Leo and I felt very peaceful. I had no sense of fear or danger, just the impending swoon of unconsciousness as it started to overtake me. I watched the whole thing as if from a very far away, very warm place, and I felt everything was going to be fine.

As soon as I came out of surgery, I felt better than I had felt in years. Tom came into the recovery room and said, "You have a very strong heart. It's a runner's heart. When I was inserting the wires, I could see how thick the walls are." What I heard him say, even though he didn't say it, was "You are a very lucky man. Your heart kept you alive these past months even when it was failing. This could easily have gone a different way."

He was right. I am a very lucky man. For one thing, I had a friend named Henry, who years ago promised to take care of me and he did, even though it meant reaching out from the beyond. First, he took me running to make sure my heart was strong enough to survive the arrhythmia. Then he made sure my knee was damaged just enough so that when the time came, and we couldn't discover what was wrong with my heart, the knee would give me one last shot at an ECG. It seemed like such a classic jazz teaching; go toward adversity, it's the way out of your dilemma.

And the knee? The knee seems to be feeling fine. It's strange, but it hasn't been much of a problem since my heart was fixed. I think maybe it served its purpose.

We only remember what we remember because of who we are and how the events of our lives have shaped us. Recalled perception tells us more about the perceiver than the perceived, more about the filter than the facts. In this way, people don't just move through time, time moves through people, and all history is a selective tradition.

Jazz isn't a kind of music; it's a way of playing music, and, by extension, a way of approaching the world. The goal, as Miles Davis once said, is to play what you don't know rather than what you do know. You are in search of your own ignorance. And it's amazing how well we learn to cover this up.

Improvisation can be taught. What is it? Trial and error. There is no trial without error. Sometimes, improvisation is simply saying yes instead of saying no. Give the moment the benefit of the doubt.

The human brain loves to improvise. In fact, it's how we learn anything. We play games. For example, to hit a moving target with a stone, we have to learn how to "lead" the target, to anticipate its future. We do this by missing a few times and then adjusting our actions to the flow of events. In other words, by trial and error. Without error, there is no trial.

Finding your own style is difficult because it means "setting it free while you're sitting astride it." This can't be taught but it can be learned. Style is distinct from habit. Style can be refined over the years, like a precious metal. Habit, good or bad, can only be repeated until it's so boring that it is dropped in favor of another.

We can teach the notes, but we can't teach the spaces between the notes. We can't teach the silences. We can't teach "at rest." We can't teach peace. We have to find it ourselves.

In June 1999, just days after he graduated from the University of Wisconsin with a major in history, Leo and I went to Minneapolis to play a gig. Billy Peterson played bass, and, as we often do when we travel, we hired a horn player to fill out the band. This time, we were joined at the Artist's Quarter by saxophonist Irv Williams. Irv was born in Arkansas eighty years ago and has lived in the Twin Cities for the past fifty of those years. He has wonderful stories about his days on the road with Duke Ellington and nights with Lester Young, but the best part of hanging out with Irv is the twinkle in his eye and the wisdom of his playing. He acts as if he's still in his mid-life, and he plays with a romantic lyricism and a calm command that is the signature of the self-realized jazzman. The sounds that come from his old horn are as cool as fresh squeezed juice on a hot day. In his music, he says only what he wants to, and he rarely repeats himself. He makes you play better when you play with him, because to hear him is to understand that your role in life is not to prove yourself but to be yourself. Showing up, as they say, is half the battle. Only when you play with Irv, there is no battle, only a party. A party with a purpose.

For years there has been talk about whether the artistic process is "the frosting or the cake." The choices miss the mark: art is the appetite. It's the hunger for life. It's what makes us want to wake up in the morning and start over. It's the reason we go to work each day and amass whatever it is we are amassing. It's the purpose for planting the seed. Without the arts, we forget our purpose, we become less human.

My favorite example of this is something Phil Woods told me. I had asked him, "What is it like to be able to play absolutely anything you can hear? It must be liberating." He just looked at me with those big sad eyes of his and said, "Oh, playing is no problem. Wanting to play. That's the problem."

This reduction of the artistic process to a search for desire — the desire for desire — is, I think, at the core of the jazz life. Those who think that musicians are merely flexing some abstract or intellectual muscle on a daily basis are really missing the point. Jazz is a transformative process, and the musician is constantly transforming himself, first of all, and his audience, by extension. It's this hunger to experience change, real, physical change, that drives the musician. If it's a need to experience "wholeness" or "completeness," then it is a "wholeness" with one's own potential that one feels (the desire to experience one's own ultimate future?). It's as if there is an almost genetic unfolding in the human heart of this potential, an internal command to follow this voice.

And isn't this similar to the theme of the Jewish High Holy Days, the belief that man can change, that we can transform ourselves and that there is a spiritual commandment that we do so? It is an act of surrender, of giving oneself over to something greater, and this, of course, is what jazz musicians do. John Coltrane was not the first to say that "music belongs to no one, it passes through us all." In the daily attempt to confront a row of piano keys, one is engaged in learning the heart's deepest desire, as a truth on the pulse, not as an abstract idea.

This is what I was thinking as I watched Leo and Irv play together. Or perhaps I was thinking nothing at all.

There were two ways home. We could either take the freeway, a direct shot through the rolling green hills of Wisconsin, or the long way, following the Mississippi River down, past small towns and great bluffs carved out over thousands of years. In the spring, if you went the long way, you could get lucky and see the eagles taking their hatchlings for a spin. The next morning, following the gig with Irv, Leo and I took the long way home, a five-hour ride, listening to music and hoping to catch one of these everyday miracles.

When we arrived in Madison, I went directly to my desk and began writing, "In the beginning, you fall in love..."

 **Epilogue**

June 21, 2001

"All comedies end in marriage. And all tragedies end in death.
Those are your choices…."

— ORSON WELLS

My old roommate Marty finally died waiting for a new liver — his old
one had been ravaged by Hepatitis C. Don Ellis, who gave up his
wife and kids to go native with us back in Madison, also died a few years back, of
cancer, having survived three wives and a hard crawl up the CBS corporate ladder. Jesse Davis, Mike Bloomfield, Tony Williams, Jerry Garcia, Art Blakey, Gil
Evans, Pepper Adams, Blue Mitchell, Rahsaan Roland Kirk, Al Gray, they too
have all passed. The list is long and growing longer by the day.

My sister Maxine lives in Toronto doing her work, and my brother Ezra is
holed up in Davenport, doing his. John Isbell is now a grandfather and Pallo
Jordan is now the Minister of Tourism for the government of South Africa. Elliot
Eisenberg is living in Amsterdam where he carries on his studies on the history
of the Left. And ever since Steve Miller retired (again), Billy Peterson has gone
back to playing bebop. Curley Cooke teaches the blues out in Seattle, and Paul
Pena, after almost thirty years of obscurity, was the subject of a documentary film
nominated for an academy award. And, in 2000, the record we made twenty-
eight years before was finally released. That same year, Mose Allison recorded a
retrospective for Blue Note Records, to celebrate his half century in the jazz business, and I was there to help him.

Tommy LiPuma is currently the CEO of the largest jazz company in the
world and Bob Krasnow is out of the music business entirely, cooling his heels in

Palm Beach. Glyn Johns is pretty much retired too; he sold his country estate in England and bought a place in the south of France. Clive Davis was replaced at Arista, the company he founded, by a rapper (a music he hated) and immediately started another new enterprise with somebody else's money. Miraslov Vitous, who I met coming out of Clive's office that day, stopped playing bass altogether for a while and developed a very successful digital sampling business, but he is starting to play jazz again.

By century's end, the jazz community had suffered many losses, both through natural attrition and institutional indifference. Most musicians were not assuaged by the periodic tributes and public television specials: why must one always die before one can live?

So when I heard that Phil Woods was very sick, I called him to get any last minute instructions and to thank him for his music. His answering machine picked up and a voice said, "We're sorry we can't take your call right now, but if you leave a message, we'll be glad to call you back. If you have work for Phil or one of his bands, please call...." and then it gave his agent's number. Well, either he was feeling a whole lot better or the instruction was to take the gig until you can't play anymore and then take the gig anyway just in case you can. Die with your boots on, Baby! Eventually, Phil called and said he had been incapacitated but now he was "back like a motherfucker," and everybody who has heard him agrees he's playing great. Perhaps it's true: that which doesn't kill you makes you stronger.

On the other hand, it can simply kill you. I thought of this the other day when, by chance, I happened to discover two boxes of my father's old letters. It was a warm summer afternoon and the sky was ominous with rain—you could just smell the coming storm on the air. I was rummaging around in a storage area, looking for nothing in particular when I came upon two large speckled files tucked behind a pile of family momentos. I had never noticed them before, which is curious, because I must have placed them there myself following my father's death thirty-three years ago. Amazing what we chose to forget. The boxes smelled like the 1940s, and they didn't appear to have been opened since.

Inside, I found, listed alphabetically and catalogued by correspondent's last name, a thorough record of Louis Sidran's life from the time he returned home from the army in early 1946 through his surrendering the dream of being a full-time writer in late 1948.

Reading these letters in chronological order was a slow, devastating descent into the disappointment of my father's life. He had just moved into the house on Carmel Ave. in Racine with my mother and her mother, and had taken a job as an associate editor at *Esquire Magazine*, commuting daily by train to Chicago. At first, the letters were full of promise. Along with editing the magazine, he was writing fiction (a couple of the stories were even attributed to "Ben Hirsh" my own first names), and in late 1946, he initiated *Esky's* first jazz issue.

He was connected in Chicago and doing fine. But then something bad happened; the details are obscure, but *Esquire* moved offices to New York City, and my father stayed behind in Racine.

He wrote to various friends at the time that he planned to become a freelancer writer, full-time. To this end, he secured an agent in New York City and sent out submissions, story ideas and proposals. He received some commissions — one thing on prize fighting for *Argosy*, another on jazz for *Coronet* — but a surprising number of turndowns. The market was tight and times were tough, he was told. One friend from the army, after complementing him profusely on his work, told him not to bother to come to New York City to look for work. "The place is crawling with writers," he wrote, "young men fresh out of the army all trying to peddle their wares." Even the ad agencies weren't hiring.

Gradually, the letters showed my father to be flying into the face of this stiff resistance, twisting, trying to catch an updraft, dodging the flak, looking for purchase. Months went by, then a year. The letters became more pointed, more revealing: he was receiving some very bad news on an almost daily basis, taking some direct hits — you could almost sense him losing altitude — yet his correspondence remained upbeat and breezy. He seemed to be challenging fate to take its best shot. Either that or he was in total denial.

Finally, he hunkered down and wrote a book. It was called *Mark the Innocent Man*, about life in the Jewish/Polish community of Chicago's Humbolt Park. The manuscript is missing, but there were a large number of letters from Henry Simon at Simon and Schuster, who had taken up his cause. In the end, after many letters back and forth, the book was not published. Word came back from the editorial board, "Too many people are writing books like yours...." In his last letter, Simon wrote, "I think I understand exactly how you feel — the blow to your plans and pride, the economic pressure the uncertainty and discouragement of the immediate future..." My father apparently wrote back to him saying, "One day we'll laugh about it."

But he wasn't laughing; he was becoming trapped, gradually, inexorably, like so many of the others, stuck in Racine on his way to somewhere else. It's not what he would have chosen, but he chose it nonetheless. He maintained his poise and accepted the capture of normalcy's net with a kind of angry grace. He became a bon vivant around town and an ad man during the day, spending his time churning out words to sell cigarettes or iced tea, children's books and gasoline, and riding the bar car home at night with the boys.

Sitting there on the floor, surrounded by this growing pile of letters, it occurred to me that perhaps, deep down, he was actually glad to get off the hook. Maybe he hadn't really been cut out for show business, for the highwire act of an artist's life. Maybe he wasn't prepared to surrender his daily pleasures for the risk of not making it. And yet, at the same time, I know it was a bitter pill for him to swallow, not being the writer he had dreamed of becoming. Within the year he would be in harness at Western Advertising Agency. Within twenty, he would be dead, dying in silence, with this bitterness on his breath.

It was so sad, going through the dozens of neatly filed rejection letters, the envelopes all opened so carefully, with a knife, not torn or ripped open with anguish or impatience, the hopes and dreams of a young man slowly drying up in front of his eyes. I imagined him reading the mail each day, and I thought about where I was at the time. 1948: I was sitting at the piano, hearing the anger boiling over behind closed doors, waiting for the ceremonial whack on the back of the head.

"He did not love his life," Bellow had said, "but he embraced his fate." I finally understood what that meant. My father was not the man he had hoped to become, but he became the man he was with all his heart.

And I recalled a moment some ten years before when an attractive, middle-aged woman with a warm smile approached me after a gig in Seattle. As I walked off the stage, she appeared out of nowhere, touched my arm and said, "Your father would have been so proud of you tonight." I looked at her with all my attention as she told how they had met in Racine years before, when he was working at Western Advertising. "He always spoke of you," she said. And then she said, "there isn't a day that goes by when I don't think of him." It took my breath away. She looked directly into my eyes and I knew. I knew that I had not really known my father at all.

Reading those letters on that rainy afternoon, the wind picking up and throwing hard drops against the window, I understood for the first time that I had chosen *not* to know him. I had chosen instead to dream my own life into being, to nurture the hurt that I carried and to use it as the fuel for my own work. I had chosen to let the legend live. In the end, I had created my own story so that I could save myself from it.

Or, as Charlie Parker once said, "If you don't live it, it won't come out of your horn."

With Steve Miller and Phil Woods,
backstage after the Ordway Theater gig (1986)

The Steve Miller crew gets their star on the walk of fame (1987) L to R:
Byron Alred, Norton Buffalo, Tim Davis, Gerald Johnson, Steve,
Kenny Lee Lewis, Lonnie Turner, Ben, Gary Mallaber, Leo (down front)

With Richard Davis
(1987)

In Japan with the Quartet and our tour manager (1987)
L to R: Gordy Knudtson, Leo, Bob Malach, Billy Peterson, Ben

With Johnny Griffin in Barcelona (1987)

With Wynton Marsalis and Marcus Roberts on the set of VH1
"New Visions" (1989)

The beekeeper, on stage in Maine (1990)

Leo plays the soundcheck (1990)

"Mr P's Shuffle" (1994) L to R: Clyde Stubblefield,
Frank Morgan, Richard Davis, Ben

With Mose Allison (1995)

With Phil Woods at the
Celebrity Lounge (1997)

Irv Williams, Ben, Leo (1999)

⁓ Discography

1971   *Feel Your Groove* (Capitol)

1972   *I Lead a Life* (Blue Thumb)

1973   *Puttin' in Time on Planet Earth* (Blue Thumb)

1974   *Don't Let Go* (Blue Thumb)

1976   *Free in America* (Arista)

1977   *The Doctor Is In* (Arista)

1978   *A Little Kiss in the Night* (Arista)

1979   *Live at Montreaux* (Arista)

1980   *The Cat and the Hat* (A&M)

1981   *Get to the Point* (Polystar)

1982   *Old Songs for the New Depression* (originally Island / currently Go Jazz)

1983   *Bop City* (originally Island / currently Go Jazz)

1984   *Live with Richard Davis* (originally Madrigal / currently Go Jazz)

1985   *On the Cool Side* (originally Windham Hill / currently Go Jazz)

1986   *Have You Met . . . Barcelona?* (Orange Blue)

1987   *On the Live Side* (originally Windham Hill / currently Go Jazz)

1988   *Too Hot to Touch* (originally Windham Hill / currently Go Jazz)

1990   *Cool Paradise* (Go Jazz)

1994   *Life's a Lesson* (Go Jazz)

1996   *Mr. P's Shuffle* (Go Jazz)

1997   *Go Jazz All-Stars* (Go Jazz)

1998   *Live at Celebrity Lounge* (Go Jazz)

2000   *Concert for Garcia Lorca* (Go Jazz)

2002   *Walk Pretty* (Go Jazz)

⤳ Radio / Television / Film

1973–1974   Host/Producer/"The Weekend Starts Now"/WMTV. Weekly
Arts program with Jane Fonda, Swami Rama, Kinky
Friedman, Steve Miller, etc.

1975–1976   Artistic Director/Jazz Programming/Soundstage/WTTW.
"Sing Me a Jazz Song" with Jon Hendricks, Annie Ross, Eddie
Jefferson, and Leon Thomas. "Dizzy Gillespie's Bebop
Reunion" with Sarah Vaughan, Milt Jackson, and Joe Carroll.

1981–1983   Producer/The Jazz Life/Pioneer Laserdisc. A series of six,
one-hour performance videos featuring Art Blakey with
Wynton Marsalis and Branford Marsalis, Johnny Griffin,
Chico Hamilton, Mike Mainieri, Nat Adderly, and Richie
Cole.

1981–1983   Host/Artistic Director for "Jazz Alive," National Public Radio.
Weekly national live jazz performances. Winner of 1982
Peabody Award.

1983–1985   Contributor to "All Things Considered," National Public
Radio. Weekly music reviews and news features.

1985–1990   Host/Producer for "Sidran on Record," National Public
Radio. Weekly interviews with jazz personalities. Winner of
International Radio Festival 1986.

1986   Music Director/"Sass & Brass"/Cinemax. A one hour special
featuring Sarah Vaughan with Herbie Hancock, Dizzy
Gillespie, Don Cherry, Al Hirt, Ron Carter, etc.

316

1988–1989	Host/Producer/Live From MIDEM. "Back to Stax" featuring Carla Thomas, Booker T. & The MG's, Sam Moore, Eddie Floyd. "Birdmen and Birdsongs" featuring Phil Woods, Red Rodney, Roy Haynes, and Frank Morgan.
1988–1991	Host/"New Visions"/VH-1 Television Network. Weekly jazz and new music program with interviews and live performances. Winner, 1989 Ace Award for "Best Cable Music Series."
1993	Music Producer/Composer/"Higher Goals"/PBS. National Daytime Emmy Nominee, Outstanding Children's Special.
1993	Music Producer/Diana Ross/*Diana Ross Live: The Lady Sings . . . Jazz and Blues*. Live pay-per-view concert with follow-up videocassette, laserdisc, and CD formats.
1994	Composer/Music Producer/*Hoop Dreams*/Fine Line Films. Winner 1994 Sundance Audience Award, New York Film Critics Award.
1998	Composer/Music Producer/*Vietnam: Long Time Coming*. Winner 1998 Aspen Film Festival, Emmy Award, DGA Award.
1996–1999	Producer "Jazz Profiles," National Public Radio. Weekly biographies of major jazz figures.

CD Track Listing

(1) "Piano Players" (from *Old Songs for the New Depression*, Go Jazz 6049) (2:20)
Marcus Miller, bass
Buddy Williams, drums
Ben Sidran, piano & vocal

(2) "Bopcity" (from *Bopcity*, Go Jazz 6048) (3:10)
Phil Woods, saxophone
Peter Erskine, drums
Eddie Gomez, bass
Ben Sidran, piano

(3) "Mitsubishi Boy" (previously unreleased recording from Japan) (3:57)
Ben Sidran, piano & vocal

(4) "On the Cool Side" (from *On the Cool Side*, Go Jazz 6009) (5:51)
Steve Miller, guitar & vocals
Billy Peterson, bass
Gordy Knudtson, drums
Ben Sidran, piano & vocal

(5) "A Good Travel Agent" (from *On the Live Side*, Go Jazz 6008) (13:04)
Phil Woods, saxophone
Billy Peterson, bass
Gordy Knudtson, drums
Ben Sidran, piano & vocal

(6) "Critics" (from *Too Hot to Touch*, Go Jazz 6010) (4:50)
Ricky Peterson, synthesizer
Billy Peterson, bass
Gordy Knudtson, drums
Ben Sidran, piano & vocal

(7) "Cool Paradise" (from *Cool Paradise*, Go Jazz 6001) (5:39)
Ricky Peterson, synthesizer
Billy Peterson, bass
Gordy Knudtson, drums
Ben Sidran, piano & vocal

(8) "Lip Service" (from *Go Jazz All-Stars Live*, Go Jazz 6007) (3:45)
Bob Malach, saxophone
Ricky Peterson, synthesizer
Billy Peterson, bass
Gordy Knudtson, drums
Ben Sidran, piano & vocal

(9) "Life's a Lesson" (from *Life's a Lesson*, Go Jazz 6013) (3:38)
Carole King, vocal
Gil Goldstein, piano
Mike Mainieri, vibes
Ben Sidran, vocal

(10) "Face" (from *Hoop Dreams* soundtrack, Go Jazz 6050) (4:18)
Bob Malach, saxophone
Rufus Reid, bass
Carl Allen, drums
Ben Sidran, piano

(11) "I'm Back" (from *Mr. P's Shuffle*, Go Jazz 6019) (5:30)
Frank Morgan, saxophone
Clyde Stubblefield, drums
Richard Davis, bass
Phil Upchurch, guitar
Ricky Peterson, organ
Margie Cox, background vocal
Ben Sidran, piano & vocal

(12) "For Margarita Xirgu" (from *The Concert for Garcia Lorca*, Go Jazz 6033)
(8:28)
Leo Sidran, drums
Manuel Calleja, bass
Bobby Martinez, saxophone
Ben Sidran, piano & vocal

Total Time (64:26)

Index

ANY OLD WAY YOU CHOOSE IT
Rock and Other Pop Music,
1967–1973
Expanded Edition
Robert Christgau
360 pp.
0-8154-1041-7
$16.95

THE ART PEPPER COMPANION
Writings on a Jazz Original
Edited by Todd Selbert
200 pp., 4 color photos, 16 b/w photos
0-8154-1067-0
$30.00 cloth

BACKSTAGE PASSES
Life on the Wild Side with David
Bowie
Angela Bowie with Patrick Carr
368 pp., 36 b/w photos
0-8154-1001-8
$17.95

BAT CHAIN PULLER
Rock and Roll in the Age of Celebrity
Kurt Loder
with a new introduction
412 pp., 30 b/w photos
0-8154-1225-8
$16.95

BEHIND BLUE EYES
The Life of Pete Townshend
Updated Edition
Geoffrey Giuliano
376 pp., 17 b/w photos
0-8154-1070-0
$17.95

BEHIND CLOSED DOORS
Talking with the Legends of
Country Music
Alanna Nash
616 pp., 27 b/w photos
0-8154-1258-4
$18.95

BETTE MIDLER
Still Divine
Mark Bego
464 pp., 40 b/w photos
0-8154-1232-0
$27.95 cloth

THE BITTER END
Hanging Out at America's
Nightclub
Paul Colby and
Martin Fitzpatrick
Foreword by Kris Kristofferson
296 pp. 32 b/w photos
0-8154-1206-1
$26.95 cloth

THE BLUES
In Images and Interviews
Robert Neff and Anthony Connor
152 pp., 84 b/w photos
0-8154-1003-4
$17.95

BONNIE RAITT
Still in the Nick of Time
Updated Edition
Mark Bego
304 pp., 29 b/w photos
0-8154-1248-7
$16.95

A CENTURY OF DANCE
Ian Driver
256 pp., 360 color and
b/w photos
0-8154-1133-2
$29.95

CHER
If You Believe
Mark Bego
Foreword by Mary Wilson
464 pp., 50 b/w photos
0-8154-1153-7
$27.95 cloth

COLONEL TOM PARKER
The Curious Life of
Elvis Presley's Eccentric Manager
James L. Dickerson
310 pp., 35 b/w photos
0-8154-1088-3
$28.95 cloth

DEPECHE MODE
A Biography
Steve Malins
280 pp., 24 b/w photos
0-8154-1142-1
$17.95

DESPERADOS
The Roots of Country Rock
John Einarson
304 pp., 16 pp. of b/w photos
0-8154-1065-4
$19.95

**DID THEY MENTION
THE MUSIC?**
The Autobiography of Henry Mancini
Updated Edition
Henry Mancini with Gene Lees
312 pp., 44 b/w photos
0-8154-1175-8
$18.95

DOLLY
The Biography
Updated Edition
Alanna Nash
354 pp., 52 b/w photos
0-8154-1242-8
$16.95

**DREAMGIRL AND SUPREME
FAITH**
My Life as a Supreme
Updated Edition
Mary Wilson
732 pp., 150 b/w photos,
15 color photos
0-8154-1000-X
$19.95

FAITHFULL
An Autobiography
Marianne Faithfull with David Dalton
320 pp., 32 b/w photos
0-8154-1046-8
$16.95

FREAKSHOW
Misadventures in the Counterculture,
1959–1971
Albert Goldman
416 pp.
0-8154-1169-3
$17.95

GO WHERE YOU WANNA GO
The Oral History of The Mamas and
The Papas
Matthew Greenwald
304 pp., 44 b/w photos
0-8154-1204-5
$25.95 cloth

GOIN' BACK TO MEMPHIS
A Century of Blues, Rock 'n' Roll,
and Glorious Soul
James Dickerson
284 pp., 58 b/w photos
0-8154-1049-2
$16.95

**HARMONICAS, HARPS,
AND HEAVY BREATHERS**
The Evolution of the People's
Instrument
Updated Edition
Kim Field
392 pp., 44 b/w photos
0-8154-1020-4
$18.95

HE'S A REBEL
Phil Spector — Rock and Roll's
Legendary Producer
Mark Ribowsky
368 pp., 35 b/w photos
0-8154-1044-1
$18.95

JOHN CAGE: WRITER
Selected Texts
Edited and introduced by Richard
Kostelanetz
304 pp., 15 illustrations, facsimiles, and
reproductions
0-1854-1034-4
$17.95

JUST FOR A THRILL
Lil Hardin Armstrong,
First Lady of Jazz
James L. Dickerson
350 pp., 15 b/w photos
0-8154-1195-2
$28.95 cloth

LENNON IN AMERICA
1971–1980, Based in Part on the
Lost Lennon Diaries
Geoffrey Giuliano
320 pp., 68 b/w photos
0-8154-1157-X
$17.95

LIVING WITH THE DEAD
Twenty Years on the Bus with Garcia
and The Grateful Dead
Rock Scully with David Dalton
408 pp., 31 b/w photos
0-8154-1163-4
$17.95

**THE LOST BEATLES
INTERVIEWS**
Geoffrey Giuliano
Afterword by Dr. Timothy Leary
448 pp., 66 b/w photos
0-8154-1226-6
$17.95

LOUIS' CHILDREN
American Jazz Singers
Updated Edition
Leslie Gourse
384 pp.
0-8154-1114-6
$18.95

MADONNA
Blonde Ambition
Updated Edition
Mark Bego
368 pp., 57 b/w photos
0-8154-1051-4
$18.95

MARIA CALLAS
The Woman behind the Legend
Arianna Huffington
416 pp., 61 b/w photos
0-8154-1228-2
$17.95

MICK JAGGER
Primitive Cool
Updated Edition
Chris Sandford
352 pp., 56 b/w photos
0-8154-1002-6
$16.95

OSCAR PETERSON
The Will to Swing
Updated Edition
Gene Lees
328 pp., 15 b/w photos
0-8154-1021-2
$18.95

**REMINISCING WITH
NOBLE SISSLE AND
EUBIE BLAKE**
Robert Kimball and
William Bolcom
256 pp., 244 b/w photos
0-8154-1045-X
$24.95

ROCK 100
The Greatest Stars of
Rock's Golden Age
David Dalton and Lenny Kaye
with a new introduction
288 pp., 195 b/w photos
0-8154-1017-4
$19.95

ROCK SHE WROTE
Women Write About Rock,
Pop, and Rap
Edited by Evelyn McDonnell
& Ann Powers
496 pp.
0-8154-1018-2
$16.95

SUMMER OF LOVE
The Inside Story of LSD, Rock &
Roll, Free Love and High Times
in the Wild West
Joel Selvin
392 pp., 23 b/w photos
0-8154-1019-0
$16.95

SWING UNDER THE NAZIS
Jazz as a Metaphor for Freedom
with a new preface
Mike Zwerin
232 pp., 45 b/w photos
0-8154-1075-1
$17.95

TCHAIKOVSKY
Letters to His Family: An Autobiography
Piotr Ilyich Tchaikovsky
Translated by Galina von Meck
612 pp.
0-8154-1087-5
$22.95

TEMPTATIONS
Updated Edition
Otis Williams with Patricia
Romanowski
288 pp., 57 b/w photos
$17.95
0-8154-1218-5

TURNED ON
A Biography of Henry Rollins
James Parker
280 pp., 10 b/w photos
0-8154-1050-6
$17.95

UNFORGETTABLE
The Life and Mystique of
Nat King Cole
Leslie Gourse
352 pp., 32 b/w illustrations
0-8154-1082-4
$17.95

WAITING FOR DIZZY
Fourteen Jazz Portraits
Gene Lees
Foreword by Terry Teachout
272 pp.
0-8154-1037-9
$17.95

WESTSIDE
The Coast-to-Coast Explosion
of Hip Hop
William Shaw
334 pp.
0-8154-1196-0
$16.95

WILLIE
An Autobiography
Willie Nelson and Bud Shrake
368 pp., 72 b/w photos
0-8154-1080-8
$18.95

Available at bookstores; or call
1-800-462-6420

COOPER SQUARE PRESS
200 Park Avenue South
Suite 1109
New York, NY 10003